The Complexity Vision
and the Teaching of Economics

The Complexity Vision and the Teaching of Economics

Edited by

David Colander

Christian A. Johnson Distinguished Professor of Economics, Middlebury College, Vermont, USA

Edward Elgar

Cheltenham, UK · Northampton, MA, USA

Published by
Edward Elgar Publishing Limited
Glensanda House
Montpellier Parade
Cheltenham
Glos GL50 1UA
UK

Edward Elgar Publishing, Inc.
136 West Street
Suite 202
Northampton
Massachusetts 01060
USA

A catalogue record for this book
is available from the British Library

Library of Congress Cataloguing in Publication Data

The complexity vision and the teaching of economics / edited by David C.
    Colander
    Includes bibliographical references.
    1. Economics—Study and teaching. 2. Complexity (Philosophy) I. Colander,
David C. II. Title.

HB74.5.C656 2000
330'.071—dc21

99–049645

ISBN 1 84064 252 1

Printed in the United Kingdom at the University Press, Cambridge

Contents

Figures and Tables

FIGURES

TABLES

Contributors

W. Brian Arthur is the Citibank Professor at Santa Fe Institute. He is a member of the Board of Trustees there and was director of the Economics Research program from 1988 to 1990 and 1995 to 1996. He received his MA in Mathematics from the University of Michigan, Ann Arbor in 1969 and PhD in Operations Research from the University of California, Berkeley in 1973. He won the Schumpeter Prize in Economics in 1990; was a Guggenheim Fellow in 1987–88 and is a Fellow of the Econometric Society. Before moving to Santa Fe he was the Dean and Virginia Morrison Professor of Population Studies and Economics, Stanford and Professor of Human Biology, Stanford, 1983–96.

His research interests include increasing returns, cognition and economics, and technology and the modern economy. Two recent books include *The Economy as an Evolving Complex System II*, edited with Steven Durlauf and David Lane, Addison-Wesley, Reading, Mass., Series in the Sciences of Complexity, 1997, and *Increasing Returns and Path Dependence in the Economy*, Ann Arbor, University of Michigan Press, 1994.

William A. Brock is Vilas Research Professor of Economics at the University of Wisconsin, Madison. Previously he was a professor at Cornell University and the University of Chicago. His interests are wide. He is a general economic theorist who has worked on monetary theory, business cycle theory, neoclassical political economy, optimal growth theory, economics of regulation, econometrics and statistics of pattern recognition, and finance. He is a Fellow of the American Academy of Arts and Sciences and the Econometric Society, has held a Guggenheim Fellowship and was Sherman Fairchild Distinguished Scholar at CalTech.

David Colander is the Christian A. Johnson Distinguished Professor of Economics at Middlebury College, Middlebury, Vermont. He has authored, co-authored, or edited 30 books and over 80 articles on a wide range of topics. He received his PhD from Columbia University and has taught at Columbia University, Vassar College, and the University of Miami as well as Middlebury. He is listed in *Who's Who?* and *Who's Who in Education?* He has been President of the Eastern Economic Association and the History of Economic Thought Society and is currently on the editorial boards of the *Journal of the*

History of Economic Thought, Journal of Economic Education, Eastern Economic Journal and *Journal of Economic Perspectives*.

Duncan K. Foley is Leo Model Professor of Economics at the Graduate Faculty of the New School University. He has taught at Barnard College of Columbia University, where he offered a graduate course on complexity and economics, Stanford University, and M.I.T. His interests include nonlinear dynamics, complexity theory, statistical equilibrium approaches to economic models, growth theory, money and macroeconomics, and Classical/Marxian economics. He is co-author with Thomas R. Michl of *Growth and Distribution* (Harvard University Press, 1999) and editor of *Barriers and Bounds to Rationality* (Princeton University Press, 1998), a collection of Peter Albins's papers to which he contributed an introductory essay on the implications of the complex systems approach for economics.

Kevin D. Hoover is Professor of Economics at the University of California, Davis, where he has been since 1985. Professor Hoover was previously a Heyworth Prize Research Fellow at Nuffield College, Oxford, and a Lecturer in Economics at Balliol College and Lady Margaret Hall, Oxford, as well as a research associate and Visiting Economist at the Federal Reserve Bank of San Francisco. He is the author of *The New Classical Macroeconomics: A Skeptical Inquiry* and numerous articles in macroeconomics, monetary economics, economic methodology and the philosophy of science. He has edited *Macroeconometrics: Developments, Tensions, and Prospects* (Kluwer, 1995) and co-edited (with James Hartley and Kevin Salyer) *Real Business Cycles: A Reader* (Routledge, 1998). Hoover serves as an editor of the *Journal of Economic Methodology*.

Roger Koppl is Professor of Economics and Finance at the Samuel J. Silberman College of Business Administration of Fairleigh Dickinson University. He has taught at Auburn University, Auburn University at Montgomery, and the Copenhagen Business School. He received a PhD in Economics from Auburn University in 1988, and an MA in Economics from New York University in 1983. He has co-edited a book on Ludwig Lachmann. He has published articles in many areas including methodology, economic history and finance. His main research interest is in economic expectations. He uses phenomenological psychology and evolutionary epistemology as the basis for a falsifiable theory of expectations.

Stephen P. Magee is the Bayless-Enstar Professor of Finance and Economics, Department of Finance, at the University of Texas at Austin. Formerly of the University of California, Berkeley, and the University of Chicago, he is the author of a variety of books and articles on international trade and public choice theory. He is currently working on biological models in economics, the benefits and the costs of legal systems, and is teaching economics and finance to senior business executives. He has worked as an economist for the White House, the Office of Management and Budget, the Council of Economic Advisers, and the Brookings Institution. He has served as an Associate Editor for the *Review of International Economics, Journal of Economic Integration, Journal of International Economics*, the *Review of Economics and Statistics* and *Economics and Politics*; he has served as a member of the Brookings Panel on Economic Activity, the National Science Foundation Advisory Committee for Economics and the Economic Advisory Board to the US Secretary of Commerce.

Peter Hans Matthews is a Professor of Economics at Middlebury College. He received his PhD from Yale in 1995. His interests include quantitative methods, both mathematical and statistical, and the history of economic thought. He received a BA (Hons) from McGill and an MA from Queen's University at Kingston. His most recent work includes 'An Econometric Model of the Circuit of Capital', forthcoming in *Metroeconomica,* 'Did Marx Know the Way to Santa Fe?', David Colander (ed), *Complexity and the History of Economic Thought* (Routledge, 2000), and 'What Else Do Bosses Do? A Neo-Hobbesian Model of the Promotion/Discipline Nexus', in the *Review of Radical Political Economics* (October 1998)

Robert E. Prasch is currently Visiting Assistant Professor at Vassar College. His previous appointments were at the University of Maine and San Francisco State University. He received his doctorate from the University of California, Berkeley in 1992. He writes in the areas of history of economic thought, institutional economics, and public policy. He has published over 30 articles, book chapters and reviews in academic journals such *as History of Political Economy, Review of Social Economy, Journal of Economic Issues, Journal of Economic Perspectives*, and the *Journal of the History of Economic Thought.*

Frederic L. Pryor is Professor of Economics at Swarthmore College and a long-time specialist in the comparative study of economic systems. Almost all of his work has focused on the use of empirical methods to extract useful information about the functioning of these systems, which have ranged from communism, capitalism, slave societies, feudalism, fascism, corporatism and animal societies. In recent years his research has turned toward the United States and he is the author of *Economic Evolution and Structure: The Impact of Complexity on the US Economy* and co-authored book *Who's Not Working and Why?*

Sunder Ramaswamy is Associate Professor and Chair of Economics at Middlebury College. He received his PhD in Economics from Purdue University in 1991, and an MA in Economics from the Delhi School of Economics, India. His principal fields of specialization are development economics, international trade, and issues in applied microeconomics. He is currently involved with a joint Reserve Bank of India and World Bank project on Indian economic reforms. In the past he has been involved with USAID and INTSORMIL projects on agricultural development in Sub-Saharan Africa. His books include *The Economics of Agricultural Technology in Semiarid Sub-Saharan Africa*, with John H. Sanders and Barry I. Shapiro (Johns Hopkins University Press, 1996) and *Economics: An Honors Companion*, with Kailash Khandke, Jenifer Gamber and David Colander (MaxiPress, Richard D. Irwin Publishers, 1995). He has also contributed numerous chapters in various books and articles either published or forthcoming in journals such as *Applied Economics, Economic Development and Cultural Change, Economics Letters, Journal of Development Economics,* and *Journal of Public Economics* .

J. Barkley Rosser, Jr. is Professor of Economics and Kirby L. Kramer, Jr. Professor at James Madison University. He received his PhD in 1976 in economics at the University of Wisconsin-Madison. He studies and teaches applications of complex nonlinear dynamics to urban/regional, environmental/ ecological, comparative, macro, and international financial economics. He has published two books: *From Catastrophe to Chaos: A General Theory of Economic Discontinuities* (Kluwer, 1991), and *Comparative Economics in a Transforming World Economy* (Irwin, 1996) with Marina V. Rosser, his wife and colleague. He is Book Review Editor of *Discrete Dynamics in Nature and Society,* and on the editorial boards of *Journal of Economic Behavior and Organization; Nonlinear Dymanics, Psychology, and Life Sciences,* and *Journal of Post Keynesian Economics.*

Michael Rothschild earned his law and MBA degrees simultaneously at Harvard. He began his career with the Boston Consulting Group. Consulting assignments exposed him to a broad array of challenging business problems, from evaluating acquisition candidates in the forest products industry to designing a new marketing strategy for a leading computer software firm. He has worked in industries as diverse as semiconductor fabrication, rail car leasing, plastics distribution, airport design, medical electronics, housing construction, and cosmetics marketing.

He is currently President of The Bionomics Institute and author *of Bionomics: Economy as Ecosystem,* a book *The Wall Street Journal* called 'revolutionary'. The Bionomics Institute applies the bionomic perspective – the concept that a market economy works much like an evolving ecosystem – to the critical problems facing corporations and governments.

James Stodder is currently Clinical Assistant Professor in the Lally School of Management and Technology, Rensselaer Polytechnic Institute at Hartford. He received his PhD from Yale in 1990, and writes on the evolution of exchage and property systems, behavioral economics, and empirical measures of inequality preference. Recent articles have appeared in *Economic Systems, Journal of Comparative Economics, Eastern Economic Review, European Review of Law and Economics, Review of Income and Wealth, Journal of Economic Education,* and the *Encyclopaedia of Political Economy.* His essay, 'Efficient Moralities: A Model of the Evolution of Exchange' will appear in the book *Reciprocity, Redistribution and Exchange*, forthcoming from Karl Polanyi Institute of Concordia University, Montreal.

Preface

The papers in the volume were originally presented at the 19th Annual Middlebury College Conference on Economic Issues. Running a conference is no easy task and I want to thank Amy Holbrook, the Economics Department Administrator, who acted as conference coordinator.

The conference was made possible by the generosity of the Christian A. Johnson Endeavor Foundation, which also funded the Chair I hold at Middlebury College. The Johnson Foundation has been a wonderful friend of the Economics Department here at Middlebury College. The Foundation has made it possible for the College to play a larger role in the economics profession than most other undergraduate schools. In doing so, it has exposed our students to a larger sense of economics than would otherwise be possible. We at Middlebury are extremely thankful to the Foundation for making that possible, and for all the help it has given us. Our special thanks go to Julie Kidd, its president.

I would also like to thank Edward Elgar, who took this project under his wing and saw to it that it became a book. As usual, the people at Elgar Publishing did a great job, and I would like to thank them, in particlar Jane Croft, Emma Gribbon, Dymphna Evans, Christine Boniface and Julie Leppard.

As you read the volume you will quickly see that this is not a mere reprinting of conference papers. It is a book whose papers fit together like pieces of a puzzle. Putting the pieces of the puzzle together took a while, and required much rewriting and reworking of papers, as well as adding additional papers where there was a missing piece. I thank the authors for putting up with my suggestions and requests to modify their papers to fit the whole.

After the papers were written they had to be prepared for publication. Melissa Dasakis did a wonderful job in coordinating this work. I thank her immensely. I also thank Aleks Wolski and Ivan Davtchev, who did excellent work on straightening out references and checking the manuscripts. Finally, I want to thank Veronica Weallans, who copy-edited the manuscript, Jenifer Gamber and Pam Bodenhorn who did a great job turning the manuscript into camera ready copy, and Helen Reiff who did the index and proofreading.

Introduction

David Colander

A new science of complexity is emerging and playing an increasingly important role in discussions of both science and the humanities. New courses in complexity are springing up; the term complexity is appearing in the popular media with increasing regularity, and new books on complexity are hitting the newsstands every day. Most of these books, courses and discussions introduce people to the mathematics, terminology and ideas of complexity. Concepts such as the Mandelbrot and Juila sets are becoming increasingly well known and terms such as butterfly effects, fractals, sensitive dependence on initial conditions, and strange attractors are making their way into everyday conversations.

This book is part of that emerging literature explosion. Its focus, however, is not on the grand theories or technical aspects of complexity; its focus is on a small subarea: complexity and the teaching of economics. It asks the question: Say that we accept that the complexity approach is worth looking into within economics; what implications does that acceptance have for the teaching of economics? Looking at such a small subarea within complexity science makes sense because it highlights some important conceptual implications of complexity. It shows that, even if the complexity research program has not yet progressed significantly, recognition that the complexity approach is a reasonable one, worth following, can change the way a subject is both taught and thought about.

The book is a collection of essays by economists about these general themes. It is organized into five parts: The Complexity Vision and Economics; The Complexity Vision and Economic Policy; Teaching the Complexity Vision in Economics: General; Teaching the Complexity Vision in Economics: Specifics; and Bioeconomics, Complexity and the Teaching of Economics. In this introductory chapter, I provide a brief introduction to complexity, and to some of the central ideas that will be discussed in more depth in the volume.

THE COMPLEXITY VISION

Joseph Schumpeter (1954) once said that to understand the ideas of a disci-

1

pline, one must understand its vision.[1] In economics there have been two underlying visions – one I call a simplicity vision, the other I call a complexity vision. As discussed in Colander (2000) different economists leaned toward different visions, but, currently, the vision that is central to the teaching of economics is the simplicity vision. This is natural because, until recently, the simplicity vision was the only game in science. If a system was truly complex – not reducible to simple structural equations – it was outside science. That has changed with the development of complexity science.

Let me be clear about what I mean by both of these visions. They have little to do with how complex one believes the economy is; all agree that the economy is very complex. They have to do with how one goes about analyzing the economy – where one searches for simplicity.

Science, whether complexity science or standard science, is the search for simplicity – a search for methods to efficiently store information about natural processes. Science takes the complexity of the world and simplifies it in a process of data compression. This data compression can take many forms; initially it takes the form of informal knowledge; then, as science progresses and deepens, that formal knowledge becomes more precise. For example, Adam Smith knew that competition guided people to serve the common good, and Kepler knew that planets follow elliptical orbits around the sun, but neither formalized that understanding.

Formalized knowledge that loses none of the insights of informal knowledge is preferable to informal knowledge, and thus science works to take broad informal knowledge and to further simplify it. Thus, Kepler's understanding of the data was compressed by Newton into an inverse square law, and economists have long been searching for a similar simplification of Adam Smith's and other earlier writers' informal insights into the workings of an economy. The questions in such a simplification process are how to simplify, and whether the simplifications lose important elements of the informal knowledge. Methodological debates in science have been, in large part, debates about alternative strategies to use to compress data.

Standard science follows the structural simplicity method of data compression: Look for a simple relationship, which can reduce data into an analytically solvable model, and find the reduced form of that model. Newton's and Einstein's famous equations are examples. Standard science has been enormously successful in many areas – the discovery that the relationships of energy and mass can be reduced to $E = mc^2$ is a stunning achievement.

Many phenomena have not been especially susceptible to the finding of simple laws. Science has generally precluded those, or, when it has not, the science that develops has been subject to enormous controversy – and often accused of trying to look like a science rather than being a science. My interest in complexity follows from my belief that economic theory has not been especially successful at finding simple structural laws that describe our economy. True, economics has reduced many of its observations to simple formulas, but it has done so only by hiding many of the observations that do not fit, and by not subjecting its propositions to 'too rigorous' empirical testing.[2]

When one does not find any simple structural simplicity, one has three options: one can define the area as outside science (there is no science of love); one can continue searching for a structural simplification; or one can start searching elsewhere for simplicity. Complexity science follows the third of these strategies. It assumes that there may be a class of phenomena – complex systems – in the physical world that, while not subject to simple structural laws, can nonetheless be simplified if viewed as iterative processes. It suggests that dynamic iterative processes have characteristics all their own that lead to certain results that can be predicted and understood. Consistent with this view, complexity looks for simplicity not in structure but in iterative processes – in dynamics rather than in statics.

It is important to note that complexity science is not a replacement for standard science; it is a supplement. It does not say that standard science is not a reasonable approach to take. It simply states that there may be other approaches that offer insight into areas that standard reductionist science has not been able to crack. These areas involve large systems of interacting entities – complex systems.

In her recent book Sunny Auyung (1998) makes a similar point. She argues that science has never been exclusively reductionist in nature; instead it has involved a two-part approach – one reductionist in nature, and one a study of large composite systems. She explains how physics has a separate branch called solid state physics, which analyzes how certain aspects of reality are understood without appeal to first principles. They appear, and are, in some way connected to first principles, but the connection is too complex for us to understand or model. The complex systems have emerged and exist, but cannot be understood through reductionism.

Through its study of iterative processes, complexity science attempts to provide insight into complex systems and to apply those general insights to specific fields. Since scientists have always known that reality is complex, a natural question is: why a new science now? If the complexity approach is a reasonable way of looking at reality, would it not have started long ago? The answer is that what is different is the computer – or, better expressed, the potential of the computer. Developments in computer technology are offering a means to gain far more insight into more complex systems of dynamic equations than previously could be imagined.

For traditionalist scientists, using the computer to 'solve' systems of equations is a bit of a cheat. Computers do not provide analytic solutions to equations, but instead provide numerical solutions using brute force. Showing something by brute computer force is not as elegant as deductively showing it from assumed first principles, and standard science prizes elegance. The bias against computer solutions runs deep, but as computational technology continues to advance, the relative cost of elegance inherent in deductive solutions will rise, swaying more and more scientists toward computational solutions. In his chapter in Part One, 'Some Santa Fe Scenery' William Brock provides an analogy. He compares the growth in computing power available to researchers with the technological changes that have occurred in automobiles, and suggests that had technical change in automobiles occurred at that same rate, a Ferrari today would cost about 10 cents. This development raises the question: Wouldn't your driving habits be different at that price?

THE RISE OF THE COMPLEXITY VISION IN ECONOMICS

When a program was put together on complexity science at what became the Santa Fe Institute, the first topic of general discussion was economics. This was for a variety of reasons. One was a mundane one – funding could be found for it; there were a number of businessmen who did not believe that standard economics was providing insight into the issues they were interested in, and they were interested whether complexity researchers might have anything to offer. A second reason was that the field of economics displayed many of the characteristics that researchers believed would characterize a complex system. It had a self-organized quality to it, and it dealt with interdependent agents. Indeed it has a long history of explanations involving the invisible hand and spontaneous order. And finally, there was an understanding of many of the issues by top researchers who had developed the standard theory. Key among these was Kenneth Arrow, who had not only developed the standard theory, but has also criticized important aspects of it. As recounted in Waldrop (1993) Arrow and Phillip Anderson were instrumental in getting the complexity research program in economics off the ground.

W. Brian Arthur was recruited to direct the program and get it statrted. Arthur's work on increasing returns fits nicely in the complexity framework. More than 20 years ago, when first thinking about how the two visions differed, Arthur drew up a list of differences. That list is given in Table I.1. It serves as a useful tool for differentiating the complexity approach to economics from the standard approach.

The table emphasizes the differences between standard economics (old) and complexity economics (new), so a few cautionary words of interpretation are probably helpful. First, neither Arthur, nor any of us who support a complexity approach, believe that complexity is a replacement for standard economics. It is simply a more general approach. For many issues the standard analysis remains relevant. Second, no one believes that standard economics does not deal with issues such as increasing returns, path dependency, or structural change; it does. The argument is that complexity can lead you more directly to such issues and place them in the center of the analysis rather than on the sides. Third, no one believes that standard economists are tied to the 'old' characteristics and are unaware of the issues that complexity raises. Good economists recognize the problems with standard economics as well as its critics do.

Where a complexity approach differs from a standard approach is in how those problems are faced. Complexity economists argue that the problems must be approached head on, from the beginning, at the deepest level. Standard economists take a more cautionary approach, trying to add such issues at the edges, and to integrate them into existing work.

The complexity vision raises deep questions about some of the fundamental assumptions of economics, and thus it has been associated with heterodox economists who have emphasized those questions in many of their critiques. I, for one, do not see that association fitting the reality. As I stated above, all good economists have raised these questions; standard economists have simply felt that the alternative approaches used by heterodox economists, which have usually involved heuristic analysis rather than formal analysis, were unacceptable. Complexity economics differs from heterodox economics in that it is highly formal; it is a science that involves simplification and the search for efficient means of data compression. Thus, complexity economics will be more acceptable to standard economists because it shares the same focus on maintaining a formal scientific framework, and less acceptable to many heterodox economists who otherwise accept its general vision.

I will stop my discussion here, not because I have answered the questions but because I do not want to take any more of the reader's time. The papers are too interesting to hold off reading. So let me now turn to a description of the chapters in the volume.

THE COMPLEXITY VISION AND ECONOMICS

This first part is designed to introduce you to the complexity vision in a much better way than my brief introduction did. The leadoff chapter by W. Brian Arthur, 'Complexity and the Economy', introduces the concept of complexity, and covers some of the same material that this introduction does but does so more elegantly, and with a slightly different slant. He points out that complex systems in general have no analytic solution; as agents adapt to the world they co-create, they create aggregate patterns. Complexity studies the devel-

Table I.1 Economics: Old and New
(from a Nov. 5, 1979 journal of W. Brian Arthur)

Old Economics	New Economics
Decreasing returns	Much use of increasing returns
Based on marginality and maximizing principles (profit motive)	Other principles possible (Order principles)
Preferences given; Individuals selfish	Formation of preferences becomes central; individuals not necessarily selfish
Society as a backdrop	Institutions come to the fore as a main decider of possibilities, order and structure
Technology as given or selected on economic basis	Technology initially fluid, then tends to set
Based on 19th-century physics (equilibrium, stability, deterministic dynamics)	Based on biology (structure, pattern, self-organization, life cycle)
Time not treated at all (Debreu) or treated superficially (growth)	Time becomes central (structure, pattern, self-organization, lifecycle)
Very little done with age	Individuals can age
Emphasis on quantities, prices and equilibrium	Emphasis on structure, pattern and function (of location, technology, institutions, and possibilities)
Elements are quantities and prices	Elements are patterns and possibilities; Compatible structures carry out some functions in each society (cf. anthropology)
Language: 19th-century math, game theory and fixed point topology	Language more qualitative; Game theory recognized for its qualitative uses; Other qualitative mathematics useful

Table I.1 Economics: Old and New — continued

Old Economics	New Economics
Generations not really seen	Generational turnover becomes central; Membership in economy changing and age-structure of population changing; Generations carry their experiences
Heavy use of indices; People identical	Focus on individual life; people separate and different; Combined switching between aggregate and the individual; Welfare indices different and used as rough measure; Individual lifetimes seen as measure
If only there were no externalities and all had equal abilities, we'd reach Nirvana	Externalities and differences become driving force; No Nirvana; System constantly unfolding
Elements are quantities and prices	Elements are patterns and possibilities
No real dynamics in the sense that everything is at equilibrium. Cf. Ball on string in circular motion. No real change happening; just dynamic suspension	Economy is constantly on the edge of time; It rushes forward, structures constantly coalescing, decaying, changing; All this due to externalities leading to jerky motions, increasing returns, transactions costs, structural exclusions
Most questions unanswerable. Unified system incompatible	Questions remain hard to answer; But assumptions clearly spelled out
'Hypothesis testable' (Samuelson) assumes laws exist	Models are fitted to data (as in EDA); A fit is a fit is a fit; No laws really possible; laws change
Sees subject as structurally simple	Sees subject as inherently complex
Economics as soft physics	Economics as high complexity science
Exchange and resources drive economy	Externalities, differences, ordering principles, computability, mind-set, family, possible lifecycle and increasing returns drive institutions, society and economy

opment of those patterns. He argues that conventional economic theory avoids addressing such issues and simplifies the questions it asks to fit the analytic methods available. Because the dynamic processes that characterize complex systems can become locked-in he argues that governments should use a 'nudging hand' to guide the economy. He concludes with the observation that 'complexity economics is not a temporary adjunct to static economic theory, but theory at a more general, out-of-equilibrium level' (p. 26).

The second chapter in Part One, 'Some Santa Fe Scenery', gives the reader an overview of the technical elements of the Santa Fe complexity approach. It is written by William Brock, a highly technical economist, under strict instructions from the editor to dispense with qualifications and nuances that are common to academic discourse, and to describe the scenery in English, something he does quite nicely.

Brock begins his chapter by pointing out that complexity is the opposite of chaos. Chaos is the study of how simple equations can lead to chaotic results; complexity is the study of how, given certain parameter values, a very complicated set of equations can generate some very simple patterns; it asks the question: How can there be as much order in the economy as there is? Complexity considers whether the patterns that develop have a property of universality about them, and whether they match real-world observations about the economy. Brock discusses how, at an early Santa Fe meeting, scientists from outside economics felt that standard economics was spending too much time on deductive, formalistic models and not enough time on work involving inductive pattern explanations. He argues that the foundations of complexity science are in the study of statistics and probability, not in calculus or set theory.

Brock then turns to the issue of how to teach complexity, and suggests that we use the teaching of ecology as a model. If ecology computer software is integrated into the texts; Brock suggests that, to teach complexity correctly, economics textbooks will need to be supplemented by fully integrated computer software that can make dynamic processes real to students. He concludes his chapter by discussing ways to integrate dynamic processes into the classroom, giving examples of using a graphing calculator for finding patterns in data, and of bootstrapping techniques.

The chapter will be tough going for many older economists, and for some younger economists who have not kept up with the latest developments in statistical methods. But, it nicely makes the point that if the future belongs to complexity economics, statistical methods, which draw as many inferences out of data as possible, will be at center stage, and the deductive analytics that currently dominates what we teach will move to the wings.

In the complexity vision a key idea is that the individual creates the world simultaneously as he or she is influenced by that world. In such a world one cannot assume far-sighted deductive rationality; individuals' rationality is shaped by the world they co-create. In the third chapter, 'Cognition: The Black Box of Economics', W. Brian Arthur explores the issue of cognition and how real world individuals find solutions to problems. He asks whether it is reasonable to make the standard economics assumption that individuals find optimal solutions to the economic problems they are posed. He points out that, while cognitive psychology has not yet understood the mind, it has decided that the best way to picture the mind is as a 'fast pattern completer', not as a rational calculating machine. What this means is that how people react to events or incentives will be dependent on their experience. More broadly, meaning will depend on previous associations rather than just our current sensory experiences. In such a world an ecology of hypotheses may or may not converge to a standard equilibrium of beliefs, but that equilibrium is a statistical equilibrium, not an equilibrium of each individual.

In the second part of the chapter Arthur relates that cognitive psychology view of the mind to economics education. He argues that education is, to a high degree, the formation of associations, and current graduate education is only giving individuals a limited set of associations, embodied in the 20 or 30 models that they learn. This focus on models eliminates the wider metaphors that are necessary to put the models in perspective. He recalls that in Belfast, they say 'If you're not confused, you don't know anything', and suggests that economics needs to recognize confusion as well as rational thought.

The final chapter in Part One, 'Looking Backwards: Complexity Theory in 2028' by Frederic Pryor is a whimsical look back at the current burst of activity in complexity theory from the future. In it Pryor argues that complexity is 'less of a unified theory and more of a vision', and that that vision needs to include a systematic view of organizational structures along the lines that he developed in his book (1996). He suggests that complexity theory is a 'rallying cry for a variety of economists dissatisfied with neoclassical economics' and that there are three groups of complexity economists – Santa Fe, esoterists, and humble practitioners. He argues that it is the humble practitioners, in their development of useful techniques of pattern recognition, who will advance our knowledge of how the economy really functions. But, he argues, humble practitioners are not sufficiently highly valued. He concludes that there is a need for complexity theorists to 'be a bit more modest and not to take all reality as their subject matter' (p. 64).

THE COMPLEXITY VISION AND ECONOMIC POLICY

The teaching of economics is very much concerned with the teaching of economic policy; yet, when one looks at the complexity literature in economics, one sees very little written about the policy implications of complexity. The two chapters in Part Two try to alleviate that. In Chapter 5, 'Complexity and Policy', William Brock and I consider the implications of complexity-based research on economic policy, trying to specify the value added brought to economic policy analysis by recent work in complex systems. In doing so we take a very narrow definition of complexity, arguing that while ideas such as lock-in and increasing returns are more quickly focused on by complexity economics, they can, and have been, arrived at by standard economics.

We distinguish between two types of worldviews – what we call the 'reporter's worldview' and the 'sophisticated economist's worldview', arguing that the complexity approach to policy is already part of the sophisticated economist's worldview. This worldview sees general equilibrium as a peda- gogical exercise, not a description of reality, and is quite content to deal with issues of path dependencies, multiple equilibria and novelty that do not fit with general equilibrium. Sophisticated economists approach issues as em- pirical questions and use standard theory only as a backdrop. Making the complexity vision explicit will make it easier for 'economic reporters' to have a worldview like a sophisticated economist's.

We then turn to the question of complexity and the activism/laissez faire debate, arguing that complexity is neutral in that debate; it favors neither ac- tivism nor laissez faire. It does however change the nature of the policy de- bate from a discussion of externalities to a discussion of ignorance and his- tory. We conclude our chapter with a discussion of changes in the way com- plexity economists will actually do policy analysis, surveying some of the different techniques complexity theorists will use, making the point that com- plexity techniques are complementary to standard economics, not substitutes for it.

Roger Koppl's chapter, 'Policy Implications of Complexity: An Austrian Perspective' responds to the Brock–Colander chapter, arguing that there is more of a laissez faire conclusion that comes from complexity than Brock– Colander suggest. His argument for laissez faire is not the libertarian Austrian argument for markets. Instead it is the 'spontaneous order, lack of knowl- edge' argument based on the empirical observation that 'the only workable systems rely heavily on voluntary exchange'. By the 'lack of knowledge' argument he means some combination of the following: (1) the equations of the models are hard to solve; (2) the equations are always changing; (3) the needed data are hard to gather; (4) the needed data are impossible to gather; (5) the equations do not exist; and (6) the equations omit entrepreneurship. He concludes that within a complexity framework political questions have very little to do with ends and everything to do with means.

TEACHING THE COMPLEXITY VISION IN ECONOMICS: GENERAL

Parts One and Two are backdrops and introductions for Parts Three and Four which focus on how the teaching of economics would change if economists took complexity seriously. In the first chapter in Part Three I consider the problems of adding complexity to an economics principles text, from the perspective of a principles textbook author. I point out that the world of a textbook writer is one constrained by a reviewing process that makes textbook writers controlled, as much as they are controlling. That translates down to a 15 percent rule – no more than 15 percent of a text can change from one edition to the next if a book is to remain a player. I then recount some of the negative reactions I got from reviewers when I attempted to include a Santa Fe view of growth in an intermediate macro text. I conclude that the publishing realities do not mean that complexity cannot be added to the texts; they simply mean that it must be added slowly, and done as only a first step, a way of preparing students to be more open to a fuller discussion of complexity in the future. The chapter then turns to some of the ways Santa Fe ideas might be integrated into current texts by more emphasis on sequential decision making, the experience curve and multiple equilibria.

In Chapter 8, 'Teaching Complexity: An Austrian Approach', Roger Koppl responds to my ideas in Chapter 7, arguing that it would be better to present an Austrian approach to economics in the text. Such an approach would put 'Santa Fe ideas at the center, not the margins'. He discusses how he uses an Austrian approach in his classes, beginning his introductory class by defining economics as 'the study of the systematic, but unintended consequences of human action'. Such an approach focuses more on process than on equilibrium. He then proceeds to recount some specific examples that he gives in class that convey the broader views that Santa Fe complexity is pushing towards.

In Chapter 9, 'Putting Induction Back: Economics without the "Con" of Pure Deduction', James Stodder suggests that the problem of current texts is that they have too little induction. He argues that 'the "con in econometrics" is a manifestation of a deeper con within economics as a whole, the con of suppressed induction' (p. 149). By that he means that economics teaches deductive models but makes little attempt to ask whether those models fit reality. To avoid that problem he suggests that we use more classroom experiments. The second part of the chapter presents three of these experiments. He concludes the chapter by arguing that taking an experimental approach to teaching economics will make teaching economics a 'learning experience for those prepared to teach it'.

The last chapter in Part Three, 'Complexity and Economic Education' by Duncan Foley, looks at longer-term issues. He asks how the way economics is taught will change if complexity is taken seriously. Foley's conclusion is very much in sympathy with Stodder's – the future teaching of economics will involve much more focus on data. By reviewing his own experience with teaching students deductive models Foley presents the problem concisely. From early on we teach students analytic methods, upping the level at each stage along the way. We promise students that the analytic models will help them understand the problems they want to understand, agreeing with them that the models they are using at that stage are too simple, but arguing that the models should be seen as stepping stones.

The complexity vision undermines that promise, and thereby undermines our ability to get students to throw themselves into deductive work as a preparation for policy work; it suggests that at the end of the analytic jumps is an abyss and that even if one reaches the highest level of analytic methods, it will not give students solutions to the real world problems to which students want answers.

He suggests that the alternative pedagogical approach to which complexity is leading is an approach based on simulation. He points out that the methodological shift toward simulation will likely be a generation shift. Students are much more comfortable with computers and simulations than are faculty, and upcoming students will be even more comfortable. He suggests that eventually the complexity revolution 'could lead to a Council of Economic Advisers where people are not running regressions but sitting in front of computer screens playing games with some model or other of the economy and deciding economic policy on that basis' (p. 172).

TEACHING THE COMPLEXITY VISION IN ECONOMICS: SPECIFICS

Part Four considers how complexity can be integrated into particular courses. In Chapter 11, 'Integrating Complexity into the Principles of Macroeconomics' Robert Prasch suggests that integrating complexity into the principles of macroeconomics course will involve more of a revival of old models than it will involve new models. He points out that a number of issues we now associate with increasing returns and path dependence were once standard fare in our principles textbooks. The acceleration principle, the principle that we are all each other's customers, the fallacy of composition and the paradox of savings, are all examples.

Prasch concludes his chapter by enumerating three benefits from introducing complexity into a principles course. First, the discussion of institutions, government, and economic policies can be put in the context of constraints of a free market system. Second, the complexity approach provides many inter-disciplinary linkages to other social sciences. And third, it underscores that history matters.

In Chapter 12, 'Teaching Macroeconomics while Taking Complexity Seriously' Kevin Hoover describes current undergraduate intermediate macro-economic textbooks as 'watered down' graduate textbooks. Intermediate macroeconomic textbooks have extensively focused on theory, and have lost touch with applications of theory to the real world. The result of this focus on theory is that students get discouraged and choose not to study economics because they do not see any connection between what they are taught in classrooms and the real economy.

Hoover's solution to this problem is to focus his intermediate macro course more on data and less on theory, although he admits a minimal amount of theory is necessary to structure the data. He writes: 'When my students are looking at data, they are not, for the most part, pursuing Baconian inductions. Rather they are looking at the economy through a set of specially tinted lenses and asking whether it looks clearer and more understandable when viewed that way' (p. 198).

Development economics has always been different, and in the next chapter, 'Development Economics and Complexity' Sunder Ramaswamy looks at the history of development economics as a case study of how complexity ideas fare in economics. He argues that the ideas that complexity raises have always been part of development economics and that what the new complexity research has to offer is the tools to deal formally with these issues. He further argues that these tools are important. Without them complexity economics is unlikely to be integrated into the teaching of economics. Instead, it will likely be segregated to heterodox economics as was development economics. Ramaswamy cautions: unless the complexity approach is converted into teachable formal models, its study, appeal, and popularity may soon disappear.

In Chapter 14, 'Integrating the Complexity Vision into Mathematical Economics' Barkley Rosser reviews the material that the standard mathematical texts present. He then briefly discusses mathematics' importance to complexity, suggesting that any text that deals in a reasonably serious way with differential or difference equations has an obvious entry point for the teaching of complexity material. After giving a number of specific examples of how complexity can be integrated into economics he suggests that to fully integrate complexity into mathematical economic texts, a qualitative jump to using computer simulations in such textbooks must occur. He suggests both MATLAB and STELLA as useful software programs to begin the qualitative jump.

The final chapter in Part Four, 'Toward the Complexification of Statistics and Econometrics Curricula' by Peter Matthews, suggests that the current teaching of statistics and econometrics is simple and beautiful, with everything in its place, much like a Mondrian painting. And that is the problem. The real world is complicated and what we teach and the real world do not relate very well. He suggests that 'complexified econometrics' will be more like a Paul Klee painting. It will directly confront multiple equilibria in which macrostructure reflects feedback and non-linearities. It will place statistical inference in a broader view of pattern detection.

Despite the differences, there are a number of 'points of contact' between the new and the old, including interaction effects and distribution functions, laws of large numbers, and the use of Monte Carlo/simulation methods. He gives examples of how these can be taught. He concludes the chapter by pointing out that to teach statistics and econometrics correctly will require a three-semester course sequence, reemphasizing the point made in other chapters that complexity moves statistics center stage in the economics curriculum.

COMPLEXITY AND BIOECONOMICS

Bioeconomics is closely related to complexity and Part Five explores that relationship. In Chapter 16, 'Bioeconomics: Lessons for Business, Nations and Life', Stephen Magee introduces the bioeconomics perspective. Man, like the animals, is rational only when being rational increases reproductive fitness. Predatory and lobbying behavior is not an aberration to be relegated to public choice theorists. It is a central allocative mechanism used by animals and reflected in their defense of territories (private property) and in their dominance hierarchies (human politics). Genetic memory and selfish gene theory provide a coherent theory of leadership, a subject largely ignored by economists.

The rationality of economic behavior in developing vs developed countries is explained by r vs. K species which thrive in high variance vs low variance environments. The metaphor of nations as species suggests that democracy is an outgrowth of economic competition and the natural selection of nations. The biological theory of punctuated equilibria provides insight into the rigidity of political institutions. The overslaughter of the mastodons by man illustrates the tragedy of commons, a pervasive problem in nature, and helps explain the economic inefficiencies of government. He argues that the law of increasing competition explains both the increasingly specialized foraging strategies of species over the last 100 million years and economic specialization. Niches get smaller and smaller through time. He concludes the paper with the biological foundations of increasing returns to prosperity, evidenced by the US, Germany and Japan having over half of the world's income. In such a world, the more we have, the more there is.

The final chapter of the book 'Complexity, Business and Biological Metaphors' by Michael Rothschild discusses the experience curve and its importance in real world business. Rothschild begins the chapter with a discussion of why he did not choose to go on in economics – it was simply too disconnected from the real-world. He became a business consultant instead, but he retained his interest in economics. He argues that principles of complexity are not inaccessible, highly mathematical, and irrelevant to business as has sometimes been suggested. On the contrary, most business people know and instinctively apply complexity ideas; they have to do so in order to survive. A product develops, competes, mutates, and eventually dies, as it is replaced by a more successful substitute.

The crux of Rothschild's argument is that it is necessary to view the economy and ongoing competition in biological terms, not the traditional deterministic, static view. To capture that dynamism it is necessary to focus the presentation on the learning that takes place. In economics texts that does not happen; no learning by firms takes place, and the learning curve, which is a central tool of businesspeople, receives almost no discussion. He supports the complexity vision because it 'directly relates to real-world business in a much more direct way than does the standard economics textbook' (p. 293).

CONCLUSION

The contributors to this volume are diverse; some are primarily teachers, others are high-powered complexity researchers, some are both, and still others are businesspeople. Some are fully committed complexity theorists; others are quite neutral towards it. What is amazing, however, is that, despite this diversity, there is a message that comes through loud and clear in all the papers. *It is in the real world where the action is; and if we want to interest students in economics, and make economics more relevant, the teaching of economics must reflect the real world, not abstract deductive models that lead nowhere fast, and may lead nowhere slowly.* Data and data analysis, inductive generalities, not deductive proofs, are where the future of economics lies.

Correct data analysis is complicated; one can find all kinds of patterns in data; determining whether those patterns are meaningful is a much more complicated job than simply running simulations on computers. There is much work to be done in exploring sensitivity analysis of simulations before simulation can be a reasonable tool. But the complexity vision suggests that simulations, and data analysis, are the future, and that work in that area will likely lead to large payoffs. In the meantime, what the complexity vision tells us is that we economists should be a bit more modest in our claims for models, a bit more focused on data and interpretations of data in our classes, and a bit less focused on abstract deductive theory.

NOTES

1. He writes: 'In order to be able to posit to ourselves any problems at all, we should first have to visualize a distinct set of inherent phenomena as a worth-while object of our analytic efforts. ... This pre-analytic cognitive act will be called vision. ... Vision of this kind not only must precede historically the emergence of analytic effort in any field but also may re-enter the history of every established science each time somebody teaches us to see things in a light of which the source is not to be found in the facts, methods, and results of the preexisting state of the science'(p. 41).
2. Economists' tendency to do this led Rosenberg (1992) to classify economics as a branch of mathematical philosophy, rather than a science.

REFERENCES

Auyang, S. (1998), *Foundations of Complex-System Theories in Economics, Evolutionary Biology, and Statistical Physics*, New York: Cambridge University Press.

Colander, D. (2000), *Complexity and the History of Economic Thought,* London: Routledge Press.

Pryor, F. (1996), *Economic Evolution and Structure: The Impact of Complexity on the U.S. Economic System*, New York: Cambridge University Press.

Rosenberg, A. (1992), *Economics: Mathematical Politics or Science of Diminishing Returns*, Chicago: University of Chicago Press.

Schumpeter, J. (1954), *History of Economic Analysis*, New York: Oxford University Press.

Waldrop, M. (1993), *Complexity: The Emerging Science at the Edge of Order and Chaos,* New York: Simon and Schuster.

PART ONE

The Complexity Vision and Economics

1. Complexity and the Economy[1]

W. Brian Arthur

COMPLEXITY

What is complexity? There are many definitions and none is absolute. But common to all studies on complexity are systems with multiple elements adapting or reacting to the pattern these elements create. The elements might be cells in a cellular automaton, or ions in a spin glass, or cells in an immune system, and they may react to neighboring cells' states, or local magnetic moments, or concentrations of B and T cells – both the 'elements' and the 'patterns' they respond to vary from one context to another. But the elements adapt to the world – the aggregate pattern – they co-create.[2] *Time* enters naturally here via adjustment and change: as the elements react, the aggregate changes, as the aggregate changes; elements react anew. Barring some asymptotic state or equilibrium reached, complex systems are systems in process, systems that constantly evolve and unfold over time. Thus complexity in the sciences is not a discipline. It is a movement that takes process seriously.

Why did the complexity movement come along in the late 1970s and early 1980s? The answer is simple. Generally, complex systems have no analytic 'solution'. The patterns that are in the process of being formed are too complicated to be worked out analytically and hence are beyond analytic study. But with the computer we can get insight into the formation of patterns by directly simulating them – computing them and observing them as they form. Complexity as a movement came along in the late 1970s and early 1980s because at that time scientists got workstations.

Complex systems arise naturally in the economy. Economic agents, whether they are banks, consumers, firms, or investors, continually adjust their market moves, buying decisions, prices, and forecasts to the situation these moves or decisions or prices or forecasts together create. But unlike ions in a spin glass that react dumbly to their local magnetic field, economic 'elements' – human agents – react with strategy and foresight by considering outcomes that *might* result as a consequence of behavior they *might* undertake. This adds a layer of complication to economics not experienced in physics or immunology.

Like most other sciences in pre-computer days, conventional economic theory chose not to study the unfolding of patterns its agents create, but rather to seek analytical solutions. To do this it needed to simplify its questions. Thus conventional theory asks what behavioral elements (actions, strategies, expectations) are *consistent with* the aggregate patterns these behavioral elements co-create. For example, general equilibrium theory asks: what prices and quantities of goods produced and consumed are consistent with (would pose no incentives for change to) the overall pattern of prices and quantities in the economy's markets? Game theory asks: what strategies, moves, or allocations are consistent with (would be optimal for a given player) given the strategies, moves, and allocations his rivals might choose? Rational expectations economics asks: what forecasts (or expectations) are consistent with (are on average validated by) the outcomes these forecasts and expectations together create? Conventional economics thus studies patterns in behavioral *equilibrium*, patterns that would induce no further reaction. In the last few years, economists at the Santa Fe Institute, Stanford, Wisconsin, MIT, Chicago, and other institutions, have begun to broaden this equilibrium approach by turning to the question of how actions, strategies, or expectations might react in general to – might endogenously change with – the aggregate patterns these create (Anderson et al. 1988, Arthur et al. 1997). And so, this 'Santa Fe approach' , or complexity approach, is not an adjunct to standard theory, but theory at a more general, out-of-equilibrium level. At this more general level, economic patterns sometimes simplify into a simple, homogeneous equilibrium; more often they are ever-changing, showing perpetually novel behavior and emergent phenomena.

Let me illustrate perpetual novelty with a classic study by Lindgren et al. (1991). Lindgren sets up a computerized tournament where strategies compete in randomly chosen pairs to play a repeated prisoner's dilemma game. Strategies that do well replicate and mutate. Ones that lose eventually die. Strategies can 'deepen' by using deeper memory of their past moves and their opponent's. A strategy's success of course depends on the current population of strategies, and so the elements here – strategies – in a sense react to, or change with, the competitive world they together create.

In his computerized tournament Lindgren discovered that the simple strategies in use at the start went unchallenged for some time. Tit-for-tat and other simple strategies dominated at the start. But then other, deeper strategies emerged that were able to exploit the mixture of these simple ones. In time, yet deeper strategies emerged to take advantage of those, and so on. If strategies got 'too smart' – too complicated – sometimes simple ones could exploit these. In this computer world of strategies, Lindgren found periods with very large numbers of diverse strategies in the population, and periods with few strategies; periods dominated by simple strategies, and periods dominated by deep strategies. But nothing ever settled down. In Lindgren's world, the set of strategies in use evolved and kept evolving in a world of perpetual novelty.

This is unfamiliar to us in standard economics. Yet there is a realism about such dynamics with its unpredictable, emergent and complicated sets of strategies. Chess play at the grand master level for example evolves over decades and never settles down. Lindgren's system is simple, yet it leads to a dynamic of endless unfolding and evolution. This is typical of complex system studies.

POSITIVE FEEDBACKS

The type of systems I have described, where elements react to the pattern the elements create, becomes interesting if they contain nonlinearities or positive feedbacks. To get some idea of how positive and negative feedback work, imagine a tray with water poured on it. First consider negative feedback: under gravity alone, the water flows away from any accumulation of water. And trivially a single, equilibrium water level is reached. A physicist would say that a single phase or single mode emerges – the equilibrium level of the water. This outcome is unique and perfectly predictable. Now let's add positive feedback. Take the same tray, polish it, and spread a thin film of water on it. Now surface tension – a form of positive feedback – becomes important. Under surface tension an agglomeration of water tends to attract neighboring molecules, so we have a mixture of positive and negative feedback of molecules attracting one another and flowing away from water. What happens? Droplets form. Do the experiment once and you get a pattern of droplets; do the experiment again and in all likelihood you get a different pattern of droplets, even though you're careful to start out with the same conditions. When there are positive feedbacks, small differences in temperature, small quantum effects, get magnified and change the outcome. The outcome is therefore history dependent. It's also a pattern: it can't be described by a single phase variable. It's not predictable. The presence of positive feedback leads to properties we associate with complexity.

In economics, positive feedback arises from increasing returns (Arthur, 1990b, 1994b). Standard economics usually assumes negative feedback, or diminishing returns, so as to ensure a unique, predictable equilibrium. If one firm gets too far ahead in the market, it runs into higher costs or some other negative feedback and so the market is shared at a predictable, unique equilibrium. When we allow positive feedbacks or increasing returns, a different outcome arises. Suppose a new technology becomes available, nuclear power for example, in alternative versions *A* or *B* or *C* (light water, heavy water, gas-cooled, etc.). And suppose each technology improves as it becomes more adopted – there are increasing returns. Then if one technology gets far enough ahead it gains advantage and eventually may dominate. (In the nuclear case, light-water reactors almost completely dominate in the US). Alternatively, consider the market for online services of a few years back, in which three major companies competed: Prodigy, CompuServe and America Online. As each gained in membership base it could offer a wider menu of services as well as more members to share specialized hobby and chatroom interests with – there were increasing returns to expanding the membership base. Prodigy was first in the market, but by chance and clever strategy American Online got far enough ahead to gain an unassailable advantage. Today it dominates. Under different circumstances, another rival might have taken the market. Notice the properties here: a multiplicity of potential 'solutions'; the outcome actually reached is not predictable in advance; it tends to be locked in; it is not necessarily the most efficient economically; it is subject to the 'adoption path' taken; and while the technologies may start equal, the outcome is asymmetrical. These properties have counterparts in non-linear physics where similar positive feedbacks are present. What economists call multiple equilibria, non-predictability, lock-in, inefficiency, historical path dependence and asymmetry; physicists call multiple meta-stable states, non-predictability, phase- or mode-locking, high-energy ground states, non-ergodicity and symmetry breaking.

Increasing returns problems have been discussed in economics for a long time. A hundred years ago in his *Principles*, Alfred Marshall (1891) noted that if firms gain advantage as their market share increases, then 'whatever firm first get a good start will obtain a monopoly'. But the conventional, static equilibrium approach gets stymied by indeterminacy: if there is a multiplicity of equilibria, how might one be reached? The process-oriented, complexity approach suggests a way to deal with this. In the actual economy, 'small random events' happen – in the technology case 'random' design improvements, word-of-mouth recommendations. Over time increasing returns magnifies the cumulation of such events to 'select' the outcome randomly. Thus increasing returns problems in economics are best seen as dynamic *processes* with random events and natural positive feedbacks – as nonlinear stochastic processes. This shift from a static outlook into a process orientation is common to complexity studies. Increasing returns problems have been studied intensively in market allocation theory (Arthur 1994b), international trade theory (Helpman and Krugman 1985), the evolution of technology choice (Arthur 1989), economic geography (Arthur 1990a, Krugman 1997), and the evolution of patterns of poverty and segregation (Durlauf 1997). The common finding that economic structures can crystallize around small events and lock in is beginning to change policy in all these areas toward an awareness that governments should avoid both extremes of coercing a desired outcome or keeping strict hands off, and instead seek to push the system gently toward favored structures that can grow and emerge naturally. Not a heavy hand, not an invisible hand, but a nudging hand.

EXPECTATIONAL PROBLEMS IN ECONOMICS

Once we adopt the complexity outlook, with its emphasis on the *formation* of structures rather than their given existence, problems involving prediction in the economy look different. The conventional approach asks what forecasting model (or expectations) in a particular problem, if given and shared by all agents, would be consistent with – would be on average validated by – the actual time series this forecasting model would in part generate. This 'rational expectations' approach is valid. But it assumes that agents can somehow deduce in advance what model will work, and that everyone 'knows' that everyone knows to use this model (the *common knowledge* assumption). What happens when forecasting models are not obvious and must be formed individually by agents who are not privy to the expectations of others?

Consider as an example my Bar or El Farol Problem (Arthur 1994a). One hundred people must decide independently each week whether to show up at their favorite bar (*El Farol* in Santa Fe). The rule is that if a person predicts that more that 60 (say) will attend, he will avoid the crowds and stay home; if he predicts fewer than 60 he will go. Of interest are how the bar-goers each week might predict the numbers showing up, and the resulting dynamics of the numbers attending. Notice two features of this problem. Our agents will quickly realize that predictions of how many will attend depend on others' predictions of how many attend (because that determines their attendance). But others' predictions in turn depend on their predictions of others' predictions. Deductively there is an infinite regress, no 'correct' expectational model that can be assumed to be common knowledge, and from the agents' viewpoint the problem is ill-defined. (This is true for most expectational problems, not just for this special case.) Second, and diabolically, any commonality of expectations gets broken up: if all use an expectational model that predicts *few* will go, *all* will go, invalidating that model. Similarly, if all believe *most* will go, *nobody* will go, invalidating that belief. Expectations will be *forced* to differ.

In 1993 I modeled this situation by assuming that as the agents visit the bar, they act inductively – they act as statisticians, each starting with a variety of subjectively chosen expectational models or forecasting hypotheses. Each week they act on their currently most accurate model (call this their *active* predictor). Thus agents' beliefs or hypotheses compete for use in an *ecology* these beliefs create. Computer simulation (Figure 1.1) showed that the mean attendance quickly converges to 60. In fact, the predictors self-organize into an equilibrium pattern or 'ecology' in which of the active predictors on average 40 percent are forecasting above 60, 60 percent below 60. This emergent ecology is organic in nature. For, while the population of active predictors splits into this 60/40 average ratio, it keeps changing in membership forever. Why

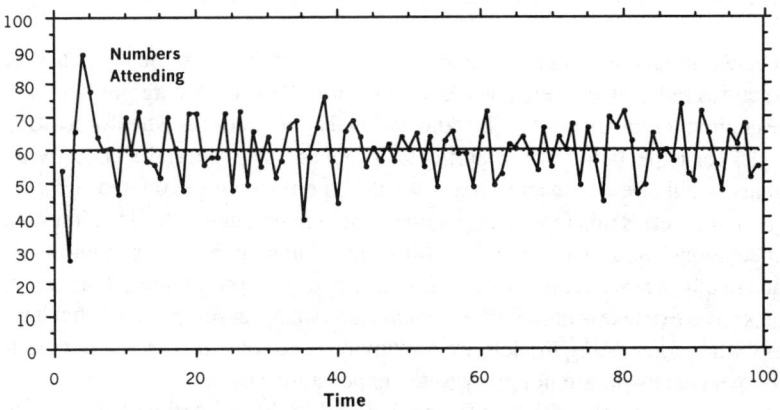

Figure 1.1   Bar Attendance in the First 100 Weeks

do the predictors self-organize so that 60 emerges as average attendance and forecasts split into a 60/40 ratio? Well, suppose 70 percent of predictors forecasted above 60 for a longish time, then on average only 30 people would show up. But then this would validate predictors that forecasted close to 30, restoring the 'ecological' balance among predictions. Even though different predictors are used continually, over time the 40–60 percent 'natural' combination becomes an emergent structure. As an expectational economy in miniature, the Bar Problem has become popular for study among physicists.

FINANCIAL MARKETS

One important application of these ideas is in financial markets. Standard theories of financial market assume rational expectations – that agents adopt uniform expectations (or forecasting models) that are on average validated by the prices these forecast (Lucas 1978). The theory works well to first order. But it does not account for actual market 'anomalies' such as unexpected price bubbles and crashes, random periods of high and low volatility (price variation), and the heavy use of technical trading (trades based on the recent history of price patterns). Holland, LeBaron, Palmer and I (Arthur et al.1997) have created a model that relaxes rational expectations by assuming, as in the Bar Problem, that investors cannot assume or deduce expectations but must discover them. Our agents continually create and use multiple 'market hypotheses' – individual, subjective, expectational models – of what moves the market price and dividend within an artificial stock market on the computer. These 'investors' are individual, artificially-intelligent computer programs that can generate and discard expectational 'hypotheses', and make bids or offers based on their currently most accurate of these. The stock price forms endogenously from the bids and offers of the agents, and thus ultimately from their expectations. So this market-in-the-machine is its own self-contained, simple, artificial financial world. Like the bar, it is a 'mini-ecology' in which expectations compete in a world these expectations together create.

Within this computerized market, we found two phases or regimes. If parameters are set so that our artificial agents update their hypotheses slowly, the diversity of expectations collapses quickly into homogeneous rational expectations. The reason is that if a majority of investors believes something close to the rational expectations forecast, then resulting prices will validate it, and deviant or mutant predictions that arise in the population of expectational models will be rendered inaccurate. Standard finance theory, under these special circumstances, is upheld. But if the rate of updating of hypotheses is turned up, the market undergoes a phase transition into a 'complex regime' and displays several of the 'anomalies' observed in real markets. It develops a rich 'psychology' of divergent beliefs that don't converge over time. Expectational rules such as 'If the market is trending up, predict a 1 percent price rise' that appear randomly in the population of hypotheses can become mutually reinforcing: if enough investors act on these, the price will indeed go up. Thus sub-populations of mutually reinforcing expectations arise, agents bet on these (therefore technical trading emerges), and this causes occasional bubbles and crashes. Our artificial market also shows periods of high volatility in prices followed randomly by periods of low volatility. This is because if some investors 'discover' new, profitable hypotheses, they change the market slightly, causing other investors to also change *their* expectations. Changes in beliefs therefore ripple through the market in avalanches of all sizes, causing periods of high and low volatility. We conjecture that actual financial markets, which show exactly these phenomena, lie in this 'complex' regime.

CONCLUSION

After two centuries of studying equilibria – static patterns that call for no further behavioral adjustments – economists are beginning to study the general emergence of structures and unfolding of patterns in the economy. In the actual economy, agents continually adjust their behaviors to the aggregate 'pattern' these behaviors create. Economic theory has always recognized this, but until recently has simplified its approach to the identification of equilibrium states, where agents' behaviors are consistent with the aggregates these behaviors imply. In the last few years, economists have turned to the wider question of how agents might continually respond endogenously to the patterns they create. Complexity economics is not a temporary adjunct to static economic theory, but theory at a more general, out-of-equilibrium level.

The approach is making itself felt in every area of economics: game theory (Lindgren 1991, Huberman and Glance 1993, Blume 1997); the theory of money and finance (Marimon et al. 1990, Shubik 1997, Brock et al. 1995); learning in the economy (Sargent 1993, Lane and Maxfield 1997, Darley and Kauffman 1997); economic history (North 1997); the evolution of trading networks (Ioannides 1997, Kirman 1997, Tesfatsion 1997); the stability of the economy (Bak et al. 1993, Leijonhufvud 1997); and political economy (Axelrod 1986, Kollman, Miller and Page 1997). It is helping us understand phenomena such as market instability, the emergence of monopolies, and the persistence of poverty in ways that will help us deal with these. And it is bringing an awareness that policies succeed better by influencing the natural processes of formation of economic structures than by forcing static outcomes.

When viewed in out-of-equilibrium formation, economic patterns sometimes simplify into a simple, homogeneous equilibrium of standard economics. More often they are ever-changing, showing perpetually novel behavior and yielding emergent phenomena. Complexity therefore portrays the economy not as deterministic, predictable and mechanistic; but as process-dependent, organic and always evolving.

NOTES

1. This chapter is an extended version of a paper that appeared in *Science*, 2 April 1999, **284**, 107–9.
2. Technically, the systems I am describing are referred to as *adaptive nonlinear networks* (the term is John Holland's) and typically if they exhibit certain properties that have to do with the multiplicity of potential patterns or with the coherence or propagation of substructures, they are said to be 'complex'.

REFERENCES

Anderson P., K.J. Arrow and D. Pines (eds) (1988), *The Economy as an Evolving Complex System*, Reading, MA: Addison-Wesley.
Arthur, W.B. (1989), 'Competing Technologies, Increasing Returns, and Lock-in by Historical Events' *Economic Journal*, **99** (394), 116–31.
Arthur, W.B. (1990a), '"Silicon Valley" Locational Clusters: When Do Increasing Returns Imply Monopoly?', *Math. Social Sciences*, **19** (3), 235–51.
Arthur, W.B. (1990b), 'Positive Feedbacks in the Economy', *Scientific American*, February, 92–9.
Arthur, W.B. (1994a), 'Inductive Reasoning and Bounded Rationality', *American Economic Review*, **84** (2), 406–11.
Arthur, W.B. (1994b), *Increasing Returns and Path Dependence in the Economy*, Ann

Arbor: University of Michigan Press.

Arthur, W.B., S.N. Durlauf and D.A. Lane (eds) (1997), *The Economy as an Evolving Complex System II,* Reading, MA: Addison-Wesley.

Axelrod, R. (1986), 'An Evolutionary Approach to Norms', *American Political Science Review,* **80** (4), 1095–111.

Bak, P., K. Chen, J. Scheinkman and M. Woodford (1993), 'Aggregate Fluctuations from Independent Sectoral Shocks: Self-Organized Criticality in a Model of Production and Inventory Dynamics'. *Ricerche Economiche,* **47** (1), 3–30.

Blume, L.E. (1997), 'Population Games', in W.B. Arthur, S.N. Durlauf, D.A. Lane (eds), *The Economy as an Evolving Complex System II,* Reading, MA: Addison-Wesley, pp. 425–60.

Brock, W.A., P. de Lima, G.S. Maddala, H. Rao and H. Vinod (eds) (1995), *Handbook of Statistics 12: Finance,* Amsterdam: North Holland.

Darley, V.M. and S.A. Kauffman, (1997), 'Natural Rationality', in W.B. Arthur, S.N. Durlauf and D.A. Lane (eds), *The Economy as an Evolving Complex System II,* Reading, MA: Addison-Wesley, pp. 45–80.

Durlauf, S.N. (1997), 'Statistical Mechanics Approaches to Socioeconomic Behavior', in W.B. Arthur, S.N. Durlauf and D.A. Lane (eds), *The Economy as an Evolving Complex System II,* Reading, MA: Addison-Wesley, pp. 41–104.

Helpman, E. and P.R. Krugman (1985), *Market Structure and Foreign Trade,* Cambridge, MA: MIT Press.

Huberman, B.A. and N.S. Glance (1993) 'The Dynamics of Collective Action', *Computational Economics*; **8** (1), 1995, 27–46.

Ioannides, Y. M. (1997), 'Evolution of Trading Structures', in W.B. Arthur, S.N. Durlauf and D.A. Lane (eds), *The Economy as an Evolving Complex System II,* Reading, MA: Addison-Wesley, pp. 129–67.

Kirman, A.P. (1997), 'The Economy as an Interactive System', in W.B. Arthur, S.N. Durlauf and D.A. Lane (eds), *The Economy as an Evolving Complex System II,* Reading, MA: Addison-Wesley, pp. 491–531.

Kollman, K., J.H. Miller and S. Page (1997), 'Computational Political Economy', in W.B. Arthur, S.N. Durlauf and D.A. Lane (eds), *The Economy as an Evolving Complex System II,* Reading, MA: Addison-Wesley, pp. 461–86.

Krugman, P.R. (1997), 'How the Economy Organizes Itself in Space: A Survey of the New Economic Geography', in W.B. Arthur, S.N. Durlauf and D.A. Lane (eds), *The Economy as an Evolving Complex System II,* Reading, MA: Addison-Wesley, pp. 239–62 and *Geography and Trade,* Cambridge, MA: MIT Press.

Lane, D.A. and R. Maxfield (1997), 'Foresight, Complexity, and Strategy', in W.B. Arthur, S.N. Durlauf and D.A. Lane (eds), *The Economy as an Evolving Complex System II,* Reading, MA: Addison-Wesley, pp. 169–98.

Leijonhufvud, A. (1997), 'Macroeconomics and Complexity: Inflation Theory', in W.B. Arthur, S.N. Durlauf and D.A. Lane (eds), *The Economy as an Evolving Complex System II,* Reading, MA: Addison-Wesley, pp. 321–35.

Lindgren, K., C.G. Langton, C. Taylor, J.D. Farmer and S. Rasmussen (eds) (1991), in *Artificial Life II,* Reading, MA: Addison-Wesley.

Lucas, R.E. (1978), 'Asset Prices in an Exchange Economy', *Econometrica,* **46** (6), 1429–45.

Marimon R., E. McGrattan and J.T. Sargent (1990), *Journal of Economic Dynamics and Control,* **14**, 329.

Marshall A. [1891], (1961), *Principles of Economics,* 9th edn, London: Macmillan.

North, D.C. (1997), 'Some Fundamental Puzzles in Economic History/Development', in W.B. Arthur, S.N. Durlauf and D.A. Lane (eds), *The Economy as an Evolving Complex System II*, Reading, MA: Addison-Wesley, pp. 223–37.

Sargent, T.J. (1993), *Bounded Rationality in Macroeconomics*, Oxford: Clarendon Press.

Shubik, M. (1997), 'Time and Money', in W.B. Arthur, S.N. Durlauf and D.A. Lane (eds), *The Economy as an Evolving Complex System II*, Reading, MA: Addison-Wesley, pp. 263–83.

Tesfatsion, L. (1997), 'How Economists Can Get ALife', in W.B. Arthur, S.N. Durlauf and D.A. Lane (eds), *The Economy as an Evolving Complex System II*, Reading, MA: Addison-Wesley, pp. 533–64.

2. Some Santa Fe Scenery

William A. Brock[*]

Complexity is a complex subject. In this chapter I try to make it a bit simpler by providing some Santa Fe scenery that gives one a visual picture of what the study of complexity is about.[1] Having done that I discuss how this picture can be taught to students. Since this chapter is an attempt to communicate to students, I am going to dispense with the qualifications and nuances that are common to academic discourse. This is done to give students a clear and uncluttered picture without the usual half dozen qualifiers in front of each noun.

The study of complexity is related to, but is different from, the study of chaos, so let me begin with a couple of words about the difference between chaos and complexity. Chaos deals with non-linear difference and differential equations generating complicated patterns – too complicated to be analyzed easily even though they are deterministic systems.

An example is a pseudo random number generator on the computer. These simple random number generating systems generate very complicated patterns that you need sophisticated statistical methods to detect. Indeed a high quality pseudo random number generator should fool any statistical test for randomness on computers of available resolutions.

The study of complexity is the opposite of the study of chaos; it is the study of how a very complicated set of equations can generate some very simple patterns for certain parameter values. Complexity considers whether these patterns have a property of universality about them. Here we will call these patterns scaling laws. An example is the US stock market: that is about as complicated as you can get. This is a highly interconnected evolutionary dynamical system of hundreds of thousands of participants, all connected together trying to beat each other, and yet certain patterns emerge. The study of complexity is the study of those patterns.

PATTERNS AND SCALING LAWS

A nice image to convey the sense of patterns and scaling laws was created by Per Bak (1996), whom we will call the sandpile man, because his image involves a pile of sand. Think of a pile of sand on a table that has a continuous flow of sand falling on the top of the pile. For a while, the sand builds up into a large conical sandpile, but at periodic times, when the sandpile builds up to what Bak calls self-organized-criticality, there is an avalanche or series of avalanches until the pile 'relaxes' back to a state where avalanches cease. To repeat, they occur as the sandpile mountain reaches certain proportions as sand drops down upon it from above. The distribution of sizes and 'relaxation times' of these avalanches follows scaling law patterns.

The study of complexity tries to understand the forces that underlie the patterns or scaling laws that develop. You can also represent the sandpile dynamics in a computer as something called a threshold cellular automaton. This is obtained by 'digitizing' the space on which the sandpile lives and representing the dynamics of the pile as a difference equation defined on this 'digitized' space.

Sandpile metaphors are a way of viewing situations where some kind of pressure builds up that is released in a chain reaction that temporarily relieves the pressure until it builds up again to a 'critical' level to be released once again. Scaling laws are a way of representing patterns in the sizes of the chain reactions and the lengths of time each reaction lasts. It turns out that in many cases the sizes and lengths are distributed according to a power law that looks much like the Pareto law of income distribution and the shape of the power law is amazingly independent of the details of the particular sandpile dynamics.

This last property is called 'universality'. To put it another way Bak's metaphorical sandpile evolves to a self-organized critical state where 'relaxation events', that is, sandslides or avalanches, occur at all size and length scales (within the constraints set by the size of the pile itself). A closely related phenomenon occurs at criticality in statistical mechanics models; for example droplets at all size scales appear just when water is at the edge of a boiling point (within the size constraints imposed by the vessel that contains the water).[2]

Most people are not interested in statistical mechanics and sandpiles, but a whole lot of people are interested in financial markets – especially chain reactions in financial markets. This makes the complexity analysis of interest because the same type of patterns shows up in finance. If researchers can understand the scaling laws underlying financial patterns, and predict when an 'avalanche' will occur, what 'size' it is, and how 'long' it will last, they will make lots of money. Thus, many people have a very strong interest in studying complexity. Later in the chapter, I will show you some patterns in finance.

ECONOMICS AND PATTERNS

Some versions of standard economics do not much look for patterns. Instead, they are a type of deductive study that is often highly formal involving proofs and lemmas. That is not the approach to science that most scientists take; this type of standard economics approach belongs to mathematical philosophy more than it does to science. It may be important, but it is not science. As some famous sage stated: 'To do science is to find patterns and explain them.' This view was expressed early on at the first conference at Santa Fe. In ecology, one of the most cogent statements of this view is Brown's book, *Macroecology* (1995). Since economics and ecology are closely related, Brown's approach is useful to us too.

Many noneconomists were surprised by the formality of some of the economics that was presented at an early Santa Fe Institute meeting (see Anderson, Arrow and Pines 1988). These scientists took a much more inductive, rather than deductive, approach to economics, that is, they emphasized patterns and argued that we are not working hard enough to explain these patterns. They argued that we are spending too much time on deductive formalistic theoretical mathematical work and not enough time on inductive pattern explanation type of work.[3]

In terms of methodology, if there is one thing that separates the Santa Fe approach from formalistic and deductive approaches, it is that the Santa Fe approach looks for patterns and constructs explanations using tools that blend ideas from evolutionary computation and statistical mechanics. Let me briefly discuss some of the patterns that appear in reality.

First, consider Zipf's Law of city size scaling. For example, a simple pattern emerges when you relate the sizes of cities in the US to their population, as discussed in Krugman (1996) in Arthur, Durlauf and Lane (1997). There Krugman displays a plot of the log of each city's population against the log of its area rank for the largest metropolitan areas in the US. The resulting graph is almost precisely a 45 degree downward sloping line. This relationship holds generally, and is a visual representation of a simple scaling law: if you multiply a city's area rank by its population, the product is close to a constant number. For example Houston is the tenth largest city in the US and has a population of 3.85 million; Spokane is the one hundredth largest city and has a population of 370,000. Gell-Mann (1994) discusses a modified version of Zipf's Law that fits data better as well as discussing the character of the scale independence of this and related scaling laws.

Second, another famous scaling relationship is due to Mandelbrot (1983). Take time-series returns on any asset, for example, foreign exchange, and look at the fraction of daily returns in the time-series data set that is greater than some amount, say X. Call this $PR(X)$. Take the log of $PR(X)$. Plot that on the vertical axis of your graph paper. Then plot the log of that number X on the horizontal axis. What you will get is almost a straight downward sloping line. This slope, alpha, is called the tail exponent.

In my view this is a remarkable and unexpected pattern. Mandelbrot did this for US cotton prices from before the Civil War. The US had gone through a lot of turmoil, a lot of shocking events – shocking both in the statistical and other senses – and yet Mandelbrot got the same value of alpha when he plotted these plots for cotton returns before the Civil War and after the Civil War. If you do this for daily data, weekly data or monthly data, you get approximately the same value of alpha. This observation led to Mandelbrot's self-similarity hypothesis. He argued (1983) that this scaling law was pervasive in nature. It was the most strikingly regular fact he had ever seen in economics, even though, if you look at returns themselves, they are essentially non-predictable – even with nonlinear methods.

The self-similarity hypothesis (which is a special kind of 'complexity theoretic' hypothesis) is that, no matter what frequency, or what market you look at, or what country you look at, you get approximately the same value of alpha. Mandelbrot said there must be some deep reason for that, and if you are going to estimate distributions for stock returns they should satisfy the self-similar property. Translated into mathematics that means, for example, if one has two random variables each distributed normally, and one adds them together, one gets a normal distribution.

The above proposition is a very important proposition underlying the complexity vision, so let me discuss some of its implications. Self similarity means that patterns form at various levels and repeat themselves. That repetition does not have to be smooth or continuous; it can be, and usually is, discrete. As we study that repetition, we can understand things. It means that the simplicity of complex systems is to be found in the study of iterative processes, not in the system. So, like all science, the science of complexity looks for simplicity, but it looks for that simplicity in iterative processes, not in the structure of the system. Put another way: simplicity is to be found in the underlying generating functions, not in the complex organization of reality. The foundations of complexity science are in statistics and probability study, not in calculus or set theory.

The most general class of distributions that satisfy the property that when you add them together you get a distribution in that family, is the so-called Pareto–Levy family of distributions. What Mandelbrot was estimating is the alpha or the Pareto–Levy exponent. When you look at financial returns data, the distribution has very thick tails. There are many more events in the tails than a Gaussian distribution would predict, and so Mandelbrot's argument was that you should be using Pareto–Levy distributions; that is the technical relation to the scaling law.[4]

What one is looking for in the data are exploitable patterns or, in statistical terms, out-of-sample predictability. Unfortunately, for those who want to make a killing on Wall Street, you will find very little out-of-sample predictability in financial returns, unless you condition on very special events and, even then, the findings of out-of-sample predictability will tend to be unstable.[5] A dramatic account of how difficult it is to find any exploitable pattern in 'deep' highly developed markets is in Kahn (1998). Kahn adduces evidence via investigative reporting that even 'quants' using the latest mathematical and computational techniques have found it extremely difficult to exploit patterns, for example, find instances of exploitable out-of-sample predictability after paying transactions costs.

COMPUTER SIMULATED MARKETS

Despite the lack of out-of-sample predictability, there are many beautiful patterns that can be found in financial data. There is a list of some of these and discussion of possible mechanisms that generate some of them in Brock's chapter in Arthur, Durlauf, and Lane (1997).[6]

The Santa Fe Institute volume edited by Friedman and Rust (1993) discusses simulated pit trading and applications to real markets as well as a tournament where people were invited to submit trading strategies with a prize going to the winner. These simulated stock markets are great teaching tools because they have the excitement of video arcade computer games and students can even try out their own trading strategies against robot traders.

Understanding the forces behind the robust patterns that scientists have observed in asset markets is useful for policy issues such as regulation of financial markets. If you look at returns on IBM, Apple, or Microsoft, and many other assets, you're going to get the same pattern. The following are some examples: (1) measures of volatility of returns are positive correlated over time; (2) measures of trading volume (detrended) are positively correlated over time; (3) measures of volatility and volume are contemporaneously correlated with correlations falling off rapidly with leads and lags; (4) returns are very hard to predict out-of-sample using past information such as past returns. Brock et al. (1996) discusses these patterns and evaluates the ability of different models in terms of their ability to generate these patterns. Brock's paper in Arthur, Durlauf and Lane (1997) reviews patterns like these and discusses recent research on building models that help explain the sources of these patterns. LeBaron, Arthur and Palmer (1998) show how their simulated stock market can generate these kinds of pattern.[7]

Rigorous and statistically precise discussion of the patterns quickly becomes complicated, which is why it is important that students get an excellent background in statistics and math if they are studying economics. But the general proposition is simple: what we see with scaling laws are hugely complex systems generating strikingly simple patterns that have a universality about them in the sense that the same kinds of patterns show up for many different types of assets and for many different time scales. Indeed some scientists consider a similarity of pattern across many different temporal and 'spatial' (where 'space' is interpreted widely, for example, different classes of assets) scales to be a hallmark signature of a 'complex system'.

DEFINING COMPLEX SYSTEMS

In this chapter I have avoided the job of defining 'complex system'. The reason is that it is hard to define. It is easier to illustrate by examples.[8]

If I were forced to give a definition the study of complexity might usefully be defined as the study of the generating functions underlying patterns like those discussed above. One nice thing about the study of patterns is that they give you a natural way to distinguish micro from macro. The macro category is separated from the micro category by the degree of survival of the phenomena to aggregation. To put it another way, the phenomenon is classified as 'macro' if it survives a type of law of large numbers, that is, if there is a strong enough dependence across individual micro units in some kind of statistical sense so that the 'averaging' effect of aggregation does not 'wash out' the phenomenon of interest. Put another way, a pattern could be called a 'macro' pattern if it still appears in data that is aggegated up from micro data. Because of 'emergent' phenomena, new macro patterns can appear at different levels of aggregation that cannot happen in micro patterns. See Brown's book, *Macroecology* (1995), for examples in ecology.

HOW TO TEACH CHAOS AND COMPLEXITY: THE EXAMPLE OF ECOLOGY

Students generally are not wild about developing the mathematical background to properly understand these kinds of patterns. But they can be enticed. Consider an example from ecology where Roughgarden (1996) has written a recent undergraduate book that might serve as some inspiration for us economists. This book uses MATLAB heavily and hooks into the 'computer/Internet' culture of today's college student. It has many examples of programs that the kids can run on their own machines and the code is in the text so that the teacher is not bothered with debugging and explaining the code.

In my view Roughgarden's book is precisely the way one needs to teach complexity. Here is why. Instead of 'beating up' on some 'strawman version' of 'conventional ecology' Roughgarden first teaches the standard, for example, logistic, Lotka-Volterra predator/prey and competition models. He then branches out into the newer Tilmanesque models of plant competition. Roughgarden's book shows the student how to extrapolate useful insights from these 'conventional' models. After using these as 'teasers' the book then starts giving the student little MATLAB computer model–running exercises, based on these simple 'building block' models. Before long the student is doing computer simulations by drawing species at random from lognormal species characteristics distributions and running these dynamical models on MATLAB when analytical tractability is no longer available. Soon the student is doing sequential colonization exercises in simulated computerized island biogeography.

After the student gets used to assembling communities and unleashing the dynamics to see where it goes (using MATLAB), Roughgarden starts putting these systems on 'patches', coupling the patches together, and letting the students simulate these patchy systems. Before long the student has been seduced into a 'cellular automaton/dynamical system' view of 'ecological process' instead of 'ecological static equilibrium'.

The student starts to see when to use 'static equilibrium' analysis and when to use 'equilibrium process' analysis. He sees where the notion of 'equilibrium' is not very useful at all to understand 'the system' and where it is useful. The student relates 'emergent structure' to 'body clumping' in the simulated sequential colonization exercise. The student sees 'emergent surprises' and gets an understanding of when to expect such surprises. As he does so he can begin to understand how and why they occur. The simulated systems generate patterns such as 'lumpy' body size distributions that teach the students something about ecological patterns in the real world.

All of this would have been impossible without the computer and software such as MATLAB. But analytics are *not* abandoned in Roughgarden. The computer and analytics work together as complements to give the student an understanding of ecology. The ecology example Roughgarden gives provides suggestions for economists integrating complexity into our teaching. Roughgarden started the book out teaching conventional ecology, but the book is setting the kids up to go further into nontraditional textbook material than Colander's 15 percent 'new stuff' rule. Recall that Colander has stressed that sales of an undergraduate textbook fall off rapidly if you include more than 15 percent 'new material' relative to the mean or median book that is currently on the market. Roughgarden's book is going to go for 30 percent, maybe more, by slipping the new material in through computer 'games' and hooking into the Internet culture of the young.

Roughgarden is an ecologist. The science of ecology, in general, stresses an approach to complexity that is attractive to students. While it takes an approach that is closely related to the Santa Fe approach, there are some differences. Let us try to explain by explaining the complexity approach of the Resilience Network (hereafter called the 'Rnet'), which is a group of systems ecologists and economists that I am also associated with.[9] The reason for spending time on this is to learn what teaching and research strategies we might borrow from ecology that might help us teach economics.

Gunderson, Holling and Light (1995) review a series of case studies that show the student how ecosystems are organized by nested processes in a hierarchy of space and time scales. Ecologists tend to view ecosystems through a lens of a nested hierarchy of differential equations where the differential equation at level h in the hierarchy operates on a timescale that is an order of magnitude faster than the differential equation at level $h + 1$.

These differential equations may be stochastic. Hence the variables driven by the differential equation at level $h + 1$ serve as potential 'bifurcation parameters' for variables driven by the differential equation at level h. Stochastic shocks to the differential equation at level $h + 1$ make the 'abrupt changes' or 'bifurcations' at level h hard to predict. This hierarchy of differential equations is then coupled across chunks of space called 'patches'.

As an example, just think of the forces that govern the population dynamics of creatures whose life cycles range from short (house flies) to long (elephants) and whose foraging ranges range from a few square meters to several kilometers.

As in the case of the sandpile dynamics, there is exogenous forcing at different levels of this hierarchy of differential equations. For example, the rotation of the earth about its axis causes night/day cycles while the rotation of the earth about the sun causes the seasonal cycles. Ecological time series and general data analysis tends to stress possible multiple stable states at each level and spatial chunk (patch) of the hierarchy of differential equations.

A data analysis tool, called a Stommel diagram, is very popular (for example Gunderson, Holling and Light 1995, Powell and Steele 1995). This is a two-dimensional diagram where measures of temporal activity are plotted against measures of spatial activity. However one sets up these diagrams one tends to see 'clumps' in time/space on the diagram with an upward slope to the distribution of clumps on the diagram.[10]

Stommel diagrams suggest one way of adducing evidence for an Rnet view of the world versus a 'sandpile' view of the world. If one prepared a Stommel diagram for sandpile activity by plotting measures of temporal activity on the horizontal axis of the diagram (measured, for example, by length of time from start to finish of each sandslide) and plotted measures of spatial activity on the vertical axis (measured, for example, by the number of grains involved in the slide or the fraction of area involved in the slide), then Bak's power law scaling suggests an even distribution of activity spread out across a log/log axis Stommel diagram. In contrast Rnet hierarchies suggest a series of 'lumpy' clumps of activity on log/log Stommel diagrams. Rnet articles cited above contain Stommel diagrams that are lumpy (see also Powell and Steele (1995) for many examples). Hence this evidence seems to support the Rnet view.

However, this comparison is unfair to sandpile models unless we build a hierarchy of sandpiles operating at different temporal/spatial scales to compare with the hierarchy of dynamics in the Rnet writings. In plain English, a hierarchy of sandpiles would correspond to a hierarchy of phenomena at different time/space scales where pressure builds up, leading to a chain reaction of relaxation until the pressure rebuilds up. Hence one would have to look closer at each lump on Rnet Stommel diagrams and see if there is evidence of a lumpy structure within that lump or see if there is evidence of a more uniformly spread out distribution of activity measure within that lump. A less lumpy distribution of activity measure within each Stommel lump is supportive of sand-pile type activity in contrast to alternative stable state activity as promoted by Rnet theorizing. The three-dimensional version of the Stommel diagram discussed in Clark (1985) where the other axis measures the 'power' of activity at each 'space/time scale' point in the 'floor' of the diagram may be needed to reveal enough difference in pattern to adduce evidence for or against any particular view.

We have no answer to the hard question discussed above. The only reason we raised the issue in the first place is to show how complexity type theorizing unleashes the mental imagination into entirely unexpected directions that stress visual computer graphic constructive devices of scientific dispute resolution that should be attractive to today's students.

In economics we can adapt some of the teaching and theorizing strategies discussed above in an attempt to stimulate our students and show them how economics can be presented in just as exciting a manner as ecology. Let me give some examples.

First let me consider an example of a Roughgarden-like approach. Consider micro textbook writing for undergraduates. A simple example for a chapter might be conventional static supply/demand analysis followed by the cobweb model for some very simple dynamics. First teach the conventional cobweb model in discrete time with adaptive expectations (next period's expected price is last period's price). This is a simple high school difference equation built up from the simplest supply and demand story where producers form price expectations today and produce for delivery one period from now.

After this background, in order to teach the student how complex patterns can arise from the simplest economically plausible dynamics, the simple 'adaptive agent' model of Brock and Hommes (1997) could be primed up for

MATLAB à la Roughgarden. In this model agents 'reproduce' according to prediction error of their 'phenotype', that is types with lower prediction error increase in number relative to types with higher prediction errors. One type is rational expectations (perfect foresight) but this requires payment of a 'cognitive' cost. The other type uses simple backward-looking 'cobweb' expectations. If supply is more elastic than demand (the usual case in agriculture), then a population of all backward-looking agents generates unstable cobweb cycles. As the amplitude of fluctuations increases it becomes worthwhile for some agents to 'purchase' rational expectations and as more agents switch to a population of more rational expectations agents, this 'far from equilibrium' force stabilizes the system.

The economy as a whole goes through 'phases' where it is 'mostly rational' and 'mostly boundedly rational'. The phases are seemingly 'random' (but are actually deterministic). This system shows how the interaction between costly 'conventional' = 'hyper' rationality, 'informational free riding' and 'evolutionary selection pressure' can generate complex patterns (actually a form of 'chaos') from a simple system.

The logic of the system is compelling because no one believes the level of rationality required in conventional rational expectations is available for 'free'. If rationality is costly it may not cover its cost to an individual 'purchaser' when everyone is using it. Hence there will be incentives to 'free ride' on the rational expectations efforts of others; this free riding causes an evolutionary selection force against 'full/costly' rationality. It is more rational to economize on costs of figuring out the 'true model' when payoff for learning the true model does not cover its cost. But when all agents are using 'cheap' methods of prediction, instability can slowly grow to the point where fluctuations become large enough to cover the cost of a better prediction method, for example rational expectations available at a cost.

This little system boils down to a pair of difference equations in the plane which can be analyzed with analytical methods, but could simply be put up on MATLAB for freshmen to play with. It's that simple. Once the students are hooked into playing around with this system they will have been moved from simple supply/demand analysis to simple cobweb expectational analysis to the analysis of the relative responsiveness of demand and supply play in economic 'stability' to the adaptive struggle of one side of the economy trying to 'informationally free ride' on the costly information gathering of other parts of the economy to a process-oriented view where there is   no general equilibrium at all.

There is a 'process' going on here (and the process is logically unavoidable because there is a tension between paying for costly rationality and the system generating enough fluctuation to cover that cost). This causes the system to never settle down to an equilibrium. There is only some idea of an 'equilibrium process'.

SOME IDEAS ABOUT TEACHING PATTERN DETECTION

Let me now turn to techniques for teaching chaos, and the detecting of patterns. I begin teaching students about pattern detection by pointing out that it is a key task of model fitters to see if there is some pattern in errors of any real-world model, whether it's a financial model, macro model or whatever. Then I teach them some techniques for finding that pattern.

Let us start on chaos. I start out with a very simple problem that can be solved on a calculator. Students, nowadays, even at the high school level, are familiar with graphic calculators, if not computers. I tell my students to type the following into a calculator or computer:

$$X(t + 1) = 2X(t) \text{, for } X(t) \text{ in } [0,1/2]$$

$$(2.1)$$

$$X(t + 1) = 2 - 2X(t) \text{, for } X(t) \text{ in } [1/2,1]$$

I tell them to draw an initial $X(0)$ at random using a uniform random number generator on [0,1] and run system (2.1) using this $X(0)$ as an initial condition. Look at the sequence of numbers produced. If you graph $X(t + 1)$ against $X(t)$ for all periods you will notice that all points lie on a tent-shaped graph. That is why (2.1) is called the 'tent map'. This is a very simple pseudo-random number generator that develops what might be called pedagogical chaos, even though the system is extraordinarily simple – any kid that has written down a do-loop on a computer can write this down and play with it on their own. You do not even have to tell them anything about math.

The remarkable properties of this system are the following: (1) The covariance of succeeding observations will be zero. To show them this, you give the students an initial starting point, $X(0)$, and ask them to calculate the covariance of succeeding observations, for example, the covariance between $X(T)$ and $X(T-1)$, over a sample of data. You get approximately zero. (2) The long-term mean will converge to one half. This is a useful exercise for students that both my graduate students and undergraduate students can do. I then ask if any of my students know what spectral analysis is. My undergraduates generally don't, but I usually have some graduate students who know what that is. I ask them to calculate the spectrum. That spectrum will be flat. Then I ask them to calculate the long-run frequency of observations between any two numbers, A < B between zero and one. This long-run frequency turns out to be B−A. In other words, this is just a simple uniform pseudo-random number generator for random numbers in [0,1].

Now I get them to see if they can detect patterns in the observations. This is something the teacher can do. Generate 1000 observations from (2.1) and give them to the students. Award a prize to the first student who figures out how these observations are generated; that is, give a prize to the student who figures out how to predict $X(t)$ given $X(t-1)$.

Now imagine that a deterministic generating mechanism like (2.1) might be lurking in the forecast errors of some model that you have fit to data. How might you detect this possibility? Well, for the tent map it would be easy to detect it, because all you would have to do is plot $X(T)$ against $X(T-1)$ for your data set and if the points all lie on some graph, you know there is a deterministic mechanism generating the data. That is obvious. But the problem is that it is easy to generate examples like the tent map that are highly dimensional, so you cannot plot $X(T)$ against $X(T-1)$ and so on, and have any chance of detecting the underlying mechanism – even though it is deterministic. Just think of the example of a computer pseudo-random number generator.

This general detection problem can be attacked with a graphical device called a recurrence plot and measure of local spatial correlation. Here is the idea. Suppose you have got a time series of N observations, for example N might be 1000. Call it $\{X(t); t = 1,2,..., N\}$. For each date t, write out the list of m consecutive observations, $(X(t) , X(t + 1)..., X(t + m-1))$. Call this $Y(t)$. This operation is called 'embedding in m-dimensional space'.

Here is how to prepare a neat object called a recurrence plot.[11] Do this for each pair of dates (t, s). Now make a plot of (t, s) in the following way. Calculate, for each pair, (t, s), the distance between $Y(t)$ and $Y(s)$ and call it $d(t, s)$. Choose a fairly small positive number, call it e, that is smaller than most of these distances, smaller than 80 percent of them, say. Now, on your plot, color the point (t, s) black if $d(t, s) < e$ and color it white otherwise. This is a recurrence plot. Using this device you can get evidence of an underlying deterministic mechanism by varying the 'embedding dimension' m and seeing if you get 'streaks' on this recurrence plot. A streak occurs if (t, s) black tends to imply $(t + 1, s + 1)$ is black.

With a little bit of practice you can learn to read recurrence plots and detect patterns such as a 'regime shift', that is a change in the dynamical process generating the data. These are detected by looking for 'white bands' on the plot. Steady-state periods are detected by looking for 'black boxes' on the plot.

However useful and fascinating a recurrence plot is, it is not a formal statistical testing procedure with confidence levels, 'p-values', and so on. Let us now describe how one might visualize the statistical procedure due to Brock, Dechert, and Scheinkman (see Brock et al. 1996 for a review article on this procedure). Here is how the test works. Let me explain with a visualization using the recurrence plot. Plot your data on a recurrence plot as explained above. Now shuffle your data so that you now have a purely random data set. That is, shuffle your observations just like you shuffle a deck of cards. Now prepare the same recurrence plot for the shuffled data. Superimpose this plot on top of the plot for your original (not shuffled) data and see if your eye can detect a significant difference. That is roughly what our testing procedure does.

Here is an attempt to translate the mathematics of our procedure into plain English. Recall the distance $d(t, s)$ between $Y(t)$ and $Y(s)$ discussed above. Ignoring endpoint problems, if you have N observations you have N squared pairs $d(t, s)$. Count the fraction of these pairs (t, s) such that $d(t, s) < e$ and call this number $C(m, e)$. Notice that m is in the notation to remind you of the dimension of the space that $Y(t)$ and $Y(s)$ live in. Now compute $C(m, e)$ for the shuffled data and call it $CS(m, e)$. Take the difference between $C(m, e)$ and $CS(m, e)$ and multiply this by the square root of N.

Brock et al. (1996) show that this quantity is approximately normally distributed if your data is generated by a purely random process. Hence a statistical test of randomness can be made up out of this procedure. Software to implement this procedure is available with the Brock, Hsieh and LeBaron book (1991).[12]

Notice that the testing procedure outlined above is only a test for independence. It has some nice properties. For example you can use it as a specification test of a class of models that you are fitting to data. This is so because under regularity conditions the asymptotic distribution of the test statistic on estimated errors of your model turns out to be the same as if it were calculated on the true errors. This is a very handy property and may account for some of the popularity of this method.

However, a finding of nonindependence of model errors by this kind of test is only a license to hunt for 'left-out structure'. The test does not tell you what that left-out structure might be. Turn now to financial applications. Any pattern we find in finance is going to have to be very subtle because of the efficient markets hypothesis. Once people find a pattern the prices are going to change to eliminate any profits from it. That is a standard arbitrage argument from financial theory and the data are quite consistent with that argument. So patterns in financial asset returns are going to be very subtle and hard to find because the easy ones will have been sucked out. So we cooked up a method that has power to detect some of these more subtle patterns, but does not imply that profits are available after paying transactions costs and properly adjusting for risk.

BOOTSTRAP-BASED TESTS OF MODELS FITTED TO DATA

This method works as follows: estimate your favorite efficient markets model on the financial returns under scrutiny. For example, estimate a class of models on returns where the returns are not themselves predictable but the volatilities are somewhat predictable. This captures part of the Mandelbrot phenomenon that if stocks get volatile, they will stay volatile for a while. That is a very well-known phenomenon. Measures of volatility of stock prices are persistent, but it is very hard to predict tomorrow whether the price itself will go up or down. If some speaker tells you that he or she can predict stock prices you should ask them why they are speaking to you rather than flying to Tahiti on their own private jet. I always respond to questions about whether our methods can predict stock prices by saying that if I could predict stock prices, I would not be here; I would be in Tahiti. I am here – so you know I cannot predict.

So now, think about what method you could use to discover patterns in a system like the stock market where the price dynamics are co-created by individuals looking for profitable patterns and trading on them? Traders use trading strategies or trading rules. So here is an example of a typical trading rule, a technical trading rule. By the standards of trading rules used in practice, this is a Stone Age tool. But it will do for illustrative purposes. You calculate a 180-day moving average; you get a buy signal when price cuts this moving average from below and a sell signal when price cuts it from above. That is an example of a mechanical type of trading rule. Notice that you have got to have a fairly large movement in stock price relative to the near-past to get a buy signal or sell signal.

Mandelbrot (1983) and others have noticed that when price makes a relatively big move, often this is followed by an increase in volatility that takes a while to settle down. This finding led researchers to build statistical models, called AutoRegressive Conditionally Heteroscedastic, abbreviated as ARCH, models. Some researchers have fit this kind of model to stock returns and have claimed that this captures all the available structure in those returns data. Notice that all this kind of model says is that if stock prices get volatile, they will stay volatile for a while. These models are one way of quantifying a pattern that I mentioned before, that is, volatility measures for the price or the returns on just about any asset are highly correlated over time.

The ARCH models described above are very popular now.[13] Let me describe how the bootstrap-based model testing method can be used to detect departures from an ARCH type model in such a way that some economics lessons are learned from the exercise. Advances in computer technology now make it possible to do simulation experiments that were impossible earlier.

Look at the learning curve in computer technology, à la Rothschild, from the mid 1980s up to the present, and imagine comparable technical progress in the automobile industry. You would have something like a ten cent Ferrari that could accelerate from zero to sixty in, perhaps, a tenth of a second. That is a car that would satisfy even me. The point is that such rapid progress in computer technology has induced fantastic progress in statistical inference methods as well.

BOOTSTRAPPING

That same progress in computer technology and in statistics curve is generating the possibility of integrating complexity into the teaching of economics. There has been a major innovation in statistics that is called bootstrapping. It allows you to replace analytic computations that used to constrain the types of statistics you could use with cheap raw computing power. This allows practical statistical inference methods to be developed where compromises to obtain tractability no longer have to be made.

We are going to describe a model evaluation procedure developed by Brock, Lakonishok and LeBaron (1992), hereafter called 'BLL', that uses the bootstrap and actual trading strategies to evaluate performance of different popular statistical models by using statistical quantities that are motivated by financial interest rather than analytical tractability.[14]

The distribution of returns to something like a technical trading strategy under the hypothesis that the returns data that you see are generated by a member of the ARCH class of data generating processes is a very complicated object by the standard of conventional econometric analysis. Use conventional statistical language and call this the 'null distribution'. But you can bootstrap, for example, the distribution of buy and sell profits as well as holding returns when you buy and you hold for 10 days, sell and hold for 10 days. You can bootstrap the distribution under the null model hypothesis that the ARCH class of models is right, that is, a member of the ARCH class actually is generating the data that you see.

That is possible now, with the cheap and powerful computer technology that is now available. Here is what you do. You read technical and fundamental trading journals. Stock traders are like members of any other profession. They have trade magazines that cater to their interests. I might add that technical trading rules have a bad name in academic finance. Evidence suggests that markets are too efficient for there to be profits in doing something as mechanical as trading based on some technical trading rule like a 180-day moving average rule. You choose some financially relevant measures of trading performance such as profits, returns and volatility of returns following buy and sell signals, and so forth.

If you want to evaluate the ARCH class of models, you fit a member of that class. Then you use that fitted model to bootstrap what is called the null distribution of your financial quantities such as returns and volatility of returns following buy and sell signals. You tick off the actual data values of these quantities on your null distribution and present a graph of this procedure to your readers. You also report probability values under the assumption that the null hypothesis is true and leave it to your readers to decide whether these actual data values are improbable enough under the assumption that a member of the ARCH class generated the data to reject that class.

Notice that using technical trading rules to implement the bootstrap-based test of your favorite class of models, for example the ARCH class, has nothing to do with whether you can make profits from technical trading. Now, we are not claiming that there are profits to be made from using the model-testing procedure advanced in Brock, LaKonishok, and LeBaron (1992). We are just saying that in the age of dirt-cheap computing power let us get rid of constraints on econometric practice that were formed in the days of expensive computer power and before advances such as bootstrapping theory. Furthermore let us design an econometrics that is tailor-made for finance, where the statistical quantities used are financially relevant (for example returns from trading strategies). In some markets technical trading rules are still being used, even though academic finance has been beating up on them for many years (and quite rightly because evidence for profits from using them after paying transactions costs is weak).

But, independently of whether these rules actually pass muster as out-of-sample predictive devices in finance we can use these rules, as well as more 'respectable' fundamentalist rules, to make up a different kind of test of 'goodness-of-fit' of a class of models and evaluate the quality of those models in a new way. What we will do is read trading magazines, take a favorite one of these trading strategies from those magazines, and bootstrap the null distribution of buy and sell returns and the volatility of these returns. Suppose the null class of models under scrutiny is the ARCH class, for example.

Bootstrapping the null distribution of returns of a trading strategy gives us a financially relevant way of measuring the significance of departures of the data from that model. This is important because in finance where you have enormous quantities of data, because any model is an approximation, just about any statistical test will reject that model if the test is any good at all. So rejection is not very interesting. What is interesting is useful information on the direction of rejection.

Here is what BLL found. On a buy signal, these standard models tend to overpredict volatility and they tend to under predict the returns. Bootstrapping the null distribution of these buy signal statistics gives you a way of measuring the 'significance' of these findings so you can assess precisely how likely it is that these findings are simply due to chance fluctuations when the underlying model is actually true. Here is another example of the use of bootstrap-based testing methods to assess how well a class of models fit financial data.

There is a class of models called the Generalized AutoRegressive Conditional Heteroscedastic in Mean (abbreviated GARCH-M). This class of models captures the observed phenomenon that if price moves a relatively large amount in the near past relative to the long-term past, then that event tends to be followed by increased volatility in prices that damps down slowly. Common sense (and a lot of financial theory) suggests that investors have to be paid to bear this increased volatility (if they can not easily diversify it away). GARCH-M is one attempt to capture this phenomenon within the context of a parametric model.

How well does the GARCH-M class perform when fitted to actual data? Well, when you unleash the bootstrap-based specification test on it you find that the GARCH-M model predicts a big positive return following a sell signal, but what you find in the data is zero or slightly negative returns following sell signals. The logic is simple. Getting a sell signal tends to mean that there has been a relatively large move in price (downward) relative to the medium-term past. This causes a slowly dying burst of volatility in GARCH-M type models. But investors have to be paid to bear this increased volatility so their *ex ante* returns must be relatively higher in GARCH-M type models. But that is not consistent with the data. The bootstrap allows you to compute the probability value of this finding under the assumption that a member of the GARCH-M class actually generates the financial data that you see. When you get done with this procedure, you have an idea of where to repair your econometric model in a financially relevant way so that it is more consistent with the data.

In doing econometric inference this way, you are tailoring your statistical quantities to be directly relevant to the application at hand, for example returns and profits for financial applications. You also are using quantities that closely capture the purposive behavior of the agents you are studying. Furthermore you are treating the financial community as if it were populated by statisticians that are hunting for the most powerful tests of the null model, against an alternative that they have a big incentive to find. Their jobs are on the line here. They do not have tenure. And if they do not find some alternatives that give them an edge, they might lose their jobs. This kind of strong incentive concentrates the attention to find relevant alternatives.

The bootstrap and the BLL method allows the econometrician to watch what traders do and use this knowledge to construct statistical quantities such as buy/sell returns of trading strategies that reflect alternatives to some model of the Efficient Markets Hypothesis such as the GARCH-M model that working traders reveal by their very behavior. Using this method the financial econometrician can 'piggy back' on the revealed behavior of traders to construct statistical quantities for use in model evaluation that are more relevant than conventional econometrics.

I have found that this kind of methodology is easier and more enjoyable to teach to students. It can be used in other application areas besides finance, for example optimal foraging theory in ecology. Students like the self-consistency property of the bootstrap. They enjoy release from compromises for the sake of analytical tractability when they do statistical work. They do not mind the extra computational work because they are 'programmed' to turn to computers anyway because of the culture of computer games, video games, Internet, and so on, in which today's youth are raised (in contrast to this writer).

Students enjoy seeing how systematic the departures are from received models and they enjoy the constructive attitude where one builds on the existing models rather than just reporting that the 'data reject the model'. Maddala and Rao (1996) contains very nice articles by Maddala and co-authors on bootstrap-based testing and related methods.

I have tried to show you how pretty some of the patterns and methods are in the above discussion. This kind of material should be just as much fun to teach and should be just as stimulating to students as anything in ecology or physics.

In macroeconomics, one could imagine designing simulational macroeconomic exercises along the lines of the simulational stock market and trading market literature discussed above. Issues of monetary policy, Okun's Law, wage-setting institutions, Phillips curve instability, Lucas Critique, policy irrelevance propositions, fine tuning, oil shocks and other supply-side shocks, demand-side shocks, credit constraints, debt deflations, inflation control measures, Great Depression type issues, and so on could be explored in a simulational macro model with realistic heterogeneity amongst the agents, with different expectational types competing on the basis of performance. Students could be encouraged to calibrate these kinds of models on historical macro data and see if they could get their calibrated systems to reproduce historically observed impulse responses to shocks. All this is far in the future, but research in computationally based complexity approaches is making this kind of teaching closer to reality.

CONCLUSION

There is much more I could say about these issues but I think I have said enough to give you some sense of the Santa Fe vision, which is very much focused on finding patterns. I have discussed how that can be taught to students. My point is that it can be made exciting for students – that students can be drawn into the math if you use a visual approach with computers, building on the technology. I am not saying it is, as yet, easy, but as the learning curve progresses, the teaching of pattern detection will become easier and easier. Since this is the direction in which I believe the science of economics is heading, I think it would be useful for economics professors to get on the learning curve now.

NOTES

*   I would like to thank David Colander for valuable help writing this chapter. He is excused from errors and any other problems in this chapter. I would like to thank the NSF and the Vilas Trust for essential support for my research.
1.   Those who want more Santa Fe scenery should take a look at Anderson, Arrow and Pines (1988), and Arthur, Durlauf and Lane (1997). They should also look at the Santa Fe Institute website: http://www.santafe.edu/.
2.   See Brock's paper in Dechert (1996) and Brock and Durlauf's papers in Arthur, Durlauf and Lane (1997) for more discussion of statistical mechanics models and sandpile models.
3.   See the discussions in Anderson, Arrow and Pines (1988) to get some flavor of the views that were expressed about economics at one of the first Santa Fe Institute conferences.
4.   The statistical analysis of the self-similarity hypothesis and related issues raised by Mandelbrot gets very complicated and is very subtle. See Loretan and Phillips (1991) for a detailed and rigorous theoretical treatment.
5.   See Brock, Hsieh and LeBaron (1991), and Campbell, Lo and MacKinlay (1997) for a review of the evidence.
6.   The papers of Arthur et al. in Arthur, Durlauf and Lane (1997), and LeBaron et al. (1998) discuss how to set up simulational stock markets that are capable of generating these patterns.
7.   Econometricians and statisticians will recognize that I am overstating the quality of patterns that develop in these markets, but the patterns sure look good to the naked eye, and that is what students respond to.
8.   See the two SFI volumes, Anderson, Arrow and Pines (1988) and Arthur, Durlauf and Lane (1997) for many examples. See also how one of the founders of the Santa Fe Institute, Murray Gell-Mann (1994) deals with this difficult question.
9.   See the references to ecologist, C. Holling, in the reference list below, as well as the journal *Conservation Biology* which is edited by C. Holling and is hosted on the WWW (www.consecol.org).
10. A very nice discussion that explains how to construct Stommel-like diagrams, and which gives many examples, is in Clark (1985). A very strong and detailed statement of such clumping phenomena and the forces behind it is Holling (1992). A recent discussion is in Peterson, Holling and Allen (1998). Stommel diagrams appear throughout these references.
11. See page 127 of Brock, Hsieh and LeBaron (1991) for an example for stock returns.
12. One can also obtain software plus a lot of interesting material on pattern detection on Dechert's webpage (http://www.dechert.econ.uh.edu/) and LeBaron's webpage (http://www.ssc.wisc.edu/~blebaron/).
13. See Bollerslev, Engle and Nelson's article in Engle and McFadden (eds) (1994).
14. There is some very beautiful discussion of bootstrap-based specification tests in the book edited by Maddala and Rao (1996).

REFERENCES

Anderson, P., K. Arrow and D. Pines (1988), *The Economy as an Evolving Complex System*, Redwood City, CA: Addison-Wesley.

Arthur, W.B., S. Durlauf and D. Lane (1997), *The Economy as an Evolving Complex System: II*, Redwood City, CA: Addison-Wesley.

Bak, P. (1996), *How Nature Works: The Science of Self-Organized Criticality*, New York: Copernicus Press for Springer-Verlag.

Brock, W. and C. Hommes (1997), 'A Rational Route to Randomness', *Econometrica*, **65** (5), 1059–95.

Brock, W. and S. Durlauf (1999), 'A Formal Model of Theory Choice in Science', *Economic Theory*, **14**, 113–30.

Brock, W., W. Dechert, J. Scheinkman and B. LeBaron (1996), 'A Test for Independence Based Upon the Correlation Dimension', *Econometric Reviews*, **15** (3), 197–235.

Brock, W., J. LaKonishok and B. LeBaron (1992), 'Simple Technical Trading Rules and the Stochastic Properties of Stock Returns', *Journal of Finance*, **XLVII** (5), 1731–64.

Brock, W., D. Hsieh and B. LeBaron (1991), *Nonlinear Dynamics, Chaos and Instability: Statistical Theory and Economic Evidence*, Cambridge, MA: MIT Press.

Brown, J. (1995), *Macroecology*, Chicago, IL: University of Chicago Press.

Campbell, J., A. Lo and C. MacKinlay (1997), *The Econometrics of Financial Markets*, Princeton, NJ: Princeton University Press.

Carpenter, S., D. Ludwig and W. Brock (1999), 'Management of Eutrophication for Lakes Subject to Potentially Irreversible Change', *Ecological Appications*, **9** (3), 751–71.

Clark, W. (1985), 'Scales of Climate Impacts', *Climate Change*, **7**, 5–27.

Dechert, W. (1996), 'Chaos Theory in Economics: Methods, Models, and Evidence', *The International Library of Critical Writings in Economics*, **66**, Cheltenham, UK: Edward Elgar.

Engle, R. and D. McFadden (eds) (1994), *Handbook of Econometrics: IV*, Amsterdam: North Holland.

Friedman, D. and J. Rust (1993), *The Double Auction Market*, Reading, MA: Addison-Wesley.

Gell-Mann, M. (1994), *The Quark and the Jaguar: Adventures in the Simple and the Complex*, New York: W. Freeman and Co.

Gunderson, L., C. Holling and S.Light (eds) (1995), *Barriers and Bridges to the Renewal of Ecosystems and Institutions*, New York: Columbia University Press.

Holling, C. (1992), 'Cross-Scale Morphology, Geometry, and Dynamics of Ecosystems', *Ecological Monographs*, **62** (4), 447–502.

Holling, C. (ed.) (1997), *Conservation Ecology*, hosted on the WWW at (http://www.consecol.org).

Judd, K. (1997), *Numerical Methods in Economics*, Cambridge, MA: MIT Press.

Kahn, J. (1998), 'Investing by The Numbers Doesn't Offer a Great Edge', *New York Times*, July 21.

Koop, G. and S. Potter (1999), 'Bayes Factors and Nonlinearity: Evidence from Economic Time Series', *Journal of Econometrics*, **88** (2), 251–81.

Krugman, P. (1997), 'How an Economy Organizes itself in Space', in W.B. Arthur, S. Durlauf and D. Lane (eds), *The Economy as an Evolving Complex System II*, Reading, MA: Addison-Wesley.

Krugman, P. (1996), *The Self-Organizing Economy*, Oxford: Blackwell Publishers.

LeBaron, B., W.B. Arthur and R. Palmer (1999), 'Time Series Properties of an Artificial Stock Market', *Journal of Economic Dynamics and Control*, **23**, 1487–516.

Levin, S. et al. (1998), 'Resilience in Natural and Socioeconomic Systems', *Environment and Development Economics,* **3** (2), 222–34.

Maddala, G. and C. Rao (eds) (1996), *Handbook of Statistics: Statistical Methods in Finance*, Amsterdam: North Holland.

Mandelbrot, B. (1983), *The Fractal Geometry of Nature*, New York: W.H. Freeman.

Peterson, G., C. Allen and C. Holling (1998), 'Diversity, Resilience and Scale', *Ecosystems*, **1**, 1–15.

Powell, T. and J. Steele (1995), *Ecological Time Series*, New York: Chapman and Hall.

Roughgarden, J. (1996), *Primer of Ecological Theory*, New York: Prentice Hall.

3. Cognition: The Black Box of Economics*

W. Brian Arthur

In his autobiography Bertrand Russell tells us he dropped his interest in economics after half a year's study because he thought it was too simple. Max Planck dropped his involvement with economics because he thought it was too difficult. I went into economics because I had been trained in mathematics and I thought, as Russell did, that economics looked easy. It took me several years to get from Russell's position to Planck's. Economics is inherently difficult. In this chapter I will explain one path by which I came to that view.

Whether one sees economics as inherently difficult or as simple depends on how one formulates economic problems. If one sets up a problem and assumes rationality of decision making, a well-defined solution normally follows. Economics here is simple: from the problem follows the solution. But how agents get from problem to solution is a black box; and whether indeed agents can arrive at the solution cannot be guaranteed unless we look into this box. If we open this box economics suddenly becomes difficult.

Once in a while as economists, we do justify our assumed connection between problem and solution. In a well-known paper, Rust (1987) tells the story of Harold Zurcher, the superintendent of maintenance at the Madison (Wisconsin) Metropolitan Bus Company. For 20 years Zurcher scheduled bus engine replacement of a large fleet of buses – a complicated problem that required him to balance two conflicting objectives: minimizing maintenance costs versus minimizing unexpected engine failures. Rust figured out the solution to this combinatorial optimization problem by stochastic dynamic programming, and matched that optimization against Zurcher's. He found a reasonably close fit. The point of Rust's article was that although this was an enormously complicated problem, Harold Zurcher found the solution and therefore, at least in this case, economists' assumption that individuals find optimal solutions to complex questions is not a bad assumption.

The Zurcher example leaves us with a broad question: Can the assumption that individuals find optimal solutions to economic problems be justified so that we can avoid studying the details of the decision process? In simple cases the answer is yes. In most cases, however, it is no. Think of an ocean that contains all the well-defined problems that interest us in the economy, with ever more difficult problems at greater depths. Near the surface lie problems like tic-tac-toe. Below that are problems at the level of checkers, and deeper still are problems like chess and Go. We might know theoretically that a solution to chess exists, say in mixed Nash strategy form, but we can't guarantee that human agents would arrive at it. So the problems that are solvable the way tic-tac-toe is solvable lie within two or three inches of the surface, but at levels deeper than this, problems cannot be guaranteed a solution. We can add to these the many problems agents face, perhaps the majority they face, that are *not* well specified. Zurcher's problem lies on the boundary of what economics agents can accomplish by way of a 'rational' solution. Deeper than this, economic 'solutions' may not match 'rationality' or may not exist.

What happens at these deeper levels? Human decision-makers do not back off from a problem because it is difficult or unspecified. We might say that when problems are too complicated to afford solutions, or when they are not well-specified, agents face not a problem but a situation. They must deal with that situation; they must frame the problem, and that framing in many ways is the most important part of the decision process. To consider that framing you have to consider what lies between the problem and the action taken. And between the problem and the action lies cognition. Between the problem and the solution there's a lot going on, and if one considers what is going on, economics becomes difficult. To paraphrase my question then: How do people make sense of a problem? How do individuals handle these more complicated problems? How do we really cognize?

In this chapter I want to consider cognition as a cognitive psychologist might look at it, and apply the findings to thinking about two different issues: economic modeling and the education of graduate students.

NOTIONS OF THE MIND

In economics we have a simple and old notion of mind. Mind is a container that holds data. The data are constantly updated by interaction with the world; and mind performs deductions based upon these data. All of this of course is implicit; in economics we don't talk about 'mind'. But we do view mind – or that which gives rise to ratiocination – as deduction upon collections of data sets. In economic theory this is reflected in treating beliefs about the world as expectations of variables conditioned upon current data (or sigma fields) – current information – and in formulating solutions based upon these. This is a shorthand, the sort of reasonable abstraction that any science makes that works well in many cases. But we need to get beyond it when we go deeper than two or three inches into the ocean of problems.

Let me look at mind and the cognitive process then from a deeper view-point – that of cognitive science. Imagine that at night you are reading a novel, say Haldór Laxness's *Independent People* and you're enjoying it. What is actually going on? Actually, that's complicated. The black and white marks on the page are focused onto the light sensors or pixels at the back of your retina. These sensory perceptions are transmitted to the rear part of your brain, and map into certain visual structures there. Somehow letters and words are parsed out, and somehow these fit together via an understanding of syntax. (Where I say 'somehow' I mean that cognitive scientists do not know the exact mechanism of what is happening.) From syntax somehow 'meaning' emerges. But what is meaning? Meaning in this case is a set of associations. You might read a sentence about rain: 'Smoothly, smoothly it fell, over the whole shire, over the fallen marsh grass, over the troubled lake, the iron-gray gravel flats, the somber mountain above the croft, smudging out every pros-pect.' These words trigger associations – associated memories really – and you form a picture, or a set of pictures. These associated memories and pic-tures in turn trigger what you might call 'affect', or feelings. The feelings are often subtle, the kind of feelings of what it might be like to be in Laxness's world – the gloom of the rain, the dreariness of the gravel flats, the oppres-siveness of the mountain, the smell of the croft in the dampness. These are subtle feelings, and these feelings actually are our intelligence, are part of our cognition. They're part of the meaning that we give to symbols. Reading and making sense of what is read consist of associated memories and associated feelings. How all this happens is not well understood by cognitive scientists; it's what French thinker Henri-Jean Martin calls a mysterious alchemy.

Here's how the Princeton cognitive psychologist Julian Jaynes (1976, p. 1) expresses this alchemy of mind:

> O, what a world of unseen visions and heard silences, this insubstantial country of the mind! What ineffable essences, these touchless rememberings and unshowable rev-eries! And the privacy of it all! A secret theater of speechless monologue and preve-nient counsel, an invisible mansion of all moods, musings, and mysteries, an infinite resort of disappointments and discoveries. A whole kingdom where each of us reigns reclusively alone, questioning what we will, commanding what we can. A hidden hermitage where we may study out the troubled book of what we have done and yet may do. An introcosm that is more myself than anything I can find in a mirror. This consciousness that is myself of selves, that is everything, yet nothing at all – what is it? And where did it come from? And why?

The point I want to make here is the meaning that's abstracted from the book is not *in* the book; it is in the mind. It's a point that starts to get recog-nized in philosophy in the 1700s by Kant, but isn't fully articulated until the twentieth century. We construct meaning by the associations we make. If this seems strange, imagine a page in Dostoyevsky shown to a Russian reader and a non-Russian reader. Each gets exactly the same data, but the Russian has the associations to parse the Cyrillic script and make the written sense data come alive. The non-Russian sees exactly the same data; but his associations if he does not speak the language are nil and there is no meaning. Meaning therefore is imposed. It emerges by our imposing associations. It's not Dostoyevsky or the book *Independent People* that brings meaning to me – that's an illusion. It's *me* that brings meaning to *Independent People*. *I*'m making sense, *I*'m imposing associations, *I* impose meaning on what I'm seeing. Not just any old meaning, but the meaning that emerges from the associations the book makes with my neural memory.

Let me give you another example because I want to hammer on this point and derive a few things from it. There's a Yeats poem that goes something like this: 'Down by the salley gardens my love and I did meet; she passed the salley gardens on little snow-white feet. She bid me to take life easy, like the grass grows on the weirs, but I was young and foolish, and now am full of tears.'[1] These words will have different effects on different people – different meanings. Ask yourself what meaning you get out of weirs. For me this has enormous meaning because I and my friends played near weirs as children. (Weirs are little dams in a stream, usually covered with algae and some form of green trailing grass.) I also know what salley gardens are. But those who are not Irish will probably be affected differently. They may wonder: what are salley gardens anyway? Maybe Salley had a garden. Maybe there's such a thing as the Salley Gardens – maybe they exist on some estate near Dublin. In the absence of knowing what salley gardens are, you probably have an image of a garden well kept, surrounded by flowers and tended by keepers. But it's not that. The word in Gaelic is s-a-i-l-e-a-c-h, and it means 'willow'. So Yeats is near willows, and therefore likely near water. If there's a weir, the water is a stream or river. Once one has these associations, immediately the initial picture shifts. My point is that different meanings can be imposed on the same data. Different meanings that come from different associations.

Data – literary or economic – have no inherent meaning. They acquire meaning by our bringing meaning to them. And different people, with different experiences, will construct different meanings.

THE MIND AS A FAST PATTERN COMPLETER

What conclusions does modern cognitive psychology draw from such examples? The first conclusion is that our brains are 'associative engines' to use a phrase of Andy Clark, a philosopher and cognitive scientist from Washington University in St. Louis (Clark, 1993). We're wonderful at association and in fact, in cognition, association is just about all we do. In association we impose intelligible patterns. To use another of Clark's labels, we are fast pattern completers. If I see a tail going around a corner, and it's a black swishy tail, I say, 'There's a cat!' But it could be a small boy with a tail on the end of a stick who's trying to fool me. But I don't do that. My mind is not built to do that. If I were strongly skeptical, I *could* do that, or if I saw some small boy playing pranks I could say, 'Well, it's either a cat or a small boy.' But in the absence of a small boy, all I'm really saying is, 'Hey! I see a cat.' But I didn't see a cat. I saw a black tail. A famous Bertrand Russell story makes the same point. A schoolboy, a parson and a mathematician are crossing from England into Scotland in a train. The schoolboy looks out and sees a black sheep and says, 'Oh! Look! Sheep in Scotland are black!' The parson, who is learned, says, 'No. Strictly speaking, all we can say is there is one sheep in Scotland that is black.' The mathematician says, 'No, still not correct. All we can really say is that we know that in Scotland there exists at least one sheep, at least one side of which is black.'

Cognitive science repeatedly tells us that we don't think deductively as the mathematician did, we think associatively as the schoolboy did. And for a very good reason: evolution has made it so. Our ability as humans a hundred thousand years ago to sniff the air and associate a fleeting humidity with the presence of water a few miles away had real survival value. Completing patterns fast, surmising the presence of water from the faintest of clues, helped us survive. Deductive logic did not; and in all but the most trivial of cases we do not use it at all. In fact, cognitive psychologists tell us that deductions themselves are primarily associative. I may say I can solve such-and-such a problem: it's a problem in spherical trigonometry. I then associate the problem with this framework. From there I associate structures and symbols with the sense data of the problem. And I proceed by such associations, stitching them together into a pattern. I'm not saying that association is all the human brain does, but cognitively, association is the main thing we do. And we do it fast. Our neural system searches fast over many associations before settling on one as a 'meaning'. Occasionally this process slows and we can see it in action, as with the three-dimensional optical-illusion pictures that were popular a few years ago that appear flat and two-dimensional until after staring for half a minute a 3-D picture 'leaps out'. So our brains process a large collection of associations into patterns – and a large set of metaphors which are merely more complicated associations with entailments. With metaphors we compare this to this and that to that, and if the comparison is good, we expect such and such to follow. Metaphor is a form of pattern association, and we process much information through metaphors. In sum, we have many different forms of associations: pictures; memories; metaphors; and theories, which are really elaborated metaphors. And this collection when it's fully operating, along with the rules for combining these (which are also associations), we call the mind.

Our minds then are extremely good at associating things, using metaphors, memories, structures, patterns, theories. In other words, the mind is not given. It's not an empty bucket for pouring data in. The mind itself is emergent. This idea is new in Western thinking but there's plenty of precedent for it in the East. The Neo-Confucian philosopher brothers Ch'eng Yi and Ch'eng Hao, writing during the Sung Dynasty about 900 years ago, both saw mind as emergent. They did not see the mind as a container, but rather as sets of ideas built one upon the other. The mind doesn't contain our ideas. It's these ideas – these associations – that instead contain the mind or constitute the mind. The mind is not fixed in any way; it consists in its associations and the apparatus to manipulate these. In this sense it's emergent. So strictly speaking I shouldn't say as I did earlier that meaning resides in the mind, because deep enough within cognitive philosophy the concept of mind itself dissolves. Meaning resides in associations which our neural apparatus connects with the data presented. We are now far from seeing reasoning as deduction that takes place in a container of variables whose values are updated by 'information'. If reasoning is largely association, it depends on the past experiences of the reasoner. The framing of a situation, the 'sense' made of it, are therefore dependent on the reasoner's history. And so is the outcome.

One final point about cognition. Sometimes we can say roughly that there is a 'correct' meaning – a single, correct association. More often, in any situation of complication, there are multiple interpretations. We may hold one or we may hold many. Often, if we are trying to solve a puzzle, or to come to a decision such as the next move in a chess game, we make many hypothetical associations and search over these, perhaps retaining more than one until further evidence presents itself. In the black tail example, if I had indeed seen a small boy a few minutes earlier, I might hold in mind both 'cat' and 'prank' until further evidence arrived.

MODELING THE COGNITIVE PROCESS

All this is fine. But as economists how do we make use of it? How might we model the thinking process in problems that are complicated or ill-defined?

I would suggest the following, by way of distillation of the observations above: in problems of complication, as decision makers, economic agents look for ways to frame the situation that faces them. They try to associate temporary internal models or patterns or hypotheses to frame the situation. And they work with these. They may single out one such pattern or model and carry out simplified deductions (at the level of tic-tac-toe) on it, if they seek guidance for action. As further evidence from the environment comes in, they may strengthen or weaken their beliefs in their current models or hypotheses. They may also discard some when they cease to perform, and replace them as needed with new ones. In other words, where agents face problems of complication or ill-definition, they use clues from the situation to form hypothetical patterns, frameworks and associations. These hypothetical patterns fill the gaps in the agent's understanding.

Such a procedure enables us as humans to deal with complication: we construct plausible, simpler models that we can cope with. It enables us to deal with ill-definedness: where we have insufficient definition, we use working models to fill the gap. Such behavior is inductive. It may appear ad hoc and messy, but it is not antithetical to 'reason', or to science for that matter. In fact, it is the way science itself operates and progresses.

More practically then, in a typical economics problem that plays out over time, we might set up a collection of agents, probably heterogeneous, and assume they make associations in the form of mental models, or hypotheses, or subjective beliefs. These beliefs might themselves take the form of simple mathematical expressions that can be used to describe or predict some variable or action; or of statistical hypotheses; or of condition/prediction rules (if situation Q is observed/predict outcome or action D). These will normally be subjective – they will differ among the agents. An agent may hold one in mind at a time, or several simultaneously, keeping track of the performance of each. When the time comes to make choices, the agent acts upon his currently most credible (or possibly most profitable) one. The others he keeps at the back of his mind, so to speak. As economists we will be tempted to say the agent rationally combines his several hypotheses. But cognitive psychology tells us we don't do this, we hold in mind many hypotheses at a time and act on the one currently most plausible. Once actions are taken the aggregative picture is updated, and agents update their confidence in each of their hypotheses.

This scheme I'm suggesting is of course also a simplification and abstraction. But it captures the idea that the agent is *imposing* meaning on the problem situation, or making sense of it by associating multiple frameworks, or belief structures, or hypotheses with it and allowing these to 'compete'. This is also a system in which learning takes place. Agents 'learn' which of their hypotheses work, and they 'learn' also in the acts of discarding poorly performing hypotheses and generating new 'ideas' to put in their place. Notice there is a built-in hysteresis: agents linger with their currently most believable hypothesis or belief model, but drop it when it no longer performs, in favor of a better one. A hypothesis or association or belief model is clung to not because it is 'correct' – there is no way to know this – but rather because it has worked in the past and must cumulate a record of failure before it is worth discarding.

A key question remains. Where do the hypotheses or mental models come from? How are they generated? Behaviorally, this is a deep question in psychology, having to do with object representation, and pattern recognition. I will not go into it here. But there are some simple and practical options for modeling. Sometimes we might endow our agents with focal models – patterns or hypotheses that are obvious, simple and easily dealt with mentally. We might generate a 'bank' of these and distribute them among the agents. Other times, given a suitable model-space, we might allow some similar intelligent search device such as the genetic algorithm to generate suitable models. The reader should note that whatever option is taken, the framework I've described is independent of the specific hypotheses or beliefs used, just as the consumer theory framework is independent of particular products chosen among.

Can such a scheme be put in practice in economics? The answer is yes. There is now a growing body of examples: the El Farol problem (Arthur 1994); the work of Sargent (1993), the Santa Fe stock market study (Arthur et al.1996). This type of study typically finds that 'solutions' – patterns of beliefs and actions predicated upon these – need to be generated by computation because of the increased complication of heterogeneous beliefs. It also typically finds a richer world, a psychological world, where an ecology of beliefs about the problem in question emerges. Sometimes this ecology of hypotheses converges to some standard equilibrium of beliefs. More often it remains open-ended, always discovering new hypotheses, new ideas.

COGNITION AND GRADUATE ECONOMIC EDUCATION

Let me turn from modeling in economics to quite a different area that can benefit from the insights of cognitive science: the education of economists.

I want to start here by drawing attention to two ways in which we make sense: two types of association, not completely different and at opposite ends of a spectrum. Let me call one 'theory' and the other 'experience'.

Theories are metaphors with entailments. If in 1705, Edmond Halley subscribed to Newton's gravitational theory and applied it to a comet that had previously appeared in 1531, 1607 and 1682, one entailment was that the comet would return in the year 1759. In using Newton's theory, Halley was making an association between a comet and the heavenly bodies Newton dealt with; and the entailments of the association allowed Halley to predict. I want to suggest that theories are *thin* associations: the theory fits if a narrow and precise set of conditions is fulfilled; and the entailments are also narrow and precise. Providing the theory fits correctly – is a good association – and is consistent within itself, then the entailments can be relied upon. Narrow fit, narrow entailments. Theories are in this way thin but powerful associations.

Experience is different. Suppose I'm an executive sent to Korea, and I've never done business there. I arrive in Korea and I'm wondering how I shall act. I have no idea of how many times I should bow to my host, or if anybody bows to the host, or whether I should take my shoes off, or if I want to close the deal do I wait till the end of dinner or do I try to close the deal up front? But I do have a lot of experience in Japan and in China, and so I use these. In this case hundreds of pictures are going through my mind. This sort of association is more dream-like. It's richer. It covers a wider set of cases. It is suggestive of what will follow given what is. But it's much less accurate and less precise and less reliable than theory. So experience in the form of a wide collection of memories and pictures of situations – *thick* association – is also powerful. Its power lies in its width of coverage and its suggestiveness. Such experience is what we seek from human conversation and from taking in stories and novels and plays. We seek to draw into ourselves other people's experiences, to make their situations into our memory pictures that we can use later. In this way we construct and conjure a whole dream-like world where logic doesn't matter and precision doesn't matter, but where suggestiveness and coverage give power.

As I said earlier, these two types of association are not completely distinct; associations arrange themselves on a spectrum from narrowness and precision to width and suggestiveness.

What has this to do with graduate economic education? A lot. A great deal of education is the formation of associations; and the spectrum ranges from collections of narrow but precise theories on one side to wide but suggestive and imprecise pictures on the other. We need both types of association to function successfully as human beings.

In economics, graduate education at least in the first year or two consists in mastering 20 or 30 theoretical economic models – thin associations. These include the principal–agent model, the overlapping generations model, the prisoner's dilemma model, and so on. The idea is that these theoretical metaphors will later become useful associations. We hope that if the student is later employed say at the World Bank, she will be able to look at a situation and say, 'This problem in African agriculture is partly a principal–agent problem. It does have some overtones of overlapping generations, and it's also got this game theory component. So I can put together a hybrid version of the three models to get insight.' All this is fine. It is fine that economics has recognized recurring structures that it has rendered into theories. We can hope and expect that a well-educated student will use these as association components later.

But models cannot be all that we teach. There's been a tendency in many graduate schools to increase teaching in theory at the expense of teaching in economic history and in case example. Students of course can still choose to study the experience-details of the economy; but they are aware that this may not enhance their graduate careers. In 1990 Colander and Klamer asked students how important having a 'thorough knowledge of the economy' was to succeeding as an economist. Three percent thought it very important, and 68 percent thought it unimportant. Important was: 'Being smart in the sense of being good at problem solving', and 'excellence in mathematics'. With this bias toward theory and away from experience, we eliminate the wider metaphors that come from history-experience – the thick associations. These allow students to put their models into perspective; they provide the vocabulary, so to speak, where theory provides the grammar; they provide a richness of thought and a breadth of association that theory cannot possibly match.

When a decision maker faces a situation of high complexity, say Bosnia in the mid-1990s, applying theory prematurely – a set of precise but narrowly applicable metaphors – can be dangerous. Let's say he is in the State Department looking at Bosnia and has been in graduate school in political science, doesn't have much experience and is full of theories. His reaction may be to shoehorn Bosnia into a pre-constructed framework. But in this situation it is better to wait and observe. And in observation to invoke a variable set of pictures on which he may conjure up a richer set of associations. Such free association comes from a study of history, not theory. 'Well, it could be a bit like the Bosnian crisis of 1908, but it's not unlike the situation under Turkish rule in 1831 when Husein seized power. On the other hand, there are elements of the ethnic rivalries of 1875 that resulted in the Austro-Hungarians taking over.' What's of use is to have thousands of such pictures from history, available for pondering and perusal. Eventually from such pondering and perusal – from dreamlike association – a composite set of hypotheses or composite picture may emerge. It's at this stage that theory might apply. Premature association without going through the richness of a wide set of pictures may be disastrous. Where I come from, Belfast – another complicated situation – we say: 'If you're not confused, you don't know anything.'

I am saying here that students need experience – details as well as theory. That is, they need economic history, not as an adjunct to theory, but as a supplier of cognitive understanding in its own right. What about teaching the history of economic thought – another threatened discipline in economic education? From the cognitive point of view, the history of economic thought bestows on us an awareness of the associations we make. Without such awareness, associations can be unconscious and poorly suited to the case in hand. Consider the English painters who came to Australia in the late 1700s or early 1800s. These artists depicted trees in Australia as they would have depicted English trees; they were well trained in English art schools and knew how to paint trees. But in Australia the leaves of most trees – often eucalyptus trees – are thinner, and the sun shines through them. Trees there look different –

lighter, more airy. It took a generation of Australian-born painters before the trees in paintings started to look like Australian trees. Before that European painters were unconsciously making European associations and imposing these upon Australia. Similarly Europeans depicted aboriginals in this early period as Europeans with dark skins. This is not to criticize artists. It is to be aware that the actions we take are built upon our unconscious associations. We need to be conscious of our associations and where they come from. We need to be suspicious of them. We need a Zen-like standing back and seeing from beginner's mind. We need an awareness that theories aren't exogenous – they were constructed by people with agendas from other times sometimes suited to the purposes of other times. We need knowledge of the history of economic thought to be fully aware of the associations we make in economics and their provenance.

So what in graduate economics education do we really want? We certainly need theory. As a theorist I'm all for theory. But we also need the rich pictures given by the study of history and institutions. We need both types of association: the theoretical, quantitative, precise frameworks and the case-based, vivid pictures in their tens of thousands. To teach only theory is equivalent to training doctors by teaching only endocrinology and pathology, and not the wide diagnostics doctors learn on grand rounds. To operate only with theory – think of driving a car – makes us beginners. It's not until we can seamlessly integrate theory and vivid pictures – theory and experience – that we become expert. I believe we are currently turning out students who lack those pictures. And in doing so, we're doing them a disservice.

DO ISSUES OF COGNITION MATTER?

Perhaps in asking my fellow economists to think about the implications of cognition, I am asking for something useful but not necessary – a luxury? I don't believe so. Consider just one example. The Soviet Union in 1990–91 decided to go capitalist. And from us economists it got much advice. But our natural bias, given the current development of economics, was to concentrate upon a worthy, but imagined, general-equilibrium outcome where institutions would be in place and markets would work smoothly and incentives would be correct.

A cognitive view of economics might have balanced this ideal view with an awareness that Russians were not arriving with empty minds to their version of capitalism. Not only did they possess old structures both economic and political, they harbored from their 70 years of communism and earlier, czarist past old associations too – of what business means, of how one interacts with authorities, of how one organizes if one wants to make money, of what one does with economic power and wealth. More enlightened advice would have built upon an understanding of how these embedded structures and understandings would play out given the new possibilities. The subsequent history of Russia's experiment with capitalism showed that these matters of cognition had great importance.

Economic agents bring to their actions not just their preferences and endowments, but also their understandings – the associations and meanings they have derived from their history of previous actions and experiences. In many of the small, standard problems of economics, we can ignore this. In the larger issues of development and reconstruction, and in constructing an economics for problems of complication and ill-definition, we cannot. We need to take cognition seriously.

NOTES

*   Editor's note: this is adapted from the conference keynote address upon which this volume is based. I asked Brian to keep the informal style as part of the chapter.
1.   The lines are lines 1, 2, 7, and 8 of an eight-line poem, 'Down by the Salley Gardens', by W.B. Yeats. From *W.B. Yeats, the Poems,* ed. Richard J. Finneran, New York; Macmillan, 1983 (p. 20). 'Down by the salley gardens my love and I did meet; / She passed the salley gardens on little snow-white feet. / She bid me take love easy, as the leaves grow on the tree, / But I, being young and foolish, with her would not agree. / In a field by the river my love and I did stand, / As on my leaning shoulder she laid her snow-white hand. / She bid me take life easy, as the grass grows on the weirs; / But I was young and foolish, and now am full of tears.'

REFERENCES

Arthur, W.B. (1994), 'Complexity in Economic Theory: Inductive Reasoning and Bounded Rationality', *American Economic Review*, **84** (2), 406–11.
Arthur W.B., J.H. Holland, B. LeBaron, R. Palmer and P. Tayler (1997), 'Asset Pricing Under Endogenous Expectations in an Artificial Stock Market', in W.B. Arthur, S. Durlauf and D. Lane (eds), *The Economy as an Evolving Complex System II*, Reading, MA: Addison-Wesley.
Clark, A. (1993), *Associative Engines*, Cambridge: MIT Press.
Jaynes, J. (1976), *The Origin of Consciousness in the Breakdown of the Bicameral Mind*, Boston: Houghton Mifflin Company.
Laxness, H. (1935), *Independent People*, New York: Vintage.
Rust, J. (1987), 'Optimal Replacement of GMC Bus Engines: An Empirical Model of Harold Zurcher', *Econometrica*, **55** (5), 999–1033.
Sargent, T.J. (1993), *Bounded Rationality in Macroeconomics*, New York: Oxford University Press.

4. Looking Backwards: Complexity Theory in 2028

Frederic L. Pryor

In October 26, 2028, three events occurred: (a) the asteroid 1997 XF-11 smashed into the earth around 3:00 pm, thereby showing that the predictions of those errant astronomers back in 1998 were really correct (contrary to the counter-claims of their jealous colleagues); (b) the Social Security system went broke as predicted; but the US government had more important problems to worry about in the following months; (c) someone just finished yet another paper reviewing complexity theory in economics, dedicated to the blessed memory of David Colander who, from the notes in that paper, appeared to be a famous impresario and book publisher in the early part of the twenty-first century. What did that paper in 2028 say?

FUTURE OF THE MOMENT

That unknown author started with the obvious point that 30 years before, complexity theory proved a rallying cry for a variety of economists dissatisfied with neoclassical economics: institutionalists seeking revenge for their marginalized status, evolutionists seeking an audience, specialists in dynamic processes and non-linear mathematics wanting to become relevant so that they could get tenure, experimentalists humbly seeking friends, unemployed specialists in comparative economic systems, sneaky Austrian economists, arrogant game theorists, ornery anti-Walrasians, frustrated economic historians, various sociopaths as well as assorted cranks who, having done poorly in their university economics classes – either as students or teachers – decided that the whole traditional canon of economics was irrelevant and/ or wrong.

The author described the emergence of three groups of complexity economists – the Santa Fe clique, the esoterists, and the humble practitioners, a matter that he returned to in a later part of his paper. That unknown author noted in passing that in the first decade of the twenty-first century complexity economists began to fracture and that the initial tolerance for dissident voices began to decline. Even within the Santa Fe clique, the fundos (fundamental-ists) focused increasingly on pure theory, trying to derive a general theory of the entire economy, while the practos (practitioners) tried to use complexity theory to solve quite specific problems in limited areas of their discipline. The fundos finally threw the practos out and took control of the Institute in 2009. Unfortunately, in the year 2011 Senator Krugman, a rising star of the Small-Government Party (one of the strange splinter groups arising after the great party realignment in 2008) took to the floor of the Senate and read selected paragraphs from various working papers of the remaining Santa Fe clique. His argument was compelling: the lack of empirical studies based on such models meant that the complexity theorists were talking primarily to themselves. The Senator drew a parallel of complexity theorists with general systems theorists who were following the lead of Ludwig von Bertalanffy and who were rightfully turned out into the streets in the 1970s.[1] Governmental grant money quickly dried up as a result, the Santa Fe Institute fell into ruins, and the search for a totally general theory of complexity became dis-credited, The obvious lesson most drew from this unfortunate episode was that it was necessary for complexity theorists to be a bit more modest and not to take all reality as their subject matter.

PROBLEMS IN COMPLEXITY THEORY

Complexity Theory as a Disposition

Complexity, our unknown author argued, was less of a unified theory and more of a vision or disposition that turned economists' attention to problems involving positive feedback, lack of a determinable equilibrium, and the importance of adaptive process of interaction between many heterogeneous people, none of whom is completely aware of how such an interaction is turning out or what others are thinking. These problems, of course, embraced only a part of the entire range of problems studied by economists. But they allowed new metaphors to be used in economics to gain understanding of previously opaque phenomena and they pushed the field away from the Newtonian model of science to which so many economist had stood in awe for so many decades.

In the pages of that manuscript, scattered by the wind after the asteroid hit, the author developed the point about complexity as a disposition or vi-sion, rather than a theory, by referring to the various articles in the book *The Economy as an Evolving Complex System, II* (Arthur, Durlauf and Lane 1997). He/she pointed out that the various essays, most of which were extremely interesting, were not unified by their results or subject matter, but rather by

their attempt to break out of the static equilibrium framework that held economists in thrall for so long and to focus on economic processes over time; to
incorporate a more realistic theory of human psychology; to look more carefully at the interactions between people, rather than between people and
some impersonal market; and to employ new metaphors to understand the
whole. That unknown author had, of course, nothing to object to this enterprise because he/she emphasized the sterility of the prevailing neoclassical
paradigm by the end of the twentieth century and the need to strike out on
new paths, taking advantage of the advances in mathematics and computing
that allowed economists to tackle more complicated subjects.

The Narrowness of Complexity Theory

As currently practiced in the first quarter of the twenty-first century, complexity economics was too narrow and it needed to be supplemented by a
more systematic view of organizational structures, rather than focusing almost exclusive attention on processes. This author noted that despite claims
of complexity theory focusing on interactions within hierarchical organization, complexity theorists never really came to grips with how the organizational structure itself molded individual decisions. This disturbed our unknown author, particularly because most important economic decisions are
made by organizations, rather than individuals acting as social atoms. He/she
also noted that although several attempts had been made to discuss the meaning and implication of complexity within organizations, such efforts were
totally ignored and the titles never made their way into any of the more
widely circulated bibliographies.[2]

Our unknown author elaborated on this theme of organizational complexity and made several crucial distinctions. Complexity of a structure, which
can be a formal organization or a system, really refers to three different
phenomena:

1. The direct information requirements of a system. More complex struc-
    tures have higher information costs, and for the United States this can
    be seen by the rising skill level of the labor force, the share of the
    labor force devoted to the creation, processing and interpretation of
    information, and the increasingly complicated global environment in
    which firms must work.
2. The increasingly greater internal interactions within a given organi-
    zation or system. Consider, for a moment, an input–output system. In
    this case such interaction would be characterized by a greater volume
    of transactions within the production system, in contrast to transac-
    tions between the production system and the environment, and there

is evidence that this is occurring. Another example comes from the financial structure – the ratio of financial to physical assets is rising rapidly and this creates many more interactions than, let us say, a peasant society where there are no bank accounts, stocks, bonds, mortgages, derivatives, or other exotic financial instruments and the only debts are those developed in the reciprocal social relations between individuals. The separation of ownership and control is yet another example of increasing interactions within a system.

3. The rising heterogeneity of a system is a third dimension of structural complexity. For instance, the population is becoming increasingly heterogeneous according to such criteria as age, family structure, ethnicity, income, wealth, and occupations. Similarly, production units, both enterprises and establishments, are becoming more heterogeneous in size.

According to this unknown author, changes in these three dimensions of structural complexity have important implications for how the economy functions and the effectiveness of the government. The structural dimensions influence the macro-stability and micro-efficiency. They influence how decisions are made in large organizations and they point our attention toward key points for empirically analyzing economic problems. Because complexity economists did not address such an issue, our unknown writer, in an attempt to be witty, declared that complexity theory was too important to leave to the Santa Fe school. We must, however, forgive him for this cheap aphorism and realize that no matter how perfect we become in the future, bad taste and flat humor will always be with us.

APPLICATION OF COMPLEXITY THEORY

Application of the complexity approach to empirical problems, our unknown author argued, is fiendishly difficult and proved the ultimate stumbling block for the general acceptance of this approach into our science in all but a limited number of cases. In the process of trying to apply empirically the ideas of complexity theory, our unknown author pointed to the sad fate of the practos who had been turned out of the Santa Fe Institute by the Fundos in 2009. This group, in turn, divided quite quickly into esoterists and humble practitioners.

The humble practitioners selected eclectically from various ideas of complexity theory and tried to find empirical evidence to support or reject them using relatively understandable statistical methods. They looked, for instance, at whether cattlemen really used rational expectations in making their breeding decisions, they tried to link the distribution of price changes in particular markets to the ways in which the markets and their participants operated; and they tried to explain why vertical integration in various production chains for foodstuffs differs so much between nations (for instance, why America has a vertically integrated fruit market but a decentralized wheat market and why in Britain the situation is exactly opposite). The humble practitioners developed some useful techniques of pattern recognition, which allowed them to make sense out of some simulation results. Although this work certainly advanced knowledge of how the economy really functioned, it lacked pizzazz and its practitioners were usually banished to obscure universities in uncomfortable climates.

By way of contrast, the esoterists worked on a grander scale, particularly because of the aforementioned difficulties in applying full-grown complexity theory to actual problems. Our unknown author noted that in a typical complexity book in the late 1990s such as *The Economy as an Evolving Complex System, II* (Arthur, Durlauf and Lane 1997), almost all of the essays have no real empirical applications, aside from a few interesting anecdotes. Two major problems underlay this surprising omission.

First, the complexity approach can explain almost anything and, therefore, it can explain nothing. We can, for instance, develop a complex model of interaction of buyers and sellers, with the buyers shopping for lowest prices and looking over their shoulders at other buyers, while the sellers face having problems in setting prices, setting advertising budgets, and obtaining the goods they want. Such a highly non-linear model cannot be solved with traditional mathematical methods, but simulations are simple and we can program and run the model quite quickly. By tweaking one or two parameters, we can also obtain all sorts of interesting results such as bubbles, boycotts, or cycles. In fact, with suitable adjustment of the parameters we can obtain almost any result that we want. But proving that some weird event is possible does not really explain why it has occurred since such results can be obtained by other models as well. Such a model, for instance, does particularly well in replicating cobweb cycles in the hog markets; unfortunately, it does not help us understand why identical hog cycles existed in Eastern Europe when these nations had centrally planned economic systems. In some cases, for instance the Schelling model of residential segregation (Schelling 1969), or Douglas Puffert's simulations of the choice railway gauge (narrow gauge versus wide gauge) in the nineteenth century (Puffert 1992), such simulations allow great insight, especially because there is no determinant outcome. It can also be useful in deciding whether any kind of structure exists, other than that created by the clashing expectations of the participants. But these occasions in economics did not turn out to be common.[3] As a result, simulation continued to be used in its traditional manner, for instance, sensitivity analyses, or ferreting out patterns when numerous variables are interacting at the same time.

Second, the econometric methods commonly used in the latter part of the twentieth century cannot distinguish between the different types of interactions that would allow us to identify the crucial causal factors in a complex system. This was originally pointed out by Charles Mansky, a well-known economist in the late twentieth century who, for instance, argued that econometricians could not easily determine whether the most important determinant of poor high school grades are the students and teachers within the school, the neighborhood effects that socialize youngsters in the area, or the social, economic, and family background of the high school pupils. Mansky, who had so much to contribute to solving such problems, unfortunately met an untimely, yet fitting, end when his computer short-circuited as he was running some multinomial logit regressions. Although some interesting non-linear econometric techniques were developed in the decades between the mid 1990s and 2028, they were extremely difficult to apply in any but the most simple economic problems. As a result, while economists working with complex models developed ever more interesting and intricate models, the subject became increasingly abstract and abstruse, and less accessible to any but those with highly developed mathematical training. Although the esoterists could not solve these problems or even communicate with most of the profession, they did have the consolation of having prestigious positions in well-known universities with comfortable climates.

A BRIEF CONCLUSION

The unknown author of the paper ended by noting that complexity theorists actually had much to tell us about the real world, even though it is sometimes difficult to know how important are the problems they were trying to solve since so few made reference to the actual economy. Some ideas of complexity theory did lead to extremely fruitful research, for instance, the importance of lock-in effects, while other ideas did not. Unfortunately, few people could follow the papers of the esoterists and the humble practitioners never received much public attention because of their status at lowly universities. Perhaps the most lasting contribution of all streams of complexity theory was the realization that a bit more modesty on the part of economists would be appropriate when they are making policy proposals because they might not fully understand the complexity of the situation. Since modesty never impressed policymakers, the influence of complexity theorists and practitioners began to wane.

Complexity theory began its slow decline in prestige in the first decade of the twenty-first century, and by 2020 sociologists stepped into the wreckage of economics and began to create 'the ultra-new economic sociology' which would solve all our economic policy problems and, at the same time, could be understood even by TV pundits.

After that asteroid hit the earth in 2028, I do not know if someone was around to reassemble the pages of this chapter on complexity theory. If someone actually read the paper, I am sure that he or she would probably fail to realize that *all* the major ideas in this chapter had been *totally* plagiarized from an obscure set of comments given at a small conference in Middlebury Vermont at the end of the previous century which focused, if I correctly recall, on the practice and teaching of complexity theory.

NOTES

1. That Senator also noted that some of the Sante Fe models were empirically wrong – for instance, when he visited El Farol bar in Santa Fe every Thursday for a month, it always had more than 60 people in it. This was because every time someone called the bar to find out how many people were there on the various Thursdays, the barkeeper always lied and named very low numbers. Once people paid the cover and then discovered how packed the bar was, they did not leave because they would lose their investment.
2. The one title our unknown author mentioned about the meaning and impact of complexity of organizational structure was an empirical study with the boring title of: *Economic Evolution and Structure: The Impact of Complexity on the U.S. Economy* by someone named Frederik Bryor, but no such author could be located in any library. Because this study featured no high-powered mathematics and, further, actually tried to study some of these relationships in an empirical fashion, it certainly deserved to be neglected.
3. The unknown author appended a sad note to his discussion about simulation methods that could explain anything by an anecdote occurring in the late twentieth century when someone raised this very point. Brian Author, who was a star in complexity theory, countered with the remark that such outcomes only occur in bad simulations and that good simulations reveal meaningful patterns no matter how they are tweaked. Shortly thereafter, Author was mortally wounded by the person who was the brunt of these remarks and who had not been properly socialized into the delightful give-and-take of debate among economists.

REFERENCES

Arthur, W.B., S.N. Durlauf and D.A. Lane (eds) (1997), *The Economy as an Evolving Complex System II,* Reading, MA: Addison-Wesley.

Puffert, D.J. (1992), 'The Economics of Spatial Network Externalities and the Dynamics of Railway Gauge Standardization', *Journal of Economic History,* **52** (2), 449–52.

Schelling, T.C. (1969), 'Models of Segregation', *The American Economic Review,* **59** (2), 488–93.

PART TWO

The Complexity Vision and Economic Policy

5. Complexity and Policy

William A. Brock and David Colander

Ultimately, the success or failure of the complexity approach to economics will have much to do with the insights it provides about policy. In this chapter we consider the implications of complexity-based research on economic policy, trying to specify the value added brought to economic policy analysis by recent work in complex systems. Doing so presents the difficult task of distinguishing what substantive ideas are captured by complexity economics that are not captured by conventional economics. This task is difficult because, as discussed in the introduction to this volume, the overlap between complexity and conventional economics depends on how broadly or narrowly one defines the terms.

For example, if one scans the *NBER Reporters* (a bastion of conventional economic policy analysis) of the last few years, one will see discussions of path dependence, evolution, lock-in, increasing returns – all the key words and ideas normally associated with the complexity approach to economics in the popular literature.[1] If one includes such work of complexity-related themes as belonging in conventional economics, as we do in this chapter, then complexity's focus on such issues cannot be the distinguishing feature of complexity economics.

If the complexity approach is not defined by the issues it looks at, what does define it? In our view it is defined by the approach it takes to understanding the economy. That approach, in turn, significantly influences the methods of analysis that it uses. Unfortunately, defining complexity by the methods used by complexity researchers is not unambiguous since there are many alternative complexity approaches. Among others, there are the Santa Fe school approach, the Brussels School approach, the Stuttgart school approach, the ecological approach, and the 'macroecology' approach. In this chapter we emphasize the Santa Fe approach and methods, but make some reference to alternative approaches.[2]

The complex adaptive systems approach is different from the conventional approach in that it takes as a first principle that complex adaptive systems do not yield to linear methods of analysis and tend to generate 'emergent structures' that come as a surprise to the analyst, whereas the conventional approach tends to assume that our economy is subject to linear methods of analysis. Methods of analysis for this complex adaptive systems approach have been primarily computational to date, but do not have to be. For example, the work of Brock and de Fontnouvelle (1999), and Brock and Hommes (1997, 1998) represents an attempt to meld together analytical and computational methods in this area by concentrating on what kinds of bifurcations can occur in these systems and how their signatures might be recognized in data generated by simulations. Whether it is computational or analytical, the complexity method involves taking seriously the complexity and self-organizing nature of the system, and then analyzing the system in the most quantitative and analytic method possible, taking that complexity seriously from the beginning of the analysis.

To argue that complexity theorists take complexity seriously is not to say that conventional researchers do not. Where the difference arises is in how the two approaches deal with complexity. The conventional approach is to make a leap of faith that the way to understand the world is to first simplify the system into a model that is analytically tractable, and to use that model as a stepping stone to understanding the complex world. Complexity researchers make a different leap of faith; they believe that, if the system being studied is complex, simplification of that system into tractable, for example, linear, models hides important elements of reality, and precludes their reintroduction. Thus, alternative simplification approaches need to be used.

In this chapter we also use a broad definition of conventional economics to avoid setting up a 'conventional economics' strawman as our basis of comparison. This allows us to focus on the added insights that work such as the urn process models (Arthur 1989, 1996), Kauffman's autocatalytic sets (see Kauffman's articles in Stein (1989)), Langton's 'artificial life' (see Testfatsion's article in Arthur, Durlauf and Lane (1997) for applications to economics), and Eigen and Schuster's 'hypercycles', that is, closed catalytic feedback loops of self-replicating molecules, (see Schuster and Sigmund's piece on evolutionary game dynamics in Prigogine and Sanglier (1987)) brings to economic policy analysis.[3]

To be more precise about our definition of conventional economics, we include most of what is contained in the *NBER Reporter,* what is found in books on increasing returns industries such as Baumol, Panzar and Willig (1982), hereafter 'BPW', Evans (1983), Krugman (1991), Katz and Shapiro (1994), Jovanovic and Nyarko (1996), Baumol (1998) and the articles in Kreps and Wallis (1997) by Crafts, Dewatripont and Roland, Aghion and Howitt, and Jovanovic. We also include the writings of 'evolutionary' economists such as Herbert Simon, J. Conlisk, Richard Day, R. Nelson and S. Winter, and many others who have been writing about issues now associated with complexity for a long time. We classify such works in evolutionary economics as 'conventional' because the themes they sounded were around before the advent of the use of techniques such as urn processes, pattern development theory, complex adaptive systems theory and artificial life techniques in the field of economics. The use of tools such as urn processes may get you to issues of increasing returns, path dependency, and lock-in more quickly, but conventional economics reached them on its own without the development of complexity theory.[4]

As should be clear to the reader, the definitions of complexity and conventional economics we have chosen make the task of finding policy implications of complexity difficult, but, we believe, the value-added approach we take highlights the policy implications of complexity better than alternative, more sympathetic expositions, would have done.

Given our definitions, our eneral conclusion should not come as a surprise to the reader. That general conclusion is that complexity theory does not significantly change much of the economic policy analysis that goes on, nor does it tell us anything definitive about economic policy. Nonetheless, we also conclude that complexity does make a difference in the way economists will be taught to think about policy, and how they will go about doing policy analysis.

THEORY, POLICY, AND MODELS

The relation between theory and policy is complicated. To get at that relationship we will distinguish between the abstract theoretical models that underlie economists' worldview and the more policy-oriented models that underlie their specific policy recommendations. We begin with a discussion of abstract theoretical models.

When a student goes to graduate school in economics, one of his or her first exercises is to work through Walrasian general equilibrium theory, starting with the Arrow–Debreu model and building up from there. This formal theory is the beginning of the formation of their economic worldview. It is a view of a perfectly competitive general equilibrium market setting in which individuals are led by market forces, in the absence of externalities, to a Pareto optimal outcome. It is what might be called the 'right price' view – it sets up economic policy as a job of finding the right price. If there are no market failures that right price is found by the market; if there are market failures, then there is a potential role for government action.

Taken at face value, Walrasian general equilibrium theory provides a very specific worldview of markets, one which sees the invisible hand of markets as 'solving economic problems'. But one must be careful about taking it at face value. Much of the pedagogical exercise is meant to bring home to students the limiting assumptions, which are necessary to prove that markets solve problems. Given those limiting assumptions Walrasian general equilibrium theory alone cannot form the basis of a worldview; it must be modified or replaced before it can have relevance to real world policy. In their education students are not taught what to replace it with, or how to modify it, so they are often left on their own to develop their modified worldview. However, in advanced courses, students are taught how to modify the basic general equilibrium framework for increasing returns, externalities, missing markets, dynamics, learning technical change, and other complications of the real world. They are also taught the basis of game theory and mechanism design theory. But all this effort still does not utilize the Complex Adaptive Systems approach that we shall discuss in this chapter.

If one scans the *NBER Reporters* or other sophisticated policy-relevant research, the image of Walrasian general equilibrium theory as the controlling worldview will appear faint. This is the case because specific thinking about policy is usually done in relation to what might be called policy models – less abstract models that are ad hoc combinations of empirical observations and principles from the general theory. Most students spend their time thinking about such policy issues in relation to these policy models since the bulk of their work involves such models; they spend little time thinking about abstract theoretical models after they have passed their comprehensive examinations.

Policy models sometimes appear somewhat ad hoc because they tend to derive their character from the problem at hand. For example, the applied policy economist will typically use one type of model in advising the government what to do about the Stock Market Crash of October 1987 but use another set of models on advising governments about how congestion should be priced in cities, how impact fees should be structured on far-flung outside developments, how externalities should be priced, and how emission permit trading systems should be designed. Similarly, she will use a different model in advising a developing country what kind of institutional design creates the appropriate incentives to produce rapid improvement in the standard of living rather than self-defeating redistributive political activity. This kind of policy model might stress the tradeoff faced by a firm towards allocating resources to produce useful products at lower costs rather than allocating resources to produce gains through the political system. Our point is that economists use multiple models in policy making and that actual policy making contains elements of art, judgment, and economic science, that is, what Scott (1998) calls 'metis' as well as 'techne'.

The metis of the policy models feeds back on the techne of the general equilibrium worldview and changes it. Policy economists, and sophisticated economic theorists, quickly learn that the Walrasian general equilibrium worldview is, at best, a first step to developing a useful worldview of the economy, and that the limiting assumptions of the model make it difficult, if not impossible, to move from that model to a real-world worldview. Recognizing this, they develop a more sophisticated worldview incorporating real-world insights and assumptions as well as modifications of general equilibrium theory, game theory and mechanism design theory. Unfortunately, that more sophisticated worldview is often ambiguous and undeveloped, since developing it formally is an enormous task. Because it is, the sophisticated economists' worldview is often only expressed to other economists who have the same training, and who share the same policy experience, and is thus hidden from noneconomists and even from some economists.

This hidden sophisticated worldview means that the first pedagogical steps toward a worldview – general equilibrium theory and game theory – are often the last step (if they make it that far) for many undergraduate economic majors. This has, understandably, led to a mischaracterization of economists' worldview by many lay writers and textbooks. We will call this Walrasian general equilibrium and game theoretic worldview, the economic reporters' worldview, because it is the way many, but happily not all, reporters characterize economists' worldview.

The complexity viewpoint has its largest effect upon this economic reporters' worldview. It directly challenges that worldview, and replaces it with what might be called a complex process worldview. Its effect on the sophisticated worldview is much more problematic, because that sophisticated worldview is seldom specified. For some economists it changes it by accepting the fact that, maybe, the simplified general equilibrium model is not only not directly relevant; it might actually limit our understanding of complex processes, by stopping us from considering certain interrelationships. For other sophisticated economists, it makes no change since they have already established their actual worldview almost independently of Walrasian general equilibrium theory.

HOW COMPLEXITY CHANGES ECONOMISTS' WORLDVIEW

In the economic reporters' worldview, simplified Walrasian general equilibrium theory provides the fallback position for policy. Complexity analysis takes that fallback position away, and thus has significant implications for policy. The reason it takes it away is that the complexity vision replaces a static conception of notions of equilibrium points with a more dynamic process conception of the economy in which there is a type of 'equilibrium process' with perpetual novelty. To put it another way, the complexity viewpoint is closer to the Hayekian, Schumpterian viewpoint of the Austrian School but uses concepts like Holland's (1995) classifier systems and Complex Adaptive System theory to formalize the Austrian viewpoint.

In the complexity view (for example Holland 1995) one no longer thinks of the economy as moving toward a preordained equilibrium – there may, or may not, be such an equilibrium; instead one thinks of the economy as an interconnected collection of co-evolving, adapting agents interacting at a variety of time/space scales, evolving in complicated ways in which path dependencies, multiple equilibria, novelty, surprise and emergent structures play major roles – a world in which there is no one right price. Such a conception has no place in the simplest versions of formal Walrasian general equilibrium theory.

In the complexity view institutions are endogenous, or self-organized. They are created by agents in the model; they cannot be assumed. Hence, a force rather like selection pressure may operate on a slower timescale to evolve the institutions in the style of Greif's article in Kreps and Wallis (1997), or Padgett's piece in Arthur, Durlauf and Lane (1997). Because institutions are evolving there is no one 'equilibrium' right price that markets are to find. Instead, there may be a 'preferable process' which finds a price. Any price that is found by that preferable process may be assumed to be as close to the right price as can be found. In the complexity view the existing reality and institutions (current reality exists, so in some sense it must work) and a knowledge of how historically evolutionary change has allowed the economy to meet new problems are necessary to answer questions about economic policy; models alone will not do so.

This means that the complexity worldview will stress history more in the manner of North's piece in Arthur, Durlauf and Lane (1997), and stress networks more in the manner of Putnam (1993) in his comparative study of performance of Italian regional governments, than does conventional analytic theory. The complexity worldview is an amalgam of Austrian, Hayekian, Northian and Schumpeterian worldviews but is more mathematically friendly, reverting to a heavy use of computational technologies when analytics fail.[5] It is interesting to note the close relationship between the complexity view and the earlier micro-simulation school championed by Orcutt and others in the 1970s.

As an example, consider the question: Do free markets and well defined property rights make society a better place? In the complexity approach, the answer to this question becomes more of a Baumol-like (1998) and Dosi (1997) exercise of comparative institutional analysis of the innovation rate, that is, an empirical, not a deductive theoretical, question as it is in conventional theory. It does not approach the issue: given assumptions X, Y, Z can we prove that competitive equilibrium is 'Pareto optimal'? Instead, it approaches it as an empirical issue whose answer may lie in areas totally untouched by simplified general equilibrium theory.[6]

As another example of how this does not change sophisticated economists' worldview, consider Frank Hahn's (a top conventional general equilibrium theorist) favorite challenge to 'conventional' economists: 'How can you tell if the economy is in a Pareto optimal state or not?' Such a challenge demonstrates an understanding of the limits of a deductive approach, and the existence of a more sophisticated worldview held by the group we are classifying as conventional economists.

To make policy recommendations within the complexity worldview one does not need a complete formal model of the economy; that is beyond our current understanding. But one can have an informal model of the economy that temporarily describes the current economy, and suggests what effect a certain policy will likely have on it.

Much of deductive standard economic theory has been directed at providing a general theory based on first principles. Complexity theory suggests that question may have no answer and, at this point, the focus of abstract deductive theory should probably be on the smaller questions – accepting that the economy is in a particular position, and talking about how policy might influence the movement from that position. That makes a difference for policy in what one takes as given – it suggests that existing institutions should be incorporated in the models, and that policy suggestions should be made in reference to models incorporating such institutions, rather than in reference to an abstract model that does not incorporate such institutions.

This historical, empirical aspect of complexity changes the type of insights economists are likely to believe they bring to policy debates. In the complexity vision economists have far less to add to policy debates once the institutions are shaped; where their policy input is most important is in institutional design – being on the crest of the new wave and providing judgment on how alternative institutional designs can make major differences in the path chosen, and hence in the ultimate outcome, and when major technological changes occur. Again, this is a very 'Northian' view (see North's essay in SFI (II)) of economic policy making. Building in the correct incentives during the design of institutions is key.

A second change brought about by complexity is that it adds a theoretical neutrality to the abstract debate about policy. In the economic reporters' worldview, that neutrality is not there; the starting point for models is either an inherent assumption of the need for policy action, as in the 'liberal' social welfare models, or an inherent assumption of the lack of the need for policy action, as in the laissez-faire perfectly competitive equilibrium models. Within the complexity worldview, one is not looking for a single model that holds for all time; one is looking for the exploitable pattern in the data that one interprets through one's broad understanding of the evolution of the economy and knowledge of existing institutions. The same debates will arise; liberals will tend to find exploitable patterns; conservatives will not. The difference is that the debate between the two will be more deeply involved in data, and less involved in abstract deductive theory, than the current debate.

A third change is that this complexity worldview makes policy recommendations less certain. It directs researchers to look for patterns and, if they find them, to determine if there is some way the existing pattern can be exploited for gain. One does not look for a policy for all time. The economic reality is a constantly evolving one; each question is slightly different; judgment about which model to use becomes an important part of policy analysis. In a complexity worldview economic models do not tell us the answer; they give us direction; the real issue is deciding what model to use when. Ultimately judgment, not models, must be used in determining policy; the question is simply at what level one wants to use the judgment.

An economist using a complexity vision will be nervous that her optimization modeling of the economy will necessarily be based on a much thinner information set than the information sets of the agents being modeled. Hence if she is put in the position of a regulator who must do something like setting policy instruments to solve a 'Phelps' type problem (compare Sargent's Marshall Lectures (1999)), she will envisage something like facing a highly interconnected 'lattice' of component agents, each equipped with something like Lucasian critique game theoretic 'common knowledge' of her policy actions, before she feels that she has a model for which she can set her controls to optimize her conception of social welfare. This realization will likely lead her to abandon any attempt at 'fine tuning', but it need not eliminate regulatory activity designed to provide some type of 'transparent' 'rule-based' policy regime that promotes stability and contract. An example of such policy actions might be the Fed action during the Stock Market Crisis of October, 1987.

As discussed by Scott (1998) Complex Adaptive System-based thinking sharpens our understanding why scientific hubris that policies can be imposed from top down is extremely dangerous. But, as also emphasized by Scott, it does not eliminate the possibility of policy action. The complexity approach adds a new avenue of policy thinking that will offer some possible guidance for policy using simulation models. The complexity-educated policy maker who has read both Gunderson, Holling and Light (1995) and Scott (1998) and has been trained in quantitative tools advanced in SFI (II) for example might think as follows. In the regulation of derivatives and other 'high-tech' financial products one must look for channels where such products might be used to erode legal regulations. One must determine what kinds of activities are covered by certain types of government insurance, such as deposit insurance, and how high-tech financial products might be used to 'hide' 'real risk exposure' and get higher returns while still being 'eligible' for deposit insurance. Finding that will help guide policy regulating those derivatives.

A fourth change in worldview is that the complexity policy analyst will always be looking for effects that do not show up immediately, but which are nonetheless there. She will simultaneously consider variables that are affected by policy at different speeds. Looking for potential trouble spots caused by such use of high technology to 'erode legal boundaries' set by regulators for private profit comes naturally to an economist who is always looking for 'slow- moving' variables that lead to nasty 'surprises' in the style of Gunderson, Holling and Light (1995). The complexity-trained policy economist will look harder to find pathways to some notion of 'edge of criticality' and will look harder at activities that might be leading to a loss of resilience. The complexity-trained policy economist will tend to try to factor in the value of a property like resilience into their benefit/cost analysis while policymaking.

A fifth change is that the process-oriented character of the complexity worldview focuses policy analysis more on existing institutions and the relationship between the feedback loops between incentives and those institutions more in the style of North's (1997) essay in SFI (II) and Putnam's study of Italian institutions (1993), than general equilibrium theory does. Put another way, there is more of a focus on 'inductive process' models than on abstract deductive models.

A sixth change is the addition of a temporal dimension to policy. The conception of path dependence and increasing returns means that the solution to problems has a temporal dimension, and that the best policy will likely change over time. Therefore, appropriate policies have a time dimension reflecting current institutional and social conditions. As Brian Arthur (this volume) points out, this has implications for the training of policymakers; they need to have specific institutional and historical knowledge to conduct policy.

This means that all solutions are temporary and changing. Complexity theory suggests that patterns develop for a time period, but are not fixed in stone. Thus, we would expect much more study than is currently done into whether the pattern upon which the policy is based is robust. Policies will become more scenario-based policy proposals with qualification attached rather than statements: this is what you should do. Complexity models will likely have multiple policy results from a specific policy. We would expect that there will be increased attention to searching for potential pathways for occurrences of abrupt changes as in mechanisms for metastability – what Holland (1995) calls 'lever points'.

We want to emphasize that it is primarily the economic reporters' worldview that will be changed. Sophisticated economists have long ago given up a simplified general equilibrium worldview. For example, this process worldview is the worldview that is closely related to that held, and used, by economists working on problems of public utilities, and state-owned enterprises, where increasing returns and technical change loom large. Thus, in a way, what complexity will do to the sophisticated economic world view is to bring it to the fore so that others can better understand it.

COMPLEXITY AND THE ACTIVISM/LAISSEZ FAIRE DEBATE

Probably the debate about economic policy that most reflects economic reporters' worldview is the debate about activism vs. laissez faire, so let us consider it a bit more closely. In economics, certain models, such as those based on social welfare functions, have been seen as activist models; others, such as the public choice model, have been seen as laissez faire models. Much of the deductive theory in economics has been conducted to demonstrate whether one or the other of these is the correct theoretical view. The complexity vision is neutral on these grounds; it favors neither activism nor laissez faire. But it does have important implications for that laissez-faire debate in that it changes the focus of that debate.

COMPLEXITY ARGUMENTS FOR LAISSEZ FAIRE

The conventional laissez faire/activist debate is centered around deductive theory and externalities. In the absence of externalities, based on a simplified Arrow–Debreu general equilibrium theory, the market 'solves' the problems. Those who believe externalities are unimportant, and that government solutions tend to end up doing more harm than the original externalities, favor laissez faire; those who believe externalities are important, and that government solutions do more good than harm, believe in activism.

As we stated above, the complexity vision takes away the reference point for theory's defense of the market. In the complexity vision there is no theoretical proof that the market solves problems. There is no unambiguous way of stating what is and is not an externality, and there is no guarantee that the market leads to the most desirable equilibrium. Thus deductive theory cannot provide a basis for the defense of laissez faire. In its place complexity places an 'ignorance argument' and the 'historical argument' in defense of laissez faire. The ignorance argument is the following: the economy is a self-organized system that is beyond our formal modeling capabilities; it has emerged through a complex set of interactions. To think that we can actually positively affect something so complex as the market in a positive way is hubris. This is what is often seen as the Austrian take on the problem, and it is a strong argument.

Another aspect of the ignorance argument concerns one's conception of the ideal state – the goal that one should be shooting for. Complexity theory directs one to think dynamically, and to see a result as part of an ongoing dynamic system; with self-organized systems, fluctuations cannot be avoided; they are part of the system. As John Holland has suggested there may be a hidden order of things that policies would undermine. Per Bak (1996, p. 198) states: 'Self-organized criticality is a law of nature for which there is no dispensation.' He concludes: 'The most robust state for an economy could be the decentralized self-organized critical state of capitalistic economics, with fluctuations of all sizes and durations.'

An 'historical argument' supplements the ignorance argument; it is the argument that, in history, many attempts to interfere with the market have led to more problems than they have resolved. Using history as a guide, in those cases it is best to not enter in. In the complexity vision, if one is going to defend laissez faire, it will be with the use of the 'ignorance' argument and the 'historical' argument; it will not be with a deductive theoretical argument.

COMPLEXITY ARGUMENTS AGAINST LAISSEZ FAIRE

The above laissez faire arguments are strong but there are also strong activism arguments which follow from complexity. These arguments follow from sensitive dependence on initial conditions, increasing returns, lock-in and path dependency, all of which, as discussed above, become important in a complexity worldview, and in the sophisticated economists' worldview.

Path dependency, increasing returns and lock-in call the competitive result into question on a number of fronts. All sophisticated economists know that, but in the translation to policy it can sometimes be forgotten. What complexity does is to make these concepts a focal point, and thereby highlight potential problems that they create for markets.

One of the problems these ideas highlight concerns fairness of competitive results. One of the often-unstated aspects of standard theory as it is interpreted by the lay public is that it provides not only a theoretical proof of the advantages of the market; it also provides a sense of fairness of the market. Individuals get what they deserve in a market economy. That sense of fairness is important in establishing a base of popular support for market results. In the standard model if individuals receive income, it is because they are more efficient. The exception to this is that they have earned this income by establishing a monopoly, but since government imposes most monopolies, activism will make things worse.

The complexity vision of economics undermines that general belief; it offers the possibility that luck – being the first one to the market – and the use of restrictive practices, are the reasons one receives high income, not one's inherent efficiency. One's competitive position comes from being on the right part of the learning curve, along with increasing returns. Thus, one could have hundreds of equally efficient individuals with one of them getting everything, and everyone else getting nothing. Technical economics does not draw fairness results from economic theory. But much writing for the lay public does, and thus this change can have an important role in changing the public's perception about the appropriateness of the market distributional result.

A closely related idea is the superstars effect of Sherwin Rosen which is extended by Frank and Cook (1995) in their book, *The Winner Take All Society* whose very title suggests that much of the high incomes captured by 'winners' are viewed as 'unfair' and not easily justified by efficiency arguments. Frank and Cook focus especially on cases where high incomes are due to a tiny marginal superiority over the next-best competitor being levered up through technological advances. Inequality generated by this kind of mechanism is not likely to be tolerated by the public at large once they understand how little of it is due to standard notions of 'merit' or 'superior efficiency'.[7]

Furthermore, the potentiality of such accumulation may lead to significant resources being wasted by competitors 'jockeying around' to get a small advantage at the beginning entry point of the process. This kind of social waste is similar to the waste of 'rent-seeking' behavior as in Colander (1984). Part of the art of good institutional design is to design institutions, that is, 'rules-of-the-game' that penalize rent-seeking behavior and reward behavior that produces value for others. Complexity's focus on cumulative processes of advantage has helped alert economists to potential areas where rent-seeking behavior is likely to be troublesome. If it were possible to measure the portion of income that was due solely to the effects of such accumulating one could imagine taxing it and using the revenues to offset more distortionary taxes rather in the manner of Frank and Cook. Of course this would be difficult in practice, but at least attention would be focused more sharply on such issues.[8]

A second activist argument directly follows from increasing returns. It concerns the view of the end result of the competitive process. Within the standard model employing assumptions of diminishing returns there is a natural limit to monopoly. Competition within an industry will lead to a balance. That is no longer the case with the complexity vision. Unregulated competition can, and often will, lead to monopoly in an industry – to one competitor winning everything. This result may be undesirable from a public policy point of view independent of efficiency. That does not mean that competition is not taking place, but significant competition will likely be from outside the industry, brought about by technological change. Thus, standard measurements of the degree of competition, such as Herfindahl indexes, will not be especially useful, and will be replaced by new measures of barriers to entry and dynamic contestability. For example, the policy analysis with increasing returns and lock-in would look at issues such as whether a forward-looking consortium can break a path towards an inefficient technology that is accumulating adherents. Again, this is a change sophisticated economists have already made; complexity simply furthers that and incorporates it into policy analysis at an earlier level.

A third way in which the complexity argument can be used to support activism is that with path dependency, it is possible that an economy can get on the wrong path, and that a slight policy adjustment early on 'could' put it on the 'right path'. The debate about QWERTY is an example of the type of debate that uses this argument; because of an historical accident we may be using an inefficient keyboard. Complexity offers the possibility that if we recognize these situations we can avoid them and, through policy, guide the economy to a preferable equilibrium.

As was the case with the arguments in favor of laissez faire, the general arguments must be supplemented with historical evidence of similar events. There have been times when activist policy has been beneficial and times when it has not. Policy analysis within the complexity approach will make use of that historical evidence to judge whether the question at hand is one where policy will help or one where it will hurt.

The QWERTY debate is a good example of how the complexity vision shifts the policy discussion. It is not surprising to us that the QWERTY debate has advocates on both sides – those who argue that the QWERTY keyboard is inefficient, and those who argue that it is not sufficiently inefficient to impose significant costs. But it is an historical, not a deductive, debate. The complexity approach does not eliminate the debate between activism vs. laissez faire; it simply shifts it from the theoretical to the abductive and empirical/historical fronts and instructs economists to look for the possibility of a strong enough process of accumulation of advantage that it is difficult to dislodge even if it appears to be locking onto an inefficient choice.

CHANGES IN PRACTICAL MODELS

While the changes to general policy thinking are considerable, the changes to actual policy models will be smaller. The reason is that actual policy making reflects a far more pragmatic approach than is reflected in general policy discussion. Policy models already do reflect history, and institutions, and policy is determined from real people facing real problems.

What complexity does is to take away the backdrop of deductive theory for practical policy models and replace it with a broader, more inclusive worldview that is much more consistent with many of the actual policy models. It changes what is considered ad hoc – in the complexity vision all policy models are necessarily ad hoc. Actual policy models have little high theory behind them; they reflect real world problems. When pushed, they break down, but generally they do not need to be pushed. Complexity theory removes the implicit belief that these policy models need to be connected to that high theory. It is OK to find patterns, and to base policy on patterns. Standard economics tries to connect theory and policy in explicit formal ways. The complexity vision suggests that that connection cannot be made formally – that the best we can do is an informal connection. Thus, complexity theory simply puts policy models in a different, more favorable, context.

Many economists have come to a policy position similar to the position to which complexity drives one, quite independently of complexity theory. They have always viewed policy that way. J.M. Clarke had a discussion of workable competition; aspects of anti-trust laws use economic theory as a backdrop, not a definitive litmus test, and the majority of the pre-1980s Keynesian and monetarist macro models were always policy models. But while that was the practice, it was not the stated methodology. The stated methodology held that formal models were preferable to informal models. This difference between practice and the stated methodology led to confusion and to a movement away from these policy models in what was taught students. Ironically, complexity theory, which is itself highly mathematical, provides a kind of theoretical foundation for the type of practical economic work that policy economists have always done. Before, such policy work was seen as hack work; in the complexity vision it is seen as the backbone of policy analysis; it is the large abstract deductive models that fall by the wayside.

CHANGES IN THE WAY ECONOMISTS DO ACTUAL POLICY ANALYSIS

Complexity brings about not only a change in the way policy is approached and thought about; complexity also brings about changes in the way policy analysis is done. For example, computer-assisted analytics and computer-assisted inferential techniques will allow researchers to locate boundaries of parameter space consistent with existing data that indicates stasis but near 'hidden' emergent nonlinearities where conventional approximation techniques are dangerous. As computer technology further develops, there will be far less emphasis on deductive models in doing policy analysis and far more on simulations and computer-assisted analysis. Instead of the current picture of an economic policy maker sitting at a desk, working on an analytic model, we would expect the picture of a policy maker sitting at a computer running simulations and using software to solve complicated analytic models that have been suggested by the patterns found in the data as discussed by Duncan Foley in this volume.

Let us consider an example: the macro policy debate on the NAIRU that appeared in the JEP Symposium in 1997. In that symposium there was a debate between those who feared expanding the economy more would ignite an inflationary spiral and those who felt it would not. Stiglitz reported that the CEA conducted econometric studies that suggested that one could grow the economy a little bit more without fear of igniting an inflationary spiral. He states that there is a 'view, more common in nonacademic circles, that the NAIRU is like a precipice: take one step over it, and you fall into a spiral of rapidly accelerating inflation ... The evidence simply does not support this view ... the world is not only continuous but approximately linear ... Thus small mistakes have only small consequences.'

The complexity approach would use some currently little used techniques to test this proposition. It would use a 'probing' strategy to check this out with special attention to probing for possible indicators that might indicate a 'poised state' of the economy. Indicators might be sought that would indicate nearness to a bifurcation point that is not revealed by the current data analysis. Computational work could be done to approximate something like Koop and Potter's (1999) 'Bayes factors' for the different views by drawing on histories and datasets of inflationary processes. Welfare distributions under the different views could then be calculated as in Pizer (1996) perhaps, in order to present policy makers with informative information on the distribution of potential costs and benefits. This might lead to further scrutiny of any sources of potential irreversibilities such as a possible 'flip' into an alternate 'stable state' as in the Carpenter, Ludwig and Brock (1997) lake, or sluggishness in changing policy if leading indicators such as some of those discussed above show caution.

The Carpenter et al. work stresses the intuitive argument that the potential presence of bifurcations and alternative stable states with potential hysteresis and irreversibilities strengthens conventional precautionary principles. It stresses the use of computational work to present a distribution of values of policy actions consistent with the ability of the data to place bounds upon the dynamical possibilities under those policy actions.

Another change that will result from the acceptance of complexity vision can be seen in how one would conduct the work on valuation of irreversibility under potential alternative stable states. Accepting complexity would likely shift the burden of proof to those acts, which have the potential to generate irreversibilities. Indicators of pathways towards social interactions in expectations formation which might cause alternative stable states could be sought after. Perhaps high frequency survey work on expectations would be in order while growing the economy a bit more. If such high frequency survey work indicated a start towards a shift in inflationary expectations, then policy would quickly back off and there would be publicly credible mechanisms set in place to convince the markets that policy would 'turn on a dime'.

A third change in the way we do policy analysis concerns the nature of the data we search out. There would likely be more expectational survey work that would give some kind of indicator how tightly interconnected relevant actors' expectations are. This could be important in practice, because the more tightly interconnected expectations are, the more likely is a 'surprise' burst of expectation revision that might be hard to reverse as well as effects that would be hard to forecast with conventional tools (see Durlauf in SFI (II)).

A fourth change will be that there will be more focus on 'process' and computationally-based methods of analysis than in 'conventional' analysis of institutional design, comparative institutions, and increasing returns industries such as public utilities. There may also be more focus on 'boundaries', more in the style of the experienced FTC commissioner who is always watching for 'sleazy' competitors who 'skate on the gray edge of legal boundaries' to get an edge on their competitors. The US Savings and Loan mess of the 1980's must always be kept in mind as a major regulatory failure.

A final change complexity brings about in policy analysis will be in the tools. They will be quite different than those currently used by conventional economists. A sampler of tools inspired by complexity include: (i) Mean Field Theory (Brock 1993); (ii) Statistical Mechanics (see Blume 1993, Brock 1993, Durlauf 1996); (iii) general bifurcation theory (see Brock and Hommes 1997); (iv) Bootstrap-based specification testing (see Brock, Lakonishok and LeBaron 1992); (v) Polya Processes and Stochastic Approximation Theory (see Arthur, Ermolier and Kaniovski 1994, Marcet and Sargent 1989, Ljung and Glad 1994); (vi) Edge of Chaos, Autocatalytic Sets,[9] (vii) Genetic Algorithms, Classifier Systems.[10] Such tools allow one to get into processes; they are highly dependent on the computer. Thus the future of a complexity based economic policy analysis will be one highly integrated with the computer.

Arnott and Leinveber (1993) have made a dramatic calculation of what an automobile would be like if technical progress in the automobile industry had progressed in the last few decades as fast as it did in the computer industry. We shall call this the '10 cent Ferrari' because it reflects that fact that an auto that performed at the level of a Ferrari would cost about 10 cents today!

This kind of technical change in the computer industry reflects a huge drop in the relative costs of computation that should have a dramatic effect on the way economics is practiced. We believe this drop in the effective price of a unit of computation is going to push economics into the computational direction.

Judd (1998) has developed the above argument. He stresses that progress in semiconductor technology has been following 'Moore's Law', which says that component density and speed has been doubling about every 18 months for silicon chips. One of Judd's arguments is that computation levers up the domain of understanding gleaned from analytical work. Another of his arguments stresses that, unlike formal mathematics, which is built up from a deep bedrock of fundamental results with a resulting high premium on deductive rigor, economic theorizing consists of a much thinner layer of economic modeling resting on top of a deep mathematical foundation. Note that the usual proof of a proposition in economics relies little on previous economic theorems and relies more on existing mathematical theorems.

Judd's introduction to his book gives an excellent example of the use of computational methods by Quirmbach who evaluated the impact of different market structures on the economic welfare generated by corporate research and development efforts. It concerned the tradeoff between the degree of competition and the level of investment. In the conventional view, if competition is expected to be too intense there will be little drive to develop useful innovations, and the investment in R&D may be too low. If firms are allowed to collude ex post, R&D will increase.

Quirmbach computed hundreds of cases and found a robust pattern that suggests that allowing collusion or monopoly ex post in order to stimulate the appropriate level of R&D ex ante is usually a bad idea. His result is not a 'theorem' in the traditional sense of economic theory, but it is an extremely valuable policy result because the robustness of his findings were unsuspected. The policy importance is obvious. Regulation and antitrust should not put up with the evils of collusion and monopoly simply in order to generate socially optimal levels of innovative activity. We can imagine doing more research along this line as computational costs continue to drop.

Indeed we could imagine building a richer class of models that exhibit path dependence and lock-in that link more closely to the underlying expectational and competitive environment rather along the lines of Porter and Spence in McCall's book (1982), and Flaherty (1980) but with more emphasis on stochastic dynamics as in the urn process-based models. A Quirmbach-type computational exercise could be used to evaluate different regulatory proposals, including no regulation at all. It may well turn out that, as in Baumol's (1998) story, there is so much fear of someone else inventing something that renders a powerful incumbent's product useless that the incumbent is driven by this fear of displacement into innovating at the optimal rate, even though it appears that he should be living the 'comfortable life' of an entrenched monopolist. The point of Quirmbach-type work à la Judd is that one can conduct combined analytical and computational modeling across a wide variety of 'game forms'. If one finds robustness of results across a wide variety of equally plausible game forms then one has more confidence in making the resulting policy recommendation.

COMPLEXITY THEORY, ECONOMICS, AND HER SISTER SOCIAL SCIENCES

Another of the implications of complexity theory for economic policy is that it will emphasize the need for economic work to consider developments in its sister social sciences. We illustrate this by mentioning some examples and thinking through some of them through the lens of Holland's complex adaptive systems.

One example is the economists' treatment of social capital in policy analysis. Economic policy discussion has been conducted with little mention of social capital. Complexity theory's emphasis on different kinds of network structures suggests, as does Putnam (1993), that the structure of networks is important in explaining the amount of social capital that self-organizes. We believe that the concept of social capital will be increasingly integrated into economic policy discussions, especially as analytical and computational advances in the analysis of network phenomena continue to be made.

Another example is that of political scientist and anthropologist, James C. Scott (1998) in his book, *Seeing Like a State*, which we discussed above. In that book he shows, via case studies, how self-organized localized networks at localized scales using detailed 'thick' information sets, which are only available by locals 'living the information', can do a better job of solving human problems than well-intentioned, but sometimes disastrous, social engineering 'optimal' planning schemes based on the necessarily 'thinner' information sets upon which such 'optimization' must be based.

A third example will be the integration of what might be called the quantification of 'social capital' by sociologists such as Coleman (1990) into economic models. Coleman stresses social capital, localized and globalized social networks containing strong and weak ties, related networks of trust, horizontal and vertical social ties, and so on. For example, the community self-policing and control of crime is a joint-goods product. Neighborhood qualities such as peace and quiet, appearance, serenity and cleanliness are examples of joint-goods production at the community level that are essential inputs into a good life.[11] There has been much recent work in the sociological literature to attempt to construct measures of social capital and show that this measure is associated with better neighborhood qualities.[12]

The conventional quantitative economist tends to shy away from this kind of literature because it is hard to formalize and, thus, hard to integrate into the corpus of modern economic theory. The complexity economists will be much more likely to make attempts to include it because tools of pattern formation analysis are being developed by complexity theorists and because computational methods are being made available that reduce the costs of analyzing hundreds and thousands of different models. To put it another way, it is now possible to computationally classify 'universality classes' of results in search of robustness of substantive economic conclusions to details of modeling that are not substantively important. This kind of evidence enhances confidence in any conclusions that are drawn. Clearly issues raised by writings on social capital such as Coleman (1990) and Putnam (1993) are important, and need to be included into the corpus of 'conventional economics'.

CONCLUSION

There is an old maxim in economics attributed to Jack Hirshleifer that all one needs to know of economics is learned in the principles course – specifically the micro principles course. This view, which is commonplace among policy makers, especially conservative policy makers, is undermined by the complexity vision. Just as complexity makes the analytics of economic theory more complex, so too does it make the application to policy more complex. In the complexity vision one never learns enough economics to decide on policy. There is a lot more to policy than supply and demand; it requires a knowledge of institutions, history, and data that are constantly changing.

That said, we also want to emphasize that much will not change. Early on in this chapter we emphasized that complexity theory will most strongly affect the conclusions coming from aggregate analysis. This point deserves to be re-emphasized, because much of the policy advice coming from economics comes from disaggregated models that are institutionally and historically, not theoretically, based.

Many of the micro policy conclusions of economics such as the general inadvisability of price controls may be unaffected by complexity-based research even though that kind of research may reveal some surprising emergence of patterns caused by imposition of such controls.

The complexity approach to policy emphasizes the need for a subtlety of understanding that accompanies a deep awareness of patterns and processes. One needs to know that patterns will sometimes self-organize in surprising ways. Sometimes processes such as the ethnic distribution of neighborhoods in, for example, Schelling-type models, may be surprisingly sensitive to small policy interventions, and sometimes they will be surprisingly stubborn to a policy intervention. Complexity analysis will direct policy analysts to search for both such possibilities.

Determining whether a pattern exists is a statistical and historical problem; thus post-complexity policy will be more strongly based in statistics and history than in deductive theory. One may come to the same conclusions as before, but those conclusions will be based more on history, and understanding of how real-world institutions work than it will be based on deductive theory.

NOTES

1. Earlier writers on multiple equilibria, path dependence, lock-in and increasing returns such as Flaherty (1980) did not use the mathematics of generalized urn schemes as did the work of Arthur, Ermoliev and Kaniosvski (hereafter AEK; compare Arthur 1989). Thus policy implications of the latter work belong in the 'complexity' classification, and the policy implications of the former work do not. See Dosi and Kaniovski (1994) for a review of the literature that uses generalized urn processes and related tools, and for a discussion of the modeling advantages inherent in such tools for capturing the idea of small chance events determining long-term 'lock-in' at a possibly undesirable long-run equilibrium. Arthur's use of this approach to discuss issues of regulation and antitrust, as well as corporate strategy, can be found in Arthur (1996). See also Arthur's web site (http://www.santafe.edu/~wba) and read the interview with Dominic Gates at (http://www.pretext.com/may98/columns/intview.htm), for a recent discussion of policy issues raised in antitrust and regulation with reference to the dispute between Microsoft and the US Department of Justice.
2. The Santa Fe approach that we wish to stress in this article involves the concepts of Complex Adaptive System as represented by Holland (1995), the books SFI (I) by Arrow, Anderson and Pine and especially SFI (II) by Arthur, Durlauf and Lane, and the work on 'evolutionary computation' as exemplified by Crutchfield, Mitchell, and others in the 'Evolutionary Computation' (EvCA) program at the Santa Fe Institute (http://www.santafe.edu with /~jcrutchfield for Crutchfield and /~mm for Mitchell). It is an approach to 'Complex Adaptive Systems' that stresses highly interconnected components made up of dynamically adapting agents embedded in a world that they co-create (see Holland 1995) assisted by the work on 'evolutionary computation' mentioned above. Samples of this kind of approach in economics and social science include Arthur et al. in Arthur, Durlauf and Lane (1997), Arthur LeBaron and Palmer (1998), Marimon, McGrattan and Sargent (1990), Sargent (1993) and Grandmont (1998). As emphasized throughout this volume there are many different strands of complexity research even when one focuses on the Santa Fe approach. In this article we will focus on three of those strands. (1) Urn process models to model economic dynamics, especially in industrial evolution in increasing returns-type industries (see Arthur 1989, Dosi and Kaniovski 1994); (2) pattern formation dynamics (see Newell's article in Stein 1989 and Krugman's 1996 use of Turing-type models); and (3) evolutionary dynamics and inductive theorizing in contrast to deductive theorizing (see Arthur, Durlauf and Lane 1997).
3. Even here there is overlap; writers such as Axelrod, Conlisk, Day, Nelson, and Winter have gotten 'close' to some of the ideas referred to in the above work.
4. As Arthur (1989), and Dosi and Kaniovski (1994) stress, this urn process type of modeling captures the dynamic character of these phenomena better than earlier modeling. However,

critics have complained that the urn process literature is 'backwards looking' whereas corporate strategy is more 'forward looking' as in Flaherty (1980) and Porter and Spence in McCall (1982). Hence, there will be cross fertilization between what we are classifying as conventional economics and what we are classifying as complexity economics. Thus a model that combines the stochastic elements of the AEK approach with the forward-looking elements of approaches like Flaherty (1980) and Porter and Spence in McCall (1982) strikes us as a worthwhile research topic. Notice that lock-in to different long-run steady states can occur in forward-looking models like Flaherty's (1980, Figure 3) and a small chance event can 'tip' the system towards a path of development from approximately equal market shares to a long-run state of highly unequal market shares. In Flaherty's (1980) dynamic rational expectations non-cooperative game theoretic oligopoly world this is due to the 'public good' character of cost-reducing investment.

5. For a precise example of what we are trying to capture as a 'complexity based' analysis of institutional change, see the discussion of Padgett's work on fourteenth-century Florentine society in a recent SFI Bulletin (http://www.santafe.edu). That discussion relates Padgett's work on institutional evolution to Fontana's work in chemical evolutions.

6. We emphasize that this change affects our characterization of the economic reporter's world view, not the sophisticated economists' worldview. Thus, this example of how a complexity theorist would approach a question used the conventional economist William Baumol's work (1998) (although he may not appreciate being classified as a 'conventional' economist).

7. An example of this which is of interest to academics is given by Frank and Cook. They show how sociologist R.K. Merton's 'Matthew Effect' is related to the lock-in idea. For example the 'best' undergraduates get into the 'best' graduate schools and get the 'best' jobs at the 'best' universities and work with the best researchers who get the best grants ... In short, a small initial advantage gets cumulated up into a large long-run advantage. This kind of cumulation of advantage from a small piece of luck at getting into the 'right' graduate school tends to strike many people as 'unfair' when it is brought to their attention.

8. There is an interesting distributional issue raised by Frank and Cook's work. Consider a leading opera singer before radio, television and satellite TV existed. The 'span' of each singer's control would be the audience reachable within the sound range of the singer's voice. Hence there would be room for many singers to co-exist. Then, the TV is invented. The slightly better singer can now crowd out all the rest and capture a rent of epsilon times a huge number. This is Rosen's superstar argument. The 'best' singer gets a huge income but the engineers that made the TV possible get modest incomes. Of course the inventor of the TV might get the patent rents, but, as Baumol points out in his *Siena Lectures* (1998), any reasonable estimate of spillovers from the technical innovativeness side of the economy to the economy-at-large appear to be huge relative to the amount captured by the innovators themselves.

9. See Crutchfield, Kauffman, Packard at http://www.santafe.edu

10. See Holland, Crutchfield, Mitchell at http://www.santafe.edu

11. Political scientist Robert Putnam's famous (1993) book, *Making Democracy Work*, does a comparative study of horizontal vs. vertical networks in his explanation of variation in efficiency of government institutions across different regions of Italy.

12. See Brock and Durlauf (1995, 1997) for a review of this type of work and the econometric inference issues that it raises.

REFERENCES

Arnott, R. and D. Leinveber (1993), 'Quantitative and Computational Innovation in Investment Management: Or "If you had everything (computationally), where would you put it (financially)?"', *First Quadrant Corporation*, No. 5, 800 East Colorado Street, Suite 900, Pasadena, CA.

Arthur, W.B. (1989), 'Competing Technologies, Increasing Returns and Lock-In by Historical Events', *Economic Journal*, **99**, 116–31.

Arthur, W.B. (1996), 'Increasing Returns and the New World of Business', *Harvard Business Review*, July–August, 101–9.

Arthur, W.B., S. Durlauf and D. Lane (eds) (1997), *The Economy as an Evolving Complex System II*, Redwood City, CA: Addison-Wesley.

Arthur, W.B., Y.M. Ermoliev and Y.M. Kaniovski (1994), 'Strong Laws for a Class of Path-Dependent Stochastic Processes', in W.B. Arthur (ed.), *Increasing Returns and Path Dependence in the Economy*, Ann Arbor: University of Michigan Press, pp. 185–201.

Bak, P. (1996), *How Nature Works: The Science of Self-Organized Criticality,* New York: Copernicus.

Baumol, W.J., J.C. Panzar and R.D. Willig (1982), *Contestable Markets and the Theory of Industry Structure,* New York: Harcourt Brace Jovanovich.

Baumol, W. (1998), *Siena Lectures* (http://www.econ-pol.unisi.it/iser.html).

Blume, L.E. (1993), 'The Statistical Mechanics of Strategic Interaction', *Games and Economic Behavior*; **5** (3) July, 387–424.

Blume, L.E. (1995), 'The Statistical Mechanics of Best-Response Strategy Revision', *Games and Economic Behavior*, **11** (2), November, 111–45.

Brock, W. (1993), 'Pathways to Randomness in the Economy: Emergent Nonlinearity and Chaos in Economics and Finance', *Estudios Economicos*, **8** (1).

Brock, W. and P. de Fontnouvelle (1999), 'Expectational Diversity in Monetary Economies', *Journal of Economic Dynamics and Control*.

Brock, W. and S. Durlauf (1995, 1997), 'Discrete Choice Theory with Social Interactions, I: Theory and II: Econometrics', Department of Economics, Madison, WI: University of Wisconsin (available at http://www.ssc.wisc.edu/~wbrock).

Brock, W.A. and C.H. Hommes (1997), 'A Rational Route to Randomness', *Econometrica*, **65** (5) September, 1059–95.

Brock, W.A. and C.H. Hommes (1998), 'Heterogeneous Beliefs and Routes to Chaos in a Simple Asset Pricing Model', *Journal of Economic Dynamics and Control*, **22** (8–9), August, 1235–74.

Brock, W., J. Lakonishok and B. LeBaron (1992), 'Simple Technical Trading Rules and the Stochastic Properties of Stock Returns', *Journal of Finance*, **47** (5), December, 1731–64.

Carpenter, S., D. Ludwig and W. Brock (1999), 'Management of Eutrophication for Lakes Subject to Potentially Irreversible Change', *Ecological Applications*, **9** (3), 751–71.

Coleman, J. (1990), *Foundations of Social Theory*, Cambridge, MA: Harvard University Press.

Colander, D. (ed.) (1984), *Neoclassical Political Economy: The Analysis of Rent- seeking and DUP Activities*, Cambridge, MA: Harper & Row, Ballinger.

Crutchfield, J., http://www.santafe.edu/

de Fontnouvelle, P. (2000), 'Informational Strategies in Financial Markets: The Implications for Volatility and Trading Volume Dynamics', General Electric Corporate R&D, One Research Circle, Niskayuna, NY, 12309, *Macroeconomic Dynamics*.

Dosi, G. (1997), 'Opportunities, Incentives, and the Collective Patterns of Technological Change', *Economics Journal*, **107** (444), September, 1530–47.

Dosi, G. and Y. Kaniovski (1994), 'On "Badly Behaved" Dynamics: Some Applications of Generalized Urn Schemes on Technological and Economic Change', *Journal of Evolutionary Economics*, **4** (2), 93–123.

Durlauf, S.N. (1996), 'Statistical Mechanics Approaches to Socioeconomic Behavior', National Bureau of Economic Research Technical Paper, **203**, September.

Evans, D. (ed.) (1983), *Breaking Up Bell*, Amsterdam: North Holland.

Flaherty, M. (1980), 'Industry Structure and Cost-Reducing Investment', *Econometrica*, **48** (5), July, 1187–209.

Frank, R. and P. Cook (1995), *The Winner Take-All Society*, New York: The Free Press.

Grandmont, J. (1998), 'Expectation Formation and Stability of Large Socioeconomic Systems', *Econometrica*, **66** (4), July, 741–81.

Gunderson L.H., C.S. Holling and S.S. Light (eds) (1995), *Barriers and Bridges to the Renewal of Ecosystems and Institutions*, New York: Columbia University Press.

Holland, J. (1995), *Hidden Order: How Adaptation Builds Complexity*, Helix Books of Reading, MA: Addison-Wesley.

Jovanovic, B. and Y. Nyarko (1996), 'Learning by Doing and the Choice of Technology', *Econometrica*, **64** (6), 1299–310.

Judd, K. (1998), *Numerical Methods in Economics*, Cambridge, MA: MIT Press.

Katz, M. and C. Shapiro (1994), 'Systems Competition and Network Effects', *Journal of Economic Perspectives*, **8**, 93–115.

Koop, G. and S.M. Potter (1999), 'Bayes Factors and Nonlinearity: Evidence from Economic Time Series', *Journal of Econometrics*, **88** (2), February, 251–81.

Kreps, E. and K. Wallis (eds) (1997), *Advances in Economics and Econometrics: Theory Applications*, Volumes I–III, Cambridge, MA: Cambridge University Press.

Krugman, P. (1991), 'History vs. Expectations', *Quarterly Journal of Economics*, **106**, 651–67.

Krugman, P. (1996), *The Self-Organizing Economy*, Oxford: Blackwell Publishers, Ltd.

LeBaron, B., W.B. Arthur and R. Palmer (1999), 'Time Series Properties of an Artificial Stock Market', *Journal of Economic Dynamics and Control*, **23**, 1487–516.

Ljung, L. and T. Glad (1994), *Modeling of Dynamic Systems*, Englewood Cliffs, NJ: Prentice Hall.

Marcet, A. and T.J. Sargent (1989), 'Convergence of Least Squares Learning Mechanisms in Self-referential Linear Stochastic Models', *Journal of Economic Theory*, **48** (2), August, 337–68.

Marcet, R., E. McGrattan and T.J. Sargent 1990), 'Money as a Medium of Exchange in An Economy with Artificially Intelligent Agents', *Journal of Economic Dynamics and Control*, **14**, 329–73.

Marimon, R., E. McGrattan and T.J. Sargent (1990), 'Money as a Medium of Exchange in an Economy with Artificially Intelligent Agents', *Journal of Eco-*

nomic Dynamics and Control; **14** (2), May, 329–73.

McCall, J. (ed.) (1982), *The Economics of Information and Uncertainty*, Chicago, IL: University of Chicago Press.

Mitchell, M., http://www.santafe.edu/

North, D.C. (1997), *The Contribution of the New Institutional Economics to an Understanding of the Transition Problem*, Helsinki: UNV/WIDER.

Packard, W., http://www.santafe.edu/

Pizer, W. (1996), *Modeling Long-Term Policy under Uncertainty*, Dissertation, Harvard University.

Prigogine, I. and M. Sanglier (1987), 'Laws of Nature and Human Conduct', G.O.R.D.E.S. Task Force of Research Information and Study on Science, Bruxelles, Belgium.

Putnam, R.D. (1993), *Making Democracy Work: Civic Traditions in Modern Italy*, Princeton, NJ: Princeton University Press.

Sargent, T. J. (1993), *Bounded Rationality in Macroeconomics,* Arne Ryde Memorial Lectures, Oxford and New York: Oxford University Press, Clarendon Press.

Sargent, T. (1999), *The Conquest of American Inflation*, Princeton, NJ: Princeton University Press.

Scott, J.C. (1998), *Seeing Like a State: How Certain Schemes to Improve the Human Condition Have Failed*, New Haven, CT: Yale University Press.

Siena Lectures (1998), *Proceedings of the XI Workshop Cycle, Growth and Structural Change*, International School of Economic Research, Univerita' de Siena, iser@unisi.it, http://www.econ-pol.unisi.it/iser.html.

Stein, D. (1989), *Lectures in the Sciences of Complexity*, Redwood City, CA: Addison-Wesley.

6. Policy Implications of Complexity: An Austrian Perspective

Roger Koppl

What policy prescription follows from complexity? Should we have more government or less? Some say that complexity does not give us a direct answer. It is neutral on policy. This is the view of Brock and Colander (Chapter 5, this volume). They argue that complexity merely directs the policy debate to different issues. Austrians are more pro-market. They think complexity implies hands off. In their private conversations, they criticize 'complexity planners' who suggest the government use a 'nudging hand'.

Austrians are often very pro-market. Many are libertarians. They advocate relatively extreme forms of laissez faire capitalism. I am not so completely pro-market. Nor does Austrian economic theory imply strict laissez faire. Libertarian ideology is an ethical and political system. It must be based on something more than social science. Often it is based on a moral argument for natural rights. The moral argument for natural rights is not a part of Austrian economics.

But there is a sense in which Austrian economics is pro-market. If Austrian economics is about right, then socialism is not a very workable system. (This point is developed below.) The only workable systems rely heavily on voluntary exchange. They are 'capitalist' in a broad sense. If you agree with that assessment of the facts, you will probably prefer some version of 'capitalism' to the alternatives. You might accept Austrian economics and reject anything like free markets. But you would do so only if you had very unusual ethical views. For example, you might have a preference for religious simplicity. Otherwise, Austrian economics does go with a more or less pro-market policy. In this chapter I try to show how Austrian economics implies a broadly pro-market policy.

In this chapter, I will outline an 'Austrian' approach to the policy implications of complexity. I will try to explain why Austrian theory implies great limits to government activity. The key is the Austrian 'knowledge problem'. The basic idea is that government regulators and planners cannot have the knowledge needed to do the job right. The Austrian economist I will draw on the most is F.A. Hayek. First, I contrast Hayek's views with the 'naive view'.

The naive view is just a straw man. But the contrast lets me make some basic points. Second, I explain the knowledge problem. I do so by quickly reviewing Austrian arguments against socialist planning. Finally, I will discuss how the Austrian knowledge problem leads to a general critique of 'intervention' in economic affairs.

HOW HAYEK'S APPROACH TO POLITICS DIFFERS FROM THE NAIVE VIEW

Hayek's approach to thinking about social and political questions is quite different from what many non-economists take for granted. To help grease the skids of understanding, I will construct a straw man for Hayek to combat. I will call the straw man's theory the 'naive view'. There are a few people, even a few serious thinkers, who hold to extreme versions of the naive view. There are bona fide examples at each end of the current 'culture wars'. Unqualified defenses of the naive view are rare, however. And yet most non-economists unconsciously adopt more moderate versions of it. Contrasting Hayek's opinions with the naive view helps clarify the Austrian policy position Hayek mapped out.

Under the naive view, how do you think about social problems? First, you ask yourself 'How would I like society to look?' The answer is generally something lovely. Society should be a wonderland of peace and love. We would all have high-paying jobs and cultural enlightenment. We are not there. Why not? The answer, under the naive view, is that evil or unenlightened people are keeping us back. The problem may be greed, ignorance, or even malicious intent.

What is to be done? We must fight ignorance and evil wherever we find them. Politics is mostly a matter of getting people to see and abhor the evil and ignorance that are responsible for our troubles. Once they are out of the way, society will, somehow, turn into something much like the workers' paradise of Marxist theory. Politics is hammering out the right values.

One might ask how, exactly, we should arrange our common affairs in this future world. Precisely how, for example, might we ensure that each person has gainful employment that does not waste society's scarce resources? How shall we ensure that the number of hospitals built will bear a reasonable relation to the number of automobiles, or jumping ropes, or philosophical treatises? These questions, to advocates of the naive view, are mere technical questions. The real *political* questions are wholly ethical in nature. Are you morally good enough to want the kind of society I want? Are you willing to stand shoulder to shoulder with me? Or do you instead nurture the bad will of the bad people?

Table 6.1 The Logic of the Austrian View

	Naive view	Hayekian liberal
Ends	A problematic political question	A political question only when there is disagreement about means
Means	A technical question, mostly outside politics	The heart of the main political differences in modern society

For advocates of the naive view it's all a question of *values* and *ends*. If you have my values, you have my politics. If you want to achieve the same *ends* as me, we are political allies. The question of *means* is merely technical.

Hayek's approach to political questions is quite different. For Hayek, political questions have very little to do with *ends* and everything to do with *means*. We cannot 'just have' whatever sort of society we want. We have a very limited scope for choice here. There are *constraints* on us that we cannot escape. Love and wisdom, compassion and knowledge, decency and information are scarce resources. The only way to get a good society is to husband them. While we have some freedom to choose how we might husband these resources, our choice is rather narrow. To maintain the current population, we have little choice but to uphold the broad laissez faire principles of eighteenth-century liberalism. Even if we disagree plenty about what exactly the good society is, we need not come into that much political conflict. For if we can agree about what the effects of different policies will be, we are likely to agree about which ones to pursue.

It comes down to ends and means. Advocates of the naive view do not believe that any significant problem of means exists. If we could just agree on ends – where we want to go – the rest is just a technical matter. The Hayekian liberal does not believe that the problem of ends is so complete. If we could just agree on means – what policies have what effects – most of our greatest differences about ends would appear less politically charged.[1] The logic of this Austrian view is summarized in Table 6.1.

THE AUSTRIAN CRITIQUE OF SOCIALISM

The central example of the Austrian approach to policy is their attack on socialism, for which Hayek and the Austrians are famous. This Austrian critique fits the logic of Table 6.1 perfectly. Socialism is a beautiful idea, they said, but it will not work. (Without irony, Hayek devoted his most overtly political book, *The Road to Serfdom*, to 'Socialists of all parties'.) The ends of socialism were never in dispute. The means, collective ownership, were found wanting. The Austrian critique of socialism matters for another reason. The Austrians found many problems with socialism including the difficulty of getting people to work hard. 'We pretend to work', went the old Soviet joke, 'and they pretend to pay us'. But the really interesting part of their argument concerned the 'knowledge problem'. It is this problem which formed the core of their attack on socialism. And it forms the core of their approach to most other questions of economic policy. The Austrian knowledge problem explains why Hayek and his followers are so skeptical of government action. Complexity theorists who are more inclined to government action are less convinced by the knowledge problem.

In an economic discussion such as this, 'socialism' means an economic system in which the means of production are owned collectively. In such a system, its advocates imagine, a central economic plan will guide production. In some versions the plan is devised through democratic processes. In other versions it is handed down by a set of experts, the central planning board. In any event, capital markets have been discarded in favor of collective planning.

From the Austrian angle, the problem with socialism is the central planning it requires. How are the planners to know what plan to set out? They must know relative scarcities and thus relative values, especially for capital goods and capital combinations. In a market, you can read that off from the prices hammered by supply and demand. But under socialist planning, you want to control supply and demand. Thus, even if you have prices, they will be controlled prices that will not tell you much about underlying scarcities. Without knowledge of relative values, socialist planners cannot really plan anything at all. They can only take wild stabs at it. For the Austrians, rational economic planning under socialism is impossible.

Consider the building of a new hospital, (Mises 1966). Should we make it several storeys tall or a low building occupying more surface area? In a market economy it is relatively easy to decide. The value of the land is a key determining variable. But in a socialist economy, there is no market price of land. No one can read-off the value of the land from its market price. The value of the land is determined by the decisions of the central planners who must determine this value in conjunction with all others. Without market prices in land and capital, the Austrians have argued, the task cannot be performed.

The Austrian argument was originally made (in 1920) by the school's leader, Ludwig von Mises. The socialists answered that they had indeed neglected the problem of economic calculation. Fortunately, modern economic theory provided a ready answer. The advanced theory of the day was Walrasian general-equilibrium theory. Leon Walras's model represented the economy as a grand set of equations describing the demands of consumers, the supplies of ultimate resource owners, and the production functions of firms. The central planning board could just figure out what those equations were and solve them. (Of course the equations would have to be modified to reflect the effects of collective ownership and a more equal distribution of wealth.) To this response the Austrians have devised a sequence of answers. When Austrians speak of the 'knowledge problem', they generally have in mind some combination of the following problems.[2]

The Equations are Hard to Solve

One might accept a general-equilibrium description of the planning problem, but point out how hard it is to solve the equations. The number of unknowns and the number of equations are both very large. Even great batteries of computers cannot be relied upon to solve the equations at all, let alone in a few hours, weeks, or months. This was a part of the Austrian argument from the start. Interestingly, it has recently been shown that general-equilibrium systems are intractable. The time it takes to calculate a solution rises exponentially with the number of variables, for example persons and goods. For any modern economy, the general-equilibrium price vector could not be calculated within the lifetime of even its youngest members![3]

The Equations are Always Changing

One might develop the last argument by pointing out that the equations that describe the planning problem are always changing. Changes in weather, population, fashion, technology, medical knowledge, resources availability, and so on, imply changes in the equation system the socialist planners should try to solve. Even if we could solve these equation systems, we could not find their solutions quickly enough.

The Needed Data are Hard to Gather

The data we would have to feed into our computers are so many and so widely dispersed that it would take too long to gather them up for use in our computers. By the time we got the data coded, they will have changed.

The Needed Data are Impossible to Gather

A more radical critique of socialist planning asserts that it is *impossible* to gather all the data needed by socialist planners. This is the idea of tacit knowledge. Gathering the data is impossible, according to this argument, because the data that should be forwarded exists in the habits and know-how of economic decision makers, and not in their conscious thought processes.

This point should be familiar to complexity theorists. The views of cognition expressed in Kaufman (1993, p. 232), Holland (1992, pp. 58–65, 1994, pp. 313–16, 1995, pp. 31–34), and others recognize that much of our thinking does not occur in the form of conscious thought processes. The complex adaptive systems called 'persons' have models of the world to guide their actions. Some of these models are explicit and can be written down. Others, however, are implicit in learned rules of behavior, phenotypes acquired by imitation, accident, and adjustment, not explicit theorizing. The agent follows rules he cannot state. He may not even know that he is following a rule. The young child follows many rules of grammar without being able to tell you about them. If I am following a rule that I do not even know exists, then I cannot be relied upon to tell you the rule. But if that rule embodies useful knowledge of the economic system, then some needed information will not be sent up to the planning experts.

The Equations do not Exist

Another radical critique denies that there are any equations to solve. There is no set of equations to describe either the results of the market process or the goals of socialist planners. Action and the passage of time always entail some elements of novelty that the planners cannot anticipate except, perhaps, in the most vague and empty way (Shackle 1972). If there are no equations to solve, what will guide the socialist economic planners? Buchanan (1982) has argued that in society, order is defined in the process of its emergence.

This point, too, should be familiar to complexity theorists. Complex adaptive systems coevolve. The environment to which subsystems adapt is constantly changing. The 'fitness landscape' is constantly changing. Thus the optimizations problems any system tries to solve are shifting and ill defined.

The Equations Omit Entrepreneurship

Entrepreneurship is missing from the standard equations of (pre-complexity) mathematical economics and from any possible centralized planning process. But it is entrepreneurship that holds the market system together (Kirzner 1973).

Entrepreneurs seek out new and untried courses of action, some small-scale, some large-scale. They experiment with new ends–means frameworks. The many acts of small-scale entrepreneurship serve to shore up gaps in the price system. Price arbitrage is the best representative of this class. This is the sort of thing Israel Kirzner has emphasized. Acts of small-scale entrepreneurship are usually equilibrating when viewed in isolation. They may accumulate, however, to send the system in new directions. Then there are the big innovations. This is the sort of thing Schumpeter (1934) emphasized. These big changes are disequilibrating. Even one such act can send the system off in a new direction. The invention of the personal computer is an example; so is Henry Ford's production line.

Entrepreneurship is governed by the type of non-directed search that complexity theorists have studied. The entrepreneur does his share of 'hill climbing'. But he also jumps, periodically, in new and untried directions. Most jumps are small; a few are big. When he succeeds, profits accrue; when he fails, losses come. These many acts of entrepreneurship are necessary to keep the different parts of the system coordinated. The fitness landscape and the adaptive responses to it are constantly changing. In such an environment, entrepreneurial leaps are necessary to keep the actions of different persons reasonably adjusted to one another. Because they are leaps, they cannot be predicted and a socialist planning board cannot simulate them.

CAPTURING SOFTWARE AND THE AUSTRIAN CRITIQUE OF SOCIALISM

The Austrian critique of socialism can be restated as an example of Arthur's (1994) 'capturing software'. The central planning board (or the political process imagined to serve that function) is the 'outside system'. The 'simpler elements' are individuals and groups of individuals such as families and trade unions. There is an 'interactive grammar' that the outside system must learn in order to get the simpler elements to perform as desired. But with central planning and economic policy in general, the simpler elements, persons and groups of persons, are not very simple. They are about as complex as the outside system, a committee of persons. Thus, the interactive grammar is very complex.

The interactive grammar 'allows many combinations of the simple elements'; it must be more complex than the elements programmed by means of it. Indeed, if the grammar is to allow many different final output combinations for the economy as a whole, it must be more complex than the economy as a whole. But the outside system is itself a part of the economy to be programmed with aid of the interactive grammar. Thus the grammar must be more complex than the outside system. To do its job, the central planning committee would have to be, in effect, more complex than itself. This is why the Austrians make the strange-sounding claim that 'rational economic calculation under socialism is *impossible*'.

Hayek (1952) produced a similar argument but applied it to the question of the mind explaining itself. I have attempted to adapt this to the context of theorizing, especially in economics and finance (Koppl 1996, 1998). The application to socialist calculation is straightforward. Long ago, an early complexity theorist made a similar point. 'The man of system', Adam Smith warned, forgets that 'in the chessboard of human society, every single piece has a principle of motion of its own, altogether different from that which the legislature might choose to impress upon it' (Smith 1759, pp. 380–1).

AUSTRIANS ON OTHER ISSUES

The Austrian critique of socialism has lost some of its initial urgency. Old-fashioned socialist ideas of central planning are much less popular today. The Austrian knowledge problem emerging from it, however, is as current as ever. The Austrian knowledge problem is solved by entrepreneurship. Many acts of small-scale and large-scale entrepreneurship keep the system going. These acts are impossible to trace, impossible to predict, and impossible to control. We cannot know what innovations are coming or how the market will react to them. Arthur's famous lock-in argument (1989) provides a good model. We cannot predict which of two new technologies will prevail. Too many of the crucial decisions occur below our threshold of observation.

Austrians draw an important rule of thumb from the knowledge problem: leave the market alone. Governments can and should amend the rules of the game from time to time. They can and should administer justice. They can and should relieve the sufferings of the destitute and protect the people from outside aggressors. Governments will always have plenty of good work to do. But we should maintain, in Hayek's words, 'a strong presumption against government's actively participating in economic efforts' (Hayek 1960, p. 221). When they do intervene, they should act on general rules, not discretion.[4]

The general resistance to 'intervention' is only a rule of thumb. Individual cases must be considered one at a time. But the Austrian knowledge problem gives us reasons to support the general presumption against activism. (I will list them presently.) The insistence on general rules, however, is a matter of principle. Hayek thought that to give governments a discretionary power of intervention 'means in effect to give it power arbitrarily to determine what is to be produced, by whom, and for whom' (Hayek 1960, p. 228). I will take up each point in turn.

When the market creates some inefficiency, entrepreneurs typically have an incentive to find it out and innovate around it. In most instances, therefore, corrective policy action is likely to be too much too late for three reasons.

First, the supposed inefficiency may not be. If the economy is an evolving complex adaptive system, then the level of complexity of the system is likely to outstrip our analytical engine. We cannot really model it adequately. We might be able to sort out some important patterns on the basis of principles known to operate. But that is not the type of detailed prediction needed to explain every business practice. Business practices that look monopolistic, or otherwise bad, in a static model may be efficiency-enhancing responses to a complex, dynamic environment. Rivalrous competition quickly cranks out a rough and ready solution to a global optimization problem that policy makers could solve, if at all, only with a very long lag.

Second, by the time a need has been identified, and policy agreed upon, and a government or regulatory action taken, the initial inefficiency is likely to have been at least partially corrected for by innovations in the private sector. By the time we get there, the fire is out.

Third, when governments practice interventionism entrepreneurs learn that they may not be permitted to carry out their plans. Without regulation, what is not prohibited is permitted. As regulation grows, however, we are slowly pushed to the opposite rule: what is not explicitly permitted is forbidden. Entrepreneurs learn to apply their talents to the political process instead of the market process. The amount of entrepreneurial energy devoted to eliminating market inefficiencies goes down. Austrians believe it is more important to maintain a culture of entrepreneurship than to correct individual instances of apparent inefficiency (Kirzner 1979).

Finally, the costs of government interventions are harder to see than the benefits. The (imagined) benefits are clear; they are the reason for the proposed action. The costs may be dispersed across time and across individuals. The benefits tend to be concrete; the costs tend to be abstract. Public choice theorists argue that politicians in a representative democracy have an incentive to exploit this fact. They have an incentive to concentrate benefits and disperse costs. Special-interest lobbying is, unfortunately, natural to representative democracy (Madison 1787). A general presumption against policy activism in economic affairs helps to reduce the threat posed by special interests. Big business is an important special interest. Corporations and groups of corporations form many competing special interest groups. The result is often some sort of 'corporate welfare'. Austrians oppose that. Austrians are not 'pro-business' or 'anti-business'. They are pro-competition.

Imagine we could know why businesses do what they do. Imagine we could know why in particular, not just in general. Imagine we could predict precisely the responses of suppliers and demanders. Imagine we could collect and process the knowledge and information dispersed throughout the economy. Then we could improve things by applying the hand of political control. For the most part, however, we do better to leave it alone. The knowledge problem creates too many obstacles to effective policy action. Returning to Arthur's notion of capturing software, we might say that the interactive grammar of interventionism is too complex to be learned by even the best of governments.

LIMITS TO THE LIMITS TO LAISSEZ FAIRE

I have given several reasons to maintain a general presumption against government action in the economic sphere. A general presumption is not a strict prohibition. Many 'interventions' do good, or at least no harm. Thus, one must consider each proposal individually, even if one applies a gaze of utmost suspicion. But there is a rather strict principle in this area with which most Austrians would agree. The principle prohibits all actions whose ends 'cannot be achieved by merely enforcing general rules but, of necessity, involve arbitrary discriminations between persons' (Hayek 1960, p. 227). This principle covers (among others) most 'measures to control the access to different trades and occupations, the terms of sale, and the amounts to be produced or sold' (Hayek 1960, p. 227).

The principle greatly restricts anti-trust. Anti-trust laws can sometimes be expressed as general rules with clear meanings easy to apprehend. But they are more often framed in vague language. Political compromise is often achieved by adopting ambiguous language. Anti-trust laws are no exception. Thus, to get an antitrust law enacted in the first place often requires the adoption of vague language. Machlup criticized US anti-trust legislation for its 'vagueness and uncertainty' which necessarily follow from 'the impossibility of defining such phrases as "unreasonable" restraint' of trade (1952, pp. 183–4). He quotes George Folk noting that 'under the "rule of reason" in the application of the antitrust laws to any given situation there is no "rule of thumb" to determine the issue' (Folk 1942 as quoted in Machlup 1952, p. 184).

The use of vague language throws the burden of interpretation upon enforcement agencies and the courts. They must rely on their discretion in deciding if a proscribed action has occurred. But precisely because they rely on discretion, their decisions cannot be predicted on the basis of any rule. Enterprises who might fall under the antitrust law cannot know what is permitted and what is prohibited. This legislatively induced uncertainty restrains action. Chapter 12 of Keynes (1936) contains a useful discussion of how uncertainty inhibits action(see also Koppl 1991 and Butos and Koppl 1997). Entrepreneurial attention is diverted to the study of the controlling agency and away from such activities as lowering costs and finding new markets (see Koppl and Yeager 1996 and the references therein). The vague language often used in antitrust legislation is objectionable because it creates ignorance and uncertainty.

When the restrictions of antitrust law are framed in vague language, enforcement agencies and the courts become discretionary actors with power, little subject to the discipline of profit and loss. They are therefore 'Big Players' in the affected markets. My 'counting argument' (Koppl 1996, 1998) is a simple combinatorial model to show that private actors subject to Big Player influence cannot formulate a complete model of the Big Player whose decisions they would predict. Absent such a model, they cannot formulate reasonable predictions about what decisions will emerge. The argument shows that one cannot form a complete model of a discretionary actor. Thus, while one might wish to say that the enforcement agency, or the judge, has an objective function (for maximizing social utility or personal utility according to one's degree of cynicism), it is not logically possible for the private actor to estimate that function. Earlier I quoted Hayek's 'Austrian' claim that giving the government discretionary power 'means in effect to give it power arbitrarily to determine what is to be produced, by whom, and for whom' (Hayek 1960, p. 228). This claim has not only historical evidence behind it, but logical force as well.[5]

TECHNOLOGICAL LOCK-IN

Today an important new form of monopoly has emerged, the high-tech monopolist created (largely) by technological lock-in. Microsoft is the leading example. The theory of technological lock-in was one of the first fruits of Santa Fe economics. Many economists such as Brock and Colander in this volume, argue that lock-in gives us a potential reason for government action and, indeed, the government's case against Microsoft is built in part on Arthur's lock-in model. To counter this argument let me consider lock-in and Microsoft with some care. I will argue that lock-in and Microsoft do not give us an exception to the presumption against government action, nor to the prohibition of discretionary policy.

Lock-in exists when you make a choice primarily because so many others have made that choice. You choose to buy an IBM or clone rather than a Mac principally because most others have made that choice. Immigrants to the US learn English because they want to speak the language so many others are using. Sometimes you choose to go with the majority because you want to be in fashion. Fashion is not lock-in. But if it is a matter of technological fit and the like, then it is lock in. The immigrant does not want to be fashionable; he wants to be understood. You choose an IBM clone because you want to read files people send you and because so many useful or entertaining programs have been written for the IBM system.

An industry subject to lock-in has increasing returns. The more a product is used, the higher the return from using another unit of it. As Arthur has explained, 'If a product gets ahead in the market it gains further advantage' (1997). Increasing returns contrast with decreasing returns, whereby, should a company 'keep expanding, eventually it would run into less demand for its brand or into higher costs of meeting demand' (1997).

Brian Arthur has argued that lock-in is both an inducement and a threat to innovation. The role for government action comes in striking a balance between the inducements and the threats. The inducement to innovation comes from the big prizes to be had. 'High tech firms put in day-and-night efforts to innovate precisely because lock-in, with its huge cash windfalls, is a potential prize for their endeavors'. We should not worry about the prospect of monopoly pricing once the prize is won. The key in high tech is performance per dollar. Innovation means higher performance. If you encourage innovation, performance per dollar will grow. The threat is not monopoly pricing of a given product. The threat is that the monopolists will spread outward across the field gobbling up other, related enterprises (Arthur 1997).

Why not let the big fish gobble up the little fish? An important source of answers is the 'Wilson–Sonsini White Paper'. This is a brief prepared by the law firm of Wilson, Sonsini, Goodrich and Rosati. The brief was part of the legal effort to prevent Microsoft from buying the software firm Intuit, the maker of Quicken and TurboTax. Brian Arthur helped author the white paper and has pointed to it with pride. It is thus a good example of complexity-based argument in favor of anti-trust. (The current case against Microsoft is not as good an example. Though it was put together under the influence of the Santa Fe vision, it cannot be said to represent that vision.)

The Wilson–Sonsini White Paper contains a section comparing the costs and benefits of horizontal and vertical integration. This is the part of interest to us. Advocates of government action against Microsoft hold that the costs of its monopolization and integration are high. They believe these costs are so high that we could improve efficiency by government action. Austrians deny it. Thus it comes down to a tally of costs and benefits. (Part of the cost of intervention might be the corruption of the principles necessary to restrain inexpedient or oppressive government action.) The Wilson–Sonsini White Paper contains a discussion of costs and benefits in section IV.C, 'Benefits of Integration'.

The white paper lists benefits of horizontal and vertical integration in computing, networks, and software. It counters them with four separate arguments. I consider each in turn. I will then return to the principle announced earlier, namely, that government interventions should be in the form of general rules that apply to all.

First, the white paper argues, 'it is possible to achieve virtually all the benefits of integration without excluding competitors'. This argument might be true, at least within its intended scope, namely, the integration of software products. But it does not address the costs of integration. It simply assumes them to be high enough to warrant corrective action. The argument seems to contain an implicit assumption, namely, that the benefits of government correction exceed the costs.

The white paper suggests, as an example, that Microsoft be obliged to license Quicken 'on a non-exclusive basis' and maintain a proprietary claim only on the software that links Quicken to other parts of the Microsoft network. Thus, 'competitors would be able to offer the product over competing networks with relatively slight inefficiency costs'. But to effect such solutions would require a permanent governmental body, such as the FTC, entrusted with the enactment of special regulations designed to keep competitors in the game without giving up the benefits of integration. But the theory of Public Choice teaches us that such agencies tend to misbehave. Firms in the affected industry would attempt to influence the agency's decisions and might succeed. This is an important form of 'rent- seeking'. The agency itself would be likely to engage in rent-seeking with Congress. The result of all this self-seeking would be inefficiencies whose costs might well exceed the costs of monopoly. We must set the costs of 'market failure' against the costs of 'government failure'.

Second, the Wilson–Sonsini White Paper claims that 'vertical integration will permit the displacement of superior products at the middle layers . . . merely because of vertical integration'. This is 'clearly a cost that should be evaluated'. I think this is true. But, again, the costs of lock-in to (possibly) inferior products must be set against the costs of attempting to impose corrective action. The Public Choice considerations raised earlier apply here too. Also, it is hard to know when an excluded product really is superior. Any candidate will have advantages and disadvantages compared to rivals. It would be hard for a government office to choose among them without the benefit of market competition. The choice is difficult or impossible in any event. Two other considerations weigh against the chance of such an office making the right choice. The office assigned to choose will be subject to political influences, legitimate and illegitimate. Thus the disinterested judgment we would desire is almost certainly not going to be made. Moreover, the decision makers have no incentive to get it right apart from public-spiritedness. They would have no incentive to work hard at getting it right.

They could easily bring in extraneous considerations such as ideology or regional loyalty or personal esthetics. They could be bribed.

Third, the Wilson–Sonsini White Paper claims that 'once Microsoft achieves dominance in a market, it has little incentive to innovate'. This seems a half-truth at best. The incentive to innovate might be stronger for a firm seeking lock-in than for a firm already locked in. On the other hand, the locked-in firm has an incentive to preserve the value of its capital. It has an incentive, therefore, to innovate in an attempt to keep competitors at bay. Arthur has used DOS as an example. 'If a clunker such as DOS locks up the PC market 10 years, there is little incentive for other companies to develop alternatives' (Arthur 1996). But an alternative *was* developed, namely the 'graphical user interface' devised by Xerox and later developed by Apple. The technology posed a threat to Microsoft who responded with Windows. Moreover, until this radical change was made, Microsoft continued to improve DOS, issuing many versions over the years.

A locked-in product or standard does not stay locked-in forever. As Arthur has noted '[t]echnology comes in waves, and a lock-in, such as DOS's, can only last as long as a particular wave lasts' (Arthur 1996). When a technology such as DOS is locked in, the winning firm may well try to ride it as long as possible. But potential competitors will seek to catch the new wave, which will crash down upon the old technology. There is plenty of incentive to innovate here. The innovations that might be lost are piecemeal improvements in the locked-out technologies. The only way to prevent that loss is to prohibit lock-in. To do so, however, would eliminate a powerful incentive to innovate, namely, the prospect of owning a locked-in technology. On net, we give the best encouragement to innovation when we keep our hands off the market.

Fourth, the Wilson–Sonsini White Paper expresses doubt over the prospect that 'vertical integration will necessarily produce efficiencies (that translate into lower prices) over, say, horizontal competition at each layer'. As evidence, however, it offers only one, purely theoretical study. Moreover, once again, no account is taken of the costs of government actions designed to get less integration.

I have expressed doubts over the costs of integration listed in the Wilson–Sonsini White Paper. Putting aside those doubts, what strategy does the paper suggest for government intervention? The key is early action. The Wilson–Sonsini White Paper says 'increasing returns analysis would suggest that government intervention will be optimal in producing competition if undertaken at the incipient stage. Once the network is successfully implemented, the social and economic costs of dismantling it are overwhelming, and, in any event, there would simply be no significant competitors to restore to the market.' But to act at such an incipient stage, the government must have a serviceable model of market expectations. 'In markets that feature increasing returns,' the report explains, 'users want to be on the same standard, so expectations (what users believe will happen) dominate user choice – as opposed, for example, to the inherent technological quality of competing product offerings.' The conclusion follows rather directly. 'In markets exhibiting increasing returns, it is therefore more appropriate to worry (from the antitrust enforcement perspective) about expectation formation among users than about current market share. In evaluating the likelihood of Microsoft's success, enforcement concerns should be directed toward factors that mold user expectations.'

Microsoft, the white paper argues, should be allowed to compete in markets subject to lock-in. But, because they have succeeded in the past, if they seem likely to win that competition, then government should intervene to prevent Microsoft from expanding the scope of its locked-in web of products and standards. The government, moreover, is charged with stepping in *before* the race is finished. The government must jump in, just before further competition is closed off.

The standard demanded of the government is too high. In markets subject to lock-in, the choice between competing technologies is decided by historical events below our threshold of observation. Were it otherwise, the firms destined to lose would not enter the field in the first place. The winner cannot be forecast, therefore, until the race is over, or nearly so. But by then the network will be largely in place and the costs of dismantling it will be high. There is perhaps a brief period in which the outcome is clear, but not yet upon us. But anti-trust officials cannot be relied upon to consistently see such occasions and act on them promptly. Even if they were to act with the required prescience and alacrity, the current legal system permits so many delaying tactics that the antitrust action would come into force only after lock-in had been achieved.

The Wilson–Sonsini White Paper proposes to address the supposed problem of technological lock-in with anti-trust measures that necessarily take the form of vague rules to the effect that some monopoly is good, but too much is bad. As I claimed earlier, however, such rules cannot be framed as the sort of general rules that do not 'involve arbitrary discriminations between persons' (Hayek 1960, p. 227). They violate the principle of liberty. This is a bad thing because of the unhappy consequences of 'arbitrary discriminations' applied by those in power.

None of what I have said here goes to deny that it may be desirable to restrict some of Microsoft's practices. For example, the Wilson–Sonsini White Paper contains a strong charge. 'Microsoft based its own compatible application program on unique components in the operating system that it had unique or early access to (e.g., Windows). Microsoft claimed it was 'open', but actually used hidden features and functions to gain competitive advantage.' I do not know whether Microsoft should be required to 'play fair' by keeping its 'open' systems truly open. It might be inexpedient to try to enforce that kind of fair play. On the other hand, it might be quite reasonable to forbid such practices. In either event, it seems that such a prohibition could be framed as a general rule applicable to all comers. It would not violate classical-liberal definitions of economic liberty.

The most alarming prospect raised by the Wilson–Sonsini White Paper may not be directly related to the other issues discussed in this chapter. And it probably has no logical link to Santa Fe complexity. It is, however, so alarmist that a brief comment may be in order.

The Wilson–Sonsini White Paper claims that Microsoft could gobble up so much on-line business that it might begin to control the content of our books and magazines. 'It is difficult to imagine that in an open society such as this one with multiple information sources, a single company could seize sufficient control of information transmission so as to constitute a threat to the underpinnings of a free society. But such a scenario is a realistic (and perhaps probable) outcome.' The threat is not real. Personal computers and the internet have made it easier, not harder, to publish one's ideas. In academia the relative ease of publishing is reflected in the explosion of new scholarly journals. Enter any Borders or Barnes & Noble to see how many books and periodicals are on sale. The number of publishers with a book on display is quite large. One may also buy any of a large number of newspapers from around the country and around the world. The number of newspapers published in the US has gone down, but the number easily available to the average reader has gone up dramatically. Now think of the internet. There has been quite an explosion here too of course. It is easy to publish a web page. Some even fear a kind of cultural Balkanization. Where, they ask, is the common forum? The number of sources of information is growing, not shrinking. (If we have a shakedown, the number may shrink back. A shakedown would not change the general trend.)

There are two reasons for this increase in the number of sources of information. First, lower costs of production. Literary activity of all sorts is a matter of the manipulation of symbols. The costs of computation have been falling dramatically. Lower costs of calculation imply lower costs of symbol manipulation. But that is only one reason for lower costs of production of literary goods. Whatever the causes, costs have been falling. The lower the cost, the greater the supply. Second, 'content' is not very subject to lock-in. Consider journalism. There is some lock-in in the competition between newspapers. I have an incentive to read the same paper as my friends and neighbors; I want to be informed of the same events they are informed of. But the effect is weak. If I find a better newspaper I can buy both. If it is a better paper, it will contain useful information that improves my decision making. Novelty is an essential feature of any literary production, be it a novel, newspaper, or magazine. If there were no novelty, the production would be something already known and familiar. Technological lock-in implies a loss of novelty. The user of a locked-in technology knows he will be operating with the same set of technical standards as everyone else. He has little uncertainty over the fit of his technical standards with those of others. The lack of novelty is part of the attraction of the locked-in technology. The buyer of a newspaper or book, on the other hand, seeks novelty. If the content were already known, it would not be necessary or desirable to buy it! The Wilson–Sonsini White Paper raised the prospect that technological lock-in could threaten the open society. Experience and argument suggest not.

CONCLUSION

In this chapter I have attempted to show what Santa Fe complexity implies for policy when it is informed by Austrian economics. Not surprisingly, laissez faire is the policy prescription. The hands-off rule is really two rules. The first is a rule of thumb. We should maintain a strong presumption against government action, but a case-by-case approach cannot be avoided. The second rule is a fixed principle. Government interventions should take the form of general rules applicable to all actors; they should not take the form of measures that entail 'arbitrary discriminations' (Hayek 1960, p. 227).

If governments are generally forbidden to intervene in economic affairs, what can they do? They can effect Adam Smith's 'simple system of natural liberty'. A few Austrians who follow Hayek especially closely, such as myself, would also encourage the government actions such as the provision of social insurance. But the main thing is to stay out of the way. Smith's 'simple system of natural liberty' consists in three duties of government: (1) administration of justice, (2) national defense, (3) public works (Adam Smith [1776] 1976, p. 208).

If we take complexity seriously, however, we should recognize that Smith's system is not simple at all. The evolved rules of a market-based society contain qualifying clauses and qualifications to the qualifications, and so on. They are complex. They are not very systematic either. They embody past solutions to old problems and many historical accidents. It is not a system, but a jumble. These rules of civil society are not very natural either. They represent mostly constraints that run contrary to human nature. We like to share, for example, and must learn to respect private property. The rules of civil society are really so many unnatural constraints without which civilization would be impossible. This is what Freud was getting at when he spoke of civilization's 'discontents'. Thus, Adam Smith's simple system of natural liberty is really a complex jumble of unnatural constraints. And a good thing too.

APPENDIX[6]

A Big Player is defined by three characteristics. First, he is 'big' because his decisions influence events in the market being studied. Second, he is insensitive to profit and loss. Third, he acts on the basis of discretion, not rules (Koppl and Yeager 1996).[7] Private actors may be Big Players, at least for a time. But they generally feel the pressure of profit and loss. Beyond the short run, Big Players are typically government actors. A discretionary central bank is a good example. In a market with only small players or one in which all potential Big Players stick to relatively simple rules, the filter of profit and loss will bring about a rough correspondence between the expectations and results. But if you have, say, one Big Player and many small players, the small players cannot contrive complete and correct models of the Big Player. The Big Player will always be something of a cipher to them. The Big Player will introduce an important element of uncertainty. In this paper I have claimed that vaguely worded anti-trust laws turn anti-trust officials (and the whole legal system) into Big Players.

An extremely simple counting argument shows why it is impossible to form a complete model of the Big Player.

A complete model of the Big Player would describe the environment in which the Big Player acts, and would predict his behavior in each of the different states of the environment. Let L denote the number of states the model can distinguish. The Big Player will not behave in the same way in all states of the environment. He has, say, R different behaviors he might exhibit. R is not greater than L. If the model is coherent and complete, each of the L states of the environment corresponds to exactly one of the R behaviors. Assume the description of the environment is minimal in the following sense. Any reduction in the number of states the model can distinguish would imply that at least one description of the environment corresponds to more than one behavior of the Big Player. (Thus, the description of the Big Player's environment includes terms to account for the passage of time and for learning by the Big Player.)

To have a complete model of the Big Player means we can vary the state of the environment (in imagination) and read off the implied variation (if any) in the Big Player's behavior. A complete model would permit us to say what in the environment 'causes' each of the Big Player's behaviors.

To explain the Big Player's behavior, we must be able to say for each of his

R behaviors what elements of the set of possible environmental states do and which do not correspond to that behavior. For each of the *R* behaviors of the Big Player and each of the *L* states of the environment we must be able to provide a description of the environment and a description of the behavior, and we must be able to say 'yes, they correspond', or 'no, they do not correspond'. It follows that we must be capable of *RL* statements. We must therefore be capable of *RL* behaviors. This number is greater than *R*. Thus, for a small player to model a Big Player, the small player must be capable of more behaviors than the Big Player. The small player must be more complex than the Big Player.[8]

A Big Player would be less complex than the typical small player if he would restrict himself to a relatively simple repertoire of behaviors. However complex the Big Player might be in other dimensions, those of his behaviors that matter to the small players would be relatively simple and easy to predict. But then he would be following a rule. By definition a Big Player uses discretion, not rules. He does not commit himself in advance to any preprogrammed response to predetermined environmental variables. He takes into account all available information at the moment of choice and weighs it and processes it in the manner that seems best at the time. He learns and changes. To predict the movements of a Big Player requires a complete model of him. As we have just seen, that model would have to be more complex than the Big Player. Small players and Big Players are at about the same level of complexity. Thus, small players cannot create complete models of Big Players. Big Players introduce an unpredictable element to the markets they affect. As a rule, such unpredictability is a bad thing because of the uncertainty it brings. (Koppl and Mramor 1997 have found an interesting exception to this rule.)

NOTES

1. Some exceptions exist, of course; abortion is a timely example.
2. For a quick overview of the socialist calculation see Lavoie 1994.
3. See Rust 1997. I thank Robert Axtell for help with this point.
4. See chapter fifteen of Hayek 1960, 'Economic Policy and the Rule of Law'. There, Hayek enters into these issues more carefully than I can do here.
5. The counting argument is given in the appendix along with a brief account of the theory of Big Players.
6. The counting argument of this appendix is presented in Koppl 1996 and again in Koppl 1998. It is inspired by Hayek (1952 and 1967) who argues that the mind cannot explain itself.
7. One might say, if one wished, that 'discretion' just means 'complicated rule'. But if the counting argument works, it matters whether the rule be complicated or (relatively) simple. Koppl and Yeager (1996) discuss the difference between rules and discretion.
8. This inference does assume that *R* and *L* are finite. Where *R* is transfinite, the result would follow only if *L* were bigger than *R*. But it is unreasonable to assume that *R* and *L* are not

finite. If one's model of the Big Player were expressed as a formal system, the number of characters in the alphabet used to write statements would be finite. The number of rules for combining symbols would also be finite. The number of well-formed formulae would be countable. Given any finite amount of time to write a symbol and any time constraint whatsoever there are only a finite number of formulae that can be written down. Thus, it seems reasonable to assume R and L are finite numbers. If either were infinite, I would be unable to survey my own model. In that case, I could not reasonably be said to be possessed of the model at all. I could not use the whole model when devising my own contingent plans. In other words, humans are but finite creatures.

REFERENCES

Arthur, W.B. (1989), 'Competing Technologies, Increasing Returns, and Lock-in by Historical Events', *Economic Journal*, **99** (1), 116–31.

Arthur, W.B. (1994), 'On the Evolution of Complexity', in G.A. Cowan, D. Pines and D. Meltzer (eds), *Complexity: Metaphors, Models, and Reality*, Reading, MA: Addison Wesley.

Arthur, W.B. (1996), 'Increasing Returns and the Two Worlds of Business', *Harvard Business Review*, July–August.

Arthur, W.B. (1997), 'Appraising Microsoft and its Global Strategy', a handout distributed at a press conference by Ralph Nader, November 13, 1997, available for downloading at <<http://www.santafe.edu>>.

Buchanan, J.M. (1982), 'Order Defined in the Process of its Emergence', *Literature of Liberty*, **5** (4), 5.

Butos, W. and R. Kopple (1997), 'The Varieties of Subjectivism: Keynes and Hayek on Expectations', *History of Political Economy*, **29** (2), 327–59.

Folk, G.E. (1942), *Patents and Industrial Progress*, New York: Harper & Brothers.

Hayek, F.A. (1952), *The Sensory Order*, Chicago, IL: The University of Chicago Press.

Hayek, F.A. (1960), *The Constitution of Liberty*, Chicago, IL: The University of Chicago Press.

Holland, J.H. (1992), *Adaptation in Natural and Artificial Systems*, Cambridge, MA: MIT Press.

Holland, J.H. (1994), 'Echoing Emergence: Objectives, Rough Definitions, and Speculations for ECHO-Class Models', in G.A. Cowan, D. Pines and D. Meltzer (eds), *Complexity: Metaphors, Models, and Reality*, Reading, MA: Addison Wesley.

Holland, J.H. (1995), *Hidden Order*, Reading, MA: Addison Wesley.

Kaufman, S. (1993), *The Origins of Order: Self-Organization and Selection in Evolution*, New York: Oxford University Press.

Keynes, J.M. (1936), *General Theory of Employment, Interest, and Money*, New York: Macmillan Press.

Kirzner, I. (1973), *Competition and Entrepreneurship*, Chicago, IL: University of Chicago Press.

Kirzner, I. (1979), 'Entrepreneurship, Choice, and Freedom', in his *Perception, Opportunity, and Profit: Studies in the Theory of Entrepreneurship*, Chicago, IL: University of Chicago Press.

Koppl, R. (1991), 'Animal Spirits', *Journal of Economic Perspectives*, **5** (3),.203–10.

Koppl, R. (1996), 'It is High Time we Take our Ignorance more Seriously', *International Review of Financial Analysis*, **5** (3), 259–72.

Koppl, R. (1998), 'Apriorism and Dualism', *Advances in Austrian Economics,* **5**, 159–79.

Koppl, R. and D. Mramor (1997), 'Big Players in Slovenia', manuscript, Fairleigh Dickinson University.

Koppl, R. and L. Yeager (1996), 'Big Players and Herding in Asset Markets', *Explorations in Economic History*, **3** (3), 367–83.

Lavoie, D.C. (1994), 'The Socialist Calculation Debate', in P.N. Boettke, (ed), *Elgar Companion to Austrian Economics*, Aldershot, UK: Edward Elgar.

Machlup, F. (1952), *The Political Economy of Monopoly: Business, Labor and Government Policies*, Baltimore, MD: Johns Hopkins Press.

Madison, J. (1787), *Federalist Paper No. 10*, in Hamilton, Alexander, Madison, James and Jay (1961), *The Federalist Papers,* New York: New American Library, Inc.

Mises, L. von (1966), *Human Action*, 3rd revised edn, Chicago, IL: Henry Regnery Company

Rust, J. (1997), 'Dealing with the Complexity of Economic Calculations', ewp-comp/9610002, <<http://econwpa.wustl.edu>>.

Schumpeter, J.A. (1934), *The Theory of Economic Development*, Cambridge, MA: Harvard University Press.

Shackle, G.L.S. (1972), *Epistemics and Economics*, Cambridge, MA: Cambridge University Press.

Smith, A. [1759], (1976), *The Theory of Moral Sentiments*, Indianapolis, IN: Liberty Classics.

Smith, A. [1776], (1976), *An Inquiry into the Nature and Causes of the Wealth of Nations*, Chicago, IL: University of Chicago Press.

Wilson-Sonsini White Paper, http://www.antitrust.org/cases/microsoft/whitep.html.

PART THREE

Teaching the Complexity Vision in Economics:
General

7.   Complexity and the Teaching of Economics

David Colander

I don't care who writes a nation's laws – or crafts its advanced treatises – if I can write its economics textbooks. (Paul Samuelson)

As the above quotation from Paul Samuelson suggests, textbooks play a central role in economics. They shape the framework within which economists look at issues, determine which questions are posed, and play a role in deciding who chooses to become an economist. Despite their importance, textbooks have received little attention from economists.

Principles textbooks do not have a good image among serious economists; they generally believe that texts reduce economists' profound thoughts into oversimplified models and maxims that reflect yesterday's ideas. Intermediate texts are seen as more closely following modern ideas, but even these oversimplify and follow new developments with a long and variable lag.

I agree with many of the criticisms of texts, and have made many of them myself. But, once I became a textbook author, I discovered the constraints under which textbook writers operate. These constraints push successful texts to their simple mantras and litanies. In large part, the degree to which my texts are successful reflects my willingness to compromise, and, to some degree, the failure of my texts to do even better than they do reflects my unwillingness to compromise – my desire to use texts to allow and encourage a somewhat different treatment of the canon than presently exists. Because of these constraints Samuelson's image of the powerful, controlling textbook writers is incomplete. *Textbook writers are controlled* as much as they are controlling.

To understand that control, one must understand the process by which textbooks are produced. Textbooks are money-making propositions, published by large corporations whose focus is on the bottom line. To see that textbooks will make money, all textbooks are heavily reviewed; we are talking 50 to 100 reviews for a principles text. These reviews are not for accuracy, nor are they to see that the ideas in the books are up to date, or even correct; the reviews exist to find out if those professors who teach the course are comfortable with the approach the author has taken. It is for that reason that texts usually reflect a merger of ideas that flourished over the past 30 years, when the now current professors went to graduate school, with a smattering of current ideas that have become popular and well known.

All successful textbook authors are responsive to these reviews. If one wants to be a player one must cater to the large portion of the market, making the book seem sufficiently traditional so that the majority of professors find it easy to teach from, using their old notes, but sufficiently new to give them a feeling that the book is 'modern'. This is the reality: successful textbooks are those that are adopted by a large group of professors, the majority of whom often are removed from the front lines of economic theory, and some of whom have had little training in economics. (In some community colleges, anyone who has been trained in business or social science is seen as an acceptable teacher of the principles of economics.) Because of the reviewing process a type of textbook lock-in occurs. Textbooks acquire a life of their own – a life which no one individual controls. If one wants to introduce new ideas into the texts one must take this textbook lock-in into account.

INTRODUCING THE SANTA FE APPROACH INTO TEXTS

In this chapter I consider the Santa Fe work on complexity in relation to economics textbooks, asking the question: how can the complexity ideas best be integrated into the texts? In my view the speed with which economics texts integrate Santa Fe ideas will play an important role in determining whether complexity remains an interest of a small group of the profession or whether it becomes the foundation of a revolution in economic thinking that I think it should be.

The complexity approach is only in its infancy, but for those of us bitten by the complexity bug, it offers a path to a much more meaningful economic theory. However, if it is to blossom, we need to increase the number of individuals open to the Santa Fe 'process' way of looking at the economy. Current texts are slowing its advance in two ways. First, they are weeding out those students most likely to look at economics within a process view, since such students find the current texts discordant with their understanding, and choose not to study economics. Second, they are setting a static vision for those who stay within economics, making it difficult for them to see the economy within a Santa Fe framework. The models and conceptual pictures presented in the current texts become mantras that are repeated again and again and, as they are, these models and conceptual pictures are no longer caricatures of economic thinking, but are the foundation of economic thinking itself. Thus, textbooks direct the mindset of future economists and, in doing so, influence the research the profession does.

Consider some of the reactions to my attempting to include a Santa Fe view of growth into an intermediate macro text. Some of the comments the reviewers wrote were:

> You may want to put these chapters on economic growth in the back of the book, or note that they may be skipped. ... I never heard of the Santa Fe Institute – you might want to give some more background on them, who they are, how long they have been in existence, sources of income etc.
>
> While I found this chapter interesting some of it is nearly useless to the average business student. In particular, I have in mind the Santa Fe approach.
>
> This chapter stretches substantially the definition of intermediate macroeconomics. The author goes beyond what is known. ... Personally, I found the chapter very interesting. I just could not figure out what an extended discussion of, say, the Santa Fe approach was doing in an intermediate macro text.
>
> My recommendation is to drop the discussion of the Santa Fe approach.
>
> It is not clear to me why the author includes this chapter. The Santa Fe approach is not part of mainstream growth economics.
>
> This chapter stretches substantially the definition of intermediate macroeconomics.

Because of these reviews, when my intermediate macro book is published, the Santa Fe view of growth will be relegated to a box. My view of integrating the complexity approach into textbooks has been significantly shaped by experiences such as these.

WAYS OF INTEGRATING THE SANTA FE APPROACH INTO ECONOMICS TEXTS

There are essentially two ways in which the Santa Fe vision can be introduced into economics texts. One way is to develop a completely new Santa Fe complexity style text. Such a text would be fundamentally different from current texts; it would logically develop the central ideas of iterative dynamic processes, introduce students to topics in the science of complexity, such as Mandlebrot and Julia sets, and then draw implications from these about economics. Such a text would find a niche and, eventually, that niche might expand. The problem with that approach is the textbook lock-in I spoke of earlier. The initial niche would be small, and it would grow slowly, if at all. Given the inertia in the teaching profession, I see a second way as being more likely to hasten the spread of the complexity approach. That second way is to knead the Santa Fe complexity ideas into simple mantras and conceptual pictures that are sufficiently compatible with existing models and conceptual pictures so that those ideas are integratable into existing texts. It is that evolutionary approach that I discuss in this chapter.

The remainder of the chapter is organized as follows: first, I briefly discuss the content and vision of current textbooks, together with their core models. Next, I discuss the Santa Fe vision and how it differs from the current vision in the texts. Finally, I discuss three general Santa Fe ideas that I believe can be added to the texts (if done discreetly) and suggest how those ideas can be integrated into the standard models found in of principles texts.

THE VISION AND MODELS OF CURRENT TEXTS

The vision behind almost all current texts is the neoclassical vision. This vision has, at its core, a conception of a deductively-determined unique equilibrium – the perfectly competitive state towards which economic forces drive the economy. It is a vision that requires the arrow of time to be downplayed, and the deductive analytics to be emphasized. It is a vision that emphasizes the reducibility of knowledge – one that sees representative agents as relevant, and one which essentially sees the interaction of the economy as reducible to a set of static models that are analytically solvable. Thus, if one had a super computer, and sufficient computing time, one could 'solve' the economic problem, and choose the 'right' prices.

In the texts, this vision is reduced to the following mantra: the world is full of tradeoffs; markets guide people in making these tradeoffs by seeing to it that prices reflect costs. Great emphasis is given to how the invisible hand of the market can direct individual choices to socially correct prices, assuming appropriate conditions.

Having presented the 'right price' vision, the texts present a discussion of those conditions that can lead to a distinction between social costs and private costs due to externalities. Much of students' training involves developing an understanding of the attributes of those 'right' sets of prices, and the problems that can prevent those right sets of prices being reached.

This neoclassical vision is embodied in a set of models and concepts. In micro, these models and concepts include: the production possibility frontier and the concept of comparative advantage; supply demand analysis; rational decision making, as inherent in indifference curve analysis; the theory of the firm and marginal cost analysis; the model of the competitive firm and monopoly; and social welfare analysis, as embodied in consumer and producer surplus. Each of these models and concepts contributes to instilling the neoclassical vision into students.

While the neoclassical micro vision is clear, the neoclassical macro vision is hazy. Until the 1980s it involved a vision of market failure on the aggregate level, with the need for government to correct that market failure with appropriate macro policies. That vision was built into the texts with the Keynesian AE/AP model at the principles level, and the IS/LM model at the intermediate level. In the 1980s that Keynesian vision has changed into a vision more consistent with the neoclassical micro vision. Aggregate markets work, except for externalities, and while there may be short-run macro externalities, in the long run the market will guide the economy to its natural rate of output and its long-run optimal growth rate.

This change in vision has caused confusion in the macro texts, and has necessitated a change in the models to make them consistent with the changed vision. Thus, we have seen the recent introduction of the AS/AD model into the principles texts, and a recent attempt by Mankiw to downplay even this model and switch the focus to long-run growth.[1] In intermediate books we have seen the Solow growth model replacing IS/LM as the first model presented to students. With the shift in emphasis, and the rise in importance of neoclassical growth theory, macro is being pulled into the same neoclassical 'right price' vision as micro.

Many economists of varying persuasions, and at various levels, do not share this textbook vision. In highly technical work, and in their informal discussions among friends, many economists recognize that one must go far beyond the neoclassical vision of the texts to understand the economy. In discussions among themselves they are quite willing to recognize, and even make fun of, the simplicity of that textbook neoclassical vision. However, when it comes to teaching, those same economists will often teach unquestionably the neoclassical vision, justifying what they do on pedagogical grounds. They argue that to present students with the problems of the mantra simultaneously with the mantra undermines the pedagogy.[2]

This approach to teaching the principles course has a significant effect on the composition of the economics profession. Those who find the neoclassical vision discordant with their understanding of economic reality drop out of economics, while those who find it resonant go on. In this manner the neoclassical vision becomes self-reinforcing, and it precludes other visions from replacing it.

THE SANTA FE VISION

The Santa Fe complexity vision is quite different than the neoclassical vision; it is one of emergence and process, not equilibria states. It is a vision of interdependent organizations and hierarchies that must be taken into account in any analysis. It is a vision in which there is no 'right price', and no definitive answers about whether the current market structure is the best we can do. Rationality is inductive rather than deductive, and the support for the market as an organizing structure comes from our lack of knowledge of social processes, rather than from our theoretical proofs that markets are the best way to organize an economy. It is a vision of continual adaptation at various levels, and of perpetual novelty. Within the Santa Fe vision, tradeoffs are much more complicated than those presented in the neoclassical vision, and the integration of economics with other fields becomes central to the analysis.

It is important to emphasize that both the neoclassical and the Santa Fe approach recognize that the economy is complex. They also both assume that underlying complexity is a simplicity. The difference between the two views is that they search for this simplicity in different places. In the neoclassical model, the simplicity is to be found in the static structure of system; production functions are homogeneous, and choice sets are susceptible to marginal analysis. In the Santa Fe vision the simplicity is not to be found in the comparative static structure of the models or in linear dynamics. In the Santa Fe approach, the simplicity is to be found in the rules underlying dynamics. It is to be found in the simple iterative dynamical laws operating within non-linear dynamical systems. In the Santa Fe vision one's understanding of a phenomenon is not of the phenomenon directly, but of *the process* that led to that phenomenon.

There are quite different limits to our understanding in the Santa Fe model and the neoclassical model. In the Santa Fe model one cannot analytically understand the system over all time and, even if one fully understood the underlying analytics, one cannot perfectly predict the future. The issue of economics is not one of getting the prices right, but of understanding the varying roles that prices are playing. Given a process many alternative equilibria are possible.

The Santa Fe vision is not a new vision. Variations of it have been around for a long time in economics. For example, Adam Smith, Frederick Hayek and J.M. Keynes all had aspects of the Santa Fe vision in their analyses. Such views, however, were downplayed by textbooks, and their contributions often forgotten. Somehow, whenever their ideas were translated into formal models, that Santa Fe vision was eliminated. The reason is that the models presented are all based on an assumption of static simplicity. Within these static models there is no room of Santa Fe simplicity and the view that complex phenomena can result from very simple dynamic laws and dynamical systems. That Santa Fe simplicity is to be found in the competitive process, not in the competitive state.

These forces pushing pedagogy away from competitive process ideas have existed for a long time and, if nothing had changed, I would believe that there was little chance of integrating the Santa Fe vision into the texts. But in the 1990s something has changed. What has changed is the possibility of formally 'solving' the dynamic model, or at least coming to tentative conclusions based on the model, within the Santa Fe vision. The second volume of the Santa Fe institute provides a glimpse of what some of those conclusions are. With computer simulations, insights into an increasing array of dynamic processes can be seen.

As this work progresses, and becomes better known, more and more professors will be amenable to introducing Santa Fe ideas into their courses. Instead of being seen as atheoretic ideas, such ideas can be seen as consistent with the latest developments in theory. Thus, used carefully, they can modernize a book. Programs embodying these solutions can be easily used and integrated into a principles course.

THE EVOLUTIONARY APPROACH TO INTEGRATING THE SANTA FE VISION INTO TEXTBOOKS

As I stated above, while it might be best to start fresh and fundamentally change the presentation of economics, textbook lock-in makes that almost impossible. First, one would find no publisher anxious to publish and push such a book. Second, the reason one wouldn't find publishers is that one would find few users. Thus, in the remainder of this chapter, I consider ways of integrating Santa Fe ideas into the texts by modifying its insights into ones that can be relatively easily amended into the models in the standard text. All the suggested ideas fall within, but push the limits of, what I call the 15 percent rule – a textbook can differ from its previous edition by 15 percent each time.

The focus of these suggested ideas will be on the broadening of the issues as presented in the principles texts so that they better fit the real world. Thus, the core of what is currently taught will remain, *but it will not be presented as the entire analysis.* It will be supplemented with concepts, terminology and models more compatible with the Santa Fe view.

The hurdle to overcome in doing this is that most economics professors are satisfied with presenting the limited model. They believe it provides a reasonable description of part of the decision-making process, and gives students a model, or at least a conceptual picture, that they can understand. For professors to want to include the Santa Fe vision, they must believe both that it is adding something to students' understanding and that it is not making the analysis too difficult to understand. Introducing Santa Fe ideas into the texts as an extension of existing ideas, rather than as a replacement for them, is the most likely way of meeting both of these requirements.

MAKING THE TEXTS SANTA FE FRIENDLY

Let me now turn to three conceptual ideas that I believe will make the texts more Santa Fe friendly. After briefly discussing these ideas, I discuss some of the amplifications of models that might be made to include these ideas in the texts.

THE BALANCING OF INDUCTION AND DEDUCTION

Current economics texts spend little time discussing induction and deduction; they simply present economics as deductive analysis. A Santa Fe-compatible book would explore the induction/deduction distinction more carefully (given the observations, what is the story that might most reasonably explain them).[3] It would emphasize how knowledge is based upon observation, and how those observations are used in combination with deduction to arrive at a decision. It would explain how economics, and every science, has always involved a balancing of induction and deduction, perhaps arriving at what Charles Peirce calls abduction.

Translating that balance down to the textbooks is difficult, as textbook models generally embody previous economists' inductive insights that have then been translated into models. Those models are taught deductively. For example, the supply/demand model embodies numerous insights about the world that previous economists have gathered from experience. Students are not taught to gather that same information, or to inductively determine a model. Instead, they are taught to go through a variety of exercises that deductively flow from an understanding of the supply/demand model.

This focus on deduction rather than induction also shows up in the textbook discussion of rationality. That discussion is closely tied to marginal utility or indifference curve analysis. With this analysis students are taught to differentiate between the income effect and the substitution effect, and are taught to think of standard optimality conditions when thinking about choice. If the economy were a two-good economy, that deductive view of choice might be sufficient, but for the broad set of choices individuals make, it is insufficient. Thus, to integrate the Santa Fe approach into the texts, it is necessary to broaden that approach – to ask students how they would decide when faced with more complicated issues.

One way to broaden it is to present some real-world choices and ask students how they made those choices. In other words: direct students toward the inductive approach, rather than simply presenting the deductive approach. It will quickly become apparent that many of the choices students make are complicated, and do not fit the simple choice model easily. One can then ask students whether it is reasonable to simplify the complicated analysis that is to be represented by the deductive choice framework. In many cases, I suspect that students will believe that it is not. For many decisions it will be obvious that the 'rational decision' will be too costly and too time-consuming. In-stead, for some decisions, individuals will rely on the others to guide them as a way of saving on decision-making costs. By integrating costly decision-making into the texts, one will have a framework for integrating an analysis of fads and speculative bubbles. The 'costly decision' framework also can be used to develop 'rules of thumb' decision making, creating a natural intro-duction to concepts such as attractors and focal points. Once these concepts are used, students who are interested in them will have an incentive to de-velop the technical foundation for them; they will be led to Santa Fe work.

Having developed the need for a broader-based choice theory, the text can draw a distinction between 'simple choice' and 'complex choice'. The analy-sis of simple choice would be very similar to what we currently have in the texts. But students would also be given a discussion of how more compli-cated choices are generally made. Issues in cognitive psychology could be introduced, and a simple example can be given, such as Brian Arthur's El Farol example. Such discussions will lead naturally to an analysis of advertis-ing, and the approaches advertisers use to make their product a focal point. Thus, this 'costly choice' extension can be used to explain questions such as: Why was Michael Jordan paid $40 million a year to endorse products? Why does Nike spend millions on placing its logo on sports stars, and on 'just do it' advertisements? and Why do localities pay so much to attract a ball team to their city? Complex choice theory can explain such phenomena; simple choice theory cannot. (See Stodder in this volume for further discussion of these issues.)

SEQUENTIAL DECISION MAKING AND DECISION TREES

In the texts, choices are invariably presented as marginal choices. In the real world, marginal choice analysis is generally insufficient. Many real-world decisions are not marginal at all; they are sequential, and non-marginal, or all-or-nothing choices. For students to have an appreciation of the Santa Fe vision, they need an understanding of such choices. Again, this understand-ing can be conveyed to students by inductively leading them through some of the decisions they have made. Consider, for example, a student's decision to take an economics class. That decision is a sequential decision that is the end product of a long string of choices. In high school the student made a decision about how much to study. Then she made a decision about which school to go to and what major to take. It is possible that she signed up for another course, only to find that the teacher was not to her liking, causing her to shuffle courses to find a replacement at the right time. The end result may be the choice of taking economics, but the choice itself can only be understood from the sequence of decisions that led her to that ultimate choice. At each point along the way, the relevant costs changed; some choices were irreversible, others were not. The same issues hold in production theory as Herbert Scarf (1994) points out. To meaningfully analyze real world decisions, non-marginal and sequential analysis is an important element.

In making sequential decisions the relevant costs are often changing and, often, the options considered will not be marginal decisions, but non-marginal. In such cases the only choice criterion one has is: total relevant costs must be below total relevant benefits. Given that criterion, there are a number of sub-criteria relevant for special cases. The current texts treat the marginal choice criterion as if it were the only case.

MULTIPLE EQUILIBRIA AND PATH DEPENDENCY

One of the major differences between the Santa Fe complexity vision and the neoclassical vision concerns equilibrium. The neoclassical vision is centered around static equilibrium; the Santa Fe vision is centered around dynamic processes of an economy far from a static equilibrium. The Santa Fe approach focuses on the competitive process, not the state of competitive equilibrium. In it the competitive state is something that is almost never even closely approached; long before an industry moves to a competitive state, a technological change will change the industry, creating a further disequilibrium. Competition often comes from without, not within, and involves changes in products. In most texts this view is lost because products are unchanging. If students are to be open to the Santa Fe approach, they need some sense of the enormous change in products that occurs, and how successful firms are continually redefining themselves, both as to what products to produce and how they operate.

Given the pervasiveness of the equilibrium concept, it seems unlikely that the current concept of equilibrium will change. The concept of equilibrium is so deeply engrained in the pedagogy of economics that the Santa Fe view that interesting dynamical systems, such as the economy, operate far from equilibrium has little place in current texts.

In thinking about this problem I was reminded of a story my six-year-old son was recently assigned to read. It is a tale of an elf who is caught, and forced by his captor to tell where his gold is buried. The captor has to go get a shovel to dig up the gold. He makes the elf tie a ribbon around the tree and promise not to remove it, so that when the captor comes back with the shovel he can identify the tree under which the treasure is buried. The elf keeps his promise, but upon the captor's return, the gold is unfindable because the elf has tied a ribbon around every tree in the forest. Essentially, this same trick can help introduce the Santa Fe vision of competitive process into texts. The concept of long-run equilibrium will not be so confining if there is not a unique long-run equilibrium. If the textbooks, early on, introduce the concept of multiple equilibria, students will recognize the importance of institutions and conventions in economics in choosing among those equilibria. Discussion of moving from one equilibrium to another can be used to introduce competitive process ideas and how the competitive process operates within institutions, and changes those institutions.

A standard example of multiple equilibria involves society's choice between driving on the right side, and driving on the left side. Two equilibria are possible. Britain and Japan have chosen one; the US and Germany another. Each choice is equally efficient, and as long as all the people while in a particular country choose the same side, there is no problem. But one side or the other must have been chosen by the country. As products evolve, society is continually making such choices, and enormous resources are spent influencing those choices. It is a dimension of competition that current textbooks miss completely.

Multiple equilibrium allows an introduction of the problem of industry standards and a number of real-world examples, such as the Beta/VHS fight, can be highlighted in case studies. When there are multiple equilibria firms will fight for growth and market share, and often will accept temporary losses if by doing so they can direct the economy to an equilibrium that benefits them in the long run. Those fights are a good introduction into the Santa Fe vision.

Having introduced the concept of multiple equilibria, one can discuss the concept of equilibrium selection mechanisms. It is here that brief discussions of evolutionary game theory and simple repeated games can be used to firm up students' understanding of such processes. Computer simulations can also be developed that consider the solution to such multiple equilibria games, and that show the importance of initial conditions, and initial positioning, and institutional structure.

INTEGRATING THESE IDEAS INTO CANONICAL MODELS

The three ideas discussed above can be integrated into text discussions in a variety of ways. In many ways, doing so would liven up the books, better relating the ideas in the texts to real-world events. For example, the competitive process is an idea that students would like. Many more real-world stories can be told about the competitive process than can be told about the competitive state. There is, however, the problem discussed above. That problem is that the dynamic concepts do not neatly fit in with the static models. While students like discussions of the real world when they are reading for fun, when they are studying for exams they lose their interest in the real world and want the texts to cover the material that will appear on their exams. Inevitably, what primarily shows up on exams, especially the multiple choice exams that predominate in introductory courses, are questions about models. Ideas that make it harder to pull definitive conclusions from models are distracting ideas, and eventually will be culled from the texts.

Thus, to integrate these ideas into the textbook canon, one must either integrate these ideas into the core models that are taught, or develop compatible models that can modify the neoclassical mantra to one more conducive to the Santa Fe vision. I now turn to a discussion of how three of the canonical models might be modified to fit the Santa Fe vision.

THE PRODUCTION POSSIBILITY FRONTIER, DECISION TREES, AND SEQUENTIAL DECISION MAKING

The first graph students are generally introduced to is the productions possibility curve. Through this graph students are introduced to opportunity costs – the infamous guns/butter tradeoff. For the Santa Fe approach to be integrated into this model additional aspects of decisions need to be added to the models: sequential decision making, increasing returns, non-linearities and learning by doing. Current texts avoid the issues by presenting the production possibility curve as a concave curve, with that shape justified by an assumption of diminishing marginal returns.

To integrate Santa Fe ideas into what is presented, the production possibility frontier must be presented (1) as a more complicated curve – one that is not concave over its whole range, and (2) as a constantly evolving curve – one that changes as decisions are made. To integrate the first idea, the text might present two ranges of the curve. The first would be the standard range where diminishing returns predominate. The second would be a range where increasing returns predominates, making the production possibility curve convex. Within this convex range, there are gains to specialization. Tradeoffs still exist, but those tradeoffs will not be marginal. In the convex range if one follows the normal marginal conditions one will be minimizing, not maximizing. These gains to specialization were very much a part of Adam Smith's view of the working of markets, but this role of specialization has disappeared from the texts.

Sequential decision making can be presented by presenting a decision tree along with the production possibility curve. The text would explain that many decisions are costly to reverse, and that, when such costly-to-reverse decisions are made, the choices facing the decision maker change. Decisions made in a costly reversibility context are fundamentally different than decisions made in a costlessly reversible context. The pouring of concrete, the sawing of a board, the cutting of a diamond, the choice of schools by students – all these can be presented as examples. Within a decision tree, sequential decision, framework, the tradeoffs are continually changing. Instead of decisions being presented in a static one-time decision framework, the decision tree leads students to picture decision making within an ongoing decision framework.

THE EXPERIENCE CURVE

One of the most important models that can help integrate the Santa Fe vision into the texts is the experience curve, also called the learning curve. This curve (see Rothschild this volume) is well known in business but is seldom discussed in economics texts. The reason is that it is a dynamic concept – costs decrease over time, not necessarily because of investment the firm has made, but because of the experience it has gained. Simply producing is a type of investment. Acceptance of such a curve undermines any simple concept of static equilibrium, and creates a tendency toward monopoly – a tendency that is quite incompatible with the standard textbook view of competition.

The learning-by-doing that accounts for the experience curve is quite different than increasing returns to scale that accounts for a downward sloping long-run cost curve. The first is a dynamic concept; the second is a timeless concept. The experience curve has nothing necessarily to do with changing the scale of production facilities; it has to do with the volume. By producing in the short run one gains a comparative advantage in the long run. Thus, when the experience curve is operative, comparative advantage is endogenous, and there is a natural tendency toward expansion and growth of those who are producing within the economic system. In the long run, the experience curve causes competition to lead to monopoly, not to a competitive state of multiple producers. In the Santa Fe vision that monopoly is prevented by the development of competition from without, such as the development of new products, which undermine that monopoly. Santa Fe competition involves continually new products and technological change, and that technological change offsets the natural tendency toward monopoly. Thus, rather than being exogenous, technological change is fully endogenous to the competitive process.

The nature of competition in an industry depends on where the economy is on its experience curve. Two types of industries might usefully be distinguished: technologically dynamic industries and technologically stagnant industries. Technologically dynamic industries are industries on the steep portion of the learning curve – the computer industry is an example. They have enormous cost reductions over time. Technologically stagnant industries are industries at the tail of their learning curve – the refrigerator industry might be an example. Their costs are relatively constant over time, and fluctuate primarily with input prices.

Current texts present all industries as technologically stagnant. Presenting the experience curve early on in the microeconomic texts part of the course will direct students to think in terms of technologically dynamic industries. Such industries will be characterized by enormous competition, new entrants and a search for an industry standard. Once a standard becomes apparent, the nature of the competition changes and some type of oligopoly market structure develops.

Rich, real world stories can be told around the experience curve, incorporating the decision tree analysis above. The lesson students learn from these stories is that in a dynamic framework the concept of 'relevant costs' is not a fixed or precise concept that can be determined from accounting data alone. Determining relevant costs requires judgment, expectations, and enormous institutional and technical knowledge. Such knowledge often is unavailable. Thus, the learning curve sets up a framework of economics within a broader uncertainty context that better helps students relate what they are learning with the real world around them.

THE AGGREGATE LEARNING CURVE

All discussions of the learning curve that I have seen have centered on individual industries. But since the aggregate economy is a complex agglomeration of industries, there should be a corresponding aggregate learning curve for the entire economy. This aggregate learning curve relates aggregate output with the growth rate in long-run productivity and thus provides a bridge between the long run and the short run in the same way that it did in the industry case. If there is an aggregate experience curve, long-run growth depends on short-run expansion, and it is impossible to separate out the two. Thus my latest attempt to introduce Santa Fe ideas into macro involves the aggregate learning curve as an important determinant of growth and an explanation of how aggregate economies can be on a different position on the learning curve. Movement along an aggregate learning curve makes technological waves of growth possible.

PATH DEPENDENCY AND THE MULTIPLIER MODEL

The multiplier model is currently out of favor as focus has shifted from the short run to the long run. From a pedagogical standpoint this has caused professors grief because the multiplier model was a wonderful crutch that provided a core model for the macro that was taught through the 1980s. With the demise of the multiplier model, there has been a demise of Keynesian economics. But with learning by doing and the experience curve, the multiplier model can be reintegrated into the theory of long run equilibrium as a simple example of path dependency. To do so one would need to have some autonomous production dependent on autonomous expenditures (creating something like the multiplier-accelerator model), but having provided that, one can develop a richer model that is open to Santa Fe ideas (see Bob Prasch this volume).

CONCLUSION

As should be clear from the discussion in this chapter, I do not see the process of integrating Santa Fe complexity ideas into the texts as easy. New ideas do not find fertile fields in entrenched professions such as the economics teaching profession. But to the degree that we succeed in making the texts more Santa Fe friendly, we will make it easier for deeper Santa Fe ideas to make their way into the profession. Thus, I think it is an important undertaking that deserves serious consideration.

NOTES

1. Although the AS/AD model is essentially a reduced form of the flexible price IS/LM model, in the principles texts it is generally presented as something quite different, so that it can be consistent with the new vision (see Colander 1995).
2. My principles book differs from most others in that it tries to present as many of these limitations of the current vision as possible, simultaneously with the presentation of the mantra. Thus, it tells students that there are potential problems with the neoclassical vision, and that there are other visions out there. But, other than for those suggestions, it maintains the 'right price' vision. I have been told that the difference costs me tens of thousands of dollars a year.
3. I would like to thank James Wible and Kevin Hoover for introducing me to the work of Charles Peirce.

REFERENCES

Colander, D. (1995), 'The Stories We Tell: A Reconsideration of AS/AD Analysis', *Journal of Economic Perspectives*, **9** (3), Summer, 169–88.

Scarf, H. (1994), 'The Allocation of Resources in the Presence of Indivisibilities', *Journal of Economic Perspectives*, **8** (1), Fall, 111–28.

8. Teaching Complexity: An Austrian Approach

Roger Koppl

David Colander (Chapter 7) has identified two ways to introducing the Santa Fe vision to undergraduate texts. We can make wholly new texts from scratch or 'knead the Santa Fe ideas . . . with existing models' (p. 123). It is revolution or evolution. Colander recommends evolution. Thus far, I agree. He goes on to suggest, however, that standard treatments 'be *supplemented* with concepts, terminology and models more compatible with the Santa Fe view' (p. 127, emphasis added). In this chapter I argue that there is a better way. That better way is an Austrian approach – to represent the Santa Fe vision as the (emerging) general theory which produces the standard results as special cases.[1] This Austrian approach has several advantages.

First, it is evolutionary. The underlying complexity theory can be stated in as much or little detail as the textbook writer feels prudent given the current state of the market. It can be set off in separate chapters or woven into the fabric of each chapter and model. It can be a soft undercurrent or the main flow.

Second, it puts Santa Fe ideas at the center, not on the margins. The student is still obliged to run through the usual models and arguments. The instructor can continue to use his old notes and the same test questions. But the student learns the old models in the full knowledge that there is a more basic and more interesting theory underlying them.

Third, it still allows the textbook writer to include Santa Fe materials as supplements. Doing so is sometimes the more convenient mode of exposition. Thus, the strategy of supplementing standard models is not even displaced in my approach.

Finally, there is a vital consideration in favor of my suggestion. It is intellectually correct. The Santa Fe vision does not lead us to throw out all that we learned in graduate school. It teaches us to use marginalist reasoning more intelligently. It teaches us to assume decreasing returns less often. It teaches us to use equilibrium as a mental tool and occasional approximation rather than a really existing resting place. When we want to learn the effects of a tariff, for instance, we use comparative-static equilibrium analysis. We use

Marshallian partial equilibrium analysis to infer that the prices of domestic tradables will rise. The old models are legitimate when kept in their proper context.

Perhaps I should expand on the point by recalling some facts of the history of our discipline. Alfred Marshall's work still forms the core of modern texts in price theory. Marshall used static, partial-equilibrium models. He used mechanical metaphors. And yet, it was Marshall who called 'economic biology' the 'Mecca of the economist' (1920, p. xii). Indeed, in Brian Arthur's now-famous tabular comparison of the new and old economics (Waldrop, 1993, p. 37), Marshall would fit far better on the right-hand side, 'new economics', than the left-hand side, 'old economics'. But, as Arthur (Waldrop 1993, p.38) has said, 'Marshall . . . didn't have the mathematical tools to do much with' increasing returns. Nor, I might add, any other distinguishing aspect of the new economics. Thus, Santa Fe complexity might best be viewed as completing Marshall's neoclassical vision by supplying the missing math. The Santa Fe group has given us the mathematical engine needed to drive us to Marshall's Mecca of economic biology.

If the example of Marshall is apposite, then the standard tools of today's undergraduate textbooks, equilibrium models included, have their place – subsidiary to the evolutionary vision of the Santa Fe Institute and to the more general models and theories now emerging from it.

WHAT IS AUSTRIAN ECONOMICS?

'Austrian economics' is the school of economic thought that began with Carl Menger's 1871 classic, *Grundsätze der Volkswirtschaftsleher*, or *Principles of Economics*. Menger was an Austrian who taught at the University of Vienna. Thus, the school of thought he founded was called the 'Austrian school' of economics. Menger's book made him one of the three co-creators of marginal utility theory and neoclassical economics. William Stanley Jevons and August Leon Walras were the others. Unlike the other two founders of neoclassical economics, however, Menger did not use equations or mathematical notation.

Menger's version of marginal utility contained a detailed analysis of how 'economizers' plan. Ever since, the 'Austrian' economists have been very interested in how things look *from the actor's perspective*. They want to be sure that all the things their theories say about how individuals act are reasonable things to say about real people. Consider the theory that inflation is caused by a wage–price spiral. This theory implies that people do not care how much their money holdings can buy. Since people *do* care about their real cash balances, Austrians reject such 'cost-push' theories of inflation. Austrians call this agent-based approach 'subjectivism'.

After World War II, members of the Austrian school stuck to their literary style and 'subjectivist' principles. The rest of the profession grew ever more mathematical. It also grew more and more attached to statistical techniques, even when there was no way to connect those techniques to the actor's perspective. These developments occurred partly under the influence of the Keynesian-neoclassical synthesis. The Austrians grew so far apart from the mainstream that by about 1970 they finally came to see themselves as a separate, heterodox school.

Friedrich Weiser and Eugen Böhm-Bawerk were early followers of Menger. F.A. Hayek and Ludwig von Mises were their students. Mises was an important influence on Hayek and the leader of the school from about 1920 to his death in 1973. The leader of the school today is Mises's student, Israel Kirzner of New York University.

AUSTRIAN ECONOMICS AND THE SANTA FE VISION

The Austrian economists who have influenced me the most include F.A. Hayek, Fritz Machlup and Alfred Schutz. Many economists would count only the first name on this list, Hayek, as an 'Austrian economist'. Machlup, they would say, was a 'neoclassical'. And Schutz would normally be labeled a sociologist, not an economist. But all three were friends and fellow members of Vienna's famous 'Mises Circle'. In any event, in this chapter I will be drawing mostly on Hayek, somewhat on Machlup, and only indirectly on Schutz.[2]

I am a Hayekian. Other Austrian economists are Misesians; others still are Lachmannians. Most of us feel the three fit together quite well, some differences amongst them notwithstanding. A few in our group, however, emphasize the supposedly great differences between Hayek and Mises. Most in this subgroup are associated with the Mises Institute. Hayek deviated from Mises in many important points, they claim, and erred in each such instance.[3] The Austrian economists in this group would probably object to most of what I say in this chapter. The majority of my Austrian colleagues, however, would not object greatly to my views even when they disagreed with some particulars.

Austrian economists (of the Hayekian variety at least) share common elements and a common past with complexity theory. Complexity theorists trace their origins in part to Ludwig von Bertalanffy's work on systems theory. Hayek cites both Bertalanffy and Norbert Wiener, creator of the related field of cybernetics. Hayek had a serious knowledge of and interest in systems theory and cybernetics. He even produced a book in 1952, based on his student essay of 1920, in which he described the central nervous system as a complex adaptive system. (Hayek cites Hebb's similar theory, but developed his ideas independently.) Though he did not use the phrase 'complex adaptive system', Hayek often used the words 'complex' and 'complexity'. He even wrote an essay entitled 'The Theory of Complex Phenomena' (1967a). He sounds like a product of the Santa Fe Institute when he describes '[t]he 'emergence' of 'new' patterns as a result of the increase in the number of elements between which simple relations exist' (p. 26). Hayek's choice of subjects, his theoretical sources, and his very language are all surprisingly close to Santa Fe complexity.[4]

The most characteristic feature of Hayek's system of thought is probably his notion of 'spontaneous order'. This notion organizes my thinking as an economist and my lectures as a teacher. A spontaneous order is a complex adaptive system. It is Adam Smith's idea of the 'invisible hand'. Models of spontaneous orders are sometimes called 'invisible-hand explanations' (Ullmann-Margalit 1978). In the classroom I generally use the phrase 'systematic, but unintended consequences of human action'.

Hayek coined the phrase 'spontaneous order' to describe '[t]he grown order . . . [the] self-generating or endogenous order' (1973, p. 37). Spontaneous orders in society are 'The Results of Human Action, but not of Human Design' (1967b). The study of spontaneous orders, Hayek argued, was originally the province of economics. But biology 'from its beginnings has been concerned with that special kind of spontaneous order we call an organism' (1973, p. 37). It was not until the arrival of 'cybernetics [as] a special discipline' that the physical sciences came to discuss these 'self-organizing or self-generating systems' (ibid).

Of course many consequences of our actions are perfectly intended. Action is purposeful and often obtains its ends. But intended consequences raise no fundamental scientific problem. Unintended consequences are puzzling. The economy runs along without a central planner. This seems a prescription for disaster. But the system holds together and permits each of us a greater fulfillment of his ends than would otherwise be possible. It is the scientific problem at the heart of economics.

Spontaneous orders have three 'distinguishing properties' (they are typical properties, not always present). First, they are complex; for spontaneous orders, the 'degree of complexity is not limited to what a human mind can master'. Second, they are abstract; a spontaneous order's 'existence need not manifest itself to our senses but may be based on purely *abstract* relations which we can only mentally reconstruct'. Third, they have no purpose; 'not having been made' by any designing minds, a spontaneous order '*cannot legitimately be said to have a particular purpose*, although our awareness of its existence may be extremely important for our successful pursuit of a great variety of different purposes' (1973, p. 38, all emphases in original).

I think it is reasonable to say that Hayek's notion of spontaneous order is, at a minimum, similar to the complexity theorists' notion of 'complex adaptive systems'. Hayek claims that such orders 'result from their elements obeying certain rules of conduct' (1973, p. 43). Each 'agent' follows a set of rules and responds to local information. The interaction of many such agents produces an overall order which was not planned by any of the agents who produced it. If the number of agents is large enough, this order may be very complex even when the rules governing each individual are quite simple. Hayek is an evolutionary theorist whose evolutionary ideas are based, in part, on a cognitive psychology similar to the sorts of things discussed at complexity conferences. As with the complex adaptive systems of the Santa Fe group, Hayek recognizes that there is 'no global controller' (Arthur, Durlauf and Lane 1997, p. 4) of the economy or any other complex adaptive system.

A paragraph on terminology may be in order. The terms unintended consequences, spontaneous order and complex adaptive system have essentially the same meanings. They are not quite identical however. Many unintended consequences are neither systematic nor orderly. But for that very reason, they do not often form the objects of scientific study. (History may study them.) A spontaneous order could be relatively simple, though few, if any, simple cases are interesting to study. In principle, a complex adaptive system could be constructed with all its aspects and behaviors perfectly planned. But it is hard to come up with examples. Such a system would have no unintended consequences. Thus the terms do not cover the same ground. But the overlap is great. This overlap contains most or all interesting phenomena in this area. For the rest of this chapter I will ignore the differences among these three concepts.

IMPLEMENTING AN AUSTRIAN APPROACH TO TEACHING COMPLEXITY

The approach I am suggesting is not new. I have been using it in my undergraduate classes for many years. Let me then describe some of the lectures embodying the approach.

I begin my introductory classes by defining economics as 'the study of the systematic, but unintended consequences of human action'. This definition is not 'true', of course. But I think it is useful. It establishes all the phenomena of our subject as aspects of theory of complex adaptive systems.

I make the notion of 'unintended consequences' concrete with a silly example. An exciting play in a football match will bring the stadium to its feet. Why? It is a systematic, but unintended consequence of human action. The phenomenon is systematic. Anytime the long bomb is thrown, the fans can be relied upon to stand up. But it is unintended. The fans in the first row stand up in order to see down the field. They intend only the 'local' end of getting a better view. The fans in the second row must now either stand up themselves or guess at the action. They stand up. This, of course, induces the fans in the third row to stand up as well. In short order, all the fans are on their feet straining to follow the ball through the air.

I follow up with a serious example: language. Any natural language is an evolved system, a spontaneous order.[5] The rules of English grammar are the unintended, but systematic consequences of human action. I may ask my students to imagine that language was the invention of some genius. How will that genius convey his (or her) splendid idea to the rest of the group? By *telling them*?

If economics is the study of the systematic, but unintended consequences of human action, the economist would seem to need a serviceable description of human action. Experience has taught economists to rely often on the view of human action as constrained choice among competing ends, not all of which can be fully satisfied. Under this description, choice is the allocation of scarce resources among competing ends. This is the Robbinsian definition of economics that dominated the textbooks for so long. Economics, however, is not about Robbins's allocational decisions; it is about the unintended consequences of them.

Introducing the standard definition under the aegis of the broader Santa Fe view of economics has two great advantages. First, it helps them to see why 'rational choice' models of action can be appropriate. Rational choice models depict people as perfect computing machines who maximize their utility functions with the greatest of mathematical ease. The rational chooser always equates his marginal rates of substitution. Second, it helps them to see that these same models are not always appropriate. The view of choice as allocation will have to give ground to other descriptions according to purpose. In the capabilities theory of the firm, for instance, choice is best viewed as execution of a habitual routine. In other contexts, concepts from cognitive psychology should be brought in.

The undergraduate model of supply and demand includes an account of the equilibration processes that bring about an equality between quantities supplied and demanded. The result of these processes, equilibrium, forms no part of the intention of any demander or supplier. Each demander seeks only his own interest in a low price. Each supplier is similarly motivated to seek out high prices. The law of one price comes into application only because of competition; it was never planned that way. In the model of perfect competition, the good's price may be compared to the meaning of a word such as 'fax'. Each trader in a competitive market makes his contribution to the good's price just as each speaker contributes to the meaning of the word 'fax'. And yet, that same price seems to the trader to be determined outside of his efforts. It is like a fact of nature. Similarly, each speaker thinks of the meaning of fax as an externally determined fact constraining his speech-acts.

The basic theory of markets is a theory of spontaneous order. Each individual seeks out his comparative advantage only to further his own ends. None of them knows what economists mean by 'comparative advantage' and each of them, perhaps, thinks his motives are perfectly non-pecuniary. But if people do in fact tend to seek out and find the market niches that bring them greater incomes, then they will tend to depart from fields in which they lack a comparative advantage and enter those in which they have a comparative advantage. The division of labor and its (imperfect!) efficiency properties are the unintended consequences of human action.

Money is an unintended consequence of human action. Undergraduates can read and understand Menger's account of the evolution of money. Menger's story is the most common example of an 'Invisible–Hand Explanation' (Ullmann-Margalit 1978). The evolution of money is also a good example of how Austrian and Santa Fe approaches can come together in the classroom. After having students read Menger, one can demonstrate the result for them in class with a simple exercise.

Take a bag filled in equal parts with black and white balls. Give it to a student who draws a ball. This student replaces the ball drawn, adds another of the same color, and removes one of the opposite color. The first student passes the bag to the next student who follows the same procedure. At each step the number of balls in the bag is unchanged, but the proportion is altered. Eventually, the bag will be filled with balls of one color only. The balls of the winning color are compared to the good that becomes money. The end result is driven by a network externality favoring convergence to a common medium of exchange. The exercise described is a non-linear Polya urn process of the sort first investigated by Brian Arthur and his co-authors (Arthur 1997).[6] Arthur used Polya urn processes to describe the results of increasing returns. As Menger showed, there are increasing returns in the choice of exchange medium just as there are often increasing returns in the choice of technology.

The deposit-expansion multiplier provides an excellent opportunity to apply Hayek's notion of unintended consequences. The concept of unintended consequences makes the deposit multiplier easier to understand. At the same time, the lecture on deposit multiplier expands the students' understanding of unintended consequences.

I set up my assumptions so as to have a simple system with inside and outside money and a multiplier equal to the inverse of the reserve ratio. Then I assume an increase in reserves and work through the T-accounts. At each step

I record the amount by which deposits, inside money, expand. After a few rounds, I ask my students to guess at the final sum. I sum the series and relate my result to the equation giving the reserve ratio.

After summing the series and deriving the deposit-expansion multiplier, I expand upon the difference between the 'mechanistic' equation thus derived and the 'free will' of bank managers. I point out that no bank manager needs to know the equation which describes the banking system as a whole. As with the 'laws' of supply and demand, the actors do not need to know how the system works in order for the model to apply. I go on to point out that we may imagine our bank managers to be driven by passion, or anxiety, or whatnot. The very human and non-mechanistic behavior of bank managers will still produce the very mechanistic results of the model if only each manager is reasonably capable of recognizing an excess or shortfall of reserves and acting appropriately on it.

Taking this approach to the deposit-expansion multiplier helps the students to see why we can use mathematics to describe human affairs even though real people are not 'mechanistic'. It is largely how the individual actions fit together that shapes the system. Experiments with 'zero-intelligence traders' (Gode and Shyam 1993) teach a similar lesson. Avoiding the fallacy of composition tells us that 'non-mechanistic' acts may produce a 'mechanistic' behavior for the overall system.

Finally, I like to present the Keynesian unemployment equilibrium (in a fixed price model) as an unfortunate example of unintended consequences. The downward spiral that lands us there is no part of anyone's intention! In a fixed-price model, however, it is the necessary consequence of a reduction in autonomous expenditures.

In each of these examples, a standard textbook model is placed in the context of complex adaptive systems. This context tells the student that the model in question assumes certain 'initial' conditions that do not always hold. They apply often enough to be of special interest, but they do not tell the whole story. The larger story is learning more about the evolution of spontaneous orders or complex adaptive systems.

CONCLUSION

I have given several examples of undergraduate lectures that treat standard topics as case studies in spontaneous order, that is, as complex adaptive systems. In some degree almost any topic in introductory and intermediate economics can be cast in the light of unintended consequences. Standard lectures on rent control and minimum wages are lessons in unintended consequences. Instructors who use experiments as teaching tools can predict their results. The students who generate those results, however, neither intend nor expect them. The students produce a small-scale spontaneous order of their own.

The theme of unintended consequences bridges the gap between the Santa Fe vision of complex adaptive systems and the fading orthodoxy of neoclassical economics. Use of the concept can help us to bring Arthur's new economics into the college classroom without completely displacing the old economics. The new economics is the general theory; the old economics is an important special case.

This approach to bringing Santa Fe ideas into undergraduate texts has the twin advantages of practicality and principle. It is practical because it is evolutionary, not revolutionary. No radical break with the old economics is required. It is principled because it is based on the correct relation between the old and new economics. As I said in the introduction to this chapter, it is intellectually correct.

NOTES

1. The Austrian school is probably too heterogeneous for me to speak of the Austrian approach.
2. I have sometimes described Ludwig Lachmann as my greatest influence. He got me thinking about the problem that has occupied me the most, subjective expectations. In my opinion, however, he made more progress defining the problem than solving it. I agree with Karen Vaughn (1994) who makes Lachmann the central figure in the emergence of an American Austrian school of thought.
3. My objections to this minority view are expressed in Koppl 1998.
4. See also Vaughn and Poulsen (1998) for a further discussion.
5. Sometimes a student will object that Noam Chomsky showed how Darwinian selection played a role in the evolution of language. But from the present perspective, that is a detail. Biology did not ordain any particular language, only a broad 'universal grammar'.
6. The Polya urn process described is non-linear because a student's probability of drawing a color will not generally equal the proportion of preceding students who drew that color. In the end, for instance, the proportion of students who drew, say, white will be greater than zero while the probability of another student drawing white will be equal to zero.

REFERENCES

Arthur, W.B. (1994), *Increasing Returns and Path Dependence in the Economy*, Ann Arbor: University of Michigan Press.
Arthur, W.B., S. Durlauf and D. Lane (1997), 'Introduction: Process and Emergence in

the Economy', *The Economy as an Evolving Complex System II*, Reading, MA: Addison-Wesley.

Gode, D.K. and S. Shyam (1993), 'Allocative Efficiency of Markets with Zero Intelligence Traders: Markets as a Partial Substitute for Individual Rationality', *The Journal of Political Economy*, **101** (1), 119–37.

Hayek, F.A. (1952), *The Sensory Order*, Chicago and London: Chicago University Press.

Hayek, F.A. (1967a), 'The Theory of Complex Phenomena', in his *Studies in Philosophy, Politics and Economics*, Chicago, IL: University of Chicago Press.

Hayek, F.A. (1967b), 'The Results of Human Action but not of Human Design', in his *Studies in Philosophy, Politics and Economics*, Chicago, IL: University of Chicago Press.

Hayek, F.A. (1973), *Law, Legislation and Liberty*, vol. I, *Rules and Order,* Chicago and London: Chicago University Press.

Koppl, R. (1998), 'Apriorism and Dualism', *Advances in Austrian Economics*, **5**, 159–79.

Marshall, A. (1920), *Principles of Economics,* 8th edn, London: Macmillan.

Ullmann-Margalit, E. (1978), 'Invisible-Hand Explanations', *Synthese*, **39** (2), 263–91.

Vaughn K.I. (1994), *Austrian Economics in America: The Migration of a Tradition,* Cambridge, MA: Cambridge University Press.

Vaughn K.I. and J. Loren Poulsen (1988), 'Is Hayek's Social Theory an Example of Complexity Theory?', George Mason University Working Paper 9807 http://www.gmu.edu/departments/economics/working/wpe9807/complexity.html.

Waldrop, M. (1993), *Complexity: the Emerging Science at the Edge of Order and Chaos*, New York: Touchstone Books.

9. Putting Induction Back: Economics without the 'Con' of Pure Deduction

James Stodder

Many economists know that neoclassical economics is much too simple, and after a few drinks we will even say so, at least to each other. Yet when facing undergraduates, we continue to draw those nice neoclassical curves as we have been taught – smooth and well-behaved, tangentially kissing at their bliss-points, which is wherever they happen to touch, always at an interior solution.

We know that the real world is complex, awash with nonconvexities, externalities, non-reversible choices, and bounded rationality. And we may even be interested in the experimental economic results that are effectively undermining the neoclassical world view, one that assumed away all these messy difficulties. But that is on the frontiers of research, we do not know how to begin *teaching* this more complex vision of economic reality.

Think back to your first economics class, when you first encountered Robinson Crusoe, or some other purposeful little *homo economicus*, and thrilled as he took his first optimizing baby steps. Perhaps you can recall that many of your fellow undergraduates mocked these nice little 'creation stories', even if you yourself did not. (Such organizing myths may have evolved in order to deselect such skeptical individuals, since they were unlikely to grow up into good neoclassical economists.)

The goal of this chapter is to reawaken that skepticism in ourselves, and to welcome back those students. We should invite them back into the classroom to *build their own models*, deduced just not from the axioms of rationality that we have forced them to adopt, but also from their own observations and experiments, and inductive reasoning on the basis of these experiences.

Consider students like the mathematician Bertrand Russell and the physicist Max Planck, both of whom decided to *not* study economics. Russell said it was because the subject was much too simple, while Planck said it was much too complicated. Given their respective exposures to economics, the simple Marshallian models of individual rationality taught in Russell's England, and the subtle Weberian studies of institutional evolution in Planck's Germany, intellectual history is likely to judge that *they were both right*. Let us imagine the development of an economic science that is neither too simple to be credible, nor too complicated to be useful.

SUPPRESSED INDUCTION: THE 'CON' OF ECONOMIC MODELING

The subtitle of my chapter is stolen from a famous critique written by Edward Leamer (1983), 'Let's Take the Con out of Econometrics'. Leamer criticized the practice of econometrics because modeling assumptions that are highly specific, and highly arguable, are usually presented as if they were the only ones worth discussing. Other plausible assumptions are not tested to see if they yield similar conclusions, even though researchers know that it is common to test dozens, if not hundreds, of model specifications to see which one gives the best fit. Applied econometric researchers have been perpetrating this 'con' for decades, and Leamer's critique is quite justified.

But if this is true of econometrics, it is also true of economics as a whole. Leamer's paper recalls one by Herbert Simon (1986) that aimed the same criticism at the entire profession. The supposed generality of most economic models is false, Simon argued, in that their predictive power comes not from their general assumption of optimizing agents, but from quite specific 'auxiliary' assumptions.

Simple Keynesian models, for example, show that government intervention can be stabilizing, given the 'money illusion' that workers are assumed to hold. Most Rational Expectations models, on the other end of the political spectrum, conclude that macroeconomic cycles are transitory and self-correcting, and this happy conclusion flows from the assumption that a money illusion is held, not by workers with respect to their wages, but by business owners with respect to the price of final product (Simon 1986, p. 33). Whether either of these assumptions is realistic is never seriously questioned. This and many other similar observations led Simon (1986, p. 39) to conclude that 'neoclassical theory, as usually applied, is an exceedingly weak theory, as shown by the difficulty of finding sets of facts, actual or hypothetical, that cannot be rationalized and made consistent with it'.

Simon's critique recalls my favorite definition of an economist – a person who knows that something works in practice, and wants to see if he can get it to work in theory. When you think about it, there should be nothing wrong with this, building a theoretical model of something you think is empirically true. The ability to capture something essential about a complicated reality on the basis of observations of a recurring pattern is what I call *inductive leveraging*. Inductive leveraging is that intuitive leap to a higher level of generality, from observation to theory. The ability to generalize on the basis of repeated patterns is, according to psychologists, a basic part of the human repertoire. Something this basic probably plays a big part in the evolutionary success of our species.

So why does this 'make it work in theory' joke seem funny to most economists, and in a slightly uncomfortable way? I think it is because we publish most of our papers as if guided solely by the opposite sort of logical inference, deductive rather than inductive. The 'con in econometrics' is a manifestation of a deeper con within economics as a whole, the con of suppressed induction.

Great leaps of inductive leveraging require inspiration, and make model building at least as much art as science. Like artistic genius, truly great model building cannot be taught. But it can still be emulated. And if inductive leveraging is essential to the most basic sorts of productive model building, then it is a scandal that we do not even acknowledge its existence. This suppression of induction is a disservice to our peers in our research, and to our someday-peers, our students. We all learned this bad faith somewhere; in fact we were schooled in it. Teaching is where it all starts, and the critique of suppressed induction must start there too.

CLASSROOM EXPERIMENTS: THE ROLE OF INDUCTION

In this section I will briefly present three simple classroom experiments. These present three of the most basic economic ideas about efficiency:

(a)   the efficiency of a competitive market;
(b)   the efficiency of equating marginal products, not average products;
(c)   money as an efficient solution to the 'double coincidence of wants' problem.

This list is so basic, it should lead many economists to ask what there is to 'experiment' about. I claim that these experiments are valuable for two reasons, reasons that may seem slightly at odds with each other. The first reason is that experiments can carry some of the pedagogic water for the instructor. And because they establish their results by inductive reasoning, they make it more likely that students will understand, believe, and remember those results.

The second reason for running these experiments is more subtle, however. These experiments can 'teach the teacher', as well as the student, something about transaction costs and the evolution of institutions. The standard efficiency results are not so obvious as most textbook accounts would have one

Table 9.1 Maximal Surplus versus Maximum Number of Traders

Cumulative quantity	Buyers' limit prices	Sellers' limit prices	Difference	
1	$63	$20	$43	
2	60	22	38	
3	57	24	33	
4	54	26	28	
5	51	28	23	
6	48	30	18	
7	45	32	13	
8	42	33	9	
9	39	34	5	
10	39	34	5	Sum (10 units): $215
11	36	36	0	
12	33	38	−5	
13	30	40	−10	
14	27	42	−15	
15	24	44	−20	Sum (15 units): $165

believe. Student solutions to these experiments will emerge that are, respectively, (a) noncompetitive, (b) non-marginal and (c) non-monetary. Given the existence of transaction costs, furthermore, these 'institutional' student solutions may actually be efficient. Induction can be carried out with contemporary and historical examples as well, providing more grist for the theoretic mill.

TRADITIONAL SUPPLY AND DEMAND: BEFORE A UNIQUE COMPETITIVE EQUILIBRIUM, MANY 'JUST' PRICES

Vernon Smith's double-auction experiment was first performed in 1956 (Smith and Williams 1992). It gives a powerful demonstration of efficiency as the maximized sum of consumers' and producers' surpluses. But it can also lead students to question the *distribution* of those surpluses.

The setup of this experiment has been described by Smith and Williams (1992), and in detail by Williams and Walker (1993). The 'just-price' interpretation presented here is my own (Stodder 1998a). In this experiment each student is designated as a 'buyer' or 'seller' of one unit of some good. Each is given a limit price for this unit, one not communicated to other participants. A seller will benefit by trading as far above this limit price, and a buyer as far below it, as luck or bargaining skill allow. These limit prices are

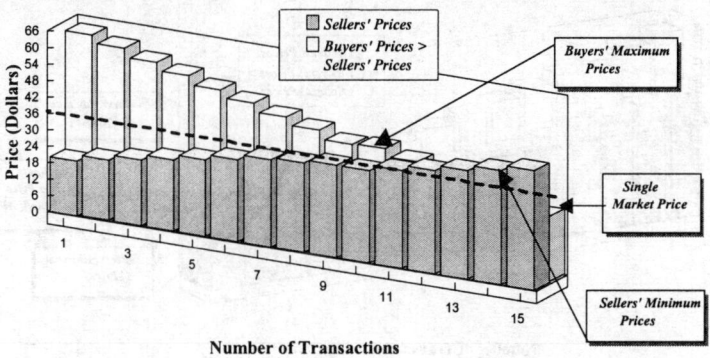

Figure 9.1   Supply and Demand – Single Market Price

given in Table 9.1.

Starting with the highest buyer's price and the lowest seller's price, these limits describe discrete units of an ordinary supply and demand function. Since the units are discrete, this should be shown as a step function or bar graph, as in Figure 9.1. This supply and demand graph is only shown *after* several rounds of bidding, when prices have converged toward a single market price – usually close to the predicted competitive equilibrium (CE).

Students in such a game find it easy to understand that this CE price maximizes the sum of 'profits' or economic surplus, the difference between the limit price of each seller and buyer who makes a trade. In Figure 9.1 this surplus is shown as the white area, to be divided above and below the final price line between the ten highest-limit buyers and ten lowest-limit sellers respectively. The remaining five buyers and five sellers are priced out of this competitive market; their inclusion would only diminish total surplus by $50, the difference between the $215 and $165 shown in Table 9.1

In such experiments it is normal for more than an efficient number of traders to find mutually-improving trades in the early rounds of the game, *before* the CE price has emerged. There is also normally a *greater range of prices* in the early rounds, before the price converges. These two points are related, and raise an interesting point about Pareto efficiency.

How can the CE price be more efficient than the earlier range of prices, some students will ask, if fewer people are able to make mutually beneficial trades? A little arithmetic or geometric reasoning shows not only that the CE price maximizes total surplus, but also that there is no *single* price outside of a narrow CE range that can achieve maximization. (With discrete units of the traded good and a monetary unit that is sufficiently divisible, the CE price is not unique. Table 9.1 shows that it will fall between $39 and $34.)

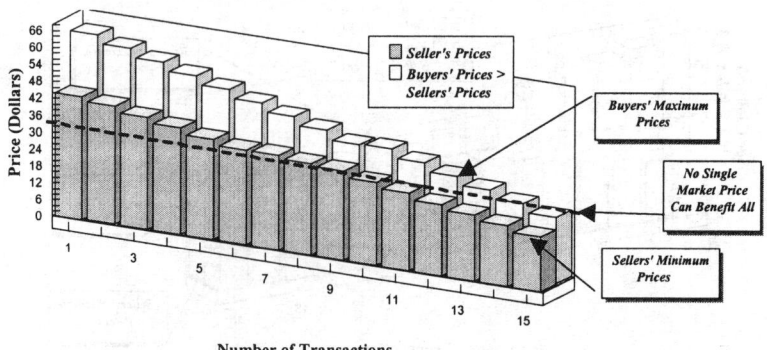

Figure 9.2   Matching of Agents – Multiple 'Just' Prices

Once there is a single market price, there is no reason for buyers and sellers to be 'matched', high-price buyers with low-price sellers, as students some- times imagine from the ordinary ordering of a supply and demand graph such as Figure 9.1. The CE price is 'impersonal' because students do not care with whom they trade at that price, and also because the reward goes to whomever was efficient or lucky enough to start with a good limit price. The invisible hand is in this sense also quite blind. This leads to arguments for and against the quality of justice dispensed by impersonal markets.

In the early rounds of the game, before traders know the prices that others are accepting, many of the unlucky, inefficient agents will be able to strike mutually-improving trades. This is easily seen in Figure 9.2 above, by reor- dering the supply curve of Figure 9.1, and starting with the highest-price, rather than the lowest-price seller. No single price is specified by this matching of high sellers with high buyers. Indeed, no single price *can* permit all trades. It is clear from Figure 9.2 that no one price allows a mutually-beneficial sale for both the first and the fifteenth unit of the good. Rather, one must now compute a variety of prices, each dividing economic surplus more or less equally between 'matched' pairs of buyers and sellers.

The CE outcome of Figure 9.1 is of course a model, an idealization to- ward which this experimental market tends only imperfectly after several rounds. The matching of high buyers with low sellers in Figure 9.2 is also a model. But it is a remarkable fact that on the first round of this auction game, almost all agents will usually find mutually improving trades. From the limit prices in Table 9.1, it is easy to confirm that even the unfortunate highest-priced seller has 7 out of 15 buyers with whom s/he can strike a mu- tually-improving deal. The matching of buyers and sellers in Figure 9.2 is actually *a better model* of this economic trade, at least for the early phases of the market, than the familiar supply and demand graph of Figure 9.1. This early phase before the 'posting' of market prices is personal because, besides their own limit price, traders do not have any impersonal market information on which to trade, only personal contacts, charm, or bluster.

In the later stages of the auction, I often find one pair of students 'reverting' to this earlier phase, happily trading at prices far from the CE even after it is clear that one of them could do much better elsewhere. Between such a pair some personal relation is usually apparent, perhaps newly struck. That relationship seems more important, at least to one of them, than maximizing his or her profit. Interestingly enough, the 'defection' of these two 'personal traders' from the impersonal supply and demand schedules typically has *no effect* on the economic surplus gained at CE by the other players. Unless one of these personal traders happens to be the one whose own limit price would have been closest to the price at which supply and demand curves cross, that is, the *least marginally-improved trader* at the CE, their defection from those curves will not affect that CE price. Such a least marginally-improved player provides a price floor (if s/he is a seller barely making any producer surplus) or a ceiling (if s/he is a buyer barely extracting any consumer surplus).

After a few rounds the students will usually have moved from the world of Figure 9.2 to that of Figure 9.1. I tell them they have traveled through millennia of economic history. They have moved from many personalized prices to a single impersonal market price. A medieval merchant or a contemporary peasant might have called the personal price between buyer and seller a 'just price'. The formal analysis of why it was just goes back at least to Aristotle (1952), and his influence on Saint Thomas Aquinas (1953) in the *Summa Theologica*. These two economic philosophers argued that the price should be set, not in order to maximize individual gains but, in Aristotle's words, to ensure that 'equality ... be restored and proportion secured' (*Eudamian Ethics,* 1242b) in the relative gains between buyer and seller. The modern economist calls this price discrimination, and it seems anything but 'just' to a western tourist when s/he is expected to pay more in a peasant marketplace.

Within a traditional economic system, however, where the identity of market actors is both known and highly relevant, this kind of 'moral economy' serves important social ends. According to political economist James C. Scott (1976), drawing on the work of Polanyi ([1944] 1957) and Thompson (1971), an economic community living close to the subsistence level will be highly risk averse, and less interested in seeing total surplus maximized than in seeing that everyone gets something. Redistribution may then be a matter of life and death, and Scott (1976) gives contemporary examples of peasants risking their lives to maintain a 'just price'. In the contemporary US, opponents of corporate downsizing argue that companies should not respond to new opportunities to maximize profits, but rather maintain personal bonds of employment and community. This is another just price argument – the provision of surplus to most economic agents is seen as more important than the maximization of total surplus *per se*.

It is easy to see that the CE price depicted in Figure 9.1 gives a greater total surplus than the just prices of Figure 9.2. In fact, the white surplus area in Figure 9.2 is smaller than that of Figure 9.1 by precisely the $50 of 'negative surplus'. Costless redistribution, through lump-sum transfers, would of course invalidate the just price idea, but the distribution of income is not so easily divorced from its generation.

Note that such lump-sum redistributions require knowledge of each agent's limit price – the very knowledge that the competitive market dispenses with, giving the market its informational advantage. It cannot be reasonable to rely on impersonal competitive markets for the maximization of economic surplus, but then to invoke omniscient government redistribution, so that the final allocation is actually Pareto-improving, and not just potentially so. The calculation of individual just prices *as part of the process* of trade – rather than setting impossible lump-sum transfers *after* trade – may be the most efficient means of equalizing distribution, subject to transaction costs. The wide historical experience of just price practices certainly makes this a plausible hypothesis.

As with all of the inductive approaches described in this chapter, this examination of supply and demand accomplishes pedagogic goals that appear to be in tension with each other – both (a) inducing the discovery of efficiency in the standard competitive market model, but also (b) relativizing and historicizing that institution. This experiment is a great introduction to the standard lessons on economic surplus, and allocational and informational efficiency. Its real power as a teaching tool, however, only emerges when *alternative* processes and allocations are also considered.

The two market outcomes, the traditional and the competitive, imply quite different social and informational relations between individuals; that is, different standards of justice *and* efficiency. Students can be encouraged to debate the relative merits of these consequences. This experiment gives a highly compressed version of the historical evolution that keeps this debate alive.

HERRNSTEIN'S 'MATCHING LAW': THE USE OF AVERAGE, NOT MARGINAL VALUES

Every economics teacher knows how easily students confuse average with marginal values. Managerial decision makers, even if they understand the difference between average and marginal products, seldom rely on the latter. Baumol (1977, pp. 34–5) conjectures this is because marginal calcula-

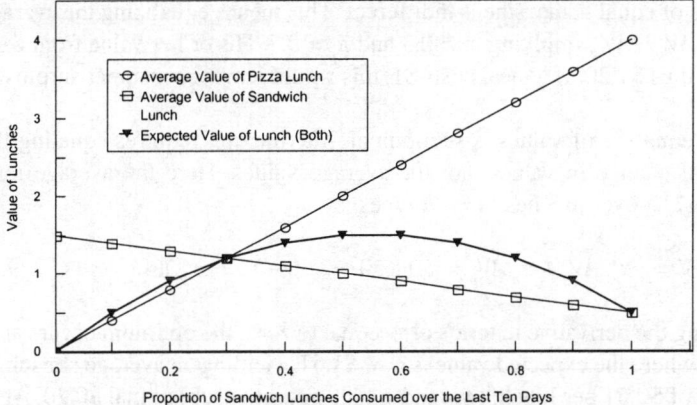

Figure 9.3   *Value of Pizza and Sandwich Lunches as a Function of the Last Ten Days' Consumption (after Herrnstein and Prelec 1991)*

tions require information the firm may not have, while average products and costs, by contrast, are always available. Does this imply that it is inefficient to try for perfect efficiency? The 'suboptimal' average rules of students and managers may actually be efficient if the data are too difficult to obtain and, like most of us, they are liable to make errors in the processing of that data.

The late behavioral psychologist, R.J. Herrnstein, in his famous 'matching law', provided the following homely illustration of suboptimality (Herrnstein and Prelec 1991). Let the average subjective value of eating a sandwich (s) or pizza (p) for lunch, be given as AV_s or AV_p. These are dollar values to the consumer, which depend on the proportion of sandwich (π_s) and pizza (π_p) lunches eaten over the last 10 days. AV_s and AV_p for a particular consumer are:

$$AV_s = 1.50 - \pi_s, \quad AV_p = 4(1 - \pi_p) = 4\pi_s, \qquad \text{since } \pi_s = 1 - \pi_p.$$

If these are the only choices, then the values for each lunch can be shown in terms of π_s, the proportion of sandwiches consumed, as in Figure 9.3. This consumer is evidently one for whom sandwiches hold a fairly steady value as a lunch staple, whereas pizzas give high value as occasional treats, but quickly lose their appeal if eaten too often.

Have students solve this individually with pencil and paper, deciding what they would do in this situation, and tell them to prepare a brief explanation of why they acted as they did. Have them assume the two lunches are equally-priced. In such an experiment, most students (and even many economists) will respond as follows. Upon entering the lunch room, the student considers which lunch gives greater subjective value. S/he then buys that item. If both are of equal value, s/he is indifferent. This means equalizing the average values, $AV_s = AV_p$, implying $\pi_s = 0.3$ and $\pi_p = 0.7$. His or her value from each meal is thus $1.20. If a meal costs $1, this would leave a consumer surplus of $0.20.

This equating of values is suboptimal. Maximizing requires equating the marginal change in values, not the average values. Here the average total value (*ATV*) over lunches of *both* types is

$$ATV = \pi_p \, AV_s + \pi_p \, AV_p = \pi_s \, (1.50 - \pi_s) + (1 - \pi_s)(4\pi_s) \qquad (9.1)$$

Setting the derivative in terms of π_s equal to zero, the optimum occurs at $\pi_s = 0.55$, where the expected value is now $1.51, yielding an average consumer surplus of $0.51 per lunch, two-and-a-half times the suboptimal $0.20. At $\pi_s = 0.55$, the optimal consumer's value from pizza is $2.20, whereas the typical student only gets $0.95 in value from a sandwich. This means that to achieve optimal satisfaction, s/he must resist having a piece of pizza whenever s/he wants one, even though it would give her more satisfaction (for the moment) than a sandwich. This degree of self-control may seem unrealistic. In fact, there is overwhelming experimental evidence that most people, and indeed most animals of every species ever studied, consistently fail to achieve such optimal control (Williams 1988).

Herrnstein's 'matching law' applies in situations when the return from each alternative (*i*) depends on the frequency, π_j, with which every alternative – including *i* – is chosen; $j = (1, 2, ..., i, ..., n)$. Generalizing Equation (9.1), the individual's total value can then be written:

$$ATV \,(\pi_1, \pi_2, ..., \pi_n) \,=\, \sum_j^n \, \pi_j \, AV_j \,(\pi_1, \pi_2, ..., \pi_n) \qquad (9.2)$$

Matching means equating the average or expected product of each alternative *i* and *j*:

$$AV_i \,/\, P_i = AV_j \,/\, P_j , \qquad (9.3)$$

where P_i and P_j are the prices of alternatives *i* and *j*, as in our lunch example where $P_i = P_j = \$1$. In the true optimality condition, the ratios of *marginal value* (*MV*) to price are equated:

$$MV_i \,/\, P_i = MV_j \,/\, P_j, \qquad (9.4)$$

From (9.2), the marginal value of each alternative *i* is:

$$MV_i \equiv \partial ATV \,/\, \partial \pi_i = AV_i + \pi_i \sum_j^n \frac{\partial AV_i}{\partial \pi_i} \qquad (9.5)$$

Matching as in (9.3) instead of (9.4) ignores the interdependencies between i and all the other j alternatives, as represented by the second term in (9.5). This term may be extremely difficult to calculate in practice.

Herrnstein and Prelec (1991, p. 147) comment that this failure to coordinate among interdependent payoffs is formally analogous to a multi-agent externality problem. Consider, for example, commuters who must choose whether to get to work by car or subway. If the cost of each is the same, each commuter optimizes by adopting the quicker mode. This becomes an example of 'matching' – commuters will crowd onto the faster alternative until the time spent on either is the same. While it is individually rational, it is socially suboptimal – every commuter does not consider the congestion her choice imposes on others.

This multi-person analogy can be pushed further. Consider the optimal consumption of sandwiches in our story as a form of subsidized 'mass transit'. Recall that the optimal consumption of sandwiches yielded a subjective value of only $0.95 per sandwich – less than the sandwich costs! To maximize total value, the high subjective return on pizzas should be used to 'subsidize' the consumption of sandwiches – more than the sandwiches themselves would merit. This is like taxing people who keep cars in the city in order to subsidize the ridership of the subway.

When asked how his matching law differed from the classic problem of the prisoner's dilemma, Herrnstein replied, 'With this dilemma, you only need one prisoner'.[1] In this sense we are all prisoners of our own desires. Failing to coordinate and control these desires, we wind up leaving each urge free to maximize 'its own' return. It is not so bad to eat too much pizza, perhaps, but matching is now used to model all sorts of serious addictions (Herrnstein and Prelec 1991; Heyman 1996). Someone may want to quit cocaine, a sexual obsession, or a life of crime, but finds the behavior too rewarding to resist in the short run. With initially high but steeply declining marginal returns, such addictions can clearly make one their 'prisoner'.

There is a suggestive analogy here between the optimal provisioning of public goods by the state, and the optimal disciplining of desires by the superego. The superego is 'super' in the sense that it can have a 'meta-preference' (a preference about one's preferences) to not be addicted. The social and religious support for such a superego is a key aim of successful anti-addiction groups like Alcoholics Anonymous. Examples can be multiplied, and students can get a richer sense of the seductiveness, as well as the sub-optimality, of matching average rather than marginal products.

But not all matching behavior is 'addictive', and it may not even be inefficient, given the constraints of accurate information and the costs of calculating marginal values. I will define addiction broadly as any behavior that is directly self-injurious (it may also be subject to social sanctions), but which the self-injuring person is nonetheless unable to control. Matching would not be so common among animal species if it were self-injurious. If not strictly 'optimal', when does matching lead to some improvement? In formal terms, when does indulging in behavior i with the higher average value (AV_i) also produce a higher marginal value (MV_i)? In our sandwich–pizza problem:

$$AV_s = 1.50 - \pi_s, \qquad AV_p = 4(1 - \pi_p) = 4\pi_s, \text{ since } \pi_s = 1 - \pi_p,$$

$$\tag{9.6}$$

$$MV_s = 1.50 - 2\pi_s, \qquad MV_p = 4 - 8\pi_p = 8\pi_s - 4.$$

It is straightforward then that $AV_s > AV_p$ implies $\pi_s < 0.30$, and thus $MV_s > MV_p$, the latter expression being negative. $MV_s < MV_p$ also implies $AV_s < AV_p$, and the former will be true whenever $\pi_s > 0.55$. In terms of Figure 9.1, this means that whenever sandwiches give a higher average payoff than pizzas – that is, whenever $\pi_s < 0.30$, the point where the sandwich and pizza lines cross – we should eat more sandwiches. If, on the other hand, pizza is giving a higher average value, and in addition we are to the right of the average value curve's peak – that is, whenever $\pi_s > 0.55$ – then we should eat more pizza.

This means that choosing the lunch with highest average value winds up producing the right marginal allocation except when π_s is between 0.30 and 0.55. If π_s is uniformly distributed on the unit interval, it falls into this narrower interval only 25 percent of the time. Otherwise, the average and marginal indicators point in the same direction. This shifts our attention from *optimization*, requiring the equality of all marginal values, and focuses it on the concept of *melioration* (Herrnstein and Prelec 1991) – requiring only that marginal values be brought somewhat closer together.

The fact that matching behavior is 'a general rule of choice' demonstrated in dozens of animal species (Williams 1988) implies that it is what evolutionary biologist John Maynard-Smith (1982) terms an *evolutionarily stable strategy* (ESS). An ESS is a non-cooperative (Nash) equilibrium that, once set by a large population, cannot be invaded by behavioral mutations in a few individuals. Since they are non-cooperative equilibria, ESS are in general neither unique nor Pareto-efficient.

The matching law therefore defines not only a constrained optimum, given the genetic limitations of most species, but probably a constrained *local* optimum. It is unlikely that raw computational power poses the main genetic obstacle. A computationally capable mutation would not face the physical constraints of, say, a human being born with wings. After all, generations of economics students have learned to solve problems like the sandwich–pizza choice, at least on tests. The mental ability required to do so without special training has almost certainly occurred in many mutations.

Rather than raw computability, the binding constraints on the success of such mutations may be the cost of acquiring data, and the cost of communicating the results to other agents who are themselves not optimal processors. An example from business practice may illustrate the point. Few managers use marginal analysis, even if they understand it perfectly well (Baumol 1977, pp. 34–5).

Unless a firm wants to experiment with radical changes in its production levels and input mix, it will usually not have data outside of a narrow range of experience. Past data, if they exist, are often not comparable due to changes in technology and product. Calculating averages, by contrast, requires only a knowledge of the firm's current operating level. If the environment is changing rapidly enough, then 'melioration', not optimization, may be the only feasible goal. By the time one collected data, estimated costs, calculated the equality of marginal payoffs, and then moved to equalize them, the true marginal payoffs would have changed.

Using both in-class experiments and business case studies, the inductive generalization of Herrnstein's matching law can show students two results that, again, seem somewhat at odds with each other: (a) the severe suboptimality of using average rather than marginal values in decision making, and (b) the extraordinary evolutionary resistance to doing things differently. Point (a) is of course the standard neoclassical lesson, and the point at which the standard textbook treatment stops. Point (b) introduces the fascinating subject of bounded rationality and a behavioral, experimentally grounded economics. The latter is a growing realm of research, associated with economists like Brian Arthur (1991) of the Santa Fe Institute.

The tension between 'lessons' (a) and (b) is also a fascinating topic for discussion. I would suggest that there are huge efficiency gains from the (inevitable?) introduction of a user-friendly estimation–simulation–optimization package that will make marginal analysis simple and practical – not just in the classroom, but in everyday business and even consumer decisions. It is time for economists to start teaching *both* lessons (a) and (b), the one in order to better understand the other.

THE EVOLUTION OF EXCHANGE, FROM GIFTS TO MONEY

Here is a simple experiment to illustrate both the efficiency of a fiat money to facilitate exchange, and also the natural evolution of other means of exchange such as gift reciprocity and middlemen/brokers. Divide students up into groups of 3, 4, 5 and 6. Pass out $n+1$ index cards to each group of n students. Have the students assign a letter to each card corresponding to one person in the group, lettering one side of the card so that Alice, Betty, Carl and David, are paired with the cards a, b, c and d.

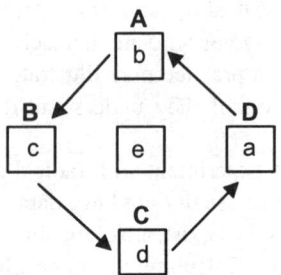

Figure 9.4 Gift Exchange

Note: Each household gives goods to those needing them, so that A, B, C and D each ends up with their preferred goods – a, b, c and d respectively. Generosity to the whole group – not just to separate individuals is the basis of status and debt. Debt status is common knowledge, and determines one's ranking in the distribution of gifts.

Tell the students to shuffle the cards and deal them out. One possible 'hand' is shown in Figure 9.4, where each person has someone else's card. A player gets one unit of value from the card with his or her letter on it, but no value from any other cards. The extra card in the group, 'e' in Figure 9.4, is worth nothing to anyone. Students will then try to make 'deals' and set up 'rules' so that they can get the card that gives value to the individual. Score will be kept for 10 rounds. The teacher can tell each student to 'earn as much as possible', deliberately leaving it vague as to whether this means maximizing one's *absolute* or *relative* score. It will be seen that groups focusing on relative scores wind up making lower absolute scores overall, so that they are in some sense 'too competitive'.

The teacher does not specify relative prices between cards; that is up to the students. I have played this game dozens of times, and I have never met a group that had any trouble arriving at the 'Walrasian clearing prices', the obvious 1 for 1 equivalencies among all the cards. The game is also a simple illustration of the powerlessness of such prices to effect improving exchanges, without an *exchange institution* to solve the 'double coincidence of wants' problem, the standard economic explanation for the invention of money, as given by William Stanley Jevons (1875). This theory of money goes back at least as far as Aristotle (*Politics*, 1257a).

In Figure 9.4, A has the b that B wants, but B has only c – nothing that A cares to accept in trade. Hence there is no 'double-coincidence of wants'. It is clearly possible to make agents A through D all better off, and Figure 9.1's circular exchange of 'gifts' is perhaps the most obvious way to do this. But there is also no efficiency-improvement possible through *bilateral, mutually improving trade* (BMIT) in Figure 9.4. An economy with considerable diversity of endowments and needs – but with neither a monetary means of exchange nor a well-stocked middleman – will clearly be unable to guarantee the attainment of efficient allocation by BMIT alone (Stodder 1995).

I have run this exchange game as a pedagogic tool in dozens of classrooms, with several hundred students. Most of the following results are, I claim, overwhelmingly clear, even on the basis of such casual empiricism:

(1) By far the most common efficient solution is to set up long term *multilateral 'gift' relations*. This is precisely what would be predicted on the basis of over a century of observations in economic anthropology (see Stodder 1995). But it appears somewhat mysterious from the point of view of any of the standard monetary theories of contemporary economics.

'Multilateral gift relations' just means giving a card to whomever needs it, with no need for an immediate or even an eventual *quid pro quo* to oneself, but with the expectation that others will be similarly 'generous' *to others*. If one fails to be so generous, all other members of the group will shun him or her. This is efficient, maximizing the expected value of each player in a four-player, ten-move game at 8 =10(0.8), that is, you score whenever your card is dealt out to anyone, which has a 4/5 card chance.

(2) About one-third of the groups become stuck in highly inefficient arrangements of *simple bilateral barter*, or else on bilateral *credit* arrangements (see below) that are only slightly less inefficient. Simple barter depends on a literal 'double coincidence of wants'; one must be able to find an improving two-way swap. In a four-player game, the chance that someone else has my card (given that I do not) is 3/4, and this must combine with the chance that I have his or her card, 1/3, giving me a probability of 1/4 of finding a bilateral swap. Together with my 1/5 probability of getting my own card in the initial deal, this means that in a game based just on bilateral swaps, my expected payoff is 10(0.25 + 0.2) = 4.5, or about half the expected value from the multilateral gift relations, which is 8.

(3) Bilateral *credit* arrangements mean that if I give you the card you want, you must promise to give me my card when you get it. Such bilateral arrangements, unlike multilateral gift relations, are typically time-dependent. The bilateral debt must be repaid within a specified number of plays, certainly before the game is over. I have never seen a multilateral gift relation show 'endgame' degeneration – people reneging on their commitments toward the end, once retaliation is unlikely or impossible. Bilateral credit arrangements, by contrast, are extremely susceptible to such endgame effects, and reneging is fairly common.

(4) 'Jealousy' in bilateral credit games is also common. Players may reason, 'Why should I help him? He's already far ahead of me.' Perhaps because multilateral gift arrangements do not rest on a bilateral comparison of benefits, such invidious comparisons seem to be much less common. Multilateral gift games are so 'uncompetitive', in fact, that they are likely to be a bit

boring for the groups playing them. The most competitive groups get very low scores, but do tend to have more fun, in the clasroom at least.

(5) As groups get larger, they are less likely to evolve multilateral gift relations, and more likely to evolve bilateral relations. This is a very clear implication from the record of economic anthropology (Stodder 1995).

(6) The 'luck' of history matters, not only in determining one's score, but also in determining what exchange institutions will evolve. Having observed hundreds of game histories, I am convinced that relatively equal 'endowments' in the first few hands of the game make it much more likely that egalitarian gift relationships are likely to evolve. This is also an arguable implication of economic anthropology (Stodder 1995).

(7) Another anthropological implication is that one player being exceptionally lucky makes him or her likely to serve as a 'big man' or centralized gift-broker with whom everyone wants to establish gift credit. Someone being exceptionally unlucky makes him a 'rubbish man' with whom no one wants to have anything to do. This result is not only remarkably close to the anthropological implications, but it is in some ways stronger, since it implies what Skinner (1948) called a behavioral 'superstition' effect on the part of those assuming that this luck, good or bad, is going to maintain itself. The subjects in this experiment should know, from the shuffling of their cards, that such luck is not predictable.

(8) No group has ever found a monetary use for the 'useless' extra card – denoting it as a fiat money with the same exchange value as the other cards. This might seem perfectly obvious in standard monetary theory, but I have never seen it occur. This fiat *quid pro quo* would effectively double the number of transfers. As long as the burden of remembering who owes what to whom does not become too great, taking on this extra transactional step appears unlikely.

A look at the history and 'prehistory' of exchange institutions is, as I have suggested, a useful complement to this experiment. The familiarity of gifts in all human societies makes gift exchange the best-known form of non-market exchange. The pioneering book by Marcel Mauss, *The Gift* ([1925] 1967) and Marshall Sahlins's work on 'generalized reciprocity' in *Stone-Age Economic*s (1972) remain popular with non-specialists in part because of the gift's emotional power to bind up friends and family, and because it seems the antithesis of egoistic market relations:

> The performance of all acts of exchange as free gifts that are expected to be reciprocated though not necessarily by the same individuals – a procedure minutely articulated and perfectly safeguarded by elaborate methods of publicity ... in which groups are linked in mutual obligations – should in itself explain the absence of the notion of gain or even of wealth other than that consisting of

objects traditionally enhancing social prestige. (Polanyi [1944] 1957, p. 47)

This suggests an efficient social accounting to rival the subtleties of the market's invisible hand, which is able to 'calculate' efficient prices and 'solve' a huge problem of allocation without market participants being in any way conscious of the larger problem. Polanyi declares ([1944] 1957, p. 50) that the equilibration of reciprocity is no less precise and just as fully socially automatic.

Figure 9.4 shows a gift exchange requiring four 'arrows' or physical transfers – the smallest number possible to achieve allocative efficiency. Nothing is wasted. There is no return of any physical *quid pro quo* – every transfer fulfills an actual need. This will be shown to represent a considerable saving in terms of *time spent carrying out all possible improving exchanges*. I call this the *time-complexity* of an exchange problem. Because of the gift's minimization of time-complexity, gift-exchange can be shown (Stodder 1995) to be most common in hunter and gatherer economies, under time pressure because of the low storability of their subsistence. Gift-exchange is also common in research organizations, perhaps for similar reasons.

As in the earlier two examples, I find that an empirical study of these exchange forms can achieve the apparently contradictory pedagogic goals of both introducing the standard model, and demonstrating its limitations. In this case we are led to understand (a) the efficiency of monetary exchange in large complex societies, but also (b) the 'artificial' or institutional basis of money, and the fact that alternative exchange relations are not only possible but for some purposes preferable.

Two important current examples of non-monetary or 'incompletely monetized' exchange (Stodder 1998) are domestic corporate barter transactions (more than $8 billion in declared *taxable* transactions in the US in 1995) and international 'countertrade' (estimated at 10 percent of world trade) (Marin and Schnitzer 1995). That this non-monetized trade is not only large but also highly countercyclical poses important challenges for macroeconomic policy, and the theory of money.

ECONOMICS AS A MATURING SCIENCE

[A]n empirically founded theory of choice ... specifies what information decision makers use and how they actually process it. This behavioral empirical base is largely lacking in contemporary economic analysis, and supplying it is essential for enhancing the explanatory and predictive power of economics. (Simon 1986, p. 25)

The banishment of induction from the study of economic reality has made our discipline, in the opinion of Nobel laureate Simon, an essentially tautological enterprise. The 'empirical leg' of our discipline, econometrics, that might be expected to be a counterweight to this deductive bias, may actually make it worse. The inductive searches that go into most econometric models are seen to be illegitimate but probably inevitable, a scandal best kept to those already initiated in the discipline, fellow practitioners of econome-TRICKS.

This sorry state of affairs is coming under increasing challenge. The suppression of induction economics has long been challenged by the historical, anthropological and institutionalist schools of economics. These champions of induction sometimes referred to their overly-deductive counterparts as 'formalists', following the critique of Polanyi (1957). But their own lack of formal technique left them for the most part as voices in the academic wilderness, always on the margins of respectability within economics at least, if not the other social sciences.

The new inductive challenge is being led by two camps with impeccable scientific credentials, behaviorists who use controlled laboratory experiments with human subjects (Smith and Williams 1992), and the Santa Fe Institute's projects on 'artificial life', computerized simulations with artificial agents. These two research projects are complementary, in that the artificial agents can be parametrized to 'act like human beings' (Arthur 1991). And the artificial life techniques of estimation with genetic algorithms and neural networks appear to do a better imitation of real human markets than equations 'derived' from economic theory and estimated econometrically. 'Measurement without theory' was once a slur cast at those estimates that were insufficiently justified by theory, even if only *ex post*. The empirical success of the neural network approach seems to be making a virtue of this former vice.

A third element of the inductive challenge can be seen coming from business schools. The professional distance between economics departments and their B-School counterparts has diminished over the last decade with the 'defection' of many economists (such as myself) to the latter camp. But I would argue that it is still a surprisingly large divide, perhaps greater than that between physics and engineering, or biology and medicine. It is significant that much of the earliest and best experiments on anomalies of choice were done in business schools, the preference reversal work of Kahneman and Tversky (1979), or the endowment effect work of Thaler (1991).

Thus the inductive offensive is already well underway on the research front. Induction and controlled experiments are now beginning to find their way back into the classroom teaching of economics. Ortman and Colander (1995) and Delemeester and Neral (1995) have produced experimental texts to accompany basic introductory economic texts by major publishers.

But the truly 'subversive' potential of a more inductive approach has hardly been appreciated, even by most of its practitioners. As Vernon Smith once remarked to me, for an experimentalist, it is sometimes hard to say if one is teaching or doing preliminary research. An introductory economics that is both inductive and deductive is going to be a lot more interesting to students, and a learning experience for those prepared to teach it.

NOTE

1. Speech to Society for the Advancement of Socio-Economics, New York, March 1993.

REFERENCES

Aquinas, St. (1953), *The Political Ideas of St Thomas Aquinas*, D. Bigongiari (ed.) translated by the Fathers of the English Dominican Province, New York: Hafner Publishing Company.

Aristotle (1952), *Eudamian Ethics*, translated by H. Rackman, Cambridge, MA: Harvard University Press.

Arthur, W.B. (1991), 'Designing Economic Agents that Act Like Human Agents: A Behavioral Approach to Bounded Rationality', *American Economic Review, AEA Papers and Proceedings*, **81** (2), 353–9.

Baumol, W.J. (1977), *Economic Theory and Operations Analysis*, Englewood, NJ: Prentice-Hall.

Delemeester, G. and J. Neral (1995), *Classroom Experiments to Accompany Taylor's Economics: A User's Guide*, Boston: Houghton Mifflin & Co.

Herrnstein, R.J. and D. Prelec (1991), 'Melioration: A Theory of Distributed Choice', *Journal of Economic Perspectives*, **5** (3), 137–56.

Herrnstein, R.J. and D. Prelec (1992), 'A Theory of Addiction', in G. Loewenstein and J. Elster (eds), *Choice Over Time,* New York: Russell Sage Foundation, pp. 331–60.

Heyman, G.M. (1996), 'Resolving the Contradictions of Addiction', *Brain and Behavioral Sciences,* December, **19** (4), 561–610.

Jevons, W.S. (1875), *Money and the Mechanism of Exchange*, London: H.S. King.

Kahneman, D. and A. Tversky (1979), 'Prospect Theory: A Theory of Decision Under Risk', *Econometrica*, March, 263–91.

Leamer, E.E. (1983), 'Let's Take the Con out of Econometrics', *American Economic Review*, **73** (1), March, 31–43.

Marin, D. and M. Schnitzer (1995), 'Tying Trade Flows: A Theory of Countertrade with Evidence', *American Economic Review*, December, **85** (5), 1047–64.

Mauss, M. [1925] (1967), *The Gift: Forms and Functions of Exchange in Archaic Societies*, London: Norton.

Maynard-Smith, J. (1982), *Evolution and the Theory of Games,* Cambridge: Cambridge University Press.

Ortman, A. and D.C. Colander (1995), in D.C. Colander (ed.), *Experiments in Teaching and in Understanding Economics, to Accompany Economics,* 2nd edn,

Chicago: Irwin Publishers.

Polanyi, K. [1944] (1957), *The Great Transformation: The Political and Economic Origins of Our Time*, Boston: Beacon Press.

Polanyi, K. (1957), 'The Economy as Instituted Process', in Arensberg and Pearson (eds), *Trade and Market in the Early Empires*, Glencoe: Free Press.

Sahlins, M. (1972), *Stone-Age Economics*, New York: Aldine de Gruyter Press.

Scott, J.C. (1976), *The Moral Economy of the Peasant: Rebellion and Subsistence in Southeast Asia*, New Haven: Yale University Press.

Simon, H.A. (1986) 'Rationality in Psychology and Economics', *Rational Choice: The Contrast Between Economics and Psychology*, Chicago: University of Chicago Press, pp. 28–40.

Skinner, B.F. (1948), 'Superstition in the Pigeon', *Journal of Experimental Psychology*, **38**, 168–72, reprinted in the same journal, (1992), September **121** (3).

Smith, V. and A. Williams (1992), 'Experimental Market Economics', *Scientific American*, **267**, December, 116–21.

Stodder, J. (1995), 'The Evolution of Complexity in Primitive Economies: Theory' and Empirical Tests', both in the *Journal of Comparative Economics*, **20** (1), February, 1–31, and May 1995, **20** (2), 190–210.

Stodder, J. (1997), 'Complexity Aversion: Simplification in the Herrnstein and Allais Behaviors', *Eastern Economic Journal*, Winter, **23** (1), 1–16.

Stodder, J. (1998a), 'Experimental Moralities: The Ethics of Classroom Experiments', *Journal of Economics Education*, **29** (2), Spring, 127–38.

Stodder, J. (1998b), 'Corporate Barter and Macroeconomic Stabilization', in *International Journal of Community Currencies*, 2 (1). www.geog.le.ac.uk/ijccr/volume2/2js.htm.

Thaler, R.H. (1991), *Quasi-Rational Economics*, New York: Russell Sage Foundation.

Thompson, E.P. (1971), 'The Moral Economy of the English Crowd in the Eighteenth Century', *Past and Present*, **50**, February, 76–136.

Williams, A.W. and J.M. Walker (1993), 'Computerized Laboratory Exercises for Micro-economics Education: Three Applications Motivated by Experimental Economics', *Journal of Economic Education*, **24**, Fall, 291–316.

Williams, B.A. (1988), 'Reinforcement, Choice, and Response Strength', in R.C. Luce et al. (eds), *Stevens' Handbook of Experimental Psychology*, Volume 2, New York: Wiley, pp. 167–244.

10. Complexity and Economic Education

Duncan K. Foley

The introduction I wrote to the collection of Peter Albin's pioneering essays on complexity in economics (Albin 1998) addresses the challenges the emergence of complexity poses to the logical structure of standard economics. Here I take up the issue of the implications of complexity for the way we teach economics. Colander's essay (Chapter 7, this volume) discusses incremental movements from current pedagogical practice: I will focus on longer term issues.

Viewing the economy as an adaptive, complex system implies fundamental changes in the way we teach the use of mathematical tools for economics, changes that threaten to exceed Colander's 15 percent rule. While complex systems can be located as a particular type of nonlinear dynamic system, no mathematical tools are available to derive general conclusions like theorems for complex systems on the basis of pure analysis. Thus it has proved impossible so far to adapt the general equilibrium comparative statics methods that have been the cutting edge of research and pedagogy in economics for the last 50 years to the analysis of complex systems. Our understanding of complex systems, in fact, relies very heavily on computer simulations of particular models. The habit of approaching economic problems through very abstract and stylized models amenable to comparative statics analysis that the current economics curriculum attempts to inculcate in students thus has limited utility in the realm of complex economic systems.

The study of complex systems seems to be leading toward a more inductive analysis that tries to draw general conclusions from the simulation of a wide variety of specific models. The advantage of this method is its ability to attack situations (for example, economies with pervasive increasing returns to scale) that are inherently resistant to classical comparative statics methods. Its disadvantage lies in the uncertain power of generalization and extrapolation that dogs all inductive arguments. We are only in the very early stages of this transformation, but I suspect that economists of the computer-game playing generations to follow us will make ever-increasing use of these simulation-based inductive methods.

COMPLEXITY IN THE ECONOMICS CURRICULUM

One support for this general argument is the reaction of students to a course on complexity that I have been teaching at Columbia for the past several years. My course on complexity begins, like many other syllabi I have examined, by studying standard dynamical systems theory. I first talk about linear systems and their limitations as models of real economies. Then I introduce nonlinearity and start the students into a consideration of nonlinear systems. As Barkley Rosser (Chapter 14, this volume) notes, nonlinearity is a necessary, but not sufficient condition for the emergence of complex dynamics. As one progresses through these systems the level of analytical mathematical difficulty rises, and eventually becomes asymptotically steep because it turns out that there are only a very limited number of simple nonlinear systems that one can say anything about analytically. You can deploy increasingly complicated analytical tools to deal with nonlinear phenomena up to Hopf bifurcations, for example, but beyond that the available results are very few and very difficult. Curiously, this increasing level of analytical difficulty is not the result of increasing conceptual sophistication in the modeling of behavior. The hallmark of complexity models is the emergence of complex dynamics from the systemic interaction of simple individual components.

At this point in the course I have to make a difficult leap and say something like: 'Well, all right. Now let's consider a situation like Brian Arthur's El Farol model (Arthur 1994). Each potential visitor wants to go to the bar as long as it's not too crowded, but hates the idea of going when the bar is too crowded. Thus each potential visitor has to predict how crowded the bar will be on the basis of some model as a basis for deciding whether or not to attend. Now, you can write down a state-based dynamical system to model this situation. But solving the model is impossible: the number of the states is extremely large, so the dimension of the resulting dynamical system is beyond the reach of analytical methods. In a version of the El Farol model where there are 100 agents, each of whom has 60 different possible models of the other patrons' behavior, you're dealing with 6,000 state variables. In an artificial stock market model, you're dealing with even more. We simply can't hope to attack this type of problem with classical analytical methods. The best we can do here is to get a feel for the dynamics of this type of model through carefully designed simulations.

In Chapter 1 in this volume Brian Arthur makes the point that it is hopeless to try to solve these models analytically, or even to say anything qualitatively by direct mathematical means about them. Perhaps this is why economists have traditionally shied away from modeling this class of complex interactions.

THE PEDAGOGICAL PROBLEM WITH STANDARD DEDUCTIVE APPROACH

The recognition of the complexity of economic systems presents a pedagogical conundrum. Traditional economic pedagogy aims to convince students that they should think abstractly. We ask them to put aside their intuition, based on their real experience of social life, which is complicated, rich, textured, and nuanced, to learn a method of analysis based on abstractions that are in many cases quite unintuitive. We ask them to view a complex, textured reality through the lens of simple models that yield precise analytical conclusions. In order to carry out this program, we teach them sophisticated mathematical tools. It is hard to keep up students' enthusiasm for working on these abstract models, which they recognize are far from reality. Students interested in real world problems are constantly looking for an alternative to the abstract methods of theoretical economics.

The view of the economy as a complex, adaptive system addresses this psychological dilemma, because it authorizes students to think of the economy in as much complex detail as they want, and thus escapes the narrow boxes of traditional abstraction. But this freedom comes at a pedagogical price: the idea of complexity tells students that much of what they have learned is not relevant to studying the more realistic models that they are really interested in.

The standard approach is often justified by telling students, in effect: 'Look. The only way you're going to think your way through difficult problems is with these abstract methods. True, we start with oversimplified models, but they will become richer and richer as you advance, and as you learn more mathematics. As you progress in your studies your ability at abstraction will improve. You will learn to manage more and more complicated models, which, while they may still be too simple, are the only path toward understanding. True, at this level, we have to choose models that have manageable mathematics, but as your knowledge of mathematics grows, the models will be improved. The result will be a more reliable understanding of economic reality than you can get in any other way.'

As a teacher of undergraduate economics I hammer away at this line, but it is not one that sells well to students. Each of these steps is painful for students. Everybody hates to abstract; at least, all my students hate it. Even once they abstract a little bit, they resist developing their embryonic abstraction to the stage of an actual model. They find the mathematics required to understand even relatively simple models difficult, and the result is pain. Learning economic models is just not as much fun as learning political science, where you can read the Bill of Rights and talk about real world issues immediately on the basis of developing further the writing and reasoning skills you were taught in high school. Put bluntly, we economists have invested a whole lot in this deductive, abstract modeling structure, and hence are going to be dubious of anything that undermines it.

The complexity point of view does undermine the standard economic approach at a fundamental level. It takes away the promised path. It says: even if you reach the highest mathematical levels, you still are not going to have the tools necessary to handle the problems you want to deal with. Complexity analysis underlines the difficulty with the deductive method, which I think underlies a lot of criticism of mathematical economics, that it focuses attention on problems the available mathematical tools can solve, rather than on the problems we are really concerned about. Available mathematical tools thus become a Procrustean bed, rather than a path to understanding.

At a conference where this chapter was presented a number of student commentators expressed some typical reactions to the standard analytic method when placed within a backdrop of complexity. 'Yes,' they say, 'we can understand the arguments for going through the abstraction and finding an analytic mathematical solution, but it is not satisfying. We generally feel that we're getting pushed around, and not getting much insight out of it. The process of abstraction always seems to lead us to an insight that somebody – Marshall, or Walras, or Jevons – had a hundred years ago, but not to a new insight for us. The teaching of insight is left behind in the process of abstraction.'

As we introduce a more inductive, complex point of view into the teaching of economics, we will find ourselves in increasingly uncomfortable dialogues with students whom we have struggled to motivate to learn traditional economic methods.

THE SIMULATION ALTERNATIVE

While I think the complexity approach is right to question traditional analytic methodology, we need to understand the limits to the alternative that students will be pushed toward as they begin to see the economic world through a complexity lens. That alternative is computer simulation, and there are serious limitations to it as well. Induction can err as easily as deduction.

Computer simulation, I believe, will ultimately dominate an economic pedagogy that takes complexity seriously. We are a long way from developing anything close to a reasonable economics pedagogy using simulation, but that is where we are heading.

It is not only in the pedagogy of simulation where there are problems; it is also in the use of simulations as a research tool. Simulations have acquired a bad name dating back to the Club of Rome Report's dire predictions, based on simulations, of imminent environmental and social collapse, which did not materialize. Recent computer modeling of climate change, global warming and weather have improved the image of simulation, but I think it is fair to say that there is no generally agreed upon methodology disciplining computer simulation and no generally accepted protocol for drawing information from simulations that transcends the simulator's priors.

If the future is to involve attacking complicated problems by taking some examples of them and simulating them, we have to make great strides in developing a methodology of simulations which allows us to put some faith in the results. Current simulation methodology is not very persuasive, because it fails to confront the logical fallacy of induction. Once you find a solution for a number of specific examples on the computer, you do not know how general the conclusions are. There is no methodology that I know that allows you to decide when you see a particular kind of phenomenon in any particular example, how generalizable it is going to be. As we use simulations in teaching economics, we have a parallel responsibility of developing the methodology of simulation as a research tool.

The El Farol problem is a good example. Simulations have shown that even though from an abstract point of view this is a very complicated state space problem, one dimension of it – namely, the proportion of customers who actually go to the bar on any given evening – stabilizes in a surprising way. But is it correct to say that stabilization is a general feature of all of these kinds of models? How much can one claim on the basis of simulation results?

I suspect all my age cohort of economists, who have been brought up on deduction and analytic models, have serious problems with such generalizations. There may be a way of answering these doubts, but it has not been spelled out yet, and until it has been spelled out, the garbage-to-solid-result ratio in simulation-based work will be high.

So the problem that complexity presents to teaching economics is that it undermines the faith in traditional analytic approaches by pointing out that the real world situations are much more complicated than the hypothesized situations simplified models deal with, but offers as an alternative a simulation methodology that cannot establish general results.

How sensitive one is to these problems will probably depend on one's generation. My cohort will have serious difficulties with the simulation solution; it runs right against the grain of the way that mathematics was taught to us. As long as complexity evolves from that mode of thinking, the computer simulations which will have to be the foundation for its analytics will be suspect.

I believe this tension will exist for a number of years, but that eventually it will be resolved. Simulation methodology will improve; as computing costs

continue to fall, replication will be easier and easier, and simulation robustness tests will be developed. At the same time students will be more and
more comfortable with simulations and computers. At some point we will
move to a shift in methodological point of view.

THE GENERATIONAL SHIFT AND THE FUTURE

I suspect this methodological shift will be a generational shift. My son is 16;
he counts any minute that he spends on homework instead of on the computer
as a minute lost to his education. He thinks he learns more from computer
games than he does from homework.

While I grant that he actually learns quite a lot from the computer – though
sometimes I wonder exactly how this works – I stand up for the value of
homework, but, again, that may simply reflect my education. His views, however, point to a very natural pedagogical path, which fits in well with complexity theory. Over time, students will arrive in class more and more familiar
with games and simulations as modes of learning. Classes will involve more
simulation, and these will evolve into interactive games. The experiments
Jim Stodder discusses (Chapter 9, this volume) are examples of this direction.

Eventually, the textbook will receive less emphasis, as students learn primarily through interaction with each other and the computer. We are a long
way from this point, but it is an alternative short-run path toward teaching
complexity from the one discussed by Colander, and may even fit his 15
percent rule. Maybe it is not 15 percent of the existing textbook that should be
changed; maybe it is 15 percent of the existing pedagogical method. Maybe
the 15 percent change should involve shifting to computer software and simulations where students will become more proficient in understanding the
world through those simulations.

Such a change will make many of us who have grown up with traditional
deductive economic models and econometrics uncomfortable. It could lead
to a Council of Economic Advisers where people are not running regressions
but sitting in front of computer screens playing games with some model or
other of the economy and deciding economic policy on that basis. We are
going to worry that they are going to take the particular for the general, and
they are going to be misled by those simulations. I suspect that we will be
right much of the time.

Terrible mistakes will be made by future generations, just as terrible mistakes were made by the previous generations and even, perhaps, are being
made by my generation. Epistemology is a very strange subject. Maybe our
confident belief that we can understand the world is more important than any

particular understanding based on particular methods. The inductive economic policy makers of the future who make their policies on the computer will make mistakes by confusing the particular with the general, but deductive policy makers can make mistakes too, by studying models that they can solve, but that do not catch the crucial realities of the problem they are confronting.

REFERENCES

Albin, P.S. (1998), *Barriers and Bounds to Rationality*, D.K. Foley (ed), Princeton: Princeton University Press.

Arthur W.B. (1994), 'Inductive Reasoning and Bounded Rationality', *American Economic Review,* **84**, 406.

PART FOUR

Teaching the Complexity Vision in Economics:
Specifics

11. Integrating Complexity into the Principles of Macroeconomics

Robert E. Prasch

The proposition that the physical world exhibits properties that can be described as 'complex' is finding more adherents in the world of natural science (Briggs and Peat 1989, Casti 1994, Coveney and Highfield 1995, Gell-Mann 1994, Waldrop 1992). With the development of the modern computer, the primary obstacle to conducting research on mathematical models that feature complex relationships is no longer germane. Over the past decade or so, some economists have drawn upon this work in order to reexamine the methods, models, and favored propositions of their profession (Albin 1998, Arthur 1990, 1994, Cassidy 1998, Colander 1996, Foley 1998). While this work is fairly new, and has not yet come to the attention of the majority of practitioners, its potential appears to be substantial. Arguably, complexity promises to change the nature and significance of economics in both its 'highbrow' and 'popular' conceptions.

Despite these trends, the issues raised by the notion of complexity have not entered into that most prominent venue of economics: the principles curriculum. David Colander argues correctly that the reasons why this is the case are largely institutional (Chapter 7 this volume). The fact is that if a textbook is to sell well in a competitive environment, it must be widely understood, and its major themes agreed upon by an overwhelming majority of the profession. It follows that by design, textbooks are purveyors and protectors of the 'conventional wisdom' as it is understood by any given generation of economists.[1]

When considering the broader meaning of the issue of complexity for the teaching of a principles course, the co-existence of positive and negative feedbacks soon suggests itself. Positive feedbacks immediately present the possibility for self-reinforcing trends in the economy – that is to say path dependence. Now, one of the first things we must acknowledge is that path dependence is not a new concept to economics or economic theory. In a number of ways, it is as old as economics itself. Elmslie (1994) has argued that positive feedbacks can be read into the work of Adam Smith. Sophisticated formulations were presented around the turn of the century by Alfred Marshall

(1920) and Allyn Young (1928). With the increasing emphasis within post-war economic thought on positivist and axiomatic methods, these ideas came to be identified with 'dissenters' from the mainstream of economic thinking – Nicholas Kaldor (1966, 1970) and Gunnar Myrdal (1944, ch. 9 and App. 3, 1957) come immediately to mind.

Nevertheless, we should note that some of the issues that we now associate with increasing returns and path dependence were once standard fare in our principles textbooks. Early editions of Paul Samuelson's *Economics: An Introductory Analysis* (1951, 1955) reveal a number of sections, not just isolated paragraphs, devoted to topics such as 'The Acceleration Principle' (Samuelson 1951, pp. 388–92, 1955, pp. 330–34). In addition, institutions explicitly designed to combat price and income instability, such as agricultural price supports, are discussed in a detailed and moderately sympathetic manner (Samuelson 1951, pp. 80–9).

Given the success of Samuelson's book, I would suggest that integrating some of the ideas associated with path dependence into the principles course is less a task requiring originality, as much as it is a task of retrieval. History shows that we have been there before. It follows that we might be able to convince textbook editors to resist the tendency towards 'path dependence' in textbook writing, and return to something that we once had. However, to be successful in this endeavor, we need to build the 'complexity vision' into the very bedrock of the principles of economics. This will ensure that these ideas do not become isolated as a 'sidebar,' like the typical discussions of Adam Smith, that only adds to the 'clutter' of contemporary textbooks.

THE TWO FUNDAMENTAL PRINCIPLES OF MACROECONOMICS

At Vassar, my introductory macroeconomics course starts by stressing two fundamental principles. I describe these ideas as fundamental because they represent dominant themes even as they distinguish macroeconomics from microeconomics. These ideas constantly reemerge as points of reference throughout the semester.

The first of these fundamental principles is the *Fallacy of Composition*. Again, there is nothing new here. Until recently, learning this logical fallacy was a core element of the first or second lecture in every economics course. I know that in the fall of 1979 the late Professor Reuben Zubrow of the University of Colorado drummed it into our heads, and a discussion of this fallacy held a prominent place through multiple editions of Paul Samuelson's textbook (Samuelson 1951, pp. 9–11, 1955, pp. 9–11). We can understand a lot about how our profession has changed by simply asking ourselves why it is that a discussion of this fallacy has disappeared from so many of today's principles texts (compare Baumol and Blinder 1997, Mankiw 1997, Miller 1997, Stiglitz 1997, Taylor 1998).[2] A discussion of this fallacy is not simply a minor point that can be left out of the principles curriculum without substantially modifying the content. In particular, a world that features unemployment demands that we attend to the fallacy of composition. As Paul Samuelson warned us a half century ago:

> There is one very important situation in which any sensible person's beliefs are likely to turn out to be the reverse of the actual economic truth. When is that? It is not during times of high or substantially full employment; it turns out that at such times one's common-sense notions usually are confirmed by the facts. *It is when there is substantial unemployment that things often go exactly into reverse.* We then move into a topsy-turvy wonderland where right seems left and left is right; up seems down; and black, white ... for a world of unemployment, the conclusions of the old classical or Euclidean economics may have to be carefully reformulated before they become applicable. (Samuelson 1951, p. 10, 1955, p. 10; original emphasis)[3]

The second fundamental principle of macroeconomics is that *we are all each other's customers.* In short, in my capacity as a consumer or as a profit-seeking firm, my expenditures necessarily represent someone else's revenues. This is a rather difficult concept to get across to students these days since we are all so attached to the 'common sense' perspective in which spending is, by definition, a diminution of savings and wealth.

As is probably well known to the members of this audience, the implications of this second fundamental principle are profound – everything from the 'Paradox of Saving', the critique of Say's Law, and the Reswitching Theorem depends, in one way or another, upon this second foundational principle.[4] In the classroom this second principle implies that under plausible conditions common sense and the method of comparative statics can run into some difficulties when studying macroeconomic phenomena. Microeconomics, dealing as it does with a single firm or person, can safely assume that there is no feedback between the expenditure of the firm on wages and the total demand for the firm's product. We do not have grounds for such confidence when we are discussing the expenditure on wages for the country as a whole (Keynes, J.M. [1936] 1964, ch. 2).

Taken together, these two fundamental principles, principles that have been virtually banished from our textbooks, can create room for concepts that are consistent with a complex understanding of the world. Moreover, they can introduce a more coherent understanding of economic history, economic institutions, and economic policy than is currently possible in the textbook world. However, these ideas do impose 'costs' in the sense that economics instructors will no longer be able to act as if all the world's issues can be readily reduced to a supply and demand problem.

IMPLICATIONS OF THE TWO 'FUNDAMENTAL PRINCIPLES' FOR TEACHING MACROECONOMIC THEORY

The most important aspect of the fundamental principles is that they create space for the introduction of positive feedbacks. In my classes, the presentation of the supply and demand model is followed by a discussion of the negative feedback properties that are the core feature of this model of the market process. This discussion includes several examples of the role of negative feedbacks in the world around us – I often point to the operation of a household thermostat, or the waves generated by dropping a rubber duck into a bathtub. The analogy to prices falling when they are too high, or rising when they are too low, seems to work rather well. I tell students that negative feedbacks are common in market systems and that the market for many, if not most, consumer goods can be analyzed along these lines.

However, I also explain that under some conditions positive feedbacks are also a distinct possibility in a free market system. In parallel to the discussion of negative feedbacks, I introduce the idea of a positive feedback mechanism and motivate it with several examples from nature. As I do this, I try to instantiate the idea that 'positive feedback' is a technical term and not an evaluative one. Even so, some students insist on believing that at some level positive feedbacks must be inherently good, simply by virtue of their name! All I can say is that whoever originally named this phenomenon was not a teacher.

At this time I introduce them to an old but valuable distinction discussed by John Neville Keynes ([1917] 1973, pp. 55–66) and rearticulated by Colander (1994). This is the difference between the 'science' and 'art' of economics, wherein the former is associated with logical analysis, and the latter is concerned with choosing the appropriate model, assumptions, and a set of non-economic considerations to be applied to any given problem in the 'real world'.

In class, I point out that a positive feedback system is one in which some activity or action generates the circumstances that allow for its own continuance on a constant or larger scale. One of my oldest and standard examples is the case of a forest fire. Given the right circumstances, a campfire or lightning strike can turn into a small fire, a small fire into a medium fire, and a medium fire into a large fire, and so on.[5] Another example of a positive feedback was the introduction of rabbits into Australia, where they have no natural predators. Given their celebrated propensity to breed, rabbits are now everywhere, and constitute a substantial problem for both ecology and farming. A final example is the behavior of herds of animals such as cattle or wildebeest – once a stampede begins, it often sets up the necessary conditions for its own continuance.

I conclude this introduction to positive feedbacks in nature by observing that such mechanisms almost always end up in some sort of disaster. The reason is that whatever activity is taking place will continue, usually at ever greater sizes or rates, until the system suffers a structural breakdown. An example of this comes from my days in the Army as a power generator mechanic. On rare occasions a positive feedback would emerge between the diesel engine and the electric generator attached to it. If one could not disengage one of several crucial cables during the first few moments of such an event, the engine would 'take off', and the result would be a rather spectacular explosion.

Examples of positive feedbacks in the economy are, in this day and age, typically contested. Indeed, it might to safe to say that many, if not most, economists simply do not believe that they exist. However, I will risk scandalizing readers by suggesting that they are not all that rare. Specifically, I believe that they are relatively common in cases wherein the actors in the market have limited information concerning states-of-the-world and/or possible outcomes. Kindleberger (1996) has done us all the service of cataloging and describing positive feedback processes in asset markets. Indeed, I have assigned this book as a way of introducing this phenomenon into the principles curriculum. I would suggest that the otherwise inexplicable crash in asset prices in October 1987 was another example. And, of course, every principles class enjoys a recounting of 'Tulip Mania' (MacKay [1841] 1980, pp. 89–97).

Positive feedbacks can also be found in relatively everyday experiences such as consumption patterns and trends. Fashion represents a somewhat innocuous positive feedback mechanism as exhibited through our choices of clothing and other consumer goods. For example, early in this century, a Vassar student was dismissed from the college for sunning her ankles on campus. Nowadays, on a warm spring day, Vassar College offers the scintillating sight of innumerable ankles. Obviously what has changed is our collective idea of appropriate attire – a social norm. As the sociologists and historians have been (correctly) telling us for years, widely observed behavior can rapidly become a norm in its own right. In addition these norms, in their turn, present a coercive force over the choices of individuals. Both good and bad can result from the fact that the behavior of a collection of persons cannot be reduced to the aggregate of individual choices – in this sense the preferences of a crowd can only be described as 'complex' (Le Bon 1952, MacKay [1841] 1980, Smelser 1962).

With regard to economics instruction, I introduce positive feedbacks into the classroom discussion at two points. The first is in a discussion of foreign exchange markets. This example is successful for a number of reasons. The first is student interest – international issues have been attractive to the students at the colleges that have employed me, so the issue of foreign exchange is often compelling in its own right. Second, while it is perhaps downplayed, it is understood, even at the level of the modern principles text, that foreign exchange markets feature 'complex' feedbacks between the expected price of a currency, the consequent changes in the expected value of foreign-denominated assets, and the demand and supply of foreign exchange. It follows that there is a degree of interdependence between expected changes in the price of currencies and the position of both the supply and demand schedules (Prasch 1998).

Again, discussing the potential for complex responses to small changes in foreign exchange markets is not new. Consider Samuelson's discussion of the kinds of problems that can be expected to arise in freely floating foreign exchange markets:

> Thus, small movements of the exchange rate are often amplified in a self-aggravating way by 'hot money', which rushes from country to country with every rumor of war, politics, and exchange rate fluctuation. When such 'capital flight' gets started in one direction on a large scale, the exchange rate may move chaotically and in extreme degree. (Samuelson 1951, p. 671, 1955, p. 627)

The realities of today's freely floating exchange rates, including the dramatic increase in the size of this market, the relative weakness of the world's major central banks, and the several spectacular crashes that we have so recently witnessed, are very interesting to students. It is a shame that our textbooks cannot be at least as insightful and interesting in their treatment of these issues as the Samuelson of 50 years ago was – when these markets were so much smaller and much more tightly controlled relative to today.

Another place where I introduce positive feedbacks into the course is in the discussion of investment. When I present the theory of investment, as part of a discussion of the 'Keynesian Cross' model and income determination, I add in a component for induced investment. Lately, I have also taken to adding an accelerator to the investment equation. The investment function then looks as follows:

$$I = I_0 + i_1 Y_t + i_2(Y_t - Y_{t-1}) \qquad (11.1)$$

As is usual in such cases, $i_1 > 0$ and $i_2 \gg 0$. While this formulation does add something of an increase in the mathematical challenges of this course, this relatively simple model can illustrate a nice positive feedback between current levels of income (Y_t), changes in the level of income ($Y_t - Y_{t-1}$), and the level of investment (*I*). Since income is, in turn, dependent on investment, we have an occasion to discuss 'cumulative causation' in the principles classroom. The time is then appropriate to discuss the fact that even across regions characterized by free trade and free capital mobility, there can be wealthy areas (Manhattan) and poorer areas (Poughkeepsie). Moreover, it can be demonstrated that positive feedback mechanisms, operating normally in a free market, will tend to reinforce these differential fortunes, *ceteris paribus*. This explanation was, of course, advanced by Myrdal (1944, 1957) and Kaldor (1966, 1970). Finally, I should point out that lectures on uneven regional development are interesting to students, who typically find some of the more well-known explanations, such as that offered by Herrnstein and Murray (1994), to be somewhat unpersuasive.

When introducing the accelerator into the principles curriculum, I once again find that I am not being innovative. On the contrary, I am simply returning to the standard textbook presentations of 50 years ago. Paul Samuelson who, along with Roy Harrod (1939), did some of the original work on growth models that featured a 'complex' interaction between an accelerator and the multiplier (Samuelson 1939), also covered these issues in his textbook (Samuelson 1951, pp. 388–92, 1955, pp. 330–34). Specifically, he stressed the problems that could emerge under what he presented as very plausible conditions, 'It is easy to see that in the acceleration principle we have a powerful factor making for economic instability' (Samuelson 1951, p. 391, 1955, p. 333).

LARGER LESSONS THAT FOLLOW FROM THE DISCUSSION OF FEEDBACKS IN THE ECONOMY

Other examples that incorporate complexity could be invoked or discussed in a principles of macroeconomics course. But the principles course is already rather busy, so I typically limit my discussion of positive feedbacks to the foreign exchange market and the accelerator. As mentioned, I also give a few informal remarks concerning the role of positive feedbacks on the formation of trends in consumption, but I do not typically accompany this discussion with a model or graph that must be studied in more depth.

My major objective, one that is ably served by raising these issues, is to convey the idea that the stability of the economic system cannot simply be presumed. In addition, I leave students with the notion that in a world of positive feedbacks and path dependence, free market outcomes are not necessarily the best that society can do. In general, I try to convey Keynes's position that the stability of the economy is something to be explained and understood by the researcher, rather than assumed (Keynes [1936] 1964, ch. 12).

At the same time, I stress that my position is not universally shared and that it is, by any measure, a minority position amongst economists and those who run our major economic and political institutions (World Bank, IMF, Washington Think Tanks, Clinton appointees, and so on). It is not too difficult to convince them of this point. A few moments with *CNBC* or the economics coverage in the *New York Times* can readily instantiate this point.

ECONOMIC POLICY

An area where the introduction of complexity themes can be most interesting is in discussions of economic policy. Having presented grounds for believing that the economy is, under some conditions, subject to destabilizing forces, I find that students are adequately prepared for a more complete understanding of the history of economic policies and the reasons behind them. This is especially true for what Former Federal Reserve Board Chairman, Arthur Burns, termed the 'automatic stabilizers' of the economic system.

An improved understanding of the problem of potential instability is useful since the public discussion of the government's macroeconomic policies has been reduced to one criterion: do they add to, or subtract from, the federal deficit? Undermining this consensus policy of a balanced budget at all costs, and separating the issue of fiscal policy from the language of virtue and vice, is of paramount importance – and much more challenging than it was even a couple of years ago.

To this end, I develop the idea of fiscal expenditure and taxation as 'automatic stabilizers'. I introduce an income tax into the equations for the Keynesian Cross, and I also introduce a counter-cyclical component into government expenditure. These two formulas now have the following look:

$$T = T_0 + tY \tag{11.2}$$

$$G = G_0 - gY \tag{11.3}$$

I will not bore the reader with a calculation of the revised expenditure multiplier that would follow from introducing the above equations into the Keynesian Cross model, but I am sure that everyone will agree that the result is to reduce its magnitude. Again, these ideas were the very cornerstone of what was once called 'functional finance'. Stabilization policy along these lines once comprised a virtual consensus endorsed by economists as diverse as Abba Lerner, Alvin Hansen, Paul Samuelson and Herbert Stein. At the very least I hope to leave my students with enough training to understand that plausible economic arguments exist to support considered market interventions and timely federal expenditures.

Indeed, in my closing lecture, I compare and contrast two 'visions' of the economic system in order to instantiate this idea. The first, following the lines of most recent textbooks, presumes stability and the ubiquitous presence of negative feedback systems. Laissez faire, free trade, balanced budgets, and 'sound' money follow from such a presumption. The second, which presumes at least some sectors and/or conditions wherein positive feedbacks can plausibly emerge, expresses support for policies that disrupt or dampen positive feedback loops, and stabilize incomes in the case of a downward spiral. Structural policies such as the welfare state, progressive taxation, a sales tax on foreign exchange, circuit breakers in asset markets, and a minimum wage, can follow from this alternative vision of the economic process.

CONCLUSION

The subsidiary pleasures that I, as an economics professor, gain from the introduction of complex phenomena and models into my principles course are three-fold. First, I can introduce economic institutions, government policies, and the conventional practices of mature market economies in an interesting manner. Instead of presenting them as curious holdovers from an unenlightened age, I can discuss these institutions in relation to the roles that they play in creating and monitoring the 'Rules of the Game' without which a free market system would destabilize itself. This presentation provides these institutions with a grounding within the curriculum that they typically do not get in the textbooks.[6]

Second, a study of the issues related to complexity allows economics to be more fully integrated into the social sciences. As mentioned, sociologists have worked on issues related to the behavior of crowds, and the behavior of groups and organizations that cannot readily be reduced to the rationality of the several individuals who comprise them. Strictly speaking, the behavior of groups and organizations is inherently complex. Acknowledging this reality means that undergraduates, who for the most part have no commitments to academic rivalries and definitions of 'turf', can enjoy the insights that come from drawing upon several disciplines as they organize their own ideas about the nature and meaning of social life and social institutions.

Third, history matters. As someone who took a major in both history and economics as an undergraduate, I never doubted the truth of this statement. Indeed, I have always sought out ways to more fully integrate historical and economic perspectives on the nature of society. Complexity, with its associated interests in irreversibility and path dependence, is one way to integrate history and economics such that the result is indeed more than the sum of the parts.

To conclude, drawing upon the complexity perspective offers the chance for an improvement in the current state of economics instruction. It is not all that 'new', so introducing it into the curriculum should present no pedagogical problem. As I have noted, until very recently notions of path dependence were present in the standard economics curriculum. Finally, a sensitivity to complexity can help us, especially those of us who teach in places where teaching matters, to integrate our insights and understandings as economists into the larger curriculum offered by our colleges. To the extent that the Chicago and Western Ontario approaches have led us to believe that sociology, history and anthropology do not matter, we have simply succeeded in isolating ourselves from our colleagues in other fields and from many talented undergraduates. This isolation is not a strength, and it does not represent progress.

NOTES

1. As one who has done a lot of work on the history of economic thought, I must confess that those of us in this subfield have not spent enough time thinking about the evolution of the textbook, and the importance of the textbook industry to the evolution of economic ideas. However, these are matters for another conference and another paper. For an excellent example of such an exercise in the field of history see FitzGerald (1979).
2. There are a few exceptions to this rule (Colander 1995, Ruffin and Gregory 1997). Speaking for myself, I was both surprised and disappointed by the PhD course in Macroeconomics that I was subjected to at UC Berkeley. It was exclusively interested in representative agent models that featured overlapping generations. Problems of effective demand, coordination, and 'false trades' were simply defined out of the field of macroeconomics. At that time (1986–87) one can honestly say that what was once called a *Fallacy* had been reformulated into the first methodological *Principle* of macroeconomics. I can attest, since I asked, that no member of the department under the age of forty thought that this was a problem or an issue. Moreover, they could not even imagine why it might be. I should add that these same professors often wondered why it was that fewer graduates students were electing to write dissertations in macroeconomics.
3. Since he was writing a textbook, Samuelson did not generally document the origins of his terms. For the record, 'Topsy-Turvy wonderland' can also be found in Lerner (1951, ch. 9), although I do not know who was the first to use this phrase in this context. Obviously, Samuelson's reference comparing classical economics to Euclidean geometry is drawn from John Maynard Keynes ([1936] 1964, 16).
4. What used to be called the 'paradox of thrift' has almost disappeared from the current crop of textbooks (compare Mankiw 1997, Miller 1997, Stiglitz 1997, Taylor 1998). Notice that several of the field's most prominent 'New Keynesians' are on this list. The paradox of thrift can still be found in Colander (1995), Ruffin and Gregory (1997), and Baumol and Blinder (1997).
5. Through experience over the years, I have found that this example is much more successful with students from out west. My hypothesis is that they have more experience with this kind of phenomenon since the summers there are so dry relative to the east. However, a few years ago there were enormous forest fires in Quebec, so some students from the northeast have become more acquainted with this phenomenon. Here in the east it is not uncommon for

students to perceive a forest fire as a negative feedback. Since the forest fires are so much smaller, the erosion problem is less severe. Therefore the destruction of forest undergrowth that occurs during a modest fire typically allows for the rapid regeneration of plant life on the forest floor.

6. Being fond of consistency, I have to admire the Chicago and Western Ontario-inspired economists who have left all institutional discussions out of their textbooks (compare McCandless 1991, Champ and Freeman 1994). Once you assume that the free market features strong negative feedback mechanisms that inevitably lead to the best possible outcomes with regard to income, employment, and utility, then all discussions of institutions are reduced to a history of folly that cannot reasonably be expected to hold anyone's attention. Hence they cut them out and present us with short books.

REFERENCES

Albin, P.S. (1998), *Barriers and Bounds to Rationality*, Princeton: Princeton University Press.

Arthur, W.B. (1990), 'Positive Feedbacks in the Economy', *Scientific American* February, 92–9.

Arthur, W.B. (1994), *Increasing Returns and Path Dependence in the Economy*, Ann Arbor: University of Michigan Press.

Baumol, W.J. and A.S. Blinder (1997), *Macroeconomics: Principles and Policy*, 7th edn, New York: Dryden.

Briggs, J. and F.D. Peat (1989), *Turbulent Mirror*, New York: Harper and Row.

Cassidy, J. (1998), 'The Force of an Idea', *The New Yorker*, January 12, 32–7.

Casti, J.L. (1994), *Complexification*, New York: Harper/Collins.

Champ, B. and S. Freeman (1994), *Modeling Monetary Economies*, New York: John Wiley.

Colander, D. (1994), 'The Art of Economics by the Numbers', in R. Backhouse (ed.), *New Directions in Economic Methodology*, New York: Routledge, pp. 35–49.

Colander, D. (1995), *Economics*, 2nd edn, Boston: Irwin.

Colander, D. (ed) (1996), *Beyond Microfoundations: Post Walrasian Macroeconomics*, New York: Cambridge University Press.

Coveney, P. and R. Highfield (1995), *Frontiers of Complexity*, New York: Random House.

Elmslie, B. (1994), 'Positive Feedback Mechanisms in Adam Smith's Theories of International Trade', *European Journal of the History of Economic Thought*, **1** (2), Spring, 253–71.

FitzGerald, F. (1979), *America Revised: History Schoolbooks in the Twentieth Century*, Boston: Little, Brown.

Foley, D.K. (1998), 'Introduction' in P. Albin, *Barriers and Bounds to Rationality*, Princeton: Princeton University Press, pp. 1–72.

Gell-Mann, M. (1994), *The Quark and the Jaguar: Adventures in the Simple and the Complex*, New York: W.H. Freeman & Co.

Harrod, R.F. (1939), 'An Essay in Dynamic Theory', *Economic Journal*, 14–33.

Herrnstein, R. and C. Murray (1994), *The Bell Curve: Intelligence and Class Struc-*

ture in American Life, New York: Free Press.

Kaldor, N. (1966), *Strategic Factors in Economic Development,* Ithaca, NY: Cornell University Press.

Kaldor, N. (1970), 'The Case for Regional Policies', *Scottish Journal of Political Economy,* **17** (3), November.

Keynes, J.M. [1936] (1964), *The General Theory of Employment, Interest and Money,* New York: Harcourt Brace.

Keynes, J.N. [1917] (1973), *The Scope and Method of Political Economy,* Clifton, NJ,: Augustus M. Kelley.

Kindleberger, C P. (1996), *Manias, Panics and Crashes: A History of Financial Crises,* 3rd edn, New York: John Wiley.

Le Bon, G. (1952), *The Crowd,* London: Ernest Benn.

Lerner, A.P. (1951), *Economics of Employment,* New York: McGraw-Hill.

MacKay, C. [1841] (1980), *Extraordinary Popular Delusions and the Madness of Crowds,* New York: Harmony.

Mankiw, N.G. (1998), *Principles of Macroeconomics,* New York: Dryden.

Marshall, A. ([1920] 1982), *Principles of Economics*, 8th edn, Philadelphia, PA: Porcupine Press.

McCandless, G.T. (1991), *Macroeconomic Theory,* New Jersey: Prentice-Hall.

Miller, R.L. (1997), *Economics Today: The Macro View,* 9th edn, New York: Addison-Wesley.

Myrdal, G. (1944), *An American Dilemma: The Negro Problem and Modern Democracy,* 2 vols, New York: Pantheon.

Myrdal, G. (1957), *Rich Lands and Poor: The Road to World Prosperity,* New York: Harper and Brothers.

Prasch, R.E. (1998), 'In Defense of a Tax on Foreign Exchange', *Journal of Economic Issues,* **32** (2), June, 325–31.

Ruffin, R.J. and P.R. Gregory (1997), *Principles of Macroeconomics,* 6th edn, New York: Addison-Wesley.

Samuelson, P. (1939), 'A Synthesis of the Principle of Acceleration and the Multiplier', *Journal of Political Economy,* December.

Samuelson, P. (1951), *Economics: An Introductory Analysis,* 2nd edn, New York: McGraw-Hill.

Samuelson, P. (1955), *Economics: An Introductory Analysis,* 3rd edn, New York: McGraw-Hill.

Smelser, N.J. (1962), *Theory of Collective Behavior,* New York: Free Press.

Stiglitz, J. (1997), *Principles of Macroeconomics,* 2nd edn, New York: Norton.

Taylor, J.B. (1998), *Economics,* 2nd edn, New York: Houghton Mifflin.

Waldrop, M.M. (1992), *Complexity,* New York: Simon & Schuster.

Young, A. (1928), 'Increasing Returns and Economic Progress', *Economic Journal,* **37** December.

12. Teaching Macroeconomics while Taking Complexity Seriously

Kevin D. Hoover

When I teach macroeconomics, I start from a simple premise: economics is about something in the world; it is about the behavior of people, individually and collectively in social organizations with respect to their material well-being. I also start with an observation: for many, perhaps most, of our students the connection between what we teach in elementary and intermediate courses and the world is really very obscure.

A family friend, Kelley, confided to me as we sat watching our kids in the swimming pool that, although she had majored in history at Emory, she was just shy of enough units to have double-majored in economics. She said, 'I loved economics. I loved the beauty of all those shifting curves and the clever deductions. But, what I never understood, was what any of it had to do with life.' Many students face Kelley's problem. It is, I believe, more acute for macroeconomics than for micro. There is a case to be made that microeconomics is a normative discipline concerned with rationality, but with little descriptive or empirical content. But macroeconomics is largely justified by its empirical relevance and its usefulness in policy analysis. Intermediate macroeconomics textbooks have become, in large measure, watered down graduate textbooks, in which theory, rather than applications, take pride of place. This development is all the more unfortunate, since even graduate students have become rather poor at knowing how to connect that theory – watered down or neat – to the real world.

COMPLEXITY AND THE IMPASSE IN MACROECONOMICS

It is commonplace to talk about a 'crisis' in economics. But I regard the situation not so much a crisis as an *impasse*. How did we get to the point where clever students like Kelley are at a loss about the linkages between economics and the economy? And what, if anything, does the disconnection between textbook theory and the real world have to do with complexity?

The disconnection is especially disconcerting in macroeconomics. For most of its history, from Sir William Petty's 'political arithmetick' in the seventeenth century through Tinbergen's early econometric models in the twentieth, empirical economics and policy analysis was largely macroeconomics. Even early econometric studies of demand curves dealt with aggregated, time-series data that presented the same methodological issues as macroeconomic data.[1] Dealing at a macroeconomic level did not pose any particular theoretical difficulty for Petty or Quesnay or even, despite the increased importance of individualism in classical economic thought, for Smith and Ricardo and the Scottish and English political economists. It certainly did not for Marx. But after the classical period in economic thought, the rise of individualism helped to form what we now know as modern microeconomics. At the same time, the spread to economics of what might be called a Cartesian or French sensibility has placed a higher value on theoretical consistency than on empirical purchase. The French approach stands in sharp contrast to Anglo-Scottish pragmatism and is by no means confined to economics.

An early example of the French approach is found in Augustine Cournot's *Researches Into the Mathematical Principles of the Theory of Wealth* (1838). Cournot gives a recognizably modern account of microeconomics. And he presents the vision of the economy represented as a giant general equilibrium system with each agent described by his own curves. Still, Cournot had the good sense to observe that such a model was only a vision and empirically impractical.

By the 1930s, economics was in an embarrassing situation. Its theory – French or English, Walras or Marshall – was individualistic, but its policy problems, data, and methods for handling data, were aggregate. The principal macroeconomic theory of the time, the Quantity Theory of Money, was aggregative and, consequently, an uneasy companion for mainstream theory. The French dealt with this by giving up relevance; the English by adopting a pragmatic inconsistency. Keynes's great methodological achievement was to claim autonomy for macroeconomics. Aggregative economics was to have its own categories, its own relationships, and its own theories, and would no longer be a poor relation to microeconomic theory. This was surely a response to complexity in the most straightforward, ordinary language (but probably not Santa Fe) sense. As Cournot had realized, there were too many agents, their relationships were too complex, for the vision of modeling them one by one to ever succeed. This meant that there was a class of phenomena – the aggregate outcomes of the individuals' complex interactions – that could be analyzed only in its own terms, if at all. Complexity in this sense was understood not only by Cournot, but by Smith, Marshall, and many others before the rise of modern microeconomics.

Keynes was triumphant in practice. Policy makers became Keynesians in spirit, if not in name. This is still true today, despite the regular declarations in the *Wall Street Journal*, the editors of which routinely confuse the Phillips curve with Okun's law, that Keynes is dead. Practice aside, Keynes's intellectual triumph was short-lived. The animating Spirit of Economics is not Keynes, but Walras, Debreu and Bourbakism. The movement in this direction began immediately on the publication of the *General Theory* in 1936 and is now complete. It is not only the new classicals, but equally the new Keynesians, who have adopted the representative–agent model as the ultimate expression of the drive for microfoundations. Macroeconomic models now consist of a single agent – or sometimes a few agents – 'representing' the actors of the economy and solving dynamic optimization problems according to the usual microeconomic rules. Lucas, for one, expresses the hope that soon the distinction between micro and macroeconomics will be erased (Lucas 1987, pp. 107–8). But this is absurd. Everything that microeconomists have taught us about aggregation theory underlines the virtual impossibility of any aggregate outcome being correctly modeled by an agent whose utility function and production function look just like those of an individual agent, but who takes the entire GDP of the economy as his output and his income. The representative-agent model does not solve the aggregation problem, the problem of complexity that Cournot rightly saw stood in the way of the practical implementation of the vision of general equilibrium modeling. Despite the appeal to the mathematics of microeconomics, this is not microeconomics or microfoundations but the simulacrum of microeconomics and microfoundations. The prevailing view is that microeconomics is the only real economics. The representative-agent model *looks like* microeconomics. But as a reaction to the problems of complexity, it is a sleight of hand. Just as the quantity theory in 1930 was an uneasy companion for the prevailing price theory, so should the representative-agent model be an uneasy companion for modern microeconomics. It is a measure of the complacency of modern economics that this unease is not felt more acutely.

The problem posed by complexity in the wider sense is not unique to economics. Physics provides an instructive analogy. In *QED* Richard Feynman writes:

> You might wonder how such simple actions could produce such a complex world. It's because phenomena we see in the world are the result of an enormous intertwining of tremendous numbers of photon exchanges and interferences. Knowing the three fundamental actions is only a very small beginning toward analyzing any *real* situation; where there is such a multitude of photon exchanges going on that it is impossible to calculate – experience has to be gained as to which possibilities are more important. Thus we invent such ideas as 'index of refraction' or 'compressibility' or 'valence' to help us calculate in an approximate way when there's an enormous amount of detail going on underneath.

> The branches of physics that deal with questions such a why iron (with 26 pro-
> tons) is magnetic, while copper (with 29) is not, or why one gas is transparent and
> another one is not, are called 'solid-state physics' or 'liquid-state physics' or 'hon-
> est physics'. (Feynman 1985, p. 114)

Feynman has an abiding faith in the fundamental unity of science and in
the reduction in principle of complex phenomena to elementary ones. Nevertheless, he also believes both in the limitations of our ability to cope with
complexity and, importantly, in the fact that we live in the complex rather
than the simplified world.

Macroeconomics stands in a similar relationship to microeconomics as
optics or chemistry does to quantum electrodynamics. 'Index of refraction',
'compressibility' and 'valence' are not the concepts of quantum electrodynamics. Yet, it is concepts like these that describe, and permit us practically to
analyze, features of the world that are important to us. We use these concepts
even though the features we care about may somehow reduce to photon exchanges, because we do not now, and may never, understand fully how to
carry out the reduction.

Nancy Cartwright, the philosopher of physics, in a passage that I have worn
out in quoting, takes the laws of physics down a peg. She makes a similar
observation to Feynman's, although she has considerably less faith in the
ultimate reduction of macro phenomena to micro:

> It is hard to find [laws] in nature and we are always having to make excuses for them:
> why they have exceptions – big or little; why they only work for models in the head;
> why it takes an engineer with a special knowledge of real materials and a not too literal
> mind to apply physics to reality. (Cartwright 1989, p. 8)

To me macroeconomics should be the realm of the economists with a special knowledge of the actual economy and not too literal minds. Complexity
in the old-fashioned sense drives us in that direction. Perhaps the greatest
contribution of the insights of the Santa Fe approach is simply to demonstrate that, even if we begin with simple rules, real situations become complex fast. Complexity forces us, for the matters that we care about, to leave
the realms of Feynman's experiments with a few photons and deal as
Cartwright's engineers with autonomous phenomena. That is in itself an
important methodological step. Whether complexity has anything more to
offer macroeconomics remains to be seen.

Let me explain my view of complexity more carefully. There is an analogy
with physics: microeconomics is constitutive, but not determinative, of macroeconomics. But there is also a disanalogy: unlike physics, micro is not
constant. People are described as bundles of preferences, and preferences
change. Modern microeconomics does not have really good ways of dealing
with such change. But Marshall (and by extension, Keynes) dealt with it by

adopting the stance of Cartwright's engineer – cultivating a not-too-literal mind. For Marshall, the human realm divided into a hierarchy of interests, of which economic interests were the lowest and not always governing or dominant. Marshall treated the optimization results of price theory as attraction points for behavior rather than predictions of behavior, as forces that influenced human decisions rather than as complete decisions in themselves. For his purposes, a static, unrealistic microeconomics served rather like the rough calculations and approximations of Feynman's 'honest physics'. I doubt that Marshall would have been overly impressed by calls to rebuild microeconomics from first principles as some advocates of the Santa Fe program suggest, because he never took price theory too literally in the first place. For my own part, I will be interested to watch the *constructive* success of the Santa Fe program, although, in the meantime, I see no reason to despair entirely of traditional microeconomics. Marshall was, I think, right: microeconomics is not everything, but in the hands of the not-too-literal minded it has considerable power. It does not determine macroeconomics, but it may nonetheless help to illuminate it.

MY COURSE

Perhaps the best way to explain how these ideas about complexity relate to economics is to tell how I teach my macroeconomics course. My goal is to get students to relate macroeconomics to the world, to real data and policy: to appreciate the relationship between the taste of the wine and its chemistry. For this the molecular physics is, at best, intermittently useful. In many ways, this course is a throwback to an older pedagogy. Many of its elements would be familiar to students of a generation ago who studied Hansen (1949), the early editions of Samuelson (1948), or such intermediate macroeconomics textbooks as Dernberg and McDougall (1960). The course is Keynesian in two senses. First, it accepts macroeconomics as an autonomous study of the economic aggregates – the inevitable result of the fact of complexity – and often emphasizes the consequences of heterogeneity. Second, it takes it for granted that suboptimal outcomes are possible and that there is no *automatic* presumption that the economy is self-regulating in the sense of always returning to the most desired state of its own accord. Business cycles are not typically regarded, as new classical real-business cycle modelers regard them, as Pareto-efficient fluctuations around a steady-state growth path. Instead, they are seen as suboptimal deviations from a desirable path. The course is not backward looking. Like many recent macroeconomics textbooks, I give pride of place to growth and emphasize the constantly changing nature of the macroeconomy.

What most distinguishes my course from others is not the theory, but the emphasis on students learning the facts about the economy. They use simple graphical and statistical techniques that help them to see how the economy actually behaves and how, or to what extent, economic theory helps us to understand the data. In Chapter 7 of this volume, David Colander reports a remark made by a reviewer of his introductory textbook that the material he includes on the Santa Fe approach 'is nearly useless to the average business student'. I do not know whether that judgment is true of Colander's book (Colander 1998). But I do believe that most of what is found in intermediate macroeconomics textbooks today is presented in a manner that renders it nearly useless to the student. The emphasis on actual data is aimed at making the economics useful.

There are limits to how deeply the students can pursue data analysis. Because most programs place very limited quantitative and statistical demands on undergraduates, I cannot use any really sophisticated econometrics. The surprising thing, I find, is that one can go very far with very simple empirical methods. When those methods fail, there is often a useful lesson for the students in why we must avoid facile inductions. For example, if one plots the real interest rate against the investment share in GDP, the fitted regression line is upward sloping. I use that to point out to the students the limitations of the scatterplot and bivariate methods. They know from other graphical investigations that both real interest rates and investment are pro-cyclical, and they therefore learn a lesson about garden-variety complexity. There are many other such lessons related to spurious and nonsense correlation, causal direction, mismeasurement and so forth.

An empirical emphasis requires a reformulation of the normal presentation of macroeconomic theory. When students read the newspapers or listen to the radio or television, the economy is presented as changing. They hear about growth rates and inflation rates. The IS/LM/AS analysis of the typical textbook, however, talks about the levels of GDP and the level of the CPI. Most people, even professional economists, have a better idea of the inflation rate than the level of the CPI, and a better idea of last quarter's growth rate than of the level of real GDP. The textbook theory is easily reinterpreted by those who understand it to speak to the more familiar categories, but the need to reinterpret it is a pedagogical barrier for many students. My approach, which is very much in the spirit of Marshall, is to start with the theory matched to familiar categories.

So much for my general approach. Let me conclude with a description of some of the particular elements. I begin with what is often regarded as the dullest material in a macroeconomics text – national income accounting. While this may be dull stuff, it is important and students often get it very wrong. An accurate understanding of the national accounts provides without much further economic analysis the tools to puncture many of the misconceptions that students have about the economy. For example, many students have a vision of the economy as one of oppressed workers and greedy capitalists; they believe that the labor share in GDP is low and profit share huge. They are surprised when they calculate the shares themselves to find the truth. Similarly, many students see the government as dominating the economy, and are surprised to see that government expenditure as a share of GDP is stable over the past 50 years. Quite a bit of useful fiscal policy analysis can be done with the national accounts alone; having students do it themselves drives home many truths. To take another example, students learn a healthy skepticism about popular economic arguments from knowing the data and how it is related. There was a widespread belief in the 1980s that the US trade deficit was caused by the government's budget deficit. The almost raw facts alone teach students that it must be more complicated than that: not only is the budget in surplus today, while the trade deficit persists, but every possible combination of trade positions and budget positions exists in the US time series or in other nations. To explain how this variety of outcomes is possible for quantities connected by an identity provides an excellent place, and an excellent case, to introduce the basic distinction between necessary accounting identities and economic behavior.

I spend a good deal of time teaching students to describe the data in useful ways. They learn, as every textbook teaches but few sufficiently emphasize, to distinguish real from nominal, as well as a complex of related skills: to convert nominal quantities to constant dollars, to calculate growth rates and index numbers, and to use shares, ratios and logarithms in the appropriate situations. These exercises may seem dull and a distraction from the economic analysis, but my experience is that students routinely get them wrong from having had insufficient practice and that it is an impediment to their understanding that the theory really does connect to the world.

After finishing with the national accounts, I move on to genuine economic analysis starting with growth. Here the approach is fairly mainstream. I start with a Cobb–Douglas production function and emphasize the roles of labor, investment and productivity in the growth process. This, of course, looks like the pseudo-microeconomics that I protested earlier. But I never meant to deny that microeconomic analogies could illuminate macroeconomics. I emphasize that we are dealing in analogies that, in the spirit of Marshall and Cartwright, must not be taken too literal-mindedly. While what I teach is not incompatible with the Solow growth model, I de-emphasize the self-adjusting mechanics of neoclassical growth. Students proceed immediately to the identification of business cycles from the historical data, and so never entertain the illusion that economies grow smoothly along steady-state paths.

My treatment of aggregate supply is really a treatment of factor markets, especially the labor market, and students never see an aggregate supply curve in price/GDP space. The analysis of labor markets is, for the most part, traditional static microeconomics, but recast so that it deals with the share of the workforce employed. In this way, the static model is easily related to the deviation of the actual growth path of the economy from a potential path defined by full employment of capital and labor. Students develop their own empirical estimates of this potential path. Some part of unemployment is regarded as involuntary unemployment in the Keynesian sense of workers being rationed in their supply of labor. It is easy to relate unemployment to its capital equivalent, capacity utilization, for which there is readily available data.

By this point, the students have a robust model, capable of dealing with a number of real world issues. Let me give an example. Several years ago, in a talk in Sacramento, David Colander argued that textbook macroeconomics was unable to account for important real world phenomena with institutional elements. He gave the example of the macroeconomics of the re-unification of East and West Germany. In contrast to Colander, I believe that simple textbook models in the hands of my students trained to cultivate a not-too-literal mind are able to address such questions. Reunification, for instance, can be seen as the sudden obsolescence of the East German capital stock, since, though it was physically unaltered, its future profitability, the basis for proper capital valuation, was largely destroyed. The consequence is just what a Cobb–Douglas production function would tell you: a fall in output, a rise in the incentives to investment, a fall in the marginal product of labor which, combined with government insistence that real wages remain high, implies high unemployment.

Having completed the discussion of economic growth, I introduce the students to different possible sources of short-run fluctuations and their implications. On the one hand, I discuss how changes in productivity and capital, as emphasized by the real-business-cycle school, may cause fluctuations in potential GDP. On the other hand, I discuss how fluctuations in demand may cause departures from potential. My students use data to examine the implications of these different views for the behavior of real wages, which involves understanding the relationship between productivity growth and wage trends, as well as the necessity of empirically isolating trends in the data. The net result is ambiguous, which is another way of driving home the complexity of the economy and of forcing the students to ask whether our simple model of aggregate supply is fully adequate.

I deal with dynamics of prices and unemployment, once again using traditional tools: the Phillips curve and Okun's law. The approach is crude, but perfectly adequate to the level of statistical capabilities of the students. I emphasize Okun's law more than most macroeconomics textbooks do, because it is so robust a relationship. I treat it as representing a causal relationship from output to unemployment and derive a version of it that demonstrates that the critical growth rate for a steady unemployment rate can be thought of as determined by the growth rates of labor productivity, population and the participation rate. This permits students to see clearly some of the ways in which the economy has changed over the postwar period and to isolate what factors would have to change if popular calls for faster sustained growth rates were to be achievable.

My treatment of the nonfinancial side of aggregate demand is relatively standard. Essentially, it is the IS curve and its components. These are once again adapted to the data by casting the real quantities as shares of potential GDP rather than real levels. On the empirical level this deals with the problem that the data are non-stationary and therefore subject to nonsense correlations. On the theoretical side, it makes it easy to see the static consumption and investment relationships as a freeze-frame of a growing economy and to related demand to unemployment and capacity utilization rates.

Where I differ radically from the treatment found in most textbooks is in de-emphasizing the LM curve. I regard the continued emphasis on the LM curve as one of the most misleading elements of macroeconomic pedagogy, a triumph of the Cartesian impulse. Financial markets are wonderfully complex. And there are robust patterns in their complexity: yield curves, the hierarchy of risk premia, and so forth. My students learn to identify and understand these patterns and to relate them to the business cycle and to policy. In the face of such complexity, to single out narrow money as the critical financial asset and to apply unwarranted aggregation and Walras's law to eliminate the vastly more important loan, bond, and stock markets (among others) in the determination of a single rate of interest of ambiguous maturity and risk category has only one advantage: it achieves closure. An IS/LM/AS model is a closed system that permits students to perform algebraic deductions, which are a great deal of fun, but not necessarily of much practical relevance. My approach emphasizes the interrelationships between interest rates. It pins down the whole structure at the short end through monetary policy and at the long end by the arbitrage between long bonds and shares reflecting the real returns on capital. What is missing is a mechanical deductive link between expansions of aggregate demand and real rates of interest. That is what the LM curve provides. But the not-too-literal minded can do without it and better appreciate the complexity of the financial system.[2]

David Colander suggests that an implication of the Santa Fe approach to complexity is that economics should be inductive rather than deductive. My course reflects the fact that I agree with this assessment – but only half way. If what Colander means is that a useful macroeconomics will always have to look to the economy itself and not simply to first principles to characterize adequately how it works, then I agree. The marginal propensity to consume or the interest-elasticity of investment or the risk-premium on corporate bonds are not things that can with any likelihood be deduced from first principles. But neither can they be induced from raw data. These parameters and even the very data from which one might derive them are infused with a conceptual picture of the economy and it is only with the presupposition of that picture that we can measure them. When my students are looking at data, they are not, for the most part, pursuing Baconian inductions. Rather they are looking at the economy through a set of specially tinted lenses and asking whether it looks clearer and more understandable when viewed that way. I suggest ways of looking at the economy that I know, either because I have tried it in advance or because of general experience, look good through those lenses. The reasoning that got me there is more what philosophers of science refer to as 'inference to the best explanation' or what the American pragmatist philosopher C.S. Peirce calls abduction: given some facts, what is a story that might explain them?[3] (Sherlock Holmes's famous elementary 'deductions' are really abductions.) While there is an element of pre-packaging from the students' point of view, occasionally they find something surprising – to them and to me. And that in itself should not surprise us. The economy after all is complex.

NOTES

1. On the history of econometric modeling of demand, see Morgan (1990) and Hendry and Morgan (1995).
2. David Colander has suggested to me that my own argument can be turned around here: the not-too-literal-minded should be able to use the LM curve despite its failure to capture some details of the economy. This is, of course, right; it explains why Robert Solow (1984) refers to the IS/LM model as the trained intuition of the macroeconomist. Pedagogically, it is a matter of judgment and experience. My experience is that it is difficult to get students to focus on those aspects of the financial markets that in fact matter for monetary policy and for investment behavior when they see the world through the LM curve. It is somewhat like those 'magic eye' pictures in which the floating object appears only when a practiced viewer stares at it just so. Many viewers never develop the knack. Sometimes it is better not to expect them to, but to provide a more accessible picture.
3. See Hoover (1994) on Peirce and Lipton (1991) on 'inference to the best explanation'.

REFERENCES

Cartwright, N. (1989), *Nature's Capacities and Their Measurement*, Oxford: Clarendon Press.
Colander, D. (1998), *Economics,* Boston, MA: Irwin/McGraw-Hill.

Cournot, A. (1838), *Recherches sur les Principes Matématiques de la Théorie de la Richesse*, Paris: Hachette.

Dernburg, T F. and D.M. McDougall (1960), *Macroeconomics*, New York: McGraw-Hill.

Feynman, R.P. (1985), *QED The Strange Theory of Light and Matter*, Princeton: Princeton University Press.

Hansen, A.H. (1949), *Monetary Theory and Fiscal Policy*, New York: McGraw-Hill.

Hendry, D.F. and M.S. Morgan (eds) (1995), *The Foundations of Econometric Analysis*, Cambridge: Cambridge University Press.

Hoover, K.D. (1994), 'Pragmatism, Pragmaticism and Economic Method', in R. Backhouse (ed.), *New Directions in Economic Methodology*, London: Routledge.

Keynes, J.M. (1936), *General Theory of Employment, Interest and Money*, London: Harcourt Brace.

Lipton, P. (1991), *Inference to the Best Explanation*, London: Routledge.

Lucas, R.E., Jr. (1987), *Models of Business Cycles*, Oxford: Blackwell.

Morgan, M.S. (1990), *The History of Econometric Ideas*, Cambridge: Cambridge University Press.

Samuelson, P. (1948), *Economics*, New York: McGraw-Hill

Solow, R.M. (1984), 'Mr. Hicks and the Classics', *Oxford Economic Papers* **36** (Supplement), 13–25.

13. Development Economics and Complexity

Sunder Ramaswamy

Arthur (1998) writes about complexity as a movement in the sciences to take 'process' seriously; and how economic agents' behavior, strategies and expectations interact and adapt to the world they co-create. North (1997) puts forth his two puzzles: (1) how to account for the uneven and erratic pattern of both historical change and contemporary development, and (2) how to model the process of change and development.

The purpose of this chapter is to point out that the ideas that the complexity approach raises, such as increasing returns, cumulative processes and path dependency, have been the preoccupation of scholars concerned with economic history and also the large cohort of development economists since the Second World War. What the new complexity research has to offer is the tools to deal formally with these issues. These tools are important. The fate of development economics suggests that without the tools, the ideas, while central to development economics, will not get integrated into standard economics. Because they were not, development economics was segregated out from standard economics. Development economists often claim that the subject matter of development economics is at once among the oldest and newest sub-fields of economics. After all, Adam Smith and other classical economists were interested in discovering the source of economic progress and analyzing the process of long-run economic change. As Sir Arthur Lewis once remarked, what Smith called the 'natural progress of opulence' is what scholars today call 'development economics' (reported in Meier and Seers, 1984). However, the field that is called development economics is recent and came about in the post-Second World War era with a primary concern for development problems of African, Asian and Latin American economies.

The two decades or so after the Second World War were the grand years of development economics with a palpable excitement among scholars and policy makers who felt that their theories, models and policies could be used to raise the income, wellbeing and economic capabilities of people everywhere. The noted scholars in the field were Paul Rosentein-Rodan, Gunnar

Myrdal, Albert Hirschman, Ragnar Nurkse, Jan Tinbergen and W.A. Lewis, to name a few luminaries. Most of these scholars believed that development was ultimately a virtuous cycle driven by external economies. They believed that modernization *leads* to more modernization. If countries fail to get such a virtuous cycle going, they remain in low-level equilibrium traps and stay underdeveloped. If one looks at the development literature of the postwar period up until the 1960s one sees fairly extensive use of concepts and terms such as strategic complementarities, low-level equilibrium traps, cumulative causation, role of institutions, 'history matters', economies of scale, and so on.

One of the early 'classics' from the development field, and a standard reading for all courses on development, was Rosenstein-Rodan's 'Problems of Industrialization of Eastern and South-Eastern Europe', published in 1943. He argued that economic underdevelopment is the outcome of a massive coordination failure, in which several investments do not occur simply because other complementary investments are not made, and these latter investments are not forthcoming simply because the former are missing. Pervasive complementarities might therefore lead to a situation where an economy is stuck in a 'low-level equilibrium' trap, while at the same time there is another, better, equilibrium, if *only* all agents could 'coordinate' their actions to reach it.[1]

He illustrated his argument for coordinated investment by imagining a country in which a large number of unemployed workers are taken from the land and put to work in a large shoe factory. Rosenstein-Rodan goes on to argue that the investment is likely to be unprofitable in isolation, but that it would be profitable if accompanied by similar investments in many other industries. Whether or not a coordinated equilibrium would arise depends on the *expectations* that each entrepreneur holds about others. To the extent that the formation of expectations is driven by past history, it may well be that a region that is historically stagnant continues to be so, whereas another region that has been historically prosperous may continue to flourish.

The parable of the shoe factory is also compelling if many different industries are involved in the coordination process to a 'desirable equilibrium'. Rosenstein-Rodan introduced the idea of the 'big push' as a policy that simultaneously creates a coordinated investment in many different sectors of the economy. The big push model of Rosenstein-Rodan is a classic case in which economies of scale at the plant level, and an elastic supply of factors of production interact to yield pecuniary external economies with real welfare significance – the movement to a high-income level equilibrium.[2]

The big push idea from a policy standpoint was not without its problems. It requires massive money like a Marshall Plan, and knowledge of the various sectoral investment requirements. In contrast to the big push idea, which is akin to a balanced growth approach, Hirschman's idea (1958) was to follow a deliberate policy of unbalanced growth, that is, to selectively promote the development of key sectors and let the notion of 'forward and backward linkages' do the work! Hirschman is not usually thought of as an economist concerned primarily with non-convexities; yet his explanation of linkages (especially backward linkages) explicitly invokes the importance of an economy achieving a minimum economic scale. Hirschman's classic *The Strategy of Economic Development* (1958) along with his other writings shaped and broadened the scope of economic development in a seminal fashion and yet his influence on the mainstream economics profession was not commensurately profound. Hirschman recognized that increased formalism of economics happening contemporaneously often failed to explain the nature of social reality. He, like many of the other development scholars, eschewed the formalism and abstract model building and increasingly adopted a style that could be characterized as 'holistic, systemic, and evolutionary' (Wilber and Francis 1986). His methodology was holistic because it focused primarily on the relations between the parts of a system and the whole. It is evolutionary because the focus is on the changes in the patterns of relations that are the essence of social and economic reality. The important contribution with which he is most identified, 'backward and forward linkages' can be identified as important elements of a dynamic development process that proceed in sequences or spurts of economic activity. His view of development is one that explains complex interrelated processes rather than one that predicts specific outcomes.

The 1950s development theorists started with a presumption of multiple equilibria[3] and posed the fundamentally important question of how to get an economy to escape a 'low-level equilibrium trap' to a better 'high income equilibrium'. There were two distinct mechanisms put forward – one worked through the economic–demographic interactions of savings, income and endogenous population growth, and the problem became one of escaping a Malthusian trap with a 'critical minimum effort' – as in the models of Nelson (1956) and Leibenstein (1957); the other approach focused on increasing returns that generate strategic complementarities among sectors in the economy, through a process of 'cumulative causation', requiring a coordinated 'big-push' for industrialization.[4]

To some students of modern day complexity theory of the Santa Fe variety, who do not have a sense of the history of economic thought, the emphasis by the early development scholars on complexity themes such as multiple equilibria, strategic complementarities, economies of scale, role of institutions and path dependence, may come as a welcome surprise. But, it should also concern them that by the mid to late 1960s, development theory of the kind put forward by Rosenstein-Rodan and Hirschman, or the ideas of

Myrdal (1957) (cumulative caustation)[5] and Nurkse (1953) (vicious circles), were fading. Mainstream economics was moving in the direction of increasingly formal and scrupulous modeling – something all these scholars either consciously eschewed, or, in some cases, believed could not be done, given the state of economic methodology and tools of the times. An important and critical puzzle was that no one had yet figured out how to explicitly model increasing returns and the underlying market structures that gives rise to them. Since increasing returns played a key role in the writings of Rosenstein-Rodan, Myrdal and Hirschman, they could not formalize the arguments they were making.

In a conversation, Nobel Laureate, Amartya Sen once remarked,

> A good economist is one who loves the discipline, is forever curious about economic issues, appreciates the fact that economics lends itself to having broad interests, and more importantly, is one who can juggle many balls, even if a little clumsily, rather than give a superb display of virtuosity with one ball.

Such a comment would resonate with many who not only study development economics but also teach it either at the undergraduate or graduate level. Over the decades the courses in microeconomics, macroeconomics, mathematical economics and econometrics have become formidably sophisticated enough to develop students' skills in the art of model building and formalism; courses on development economics, on the other hand, while introducing a lot of theory and empirical testing were nevertheless 'clumsy' à la Sen. I can recall, as a graduate student at the Delhi School of Economics, that the papers we were reading for the graduate course on development economics were not necessarily as elegant or tractable as in the other courses but were focused on the important questions about the human condition from an economics perspective – issues of poverty, demography, industrialization, and so on, for many of which we did not always have answers. In short no one could accuse the development economics I learned as 'displaying a superb virtuosity with one ball'. But, while it seemed natural to focus on development economics in a country like India, it became apparent by the mid 1980s, that in most western universities, the field itself had lost a lot of meaning and claims to grandeur.

WHY DID DEVELOPMENT ECONOMICS FADE AWAY?

The natural question, given the importance of the question and the richness of the answers, is 'what happened?' In his humorous and perceptive account of the economics profession, Leijonhufvud (1981) remarks on how the pecking order and status relationships within the Econ tribe are determined by the skills and abilities in making certain types of implements called, 'models':

The priestly caste (the Math-Econ) for example, is a higher 'field' than either Micro or Macro, while the Develops just as definitely rank lower. Second, we know that these caste rankings are not permanent and can change over time. There is evidence, for example, that both the high rank assigned to the Math-Econ and the low rank of the Develops are, historically speaking, rather recent phenomena. The rise of the Math-Econ seems to be associated with the previously noted trend among all the Econ towards the ornate, ceremonial models, while the low rank of the Develops is due to the fact that this caste in recent times has not strictly enforced the taboos against association with the Polscis, Sociogs, and other tribes. Other Econ look upon this with considerable apprehension as endangering the moral fiber of the tribe and suspect the Develops even of relinquishing model-making.

Krugman (1994, pp. 349–50) in a recent essay seems to confirm Leijonhufvud's satirical account by claiming that

economic theory is essentially a collection of models. Broad insights that are not expressed in model form may temporarily attract attention and even win converts, but they do not endure unless codified in a reproducible – and teachable – form. Like it or not, however, the influence of ideas of that have not been embalmed in models soon decays.[6]

This could be one crucial reason as to why 'development economics' – despite generating some formidable ideas in the 1950s and 1960s – has never achieved a high status. In this light, it is instructive to see the Murphy, Shleifer and Vishny paper, 'Industrialization and the Big Push' (1989) that effectively resurrects the big push idea in spirit to convey what Rosenstein-Rodan was trying to do. Their model would be the sort of exercise that Krugman would have felt was needed in the 1950s. One of the main reasons, however, for why this did not happen then, as already mentioned, was the difficulty surrounding the *explicit* modeling of increasing returns and underlying market structure that generates these forces. Murphy, Shleifer and Vishney (1989) focus on the necessary condition of external economies, and what a model of external economies must include. Their work provides a model of the underlying imperfect market structure (as a set of limit price monopolies) that generate these scale economies.

One of the interesting insights of Murphy et al.'s formalization of Rosenstein-Rodan's big push model was to show that the big push idea was not that far-fetched; especially to skeptics who believed that if modern technology is better, then rational actors would simply adopt it. But Murphy et al. explicitly modeled the interaction between economies of scale and market size that result in low-level equilibrium traps, something that Rosenstein-Rodan had written informally about four decades ago. As Arthur (1994) points out, the revival of the big push idea by Murphy et al. has renewed the interest in increasing returns among development economists.

It is becoming increasingly clear that we need to understand positive feedbacks, the role of institutions, path dependence, interaction between economic agents, and so on, to really understand the process of growth and development. It is heartening to see some of this finally filter back not just into research à la Murphy, Shleifer and Vishney (1989) but also in some of the new and well-received texts on development economics – Basu (1997) and Ray (1997) are good examples. Both books are very strong on building the analytical foundations of development theory and expose the student to some of the most recent advances in game theory and growth theory, and consciously use concepts of positive feedbacks, coordination failures, and the role of history and expectations, in a consistent manner to explain the process of development or lack thereof.

CONCLUSION

Development economics provides a useful case study for complexity theorists to keep in mind. The ideas are not enough. To succeed in a textbook institutional environment, the ideas must be embedded in simple models. Those not so embedded fade away. Having the tools now to go along with the 'grand ideas' is breathing new excitement into the study and teaching of development economics. Dusting off the ideas already found on the intellectual shelves – the emphasis on strategic complementarities, increasing returns, multiple equilibria, the role of history and expectations – to expand our understanding of the complex phenomena of growth and development is a fascinating and extremely important research agenda.

If one used Brian Arthur's definition of complexity presented at the start of this chapter, development economics has been the study of complexity. But economics has a process, too, and the history of development economics suggests that unless the story of complexity is embodied in teachable formal models, the study of complexity will fade.

NOTES

1.   Rosenstein-Rodan's characterization of the process of the economic development could be summed up as 'natura facit saltum' – nature does make a jump, the opposite of the dictum, 'natura non facit saltum' that Alfred Marshall thought appropriate for economics (cited in Meier and Seers, 1984, p. 207).
2.   One of the key elements of the Santa Fe approach is the notion of increasing returns or positive feedbacks. There are of course a number of approaches to increasing returns that

can be identified in the economics literature (see Arthur, 1994). There is the 'history-depen-
dent, dynamic approach' that he adopts and which also formed the backdrop for many of the
development theorists of the 1940s and 1950s (such as Rosenstein-Rodan's idea of the 'big
push'). There is also the 'imperfect-competition, static approach' that made its way into
international trade theory and is now called the 'New Trade Theory' and is commonly associated with the works of Paul Krugman and Elhanan Helpman, among others, and finally the
'deterministic-dynamic approach' of Paul Romer and others who have written on endogenous growth processes.

3. Multiplicity of equilibria, as Bardhan (1993) points out also creates more space for noneco-
nomic factors – cultural, social, and political – in influencing the process of economic movement toward an equilibrium.

4. The economic–demographic models as well as the subsequent models of learning and international specialization focus on the decisive role of 'history' and initial conditions. Development policy in this context is to compensate for an historical handicap. On the other hand,
'big-push' models emphasize the role of 'expectations' (on investment by other firms) and
the self-fulfilling nature of such expectations. In this case, the role of development policy is
to *coordinate* expectations around high investment. The writings of the development scholars in the 1950s reflect the important role accorded to 'history' and 'expectations' in equilibrium selection.

5. The idea of 'cumulative causation' of course was already present in Young (1928).

6. Sir Arthur Lewis's classic paper (1954) on surplus labor and the development of the dual
economy was an interesting exception in that it provided an explicit model that helped launch
hundreds of other papers. According to Krugman (1994, p. 47), since many of the ideas
proposed by the development theorists proved intractable to model formally, most of them
opted out of the mainstream, preferring to use 'suggestive metaphors, institutional realism,
interdisciplinary reasoning, and a relaxed attitude towards internal consistency. The result
was wonderful writing, some inspiring insights and an intellectual dead end'. Whether
Krugman's view is correct or overemphasizes the professional attachment to 'model building' is debatable, but the fact remains that these ideas did fade to the intellectual periphery
for a while. Taylor (1994) offers a slightly different view in that by the 1970s, the views of
Rosenstein-Rodan, Hirschman, Myrdal and Nurkse, simply did not fit the spirit of the times,
and that here was a case of an intellectual pendulum shift.

REFERENCES

Arthur, W.B. (1994), 'Increasing Returns and Path Dependence in the Economy',
Ann Arbor: University of Michigan Press.

Arthur, W.B. (1998), 'What Complexity can Teach us About the Economy', Presented at the 19th Annual Middlebury College Conference on Economic Issues,
Middlebury, VT.

Bardhan, P. (1993), 'Economics of Development and the Development of Economics', *Journal of Economic Perspectives*, **7**, 129–42.

Basu, K. (1997), *Analytical Development Economics*, Cambridge, MA: MIT Press.

Hirschman, A. (1958), *The Strategy of Economic Development*, New Haven: Yale
University Press.

Krugman, P. (1994), 'The Fall and Rise of Development Economics', in L. Rodwin
and D. Schon (eds), *Rethinking the Development Experience*, Washington, DC:
Brookings Institution.

Leibenstein, H. (1957), *Economics Backwardness and Economic Growth*, New York:

John Wiley.

Leijohnhufvud, A. (1981), *Information and Coordination*, Oxford: Oxford University Press.

Lewis, W.A. (1954), 'Economic Development with Unlimited Supplies of Labor', Manchester School, pp. 139–91.

Meier, G.M and D. Seers (1984), *Pioners in Development*, Oxford: Oxford University Press.

Myrdal, G. (1957), *Economic Theory and Under-Developed Regions*, New York: G. Duckworth.

Murphy, K., A. Shleifer and R. Vishny (1989), 'Industrialization and the Big-Push', *Journal of Political Economy*, **97**, 1003–26.

Nelson, R. (1956), 'A Theory of Low Level Equilibrium Trap in Underdeveloped Economics', *American Economic Review*, **46**, 894–908.

North, D. (1997), 'Some Fundamental Puzzles in Economic History and Development', in W.B. Arthur, S.N. Durlauf and D.A. Lane (eds), *The Economy as an Evolving Complex System II*, Reading, MA: Addison-Wesley.

Nurkse, R. (1953), *Problems of Capital Formation in Underdeveloped Countries*, Oxford: Oxford University Press.

Ray, D. (1997), *Development Economics*, Princeton: Princeton University Press.

Rosenstein-Rodan, P. (1943), ' Problems of Industrialization of Eastern and South-Eastern Europe', *Economic Journal*, **53**, 202–11.

Taylor, L. (1994), 'Hirschman's Strategy at Thirty-Five', in L. Rodwin and D. Schon (eds), *Rethinking the Development Experience,* Washington, DC: Brookings Institution.

Wilber, C. and Francis, S. (1986), 'The Methodological Basis of Hirschman's Development Economics: Pattern Model vs. General Laws', *World Development*, **38**.

Young, A. (1928), ' Increasing Returns and Economic Progress', *Economic Journal*, **14**, 181–94.

14. Integrating the Complexity Vision into Mathematical Economics

J. Barkley Rosser, Jr.*

This chapter will contemplate how the idea of economic complexity can be introduced into the teaching of mathematical economics. This means that it will not seek to instruct mathematically-oriented economists as to how they should go about their business. Neither will it seek to present any new breakthroughs or applications of economic complexity. Rather it will consider which concepts of complexity and what kinds of applications of those concepts would be most suitable for inclusion in textbooks on mathematical economics for the training of economists more generally. Needless to say, this will also entail a consideration of how courses in mathematical economics are currently taught and how that might change, in terms of heuristic approaches as well as in terms of content taught.

THE STATE OF THE MATHEMATICAL ECONOMICS COURSE

Mathematical economics as a course sits at a somewhat peculiar position in the economics curriculum. It is taught at both the undergraduate and graduate levels. But in the former it is generally viewed as a very advanced course that only the top students take, whereas in the latter it is often taught as a somewhat remedial course for starting graduate students who are not quite up to speed on their mathematical background and need either some review or reinforcement if not outright basic training in concepts necessary for them to survive the first year microeconomic and macroeconomic theory courses that they must take. Thus most textbooks in the field contain certain core topics that are viewed as the bare necessity, notably simple matrix algebra and calculus. They also contain applications of those concepts in both microeconomics and macroeconomics, usually with little pattern or consistency, even in those claiming to have an emphasis on 'teaching economics'. Beyond these core concepts what else is covered varies considerably from book to book.

What the common canon consists of first emerged in books that were written as more general monographs for the edification of economists, rather than initially as textbooks for established courses, most notably Allen (1938, 1959) and Samuelson (1947). Both of these classics came to be used as main or supplementary textbooks in many graduate economics programs for many years. It is not surprising that the appearance of the first edition of Allen coincided with the upsurge of use of calculus and other mathematical techniques in economics more generally in the 1930s,[1] even though that first edition lacked some elements of the common core, such as matrices. Of course there were many other books that contributed elements of what would become the core,[2] but these two represented more comprehensive coverage with emphases on the application of mathematical techniques more broadly. But, in contrast to Allen, Samuelson's *Foundations of Economic Analysis* had a goal of presenting an overview of economics as a whole while simultaneously showing how it could be presented using the constrained optimization method of the multivariable calculus.

The book that defined the canon for textbooks in mathematical economics in the way Samuelson's *Economics* did for introductory textbooks in economics for decades was Chiang's *Fundamental Methods of Mathematical Economics* (1967, 1974, 1984) which has gone through three editions. In the tradition of Samuelson's *Economics,* Chiang's book strives for inclusiveness and comprehensiveness, presenting itself as a book that the aspiring economics graduate student can keep around as a reference on many mathematical topics that might come up for many years after taking the course, even if not all of the book or the topics were covered in the course. Indeed, at 788 pages it is longer than any of its rivals in the field,[3] although not much more so than Takayama (1974, 1985) who covers optimal control theory, unlike Chiang.[4]

In the third edition of Chiang (1984) we find the following breakdown of topics. There are six parts with 21 chapters. The introduction contains two chapters, one on some general issues and the second on such mathematical concepts as real numbers, sets, and functions. The second part on static (or equilibrium) analysis has three chapters and presents matrix algebra as well as the concepts of partial and general equilibrium. The third part on comparative-static analysis has three chapters and presents basic differential calculus with some multivariable elements such as Jacobian determinants. The fourth part on optimization problems has four chapters covering such things as higher order derivatives, exponentials and logarithms, concavity and convexity, and the use of Langrangian multipliers to solve optimization problems with equality constraints with production function theory as an application. The fifth part on dynamic analysis has six chapters covering basic integral calculus and growth models, first-order and higher-order differential equations, first-order and higher-order difference equations, with the cobweb model and the multiplier-accelerator model being examples used, and then simultaneous differential and difference equations including a presentation of phase diagrams and the Taylor expansion with applications to dynamic input–output models and inflation–unemployment models. The final part on mathematical programming has three chapters covering both linear and nonlinear programming.[5] This is the standard canon of textbook mathematical economics as it has been for several decades now, a broad overview of mathematical techniques with a healthy smattering of applications that the typical graduate student would be likely to encounter in his or her theory classes.

Besides being universally shorter, more recent rivals to Chiang have gone in several directions. Of course all attempt to have more up-to-date applications compared to the occasionally almost dinosauric examples found in Chiang. One approach is to be much simpler with many fewer topics. Thus, Toumanoff and Nourzad (1994) do not cover integral calculus, differential or difference equations, or nonlinear programming. Another is to replace many topics with something viewed as more current. Thus Baldani, Bradfield and Turner (1996) remove what Toumanoff and Nourzad do as well as linear programming, but then add a chapter on envelope theorems and four chapters (out of 18 total) on static and dynamic game theory. Some attempt to be a bit more advanced than Chiang, while basically following his approach. Thus Klein (1998) covers most of what he does in a more compressed manner, as well as optimal control theory with applications to infinite horizon optimization problems. Others focus more on presenting economic concepts first with the mathematics being brought in as one goes along, for example Silberberg (1978, 1990). Some books that are not strictly mathematical economics textbooks follow such an approach but with an emphasis upon the application of a particular mathematical idea or approach, such as Nikaido (1968) and Mas-Colell (1985).

Others specialize in following more idiosyncratic paths in terms of presentation and examples, while still covering most of the same mathematical topics found in Chiang. Thus, one finds methodologist Hands (1991) presenting somewhat more unusual examples in boxes, ranging from international trade theory with monopolistic competition through analytic Marxian value theory to the Scarf and Gale counterexamples to Walrasian stability. In one box (ibid., pp. 65–7) he discusses chaos theory, the only example I am aware of in an existing mathematical economics textbook of a discussion of economic complexity as defined below.

One final point of some significance must be noted about all of these books. None involves any use of computer simulation exercises. It is reasonable to expect that this is something that will change. But there are important pressures to remain dependent on the existing path. A central purpose of these books is to provide students with the tools they need to pass graduate theory courses and ultimately a graduate preliminary or qualifying exam. Such exams are not carried out in interactive computer simulation environments, but involve solving problems with pen or pencil and paper. As long as this remains the pedagogical bottom line, this need for these books to instruct in how to solve such problems will remain paramount, irrespective of exactly which such problems are viewed as most important. Given that an increasing amount of complex dynamics is studied through computer simulation, this is a profoundly important barrier to its integration into standard mathematical economics textbooks.

WHAT IS ECONOMIC COMPLEXITY? A GENERAL PERSPECTIVE

In *The End of Science*, Horgan (1997) complains about 'chaoplexologists' and how there are at least 45 different definitions of 'complexity', according to a compilation by Seth Lloyd, with most of these involving measures of information, entropy, or degree of difficulty of computability of a system.[6] Obviously there is no single or simple way to define something as complex as complexity, although we shall try to do so. Like many others such as the popularizer Waldrop (1992), Horgan sees it as to some degree whatever people at the Santa Fe Institute do, the Mecca of complexity theory. Thus, it is tempting to fall back on this and say that it is what one finds in such volumes as Anderson, Arrow and Pines (1988) or Arthur, Durlauf and Lane (1997a). But this really will not do.

Now another issue involves how narrow a definition one should use. Thus, in his critique of complexity theory, Horgan sneers that it is just the latest in a long line of failed fads and that its days are numbered too as it inevitably encounters its limits and ends. These earlier fads that he dismisses include cybernetics (Wiener 1948, 1961), catastrophe theory (Thom 1972), and chaos theory (Gleick 1987, Ruelle 1990). Unsurprisingly and understandably, some advocates of complexity theory have attempted to disassociate it from these allegedly discredited or passé earlier ideas and movements.[7] But perhaps the advocates of complexity theory should follow the example of the Impressionist painters who adopted the name bestowed upon them by their critics and accept with pleasure the charges that have been made by Horgan and others. In short, as argued in Rosser (1991), there is a fundamental linkage between these various approaches, a linkage that should not only be admitted and recognized, but celebrated. Current complexity theory is indeed the offspring of these earlier ideas.

A useful 'big tent' definition can be found in Day (1994). Complex dynamics are those that for nonstochastic reasons do not converge to either a unique equilibrium point or to a periodic limit cycle, or that explode. This implies some form of erratic oscillations of an endogenous nature, not merely the result of erratic exogenous shocks.[8] A necessary but not sufficient condition for such complex behavior is that the dynamical system as defined by its differential or difference equations contains some element of nonlinearity. This is a common element that one finds all the way from the nonlinear feedback mechanisms in the old cybernetics and general systems models, through the multiple equilibria with associated potential discontinuous behavior of the catastrophe theory models, through the butterfly effect phenomenon and irregularities arising with sufficiently great nonlinearity in the chaos models, and including the various kinds of self-organizing emergent phenomena and path dependence associated with increasing returns found in some of the more recent Santa Fe-type complexity models.

This is not the place to carry out an in-depth review of the various varieties of complex dynamics.[9] However, we shall attempt a very brief and superficial review of several of the concepts that might conceivably show up in future mathematical economics textbooks. We shall not review further ideas associated with cybernetics as most of those that are useful are by now more or less fully embedded in the systems and models used by those associated with the Santa Fe Institute.[10]

As regards catastrophe theory, what is probably the most important idea associated with it can be learned without getting into the detailed mechanics of catastrophe theory itself. That idea is that nonlinearity can imply multiple equilibria with discontinuous endogenous shifts arising from continuously varying exogenous changes. Such an idea has been used to explain business cycles through a cusp catastrophe model with a Kaldorian investment function (Varian 1979), sudden shifts in city size when there are both increasing and decreasing returns to city size (Casetti 1980, Dendrinos and Rosser 1992), as well as explaining how the demand for a currency as a reserve currency can suddenly collapse (Krugman 1984). A few math econ textbooks have some presentation of multiple equilibria, usually in conjunction with some stability analysis (Hands 1991; Baldani, Bradfield and Turner 1996), but rarely is much done with this. Samuelson (1947) and Mas-Colell (1985) are exceptions to that generalization, but then as noted above neither is properly a math econ textbook, despite occasional use in such courses.

A more likely candidate for explicit treatment is chaos theory which opens up a variety of related complex dynamic phenomena. There remains some disagreement regarding exactly what chaos is in deterministic systems, but one element that is by now universally agreed upon is sensitive dependence on initial conditions (SDIC), more popularly known as the 'butterfly effect'. This involves a local instability that arises when there is a slight change in a parameter value or a starting value.[11] The system will then rapidly diverge from the path it would have followed otherwise.[12] At the same time the system's behavior will remain bounded while appearing to be random in some sense and will even eventually return arbitrarily close to its original path, however briefly. Such behavior can arise even in quite simple single equation models such as the logistic equation as studied by May (1976) which has been extensively employed in economic models exhibiting chaotic dynamics. We note that even though the dynamics involved are not truly mathematically chaotic, an analogue of the butterfly effect shows up in the models of path dependence with regard to the role of chance at certain critical points when the choice of a path is made (Arthur 1989).

Horgan (1997) argues that chaos theory has reached its limits partly by focusing on the important figure of Mitchell Feigenbaum who, according to Horgan, has not had a serious new idea about chaos theory since 1989. Whether or not this is the case, there have certainly been some interesting new developments in economics regarding the application of chaos theory, at least theoretically. Among these are the idea of controlling chaos (Kaas 1998), the analysis of multi-dimensional chaos through the use of global bifurcations (Goeree, Hommes and Weddepohl 1998), and the discovery that simple adaptive mechanisms can mimic truly chaotic dynamics leading to the possibility of 'learning to believe in chaos' (Grandmont 1998, Hommes and Sorger 1998; Sorger 1998). Applications of chaos theory to economic applications that are used in such math econ texts as Chiang include cobweb dynamics models (Chiarella 1988, Hommes 1991), duopoly dynamics (Rand 1978, Puu 1998), and business cycle models (Benhabib and Day 1982, Grandmont 1985).

Closely related to chaotic dynamics, but distinct, is the concept of strange attractors. An attractor is the set to which a dynamical system asymptotically tends to move if it is within what is known as the basin boundary of the attractor. Strange attractors have complicated shapes that possess a non-integer dimensionality that is labeled 'fractal' (Mandelbrot 1983). Many systems that follow strange attractors also exhibit chaotic dynamics. But it is possible for non-chaotic systems to have strange attractors and for chaotic systems not to have strange attractors (Eckmann and Ruelle 1985). Any system that has a strange attractor will exhibit complex dynamics according to our definition given above. The first economic model constructed that possessed a non-chaotic strange attractor was due to Lorenz (1992, 1993b) and is a variant of the same Kaldor (1940) trade cycle model studied by Varian (1979).

Even though there may be neither chaotic dynamics nor strange attractors, if there is more than one attractor point (often a multiple equilibria situation), then it is possible that the boundaries separating the basins of attraction of each attractor may have an erratic or fractal shape (McDonald, Grebogi, Ott and Yorke 1985). In such a case, small exogenous shocks can cause very large changes as the system jumps easily from one basin of attraction to another. The model of Lorenz (1992, 1993b) noted above was also the first economic model to exhibit such fractal basin boundaries, yet another source of potentially complex dynamics. Other examples include Brock and Hommes (1997a) for market prices, Rosser and Rosser (1996) for transition economy dynamics, and Feldpausch (1997) for ecological-economic systems.

WHAT IS ECONOMIC COMPLEXITY? THE SANTA FE PERSPECTIVE

So far the models we have looked at could involve equilibria, however complex or unreached, and possibly even fully informed, homogeneous and rational agents. However, some associated with the Santa Fe Institute (SFI) have argued for a narrower, 'small tent' definition of complex dynamics, averring that these earlier models are not truly complex. Those advocating such a position have not put forward a succinct definition of what complex dynamics are, and indeed may well face the Horgan criticism regarding too many such definitions or no definition at all. Rather they have preferred to put forward sets of characteristics or principles that should be associated with truly complex systems.

Arthur, Durlauf and Lane (1997b) list six such principles or characteristics: (1) dispersed interaction, that there are many probably heterogeneous agents interacting only with some of the others possibly over space; (2) no global controller or competitor that can exploit all opportunities in the economy or the interactions in the system;[13] (3) cross-cutting hierarchical organization with many tangled interactions;[14] (4) continual adaptation by learning and evolving agents; (5) perpetual novelty as new markets, technologies, behaviors and institutions create new niches in the 'ecology' of the system, and (6) out-of-equilibrium dynamics with there possibly being no equilibrium at all or one or many that are constantly being changed or created with the system never being near some global optimum. All of this is seen as being consistent with notions of bounded rationality rather than full rational expectations on the part of agents (Sargent 1993). Although there continues to be considerable amounts of work done analytically fitting these criteria, increasingly the trend is for such studies to be carried out using computer simulations.

A number of approaches have arisen that incorporate many of these elements for developing economic models. One is to explicitly model the behaviors of a set of identified heterogeneous agents who evolve strategies over time in response to events and the behavior of the other agents. One useful technique for modeling such adaptive behavior by such agents has been the use of genetic algorithms developed by Holland (1992). Dawid (1996) reflects a broad application of this approach to various economic issues. A closely related approach involves the use of 'artificial life' algorithms (Langton 1989). Epstein and Axtell (1996), Tesfatsion (1997) and Axtell (1999) provide economics applications.

One major adaptation of these approaches has been the development of inductive learning models of financial market behavior with heterogeneous agents. The famous paper on noise traders by Black (1986) and the stock market crash of 1987 stimulated the emergence of models with heterogeneous agents, including some with chaotic speculative bubble dynamics (Day and Huang 1990).[15] More recently researchers at the SFI have developed a model along these lines of stock market dynamics with numerous 'adaptively rational' agents (Palmer et al. 1994, Arthur et al. 1997a). These models show a variety of the complex behaviors in the above list. The market never settles down to an equilibrium, although it may exhibit considerable regularity for periods of time, only to experience outbreaks of bubble-like behavior from time to time.

An important analytic analogue of this simulation model is due to Brock and Hommes (1997a). Rather than allowing agents to evolve a multiplicity of strategies, they restrict them to two, a stabilizing but information-costly rational expectations one and a destabilizing but information-cheap rule-of-thumb one, drawn from cobweb dynamics. They also draw on another strand of ideas that have been widely influential at SFI, that of interacting particle systems (IPS), also known as spin glass models (Kac 1968, Spitzer 1971), originally developed to explain phase transitions in states of matter such as the boiling or freezing of water and first applied in economics by Föllmer (1974). Brock (1993) and Durlauf (1997) discuss the mean-field variant of such models. In these models agents make discrete choices that depend on the general state of others' choices as well as their own willingness to change their choices.[16] Brock and Hommes (1997a) analytically establish a wide array of complex dynamics for this model, including such already mentioned phenomena as chaotic dynamics and fractal basin boundaries.

Rosser and Rosser (1997, 1998) use the IPS framework to examine macroeconomic collapse in transitional economies. This is seen as the implosion of a transitional economy to a high unemployment regime as a phase transition resulting from institutional breakdown generates a coordination failure in the economy. The negative dynamics arise when unemployment becomes so high that taxes for unemployment compensation push wages up in the private sector more than the high unemployment rate is pushing them down. Other examples of applications of this IPS approach include Durlauf (1996) to neighborhood composition dynamics and Kulkarni, Stough and

Haynes (1997) to highway congestion dynamics.

An unsurprising extension of this kind of modeling involves laying out explicitly the specific relations between agents in a spatial or lattice framework. One set of models resulting from this approach are the 'sandpile' or 'self-organized criticality' models (Bak 1996).[17] Given a specific lattice arrangement, the system self-organizes to a poised out-of-equilibrium state that is then subject to a skewed distribution of 'avalanches' of varying sizes that arise from steady exogenous shocks, as with sand pebbles being dropped on a sandpile. These various responses reflect the ricocheting through the lattice of these external impacts. This approach differs from the IPS one in that exogenous shocks trigger the reactions, whereas in the IPS models the variation of a control parameter that is analogous to temperature in the original statistical mechanics literature is what triggers the discontinuous behavior. The most prominent example of an application to economics is a model of macroeconomic fluctuations due to Bak et al. (1993).

Another strand that is sometimes placed into a spatial context involves the issue of increasing returns and path dependence. The non-spatial variety generally focuses on technology and the question of lock-in (Arthur 1989). However, the more spatial variety in the form of self-organizing models of urban and regional economic organization has drawn on the Brussels School work of Ilya Prigogine (Allen and Sanglier 1981, Prigogine and Stengers 1984) and the synergetics approach of Haken (1977) in Stuttgart (Weidlich and Haag 1983, 1987). Arthur (1988) and Krugman (1996) also discuss such models.

Finally, although game theory has been viewed by some as an example of distinctly non-complex dynamics, there has recently been a trend towards modeling dynamic evolutionary games that has opened the door to what appear to be complex dynamics. Some of these involve incorporating mean-field IPS elements as well as specific neighbor interaction effects in the evolutionary process. Examples include Foster and Young (1990), Blume (1993), Lindgren and Nordahl (1994), Lindgren (1997) and Darley and Kauffman (1997).

Clearly, although we have characterized this view of complex dynamics as being 'small tent', it encompasses a wide variety of approaches and models, again so many that it is open to the complaints and criticisms of Horgan that 'complexity leads to perplexity'. Nevertheless, with its very openness and its reliance on the increasingly important tool of computer simulation, one would be hard-pressed to agree with Horgan that this particular variant of complexity is about to run out of steam or into any truly serious limits any time soon.

WHAT IS TO BE DONE?

In some textbook publishing circles one hears of a '15 percent rule', that no new textbook should deviate from existing dominant texts in a particular field by more than 15 percent in content if it is to do well in the market.[18] Unfortunately, a strong reason for this is the sheer inertia, if not outright laziness, of professors who like to teach out of old notes with little variation over time, even as they change the textbooks they use. We have implicitly already seen this rule at work in mathematical economics in that Chiang replaced Allen as the dominant text and has a very similar outline of its chapters and topics covered. One must add to this the inertia in math econ already noted above by the need to teach students to solve 'paper and pencil' calculation types of problems that limits introducing computer simulation techniques, at least in a major way, for the near future. Any effort to integrate the complexity vision into the teaching of mathematical economics must take into account these facts if it is to be remotely successful.

Given these constraints, there is no way that all of the various topics so briefly covered above can be seriously taught in a math econ textbook. Nevertheless, there appear to be some real openings for at least some topics and some coverage, especially in some of the books. Of course one way to go is that of Hands (1991), to introduce complexity ideas as special oddball topics placed in boxes, a recent trend in textbooks in general.[19] But this seems to be a somewhat limited and limiting approach. One would hope to have a deeper and fuller integration of the topic or topics into the core material itself, not have it merely presented as some kind of oddball special case freak show for students to gawk at as they pass on by to the 'really important stuff'. But which topics will get covered and how will depend on the nature of the textbook, with more coverage likely in those books that are more oriented to dynamics, are more high level, and are more comprehensive.

The least amount of coverage is likely to happen in the narrowest and lowest level books, such as Toumanoff and Nourzad (1994) that barely covers the minimum of the most basic core of simple linear algebra and differential calculus. However, even in a book such as this there are openings. One that may also be useful in other kinds of textbooks involves the idea of increasing returns and path dependence. This book has a chapter on production theory and virtually all discussions of production theory have some kind of discussion of returns to scale. There is an obvious entry point for bringing in the Arthur type arguments as well as such possible material as that of the learning curve as presented by Rothschild (1990). Of course these arguments involve dynamics to some extent, but do not necessarily involve differential or difference equations per se, which tend not to show up in such chapters in such books. Indeed, Toumanoff and Nourzad have no coverage of them at all.

Yet another possible opening for such a text is the basic question of multiple equilibria and the possibility of discontinuous dynamics that can arise in such situations. One does not need to bring in catastrophe theory for such a discussion, indeed it is probably not advisable given the rather specialized material on gradient dynamics and so forth that is involved. The sort of models discussed above are probably too specialized or esoteric for a book like Toumanoff and Nourzad, dealing with foreign exchange markets, Kaldorian business cycle models, or urban economics. But what can happen when there is a backward-bending supply curve with an increasing demand may be more amenable and more basic. This example depicts what many bioeconomists think holds for many fisheries and possibly explains the real-world phenomenon of the collapses of fisheries (Copes 1970, Clark 1976), something very much in the news and to which students can relate.[20]

When we get to the broad center of established math econ texts as represented by Chiang, there is a very obvious opening in addition to those already listed. Any text that deals in a reasonably serious way with differential or difference equations has that section as an obvious entry point for complexity material, especially as we have defined it as essentially being a special case of nonlinear dynamics. Chiang in particular in his presentation of difference equations uses two examples that have been shown as potentially exhibiting chaotic dynamics and in some cases a wide variety of other complex dynamics, the cobweb model and the multiplier-accelerator model. With regard to the first, one can start out rather simply, and then allowing for nonlinearities of the supply and demand curves or various lags, one can begin to derive more complex dynamics. The classic agricultural examples can be used as with Chavas and Holt (1993). Furthermore the questions of heterogeneous agents and their interactions can be brought in by introducing the kind of analysis in Brock and Hommes (1997a). One probably would not want to go to the full array of complex dynamics that they investigate, but a door can be opened here as well for the use of computer simulation methods as the student varies the parameters and assumptions. In such cases the student may well discover some of these more unusual outcomes on his or her own initiative. A variety of software systems may be useful for this including MATLAB and STELLA (Ruth and Hannon 1997). But this awaits the qualitative jump to using computer simulation in such textbooks which is probably near but has not yet arrived.

It is a curious testament to the inertia invoked by the 15 percent rule that certain kinds of examples have persisted in math econ texts even up to relatively recent and high-powered ones, even when such examples have largely disappeared from the field texts from which they are presumably drawn. Thus, even as recent and relatively advanced a text as Klein (1998) still presents the multiplier-accelerator model, following on the example of Chiang, even though one would be hard pressed to find an intermediate or advanced macroeconomics text that contains it. But, of course, modern new classical macroeconomics tends to emphasize exogenous shock models with rational expectations with representative agents, the very antithesis of what the complexity vision sees for macroeconomics (Colander 1996). Such models do not display the kinds of endogenous fluctuations that a nice difference equation model generates. One could of course be more up-to-date and use an overlapping generations model such as one finds in Benhabib and Day (1982) or in Grandmont (1985). But it remains possible to use a nonlinear version of the traditional multiplier-accelerator model[21] to show at least chaotic dynamics (Blatt 1983, Gabisch 1984), if not more complex outcomes. Most of these outcomes can be shown analytically, although it is certainly possible to develop these results in a simulation environment where students can see such things as transitions to chaos.

It remains unclear what might be the best way to introduce the full array of Santa Fe types of models as discussed above. Certainly they will need to await the fuller introduction of computer simulation techniques into these textbooks. We may see students some day in math econ courses spending time running descendants of the artificial life program SUGARSCAPE (Epstein and Axtell 1996). But, much as Horgan criticizes these models as mere artificialities that do not really tell people what is going on in real societies, so many math econ professors may well be concerned that excessive time spent on what may be very intriguing programs of such sorts is really a diversion from learning the hard core sorts of material that they need to learn for their prelims, such as how to test for second-order conditions in a multivariable constrained optimization problem by solving for the determinants of Jacobian matrices. The full implementation and use of such Santa Fe type complexity programs may need to await a clearer way of tying them to demonstrating core material.

One option that may be becoming more possible is through dynamic evolutionary game theory as described above. There certainly is a trend towards the increasing use of game theory in microeconomics in general, although much of this is very non-complex. This trend has even begun to show up in some math econ texts as in Baldani, Bradfield and Turner (1996). A real opening here might be the introduction of programs with iterated versions of some classic game theory cases such as the prisoner's dilemma, as discussed for example in Lindgren (1997). As noted, Lindgren deals with a number of other complexity phenomena and issues such as the mean-field IPS approach and questions regarding sequential decision making and decision trees. It may well be that in the longer run, evolutionary dynamic game theory will provide an entry for using computer simulation techniques to demonstrate various kinds of complex dynamics in mathematical economics textbooks.

CONCLUSIONS

We have reviewed the troops in existing mathematical economics textbooks intended for use at either the upper undergraduate or low to middle graduate level. These universally cover certain core topics, especially basic linear algebra and differential calculus, and most cover a number of other topics such as linear programming, difference and differential equations, and sometimes optimal control theory or game theory. Almost none of these cover anything that can be called complex dynamics, although when they do so, it may be as a special oddball case to be put in a special box. We have also reviewed a wide variety of complex dynamics with a heavier emphasis on those associated with chaotic dynamics or with the variety of approaches that have emerged from the Santa Fe Institute.

It is recommended that, at least initially, examples should be brought into topical areas where they fit easily in an analytical form and where examples are already being used that can easily be shown to exhibit complex dynamics of one sort or another. Leading candidates include increasing returns in sections on production theory, multiple equilibria in sections on equilibrium, fuller examination of cobweb models when these are used in sections on difference equations, and likewise of multiplier–accelerator models when these appear.

The fuller integration of the Santa Fe types of complex dynamics will probably have to come with the introduction of computer simulation software packages into math econ textbooks, something which may be resisted more than many might expect given the nature of the course and the expectations of its necessary role, especially in preparing graduate students in economics for passing their graduate micro and macro theory courses and then their prelim exams. Nevertheless, this introduction will surely eventually arrive and the introduction of Santa Fe ideas will then be much easier, with models of evolutionary, dynamic game theory possibly being an opening wedge in this endeavor. Yet another may well be the kinds of models of financial markets that have been developed with heterogeneous agents with evolutionary strategies, although the entry point for such models may arise from looking at the simple cobweb model initially and then expanding the study of it by simulation software.

Thus, there will certainly be resistance to integrating the complexity vision into mathematical economics textbooks. But there appear to be a number of promising entry points for introducing and integrating analytical models of economic complexity in the near future, with the prospects likely to improve as time proceeds and computer simulation exercises become standard in such textbooks.

NOTES

*   The author acknowledges receipt of useful materials from Bruce Brunton and David Horlacher and useful comments from David Colander. The usual qualifying caveat applies.
1.   Cournot (1838) is generally credited with first using calculus in an economics application. Walras (1874) used systems of linear equations, if not matrices explicitly, as well as calculus, and first formalized the idea of general equilibrium. Some argue that matrices are implicit in Quesnay's *Tableau Économique* from the mid-1700s. Mirowski (1986) argues that these applications are not proper and that the first true mathematical economist was Marx. For discussion of early appearance of complex dynamics in economics see Rosser (1999a).
2.   Important among these were Koopmans (1951) and Dorfman, Samuelson and Solow (1958) for linear programming and Burmeister and Dobell (1970) and Intriligator (1971) for growth theory and optimal control theory, the latter not necessarily in the basic common core.
3.   There seems to have been a general trend in recent years, with a few exceptions, to shorter textbooks in many fields of economics. This author is aware of an unofficial rule among some publishers of an upper limit of 600 pages for upper level textbooks. This may be a good thing.
4.   Chiang (1992) more than makes up for this lacuna.
5.   Actually this outline is not that different from that found in Allen (1959). A few differences are that Allen has matrices and linear algebra near the end, does not cover linear or nonlinear programming, but has some calculus of variations, arguably the foundation for optimal control theory.
6.   For a list of the 45 concepts, if not their precise definitions or references to those, see footnote 11 to Chapter 8 on pp. 303–4 in Horgan (1997).
7.   In some cases the discrediting during the busts after the booms of the fads has been way overdone by the economics profession. Thus, the most prominent criticism of catastrophe theory's use in economics came from Zahler and Sussman (1977) who criticized Zeeman's (1974) stock market model because it had heterogeneous agents with some not possessing rational expectations. However, making such assumptions has become standard in many financial economics models, not just those coming out of Santa Fe, and this criticism now looks ridiculous. But the baby got thrown out with the bathwater and most people have forgotten why, only that it was for supposedly good reasons.
8.   Although this is labeled a big tent definition, it does not cover some uses of the term 'complexity' in economics, for example by Pryor (1995) or by Stodder (1995, 1997).
9.   Some useful summarizing sources include Anderson, Arrow and Pines (1988), Arthur (1994), Arthur, Durlauf and Lane (1997a), Bak (1996), Barnett, Geweke and Shell (1989), Brock (1993), Brock, Hsieh and LeBaron (1991), Day (1994), Dechert (1996), Guastello (1995), Holland (1992), Kauffman (1993), Lorenz (1993a), Mandelbrot (1983), Nicolis and Prigogine (1989), Peitgen, Jürgens and Saupe (1992), Puu (1997), Rosser (1991, 1996, 1998, 1999b) and Zhang (1991), although some of these do not cover the full range of topics involved.
10. One line of development here is from the work of Forrester (1961) who argued that complex nonlinear feedback cybernetic systems could generate 'counterintuitive' sudden changes. His work directly influenced the chaos theory models of Sterman (1989) and his associates, many of whom are now doing more Santa Fe type complexity models.
11. Gleick (1987) identifies Lorenz (1963) as having both discovered and coined this idea, although it had been known in some form since at least Poincaré (1880–90). In his 1963 article Lorenz does not call it either sensitive dependence on initial conditions or the butterfly effect. He coined this term in a speech. This may account for the different versions of just where the butterfly flapping its wings is supposedly located that is causing hurricanes in which other distant location.
12. A sufficient condition for this to hold is that the largest real part of the Lyapunov exponents be positive (Oseledec 1968). Dechert (1996) contains discussions of the methods and diffi-

culties involved in empirically estimating these. There is great skepticism that any economic time series actually exhibits true mathematical chaos (Jaditz and Sayers 1993, LeBaron 1994), despite some who argue to the contrary (Blank 1991, Chavas and Holt 1993).

13. This aspect is very consistent with ideas of some Austrian economists who emphasize that complex dynamics lead to emergent self-organization in decentralized free market economies (Hayek 1948, 1967, Lavoie 1989).

14. For discussions of hierarchy dynamics see Nicolis (1986), Holling (1992), Rosser (1994, 1995), and Rosser et al. (1994). See Simon (1962) for the foundations of hierarchy theory.

15. For an application of this model see Ahmed et al. (1997). For broader reviews see Brock (1997), Brock and Hommes (1997b), and Rosser (1997).

16. The emphasis on agents concerning themselves with the opinions and expectations of others was emphasized by Keynes (1936) in his famous 'beauty contest' example. Logical problems that can arise when agents begin thinking seriously about other agents thinking about their thinking and so forth have been analyzed by Binmore (1987) and Koppl and Rosser (1998).

17. Somewhat related to this approach is the 'edge of chaos' model of evolutionary dynamics (Kauffman 1993, 1995, Kauffman and Johnsen 1991). However, this has yet to directly generate any economics applications, despite some influence on discussions and modeling.

18. This author first heard of this from David Colander, but has heard it repeated by some textbook publishers as well.

19. It is a bit odd that Hands placed his box on chaos theory early in the book in the chapter on single-variable calculus models rather than in the chapters dealing explicitly with dynamics.

20. Hommes and Rosser (1999) show how chaotic dynamics can arise in this fishery example with agents following simple adaptive rules with consistent expectations.

21. Samuelson (1939) first suggested possible nonlinearity of the consumption function in the multiplier-accelerator model.

REFERENCES

Ahmed, E., R. Koppl., J.B. Rosser, Jr. and M.V. White (1997), 'Complex Bubble Persistence in Closed-End Country Funds', *Journal of Economic Behavior and Organization*, **32**, 19–37.

Allen, P.M. and M. Sanglier (1981), 'Urban Evolution, Self-Organization, and Decision Making', *Environment and Planning A*, **13**, 167–83.

Allen, R.G.D. (1938) (1959, 2nd edn), *Mathematical Analysis for Economists*, London: Macmillan.

Anderson, P.W., K.J. Arrow and D. Pines (eds) (1988), *The Economy as an Evolving Complex System*, Reading, MA: Addison-Wesley.

Arthur, W.B. (1988), 'Self-Reinforcing Mechanisms in Economics', in P.W. Anderson, K.J. Arrow and D. Pines (eds), *The Economy as an Evolving Complex System*, Reading, MA: Addison-Wesley, pp. 9–31.

Arthur, W.B. (1989), 'Competing Technologies, Increasing Returns, and Lock-In by Historical Events', *Economic Journal*, **99**, 116–31.

Arthur, W.B. (1994), *Increasing Returns and Path Dependence in the Economy*, Ann Arbor: University of Michigan Press.

Arthur, W.B., S.N. Durlauf and D.A. Lane (eds) (1997a), *The Economy as an Evolving Complex System II*, Reading, MA: Addison-Wesley.

Arthur, W.B., S.N. Durlauf and D.A. Lane (eds) (1997b), 'Introduction', in their,

The Economy as an Evolving Complex System II, Reading, MA: Addison-Wesley, 1–14.

Arthur, W.B., J.H. Holland, R.P. Baron and P. Tayler (1997), 'Asset Pricing Under Endogenous Expectations in an Artificial Stock Market', in W.B. Arthur, S.N. Durlauf and D.A. Lane (eds), *The Economy as an Evolving Complex System II*, Reading, MA: Addison-Wesley, pp. 15–44.

Axtell, R.L. (1999), 'The Emergence of Firms in a Population of Agents: Local Increasing Returns, Unstable Nash Equilibria, and Power Law Size Distributions', Santa Fe Institute Working Paper 99-03-019E.

Bak, P. (1996), *How Nature Works: The Science of Self-Organized Criticality*, New York: Copernicus Press for Springer-Verlag.

Bak, P., K. Chen, J. Scheinkman and M. Woodford (1993), 'Aggregate Fluctuations from Independent Sectoral Shocks: Self-Organized Criticality in a Model of Production and Inventory', *Ricerche Economiche*, **47**, 3–30.

Baldani, J., J. Bradfiel and R. Turner (1996), *Mathematical Economics*, Fort Worth: Dryden Press.

Barnett, W.A., J. Geweke and K. Shell (eds) (1989), *Economic Complexity: Chaos, Sunspots, Bubbles, and Nonlinearity*, Cambridge, UK: Cambridge University Press.

Benhabib, J. and R.H. Day (1982), 'A Characterization of Erratic Dynamics in the Overlapping Generations Model', *Journal of Economic Dynamics and Control*, **13**, 379–400.

Binmore, K. (1987), 'Modeling Rational Players I', *Economics and Philosophy*, **3**, 9–55.

Black, F. (1986), 'Noise', *Journal of Finance*, **41**, 529–43.

Blank, S.C. (1991), '"Chaos" in the Financial Markets? A Nonlinear Dynamical Analysis', *Journal of Futures Markets*, **11**, 711–28. Also in Dechert (1996), 479–96.

Blatt, J.M. (1983), *Dynamic Economic Systems: A Post-Keynesian Approach*, Armonk, NY: M.E. Sharpe.

Blume, L.E. (1993), 'The Statistical Mechanics of Strategic Interaction', *Games and Economic Behavior*, **5**, 387–426.

Brock, W.A. (1993), 'Pathways to Randomness in the Economy: Emergent Nonlinearity and Chaos in Economics and Finance', *Estudios Económicos*, **8**, 3–55. Also in Dechert (1996), 3–55.

Brock, W.A. (1997), 'Asset Price Behavior in Complex Environments', in W.B. Arthur, S.N. Durlauf and D.A. Lane (eds), *The Economy as an Evolving Complex System II*, Reading, MA: Addison-Wesley, 385–423.

Brock, W.A. and C.H. Hommes (1997a), 'A Rational Route to Randomness', *Econometrica*, **65**, 1059–95.

Brock, W.A. and H.C. Hommes (1997b), 'Models of Complexity in Economics and Finance', in C. Heij, H. Schumacher, B. Hanzon and K. Praagman (eds), *System Dynamics in Economic and Financial Models*, New York: John Wiley & Sons, pp. 3–44.

Brock, W.A., D. Hsieh and B. LeBaron (1991), *Nonlinear Dynamics, Chaos, and Instability: Statistical Theory and Economic Evidence*, Cambridge, MA: MIT Press.

Burmeister, E. and A.R. Dobell (1970), *Mathematical Theories of Economic Growth*, New York: Macmillan.

Casetti, E. (1980), 'Equilibrium Population Partitions Between Urban and Agricultural Occupations', *Geographical Analysis*, **12**, 47–54.

Chavas, J.P. and M.T. Holt (1993), 'Market Instability and Nonlinear Dynamics', *American Journal of Agricultural Economics*, **75**, 819–28. Also in Dechert (1996), 322–9.

Chiang, A.C. (1967) (1974, 2nd edn) (1984, 3rd edn), *Fundamental Methods of Mathematical Economics*, New York: McGraw-Hill.

Chiang, A.C. (1992), *Elements of Dynamic Optimization*. New York: McGraw-Hill.

Chiarella, C. (1988), 'The Cobweb Model: Its Instability and the Onset of Chaos', *Economic Modelling*, **5**, 377–84.

Clark, C.W. (1976), (1990, 2nd edn), *Mathematical Bioeconomics*, New York: Wiley-Interscience.

Colander, D.C. (1996), 'Overview', in D.C. Colander (ed.), *Beyond Microfoundations: Post Walrasian Macroeconomics*, Cambridge, UK: Cambridge University Press, pp. 1–17.

Copes, P. (1970), 'The Backward-Bending Supply Curve of the Fishing Industry', *Scottish Journal of Political Economy*, **17**, 69–77.

Cournot, A. (1838), *Récherches sur les Principes Mathématiques de la Théorie de la Richesse*, Paris: Hachette.

Darley, V.M. and S.A. Kauffman (1997), 'Natural Rationality', in W.B. Arthur, S.N. Durlauf and D.A. Lane (eds), *The Economy as an Evolving Complex System II*, Reading, MA: Addison-Wesley, pp. 45–80.

Dawid, H. (1996), *Adaptive Learning by Genetic Algorithms: Analytical Results and Applications to Economic Models*, Heidelberg: Springer-Verlag.

Day, R.H. (1994), *Complex Economic Dynamics, Volume I: An Introduction to Dynamical Systems and Market Mechanisms*, Cambridge, MA: MIT Press.

Day, R.H. and W. Huang (1990), 'Bulls, Bears and Market Sheep', *Journal of Economic Behavior and Organization*, **14**, 299–329.

Dechert, W.D. (ed.) (1996), *Chaos Theory in Economics: Methods, Models and Evidence*, Aldershot: Edward Elgar.

Dendrinos, D.S. and J.B. Rosser, Jr. (1992), 'Fundamental Issues in Nonlinear Urban Population Dynamic Models', *Annals of Regional Science*, **26**, 135–45.

Dorfman, R., P.A. Samuelson and R.M. Solow, (1958), *Linear Programming and Economic Analysis*, New York: McGraw-Hill.

Durlauf, S.N. (1996), 'Neighborhood Feedbacks, Endogenous Stratification, and Income Inequality', in W.A. Barnett, G. Gandolfo and C. Hillinger (eds), *Dynamic Disequilibrium Modelling: Proceedings of the Ninth International Symposium on Economic Theory and Econometrics*, Cambridge, UK: Cambridge University Press, pp. 505–34.

Durlauf, S.N. (1997), 'Statistical Mechanics Approaches to Socioeconomic Behavior', in W.B. Arthur, S.N. Durlauf and D.A. Lane (eds), *The Economy as an Evolving Complex System II*, Reading, MA: Addison-Wesley, pp. 81–104.

Eckmann, J.P. and D. Ruelle (1985), 'Ergodic Theory of Chaos and Strange Attractors', *Review of Modern Physics*, **57**, 617–56.

Epstein, J.M. and R. Axtel (1996), *Growing Artificial Societies from the Bottom Up*,

Cambridge, MA: MIT Press.

Feldpausch, C.M. (1997), *The Political Economy of Chaos: Multiple Equilibria and Fractal Basin Boundaries in a Nonlinear Environmental Economy*, PhD Dissertation, American University.

Föllmer, H. (1974), 'Random Economies with Many Interacting Agents', *Journal of Mathematical Economics*, **1**, 51–62.

Forrester, J.W. (1961), *Industrial Dynamics*, Cambridge, MA: MIT Press.

Foster, D. and P. Young (1990), 'Stochastic Evolutionary Game Dynamics', *Theoretical Population Biology*, **38**, 219–32.

Gabisch, G. (1984), 'Nonlinear Models of Business Cycle Theory', in G. Hammer and D. Pallaschke (eds), *Selected Topics in Operations Research and Mathematical Economics*, Heidelberg: Springer-Verlag, pp. 205–22.

Gleick, J. (1987), *Chaos: The Making of a New Science,* New York: Viking Press.

Goeree, J.K., C.H. Hommes and C. Weddepohl (1998), 'Stability and Complex Dynamics in a Discrete Tâtonnement Model', *Journal of Economic Behavior and Organization*, **33**, 395–410.

Grandmont, J.M. (1985), 'On Endogenous Competitive Business Cycles', *Econometrica*, **53**, 995–1045.

Grandmont, J.M. (1998), 'Expectations Formation and Stability in Large Socioeconomic Systems', *Econometrica*, **66**, 741–81.

Guastello, S.J. (1995), *Chaos, Catastrophe, and Human Affairs: Applications of Nonlinear Dynamics to Work, Organizations, and Social Evolution*, Mahwah: Lawrence Erlbaum & Associates.

Haken, H. (1977), (1983, 3rd edn), *'Synergetics' Nonequilibrium Phase Transitions and Social Measurement*, Berlin: Springer-Verlag.

Hands, D.W. (1991), *Introductory Mathematical Economics*, Lexington: D.C. Heath.

Hayek, F.A. (1948), *Individualism and Economic Order*, Chicago: University of Chicago Press.

Hayek, F.A. (1967), 'The Theory of Complex Phenomena', in F.A. Hayek, *Studies in Philosophy, Politics, and Economics*, London: Routledge & Kegan Paul, pp. 22–42.

Holland, J.H. (1992), *Adaptations in Natural and Artificial Systems*, 2nd edn, Cambridge, MA: MIT Press.

Holling, C.S. (1992), 'Cross-Scale Morphology, Geometry, and Dynamics of Ecosystems', *Ecological Monographs*, **62**, 447–502.

Hommes, C.H. (1991), *Chaotic Dynamics in Economic Models. Some Simple Case Studies*, Groningen: Wolters-Noordhoff.

Hommes, C.H. and G. Sorger (1998), 'Consistent Expectations Equilibria', *Macroeconomic Dynamics*, **2**, 287–321.

Hommes, C.H. and J.B. Rosser, Jr. (1999), 'Consistent Expectations Equilibria and Complex Dynamics in Renewable Resource Markets', mimeo, University of Amsterdam and James Madison University.

Horgan, J. (1997), *The End of Science: Facing the Limits of Knowledge in the Twilight of the Scientific Age*, paperback edition, New York: Broadway Books.

Intriligator, M.D. (1971), *Mathematical Optimization and Economic Theory*, Englewood Cliffs: Prentice-Hall.

Jaditz, T. and C.L. Sayers (1993), 'Is Chaos Generic in Economic Data?', *Interna-*

tional Journal of Bifurcations and Chaos, **3**, 745–55.

Kaas, L. (1998), 'Stabilizing Chaos in a Dynamic Macroeconomic Model', *Journal of Economic Behavior and Organizaiton*, **33**, 313–32.

Kac, M. (1968), 'Mathematical Mechanisms of Phase Transitions', in M. Chrétien, E. Gross and S. Deser (eds), *Statistical Physics: Phase Transitions and Superfluidity, vol. 1*, Brandeis University Summer Institute in Theoretical Physics (1966), 241–305.

Kaldor, N. (1940), 'A Model of the Trade Cycle', *Economic Journal*, **50**, 78–92.

Kauffman, S.A. (1993), *The Origins of Order: Self-Organization and Selection in Evolution*, New York: Oxford University Press.

Kauffman, S.A. (1995), *At Home in the Universe: The Search for Laws of Self-Organization and Complexity*, New York: Oxford University Press.

Kauffman, S.A. and S. Johnsen (1991), 'Coevolution to the Edge of Chaos: Coupled Fitness Landscapes, Poised States, and Coevolutionary Avalanches', *Journal of Theoretical Biology*, **149**, 467–505.

Keynes, J.M. (1936), *General Theory of Employment, Interest and Money*, London: Harcourt Brace.

Klein, M.W. (1998), *Mathematical Methods for Economics*. Reading, MA: Addison-Wesley.

Koopmans, T.C. (1951), *Activity Analysis of Production and Allocation*, New York: John Wiley & Sons.

Koppl, R. and J.B. Rosser, Jr. (1998), 'Everything I Might Say Will Already Have Passed Through Your Mind', mimeo. Fairleigh Dickinson University and James Madison University.

Krugman, P.R. (1984), 'The International Role of the Dollar: Theory and Prospect', in J.F.O. Bilson, R.C. Marston (eds), *Exchange Rate Theory and Practice*, Chicago: University of Chicago Press, pp. 261–78.

Krugman, P.R. (1996), *The Self-Organizing Economy*, Oxford: Blackwell Publishers.

Kulkarni, R.G., R.R. Stough and K.E. Haynes (1997), 'Spin Glass and the Interactions of Congestion and Emissions: An Exploratory Step', *Transportation Research C*, **4**, 407–24.

Langton, C.C. (1989), *Artificial Life*, Redwood City: Addison-Wesley.

Lavoie, D. (1989), 'Economic Chaos or Spontaneous Order? Implications for Political Economy of the New View of Science', *Cato Journal*, **8**, 613–35.

LeBaron, B. (1994), 'Chaos and Nonlinear Forecastibility in Economics and Finance', *Philosophical Transactions of the Royal Society of London A*, **348**, 397–404.

Lindgren, K. (1997), 'Evolutionary Dynamics in Game-Theoretic Models', in W.B. Arthur, S.N. Durlauf and D.A. Lane (eds), *The Economy as an Evolving Complex System II*, Reading: Addison-Wesley, pp. 337–67.

Lindgren, K. and M.G. Nordahl (1994), 'Evolutionary Dynamics of Spatial Games', *Physica D*, **75**, 262–309.

Lorenz, E.N. (1963), 'Deterministic Non-Periodic Flow', *Journal of Atmospheric Sciences*, **20**, 130–41.

Lorenz, H.W. (1992), 'Multiple Attractors, Complex Basin Boundaries, and Transient Motion in Deterministic Economic Systems', in G. Feichtinger (ed.), *Dy-*

namic Economic Models and Optimal Control, Amsterdam: North-Holland, pp. 411–30.

Lorenz, H.W. (1993a), *Nonlinear Dynamical Economics and Chaotic Motion*, 2nd edn, Heidelberg: Springer-Verlag.

Lorenz, H.W. (1993b), 'Complex Transient Motion in Continuous-Time Economic Models', in P. Nijkamp and A. Reggiani (eds), *Nonlinear Evolution of Spatial Economic Systems*, Heidelberg: Springer-Verlag, pp. 112–37.

Mandelbrot, B.B. (1983), *The Fractal Geometry of Nature*, 2nd edn, San Francisco: W.H. Freeman.

Mas-Colell, A. (1985), *The Theory of General Economic Equilibrium: A Differentiable Approach*, Cambridge: Cambridge University Press.

May, R.M. (1976), 'Simple Mathematical Models with Very Complicated Dynamics', *Nature*, **261**, 459–67.

McDonald, S.W., C. Grebogi, E. Ott and J.A.Yorke (1985), 'Structure and Crisis of Fractal Basin Boundaries', *Physics Letters A*, **107**, 51–4.

Mirowski, P. (1986), 'Mathematical Formalism and Economic Explanation', in P. Mirowski (ed.), *The Reconstruction of Economic Theory*, Boston: Kluwer-Nijhoff, pp. 179–240.

Nicolis, G. and I. Prigogine (1989), *Exploring Complexity: An Introduction*, New York: W.H. Freeman.

Nicolis, J.S. (1986), *Dynamics of Hierarchical Systems: An Evolutionary Approach*, Berlin: Springer-Verlag.

Nikaido, H. (1968), *Convex Structures and Economic Theory*, New York: Academic Press.

Oseledec, V.I. (1968), 'A Multiplicative Ergodic Theorem: Ljapunov Characteristic Numbers for Dynamic Systems', *Transactions of the Moscow Mathematical Society*, **19**, 306–33.

Palmer, R.G., W.B. Arthur, J.H. Holland, B. LeBaron and P. Tayler (1994), 'Artificial Economic Life: A Simple Model of the Stock Market', *Physica D*, **75**, 264–74.

Peitgen, H.O., H. Jürgens and D. Saupe (1992), *Chaos and Fractals: New Frontiers of Science*, New York: Springer-Verlag.

Poincaré, H. (1880–90), *Mémoire sur les Courbes Définies par les Équations Différentielles I-VI*, Oeuvre I, Paris: Gauthier-Villars.

Prigogine, I. and I. Stenger (1984), *Order out of Chaos: Man's New Dialogue with Nature*, New York: Bantam Books.

Pryor, F.L. (1995), *Economic Evolution and Structure: The Impact of Complexity on the U.S. Economic System*, New York: Cambridge University Press.

Puu, T. (1997), *Nonlinear Economic Dynamics*, 4th edn, Heidelberg: Springer-Verlag.

Puu, T. (1998), 'The Chaotic Duopolists Revisited', *Journal of Economic Behavior and Organization*, **33**, 385–94.

Rand, D. (1978), 'Exotic Phenomena in Games and Duopoly Models', *Journal of Mathematical Economics*, **5**, 173–84.

Rosser J.B., Jr. (1991), *From Catastrophe to Chaos: A General Theory of Economic Discontinuities*, Boston: Kluwer Academic Publishers.

Rosser, J.B., Jr. (1994), 'Dynamics of Emergent Urban Hierarchy', *Chaos, Solitons and Fractals*, **4**, 553–61.

Rosser, J.B., Jr. (1995), 'Systemic Crises in Hierarchical Ecological Economies, *Land Economics*, **71**, 163–72.

Rosser, J.B., Jr. (1996), 'Chaos Theory and Post Walrasian Macroeconomics', in D.C. Colander (ed.), *Beyond Microfoundations: Post Walrasian Macroeconomics*, Cambridge, UK: Cambridge University Press, pp. 87–107.

Rosser, J.B., Jr. (1997), 'Speculations on Nonlinear Speculative Bubbles', *Nonlinear Dynamics, Psychology, and Life Sciences*, **1**, 275–300.

Rosser, J.B., Jr. (1998), 'Complex Dynamics in New Keynesian and Post Keynesian Models', in R.J. Rotheim (ed.), *New Keynesian Economics/Post Keynesian Alternatives*, London: Routledge, pp. 288–302.

Rosser, J.B., Jr. (1999a), 'The Prehistory of Chaotic Economic Dynamics', in M.R. Sertel (ed.), *Proceedings of the Eleventh World I.E.A.Congress, Volume 4: Contemporary Economic Issues: Proceedings of the Eleventh World Congress of the International Economic Association,Tunis, Volume 4: Economic Behaviour and Design*, London: Macmillan, pp. 207–24.

Rosser, J.B., Jr. (1999b), 'On the Complexities of Complex Economic Dynamics', *Journal of Economics Perspectives*, **13** (4), Fall, 169–92.

Rosser, J.B., Jr. and M.V. Rosser (1996), 'Endogenous Chaotic Dynamics in Transitional Economies', *Chaos, Solitons and Fractals*, **7**, 2189–97.

Rosser, J.B., Jr. and M.V. Rosser (1997), 'Complex Dynamics and Systemic Change: How Things Can Go Very Wrong', *Journal of Post Keynesian Economics*, **20**, 103–22.

Rosser, J.B., Jr. and M.V. Rosser (1998), 'Discrete Dynamics in Transitional Economies', *Discrete Dynamics in Nature and Society*, **1**, 269–81.

Rosser, J.B., Jr., C. Folke, F. Günther, H. Isomäki, C. Perrings and T. Puu (1994), 'Discontinuous Change in Multilevel Hierarchical Systems', *Systems Research*, **11**, 77–94.

Rothschild, M. (1990), *Bionomics: Economy as Ecosystem*, New York: Henry Holt.

Ruelle, D. (1990), *Chance and Chaos*, Princeton: Princeton University Press.

Ruth, M. and B. Hannon (1997), *Modeling Dynamic Economic Systems*, New York: Springer-Verlag.

Samuelson, P.A. (1939), 'A Synthesis of the Principle of Acceleration and the Multiplier', *Journal of Political Economy*, **47**, 786–97.

Samuelson, P.A. (1947), *Foundations of Economic Analysis*, Cambridge, MA: Harvard University Press.

Sargent, T.J. (1993), *Bounded Rationality in Macroeconomics*, Oxford: Clarendon Press.

Silberberg, E. (1978), (1990, 2nd edn), *The Structure of Economics: A Mathematical Analysis*, New York: McGraw-Hill.

Simon, H.A. (1962), 'The Architecture of Complexity', *Proceedings of the American Philosophical Society*, **106**, 467–82.

Sorger, G. (1998), 'Imperfect Foresight and Chaos: An Example of a Self-Fulfilling Mistake', *Journal of Economic Behavior and Organization*, **33**, 363–83.

Spitzer, F. (1971), 'Markov Random Fields and Gibbs Ensembles', *American Mathematical Monthly*, **78**, 142–54.

Sterman, J.D. (1989), 'Deterministic Chaos in an Experimental Economic System', *Journal of Economic Behavior and Organization*, **12**, 1–28.

Stodder, J.P. (1995), 'The Evolution of Complexity in Primitive Economies: Theory', *Journal of Comparative Economics*, **20**, 1–31.

Stodder, J.P. (1997), 'Complexity Aversion: Simplification in the Herrnstein and Allais Behaviors', *Eastern Economic Journal*, **23,** 1–16.

Takayama, A. (1974), (1985, 2nd edn), *Mathematical Economics*, Fort Worth: Dryden Press, Cambridge, UK: Cambridge University Press.

Tesfatsion, L. (1997), 'How Economists Can Get ALife', in W.B. Arthur, S.N. Durlauf and D.A. Lane (eds), *The Economy as an Evolving Complex System II*, Reading, MA: Addison-Wesley, 533–64.

Thom, R. (1972), *Stabilité Structurelle et Morphogenèse*, New York: Benjamin. English translation, (1975), *Structural Stability and Morphogenesis*, Reading: Benjamin.

Toumanoff, P. and F. Nourzad (1994), *A Mathematical Approach to Economic Analysis*, Minneapolis/St. Paul: West Publishing.

Varian, H.R. (1979), 'Catastrophe Theory and the Business Cycle', *Economic Inquiry*, **17**, 14–28.

Waldrop, M.M. (1992), *Complexity: The Emerging Science at the Edge of Order and Chaos*, New York: Simon & Schuster.

Walras, L. (1874), *Éléments d'Économie Politique Pure*, L.L. Corbaz., English translation (1954), by W. Jaffé, *Elements of Pure Economics*, Homewood: Richard D. Irwin.

Weidlich, W. and G. Haag (1983), *Concepts and Models of a Quantitative Sociology: The Dynamics of Interaction Populations*, Berlin: Springer-Verlag.

Weidlich, W. and G. Haag. (1987), 'A Dynamic Phase Transition Model for Spatial Agglomeration', *Journal of Regional Science*, **27**, 529–69.

Wiener, N. (1948), (1961, 2nd edn), *Cybernetics: or Control and Communication in the Animal and the Machine*, Cambridge, MA: MIT Press.

Zahler, R. and H. Sussman (1977), 'Claims and Accomplishments of Applied Catastrophe Theory', *Nature*, **269**, 759–63.

Zeeman, E.C. (1974), 'On the Unstable Behavior of the Stock Exchanges', *Journal of Mathematical Economics*, **1**, 39–44.

Zhang, W.B. (1991), *Synergetic Economics: Time and Change in Nonlinear Economics*, Heidelberg: Springer-Verlag.

15. Toward the Complexification of Statistics and Econometrics Curricula*

Peter Hans Matthews

One of the most beloved pieces of furniture in our house is a small, hand-made bookcase intended to evoke Gerrit Rietveld's *Red and Blue Chair* (1918), a classic example of *de Stijl*, the movement most associated with Piet Mondrian. The more I considered the 'complexification' of the statistics and econometrics curriculum, the more the bookcase reminded me of traditional (liberal arts) courses – simple, beautiful and, like the 'L' in BLUE, linear. After a time, even the *a priori* and exclusive commitments of Rietveld and Mondrian to black, white and the three primaries seemed to echo the (deductive) reliance of the 'old econometrics' on a small number of primitives. While *de Stijl's* ambitions were perhaps never 'attainable', it is difficult to dismiss Mondrian's status as 'one of the supreme artists of the twentieth century' (Hughes 1988, p. 200), no less difficult, in fact, than it is to dismiss the substantial achievements of the old econometrics.

Still, if there is to be a 'new econometrics', its character will be better reflected in another piece of 'art' in our house, an exhibition poster of Paul Klee's *Unstable Equilibrium* (1922). The picture resonates with most economists, even if it was Klee's interests in the hard, not soft, sciences that inspired it: there are the familiar 'arrows of motion' for example, that with one curious exception radiate outward – not from a point, however, but from some vertical axis. There is also a small(ish) white border that (or so I interpret it) somehow contains this explosiveness, and which therefore hints at the existence of some non-linear 'border dynamics'. Klee's world, and the world econometricians must now confront, is one in which there is more than one equilibrium – some of which are stable, some of which are not – and in which 'macrostructure' often reflects the existence of some sort of 'feedback' and/or other non-linearities.

The question considered here is not whether, or even how, econometricians will do so, but rather the terms on which our students are introduced to it. Colander's '15 percent rule' reminds us that the publishers of textbooks, and perhaps most of their readers, are resistant, and often for sensible reasons, to curricular revolutions. No revolution is needed here, however. As the second section of the chapter illustrates, the 'complexification' of the statistics/ econometrics curriculum starts with a subtle epistemological shift: students learn to understand (even) traditional inference as part of a broader concern with 'pattern detection' or what Hoover (1999) calls 'abduction'. Furthermore, where new(er) tools must be introduced, connections to older, more familiar methods are often not difficult to establish: the BDS statistic, discussed in more detail below, could be presented as an extension of the 'preSanta Fe' literature on non-linearities, for example, which is treated in most current texts. It does alter 'rates of curricular substitution', however – in the sequence of courses envisioned here, RESET and CUSUM tests will become more prominent, for example, while the method of principal components will become less so. In addition, as the 'case studies' in the second section also reveal, I believe that students should learn the most basic methods in context, *before* their first statistics course, as part of a (directed, to be sure) search for 'stylized facts'. It also reflects the dual principle that what students learn about pattern detection in statistics and econometrics courses should influence their perspectives on the *construction* of theoretical models.

The third section of the chapter serves to reinforce the notion that there are dozens of 'points of contact' between traditional tools and methods and a Santa Fe-based curriculum. The examples discussed there include the connection(s) between 'interaction effects' and distribution functions, laws of large numbers and the evolution of macrostructure, identification and the presence of positive feedback, GARCH models and the use of Monte Carlo/ simulation methods. In each case, the extension(s) needed for 'complexification' are, if not trivial, feasible, and most readers will be able to provide examples of their own.

PATTERNS, NONLINEARITIES AND COGNITION

The econometrics of positive feedback, for example, are best understood in context, so that the familiar (to both students and teachers now) 'self-reinforcement' mechanism characteristic of endogenous growth models provides a convenient point of departure. The surprise, then, is that this remarkable renaissance, rooted in the perceived *empirical* failures (Lucas 1988) of the neoclassical parable, has produced so little persuasive econometric research. In their provocative application of Leamer's (1983) 'extreme bounds test' – a test *all* econometrics students, 'old' or 'new', should be familiar with – Levine and Renelt (1992) found that once initial income, school enrollment, population, and rate of investment were accounted for, *no* other variable proved robust in standard cross-sectional specifications. The problem, of course, is that an enhanced (with human capital) neoclassical model also asserts that all four of these 'focus variables' will be correlated with per capita output *out of equilibrium*, an observation that complicates the identification of returns to scale and/or other forms of positive feedback (Mankiw, Romer and Weil 1992).

Sala-i-Martin's (1997) subsequent efforts to reverse Levine and Renelt's (1992) results, on the basis of a (perhaps much) less strict bounds test, were no less provocative. His now infamous 'two million regressions paper' is the sort of 'computation intensive' exercise that will be characteristic of the new econometrics, complex or otherwise, and it restored 22 of the 59 'doubtful variables' he reconsidered to robustness. Fewer than half were 'economic' in the narrow sense, however: the list includes three regional variables, four political variables, five religious variables and one for former Spanish colonies. While the Santa Fe vision can (and does) accommodate this sort of 'institutionalism' – North's (1997) contribution to the second volume is an influential example – this was not the positive feedback Romer (1994) and others first envisioned. Furthermore, the list of 'economic variables' that failed (even) Sala-i-Martin's test includes the rate of inflation, indices of financial sophistication and measures of public expenditure/deficits.

Should critics therefore conclude that the contributors to the literature have 'mined', perhaps even 'tortured', their datasets, often without the benefit of a loss function (McCloskey 1985)? No. On the one hand, there have been successes: Durlauf and Johnson (1995), for example, find that a neoclassical model with 'multiple growth regimes', in which the non-linearities result from 'threshold effects' performs quite well.[1] On the other hand, Levine and Renelt's (1992) characterization holds for *linear* models, in which the presence of non-linear(izable) feedback could well be obscured. If there is self-reinforcement, in other words, it has proven more difficult to detect than first expected, but researchers (and their students) have no doubt benefited from the effort.

More important, perhaps, the standard, if seldom heeded, advice not to mine data and/or 'cook results' should perhaps be reconsidered here: this still newish literature could be understood as an unfinished and (to be sure) inefficient exercise in *pattern detection*.[2] (Those who read the literature with some care, for example, were not surprised that inflation failed either the Leamer or Sala-i-Martin tests – the relevant coefficient was often insubstantial, in both the statistical and economic senses.) This becomes relevant inasmuch *as the pursuit of pattern and order, and the consequent attention to abductive methods, are the* sine qua non *of a 'complexified' statistics and econometrics curriculum*. Indeed, the premise that economic data sometimes reveal 'structure' not evident in the standard tests of *a priori* linear models should be one of the definitive characteristics of a Santa Fe-based course.

It is essential, however, that students consider the question 'What are the structures/empirical facts in need of explanation?' well *before* enrollment in a first statistics/econometrics course, and that the simplest methods of 'pattern inference' be introduced sooner rather than later. For what it is worth, I tend to devote the first two, even three, weeks of a first course in macroeconomics to classroom discussions of possible patterns in American data since the Great Depression, in lieu of the usual detailed treatment of production possibilities sets, etc. I have noticed, for example, that students invited to 'deconstruct' the behavior of real GDP in the first or second lecture/discussion of the semester tend, *on their own*, to resolve the series into a deterministic trend and 'residual', note the reduced size of these residuals over the post war period, discern the existence of some sort of 'trend break' in the 1970s and even note the (changing) asymmetries in the business cycle. An introduction to, and some experimentation with, scatter plots, best-fit lines and other tools for 'data exploration' in discussion periods allows most students to discover other (in some cases, pseudo) structures for themselves, from Okun's Law to the short-run Phillips curve. Before the first week ends, in other words, students have started to acquire a sense, 'correct' or otherwise, of what a sensible macroeconomics should explain, a *raison d'être* few(er) textbooks now provide. If, over the month that follows, there is further 'experimentation' with a more diverse data set, both inside and (in the form of problem sets, and so on) outside the classroom, the resultant 'sense of order' serves as an anchor for theoretical discussions. (This 'search for order' is perhaps also the occasion for an introduction to the resources available to economists on the internet, from data sources and various 'chart makers' to the Santa Fe Institute's own Web site.)

Furthermore, these 'pattern hunts' can become (even) more sophisticated than hinted here. If the dissection of the real GDP series is expanded from one lecture to two, or perhaps two to three, students can be introduced to several 'variable trend' alternatives to their initial trend/residual characterization. Even without a detailed and, in this context, unproductive discussion of unit roots, and so on, most students *could* acquire an intuitive sense of the issues at the level of, for example, the non-technical sections of Stock and Watson (1988). The rationale for such a discussion, of course, is that these 'alternative structures' have distinct consequences for the substance of the course, and it is critical that economists and their students also discuss these in some detail: if the first lends itself to a natural division between the macroeconomics of the short and long periods, the second undermines it.[3] Here and elsewhere, of course, the instructor's own sense of the 'economic order' should inform the curriculum – to the extent s/he believes the series can be better described in terms of a 'trend plus break(s)' (Perron 1989), for example, or to the extent s/he believes this offers a better platform for the course, some textbooks and/ or datasets will be favored over others. (Furthermore, students in a second or third econometrics course in which time series methods are featured *need* to consider these alternatives in more detail, as discussed in (for example) Hamilton (1994).)

As a third, and more 'complex', alternative, students could also (or perhaps instead) calculate (proportional) rates of increase from one period to the next y_t, and then construct plots of $\ln(y_t)$ against $\ln(\text{Prob } y_t > b)$, as a prelude to subsequent discussions of 'power laws' and Pareto–Levy distributions in more advanced courses. To the extent that this exercise is successful, it could then be repeated (in a problem set, perhaps) with more/less frequent data, to determine whether the so-called 'tail exponent' is indeed constant, which leads, for those who are interested, to a discussion of 'self-similar' orders (Brock 1999).

The principle that 'order' and/or 'transcendental laws' will sometimes manifest themselves as unconditional distributions is an important one for students to master, even if the distributions students discover for themselves in first level courses are often 'degenerate' – that is, versions of Klein's (1962) 'five great ratios' or Simon's (1990) 'great and almost great magnitudes in economics'. The surprise, perhaps, with Simon's list – one that includes four of Klein's five ratios – is how much (to use his term) 'mushier' these have become over the last decade or so. Indeed, it would be productive to return to the list(s) in a first statistics course, and to discuss there whether this 'mushiness' reflects (i) the collapse of the relevant empirical law(s), (ii) evidence that these laws were (perhaps from the start) more subtle than this, or (iii) the need for a careful distinction between *unconditional* and *conditional* distributions/laws.

Even if, when all is said and done, we find the case for Klein's constant ratios less than persuasive, students benefit from a sense of their (approximate) size(s). Despite the 'drift' in labor's share in output, for example, in the 1980s, I recall that when I first read the appendices in Gordon's textbook as a student, it was not the more or less constant distributive shares that surprised me, even if the conclusion that production was (therefore?) Cobb–Douglas seemed a *non sequitur* of sorts, but rather the observation that these shares were more or less constant, *but different*, elsewhere. The inference that distribution was less 'technical' than 'social' seemed both inevitable and fundamental then.

If it is important that students become familiar with (in particular) financial and macroeconomic data, and start, at least, to search for patterns before their first course in economic statistics, it is also important, I believe, that this search not be limited to economic data. Economists' recent interest in self-similar structures, for example, is in some measure a reflection of our sense that these orders exist in 'nature', and the current enthusiasm for these could, and should, be shared with students. Brock (1996) reviews some of the most important economic (Gibrat's Law, Pareto's Law and Mandelbrot's Plate 340, for instance) and non-economic (Per Bak's (1996)) archetypal 'sandpile' examples, but there are others, of course, that would interest students here and elsewhere.[4]

Bak (1996), for example, concludes on the basis of some data and an instructive simulation exercise that traffic is a wonderful example of $1/f$ noise. Likewise, Schroeder's accessible *Fractal, Chaos and Power Laws* (1991) introduces readers to Voss and Clark's (1978) remarkable paper, which concluded that the spectra of *both* frequency intervals and amplitudes of successive notes in the first of Bach's Brandenberg Concertos are (well) described as $1/f$ power laws. (Experience tells me that students with both musical and statistical abilities will either be fascinated or dismissive, but never indifferent.) In fact, Schroeder fancifully speculates that Birkhoff's 'theory of the aesthetic' could even be formalized along these lines. The characterization of Bach's music also serves to underscore an important *caveat* for students: the inference that the unconditional distribution of asset returns is self-similar is no more the basis for profitable speculation than the unconditional distribution of frequencies is the 'secret' to successful composition. Or, from another perspective, the difference between the musician and the listener is not the unconditional distribution of frequencies and/or amplitudes, but the conditional! There are dozens, perhaps hundreds, of other examples, from the size/frequency of meteors or animal species (Schroeder 1991) to Zipf's Law of Word Choice (Li 1991).

It remains to consider the precise nature of 'pattern hunts' in statistics and econometrics courses. Brock's (1999) 'tent map exercise', described in detail in one of his contributions to this volume, strikes me as a useful point of departure and I, too, would be tempted to offer a small prize to the student who either constructs a 'best prediction rule' or 'proves' (incorrectly, of course) that the series is unpredictable as part of a first or second problem set. It is a useful feature of the exercise that better and/or more advanced students will (or so I suspect) reach the mistaken conclusion that $X(t)$ is a series of draws from a $U(0,1)$ distribution – in effect, the output of some (pseudo-) random number generator – more often than less experienced students will: the fact that the covariance of successive observations will be small or that the spectrum of $X(t)$ is flat reminds them (and us) of the limitations of 'standard' statistical tools.

Likewise, Brock's (1999) transition from simple tent maps to 'recurrence plots' could, in principle, be reproduced in the classroom. (The caveat is needed here because the effective use of these plots seems to me an acquired skill, one that requires investment in human capital.) On the other hand, even without a detailed treatment of the plots themselves, the notion of a 'correlation integral', and the intuition, if not the technical foundations, for the BDS statistic (Brock and Potter 1993) could be introduced to students. It is important, however, that students also understand that BDS test inference can be sensitive to both the 'embedding dimension' and the standard for 'nearness' (metric) and that its power in small(er) samples is suspect, a matter of particular concern in courses that feature national income and product data.[5]

The BDS statistic is, of course, one tool in a now abundant chest of 'linearity tests' against unspecified alternatives. Some of these tests – those based on frequency domain representations, for example – will be too exotic for the sort of course(s) envisioned here, but others – the 'plain vanilla' tests mentioned in most primers – call for renewed attention. That is, the possibilities of 'low dimensional chaos' aside, a Santa Fe-inspired econometrics course should, at the least, underscore the detection of (even mild) non-linearities in economic data. In particular, students should first become (more) familiar with the RESET test (Ramsey 1969) and the CUSUM and CUSUMSQ plots. It will be 'obvious' to most, for example, that if the classical linear model:

$$y = \beta_0 + \beta_1 x_1 + \dots + \beta_k x_k + u$$

is estimated, and the 'correct' model is (for example) a polynomial of some kind, the estimated coefficients $\hat{\delta}$ in the 'auxiliary regression'

$$\hat{u} = \gamma_0 + \gamma_1 x_1 + \dots + \gamma_k x_k + \delta_1 \hat{y}^2 + \dots + \delta_h \hat{y}^h + \epsilon$$

should not (all) be 'close' to zero.[6] The standard RESET test is, in this case, an F-test of $H_0 : \delta_1 = \dots \delta_0 = 0$, with $h = 2$ or 3 the most common *a priori* choices. (As the previous footnote underscores, rejection of H_0 is *not* evidence of a polynomial or other specific alternative, but rather, as Brock (1999) describes it in another context, the license to hunt for more structure.) Tsay's (1986) test, mentioned in few(er) primers, could then be introduced as a natural, if less parsimonious, extension of the RESET auxiliary regression, one that includes second-order terms. This said, the benefits of either test will be lost unless students either read about (Vitaliano (1987) or Baghestani (1991) are accessible papers) or, even better, estimate for themselves models in which (mild) non-linearities are indeed present.

More important, perhaps, students should also become familiar with recursive estimation and the CUSUM and CUSUMSQ plots (Brown, Durban and Evans 1975) as (informal, at this level) tests of structural stability and/or linearity. Given the relative price of 'computation intensive' methods, it is now (almost) costless, for example, to estimate the recursive model:

$$y_t = \beta_0(m) + \beta_1(m)x_{1,t} + \dots + \beta_k(m)x_{k,t} + u_t$$

$t = 1, \dots, m$, for all m between some h and T – that is, to produce a sequence of recursive (OLS) estimates $\hat{\beta}(m)$. If the statistical model is 'correct' and its parameters are stable, it follows that each of the sequences of estimates $b_j(m)$ should 'settle down' as m increases. It is also more or less 'intuitive' that sharp fluctuations in $b_j(m)$ provide (limited, to be sure) evidence of a structural break, while 'trends' in one or more of the $b_j(m)$ are consistent with misspecified functional form. To formalize this intuition, let v_m be the recursive residuals or 'step ahead' forecast errors and w_m the standardized transformation of this series. The cumulative sum (or CUSUM(m)) of these is then defined to be

$$(1 / \hat{\sigma}) \sum_{t = h + 1}^{m} w_t$$

and CUSUMSQ(m) as

$$\sum_{t = h + 1}^{m} w_t^2 / \sum_{t' = h + 1}^{T} w_{t'}^2$$

the ratio of the sum of the squared recursive residuals to the residual sum of squares over the full sample, which implies that CUSUM should remain 'close to zero' and CUSUMSQ should rise 'steadily' between 0 and 1 if the model is both correct and its parameters stable.

As it turns out, the derivation of asymptotic distributions for CUSUM and CUSUMSQ statistics are too difficult for the course(s) envisioned here – the construction of confidence intervals for CUSUM, reviewed in Stock and Watson (1988), relies on the properties of Brownian motion, for example – but this should not undermine their considerable usefulness in the classroom. (Students in 'computation intensive' courses, however, should be able to explore the properties of either on the basis of Monte Carlo/bootstrap methods.) The formulae themselves are simple and, more important, these low power tests contain less information than the CUSUM and CUSUMSQ plots themselves, which are an important but underappreciated diagnostic tool.

Harvey's (1990) review of Brown, Durbin and Evans's (1975) illustrative application, the demand for local telephone service in the UK, is instructive: while neither the CUSUM nor the CUSUMSQ statistics leave their respective 'confidence bands', there *is* some evidence of a structural break, and the CUSUM plot 'dates' this break well. (In this particular case, the existence of a sharp (downward) movement in the cumulative sum hints that the problem is in fact the switch to a 'new' demand function, not the mis-specification of its functional form, which is more difficult to discern.) Students in search of other illustrations will find them in the (still) active empirical literature on the demands for M1 and/or M2 – see Cuthbertson, Hall and Taylor (1992) or Dufour (1986).

There are other common tests that deserve increased attention, the most familiar of which involve Box-Cox (BC) transformations of variables (Spitzer 1982). In particular, students should be able to estimate and evaluate models in which the BC coefficient differs across variables, a specification that includes the common linear, log-linear, and various semi-log and reciprocal relationships as special cases. It is also important that students understand the economic rationale, or in some cases the absence of same, for each – that is, no one, students and/or instructors, should estimate a linear rather than a log-linear (or vice versa) model unless s/he has (a) considered its economic rationale, and (b) tested this choice. Consider the familiar human capital model, for example, with the (natural) logarithm of wages as the dependent variable, and education, tenure, and so on, as independent variables, a specification labor economists feel little need to motivate, even in textbooks. Rosen (1977, p. 13) reminds us, however, the theoretical foundation(s) for the semi-log specification are themselves a matter of some debate, in which case its use should be (but seldom is) rationalized on the 'goodness of fit' or is itself a 'testable' theoretical restriction.

These difficulties are in turn a reminder, however, that an econometrics curriculum that features non-linearities should perhaps first devote some attention to functional form(s). To reprise an earlier theme, it is not the wholesale reconstruction of the curriculum that is needed, but rather a different perspective on it: Frank Fisher's 'Iron Law of Non-Linear Econometrics' (Mankiw 1996) – Don't Do It! – needs to be repealed, or perhaps amended. This said, if it seems obvious (to most of us, at least) that the 'laws of motion' of capitalist economies are often non-linear, it is also the case that the pursuit of non-linearities can be overzealous, as the 'overfitting' of Hendrick–Prescott filters and some 'neural net' methods illustrate.[7]

It should also be remembered, however, that the dominance of the 'classical linear model' (or CLM) was in some measure rooted in both statistical and computational constraints on research – as late as the mid-1980s, Lau's (1986) review of functional forms in econometric model specification included 'computational facility' as one of the five selection criteria, where this was often (but not without fail) understood to mean linear in parameters. It would be fair to conclude that despite substantial, and often remarkable, research on the asymptotics of non-linear least squares (NLLS) estimators in both single and multiple equation frameworks, both the computational burdens and (sensible) concerns about the small sample properties of these estimators limited their use.[8] Given the inexpensive but powerful software now available for (even) personal computers, however, researchers can calculate and test NLLS estimates, minimize non-linear likelihood functions or produce 'bootstrapped' confidence intervals at little or no cost.

This does *not* mean, of course, that students should learn to *start* their specification searches with contrived non-linear functions except, perhaps, to experiment with NLLS and, more important, to discover for themselves the poor 'out of sample' behavior of most such models. Even in those cases where the student and/or instructor has reason to believe the 'correct' statistical model is non-linear(izable), the set of 'linear in parameters' models is much richer than some textbooks hint. Other than the log-linear, semi-log, reciprocal and polynomial, all of which have been mentioned, students should also be familiar with both the transcendental and translog models, for example. In particular, students should understand the precise sense in which the latter is considered a 'flexible functional form', the source of its considerable appeal to microeconometricians.

Likewise, the set of non-linear(iazable) forms discussed in these courses need not be substantial. Indeed, two of the most important have been mentioned: Box-Cox, the basis for the basic test(s) described earlier, and the logit, most familiar in the context of qualitative choice models, but now important to neural net modelers, too. Students with an intermediate course in microeconomics in their 'portfolio' will not be surprised to find that CES functions are also (often) useful. Context, and the particular interests of researchers and students, will influence the introduction of other non-linear forms: the traditional reliance on competitive market models to motivate the identification problem, for example, is a natural platform for the discussion of estimation of disequilibrium models (Quandt 1982). In this context, students must confront the problem that even when the demand D_t and offer S_t are linear, the otherwise intuitive model $Q_t = \min(D_t, S_t)$ is not, and cannot be linearized. This is of course one of the simplest, but most important, 'regression or régime switching' models, and in courses that feature time series methods, instructors will then find it less difficult to motivate this important and 'complex' literature.[9]

Last, it seems appropriate to return, for a moment, to the broader theme of 'pattern detection' in the social sciences. In particular, it also strikes me that a 'Santa Fe sensitive' curriculum should underscore its (potential) contribution to the *construction*, as well as the evaluation, of economic models. For example, a classroom discussion of the estimation of the traditional – that is, adaptive – 'cobweb model', a standard variation on the identification problem discussed later, could be extended to allow for 'least squares' or other statistical learners, following Bray and Savin (1986). (Students who find the classic corn and/or livestock parables 'remote' will often be interested in major/occupational choice cobwebs (Freeman 1976), so much so that this also provides a platform for the discussion of 'as if-ism' in economics.) In still more advanced courses, one could (even) consider variants of the Hommes and Sorger (1998) model, in which a 'consistent expectations equilibrium' or CEE is consistent with two-period cycles, or even chaos.

There is no reason that classroom discussion should be limited to cobweb models, however. In the liberal arts environment, the second or third econometrics course is often not completed until the final semester or two, which means that if the connections between 'boundedly rational' individuals/institutions who use statistical methods to 'learn' about their environment and macroeconomic outcomes must be established there, if at all. Likewise, it should be possible for students to explore, on their own, Arthur's (1994) El Farol 'experiment', with its remarkable 'emergent ecology', and/or the Santa Fe Institute's 'artificial stock market' (Arthur 1997). Econometrics students would also be surprised to discover that similar methods have even been used to characterize the 'social articulation of desire' (Cornwall 1997), as individuals 'learn', in a statistical sense, about their own sexual preferences through their interactions with others.

Finally, there is now an obvious and acute need to articulate and test even crude models of 'human pattern detection', the sort of research that first-rate students could, with some assistance, initiate for senior theses, and so on. Rotheli (1998), for example, evaluates an influential model of pattern formation with experimental subjects who confront an unknown (to them) Markov process, and finds that despite evidence of 'learning', there is no convergence to 'rational' expectations.

POINTS OF CONTACT

There are, as the introduction alluded to, natural 'points of contact' between the traditional curriculum and a 'complexified' one. What follows are brief discussions of five such examples, in order of their probable appearance in a three course sequence.

Aggregation

The presence of 'interaction effects', either 'neighborhood' or 'global', is of course a definitive feature of the Santa Fe vision, and macroeconomists have understood for some time that these effects undermine the usefulness of 'representative agent' models. It is perhaps less obvious, however, that the relevant aggregation difficulties can be introduced, with little effort, in a first or second statistics course. Kirman's (1997) recent elaboration of Allen's (1982) influential paper, for example, (re)constructs definitions of 'macroeconomic phase' and 'microeconomic characteristics' in measure-theoretic terms. This does not mean, however, that students' introduction to statistics needs to be measure-based – the intuition behind Kirman (1997) can be communicated on the basis of conditional and unconditional discrete pdfs, which will be familiar to all. In particular, and as Kirman (1997) reminds readers, even if one 'knows' the conditional probabilities that each actor is in a particular 'state of the world', the probabilities of 'macroeconomic phases' will sometimes be indeterminate if 'substantial' interaction effects exist. In much less formal terms, interaction complicates, and in some cases undermines, the search for the microfoundations of macroeconomics.

To their credit, of course, serious econometricians have for some time been more sensitive to such issues than most. In an instructive paper on the (mis)use of representative agent models to construct macroeconometric models, for example, Geweke (1985) reminded pre-Santa Fe readers that (at the least) three difficulties required further attention: 'the fact that [representative agent] models ... *can* be constructed is unrelated to whether or not these models are adequate', 'some of this [research] has proceeded using [representative agent models] whose behavior cannot be aggregated exactly' and 'it is ... presumed that the aggregator function is structural with respect to ... intervention.' (Each of these is then illustrated with a simple neoclassical model that most, but perhaps not all, students could easily understand.)

The point, in a nutshell, is this: statistical/econometric methods can be used to illustrate the commonsensical proposition that there is still a rationale for macroeconomics per se, for the pursuit of 'laws of motion' that operate at the national and/or international (that is, macroscopic) levels. Indeed, for purposes of such discussion, I have sometimes introduced the familiar linear consumption function – or, if one prefers, the apparent co-integration of consumption and disposable income – as a possible 'emergent structure' of sorts, a simple 'empirical law' with obscure, perhaps even non-existent, microfoundations, notwithstanding the contributions of Hall (1978) and others.

Laws of Large Numbers

Economic statistics students confront their first (formal, at least) statement of the 'law(s) of large numbers' (hereafter, LLN) soon after the start of the course. It is reasonable to suppose, then, that students could perform the following 'thought experiment' after a few weeks:

Imagine a large (infinite, in fact) urn with one red and one black ball. Draw one of these balls and, no matter what its color, return it and add another red with probability 1/2, and another black with probability 1/2. (If it helps, assume that a fair coin is tossed to determine the color of the next ball.) Repeat this ad infinitum. What is the proportion of red balls in the limit?

No student will fail to see that the draws are, in this case, superfluous – the process is not, in other words, 'dependent' on its own history – or that the proportion of red balls will 'settle down' (this can be made more precise, of course) to 1/2. Suppose, however, that we tweak the experiment:

Consider an alternative 'urn process' in which, after replacement, one adds a second ball of the same color with likelihood 3/4, and one of the other color with likelihood 1/4. What are the proportions of red and black balls in the limit in this case?

The answer will *not* be obvious to most students now – the composition of the urn now *seems* 'history sensitive' – and calls for simulation, either inside or outside the classroom.[10] Indeed, the conclusion that in this case, too, the proportions will settle down to (1/2,1/2) will surprise those students who would otherwise conflate the presence of 'positive feedback' and the evolution of 'macrostructure'. In more advanced courses, this could in turn serve as the prelude to a discussion of other, more elaborate, LLNs, as reviewed in, for example, White (1984).

It is the third version of this experiment, however, in which the 'path dependence' is more pronounced, that establishes the connection to Santa Fe:

Consider another 'urn process' in which researchers replace and then add another ball of the same color. What is the behavior (in the limit, of course) of the proportions of red and black balls now?

Few students not familiar with the literature will be able to sense, let alone prove, the result, so this, too, will require computer simulation. The surprise, of course, is that while the proportions will indeed 'settle down' in each of these simulations, these 'limit proportions' will be different from one student to the next. In more precise terms, the limit is a U(0,1) random variable.

To be (a little) more formal, students could be invited to cast their answers in terms of some 'urn function' $q_t = q(p_{t-1})$, where p_{t-1} is the proportion of red balls in the urn before the tth draw, and q_t is the likelihood that another red ball is added then. (In the first experiment, $q_{t+1} = 1/2$; in the second, $q_{t+1} = (1/4) + (1/2) p_t$; and in the third, $q_{t+1} = p_t$.) Most will infer that p_t will tend toward one of the stable fixed points of $q(p)$.

Readers will recognize this as the benchmark 'Polya process', which Arthur, Ermoliev and Kaniovski (1987) extended in their remarkable paper to n colors and nonlinear q_t functions that are themselves time sensitive, provided these tend, in a precise sense, to some limit function q. While Arthur et al.'s proof would be outside the scope of most courses, the essentials of the paper – in particular, the connection between the potential for a finite number of stable limit points and what the paper calls the 'emergence of [alternative] macrostructure[s]' would then be accessible to all. Indeed, it is a small(ish) step from these experiments to the archetypal 'complex parables' about 'lock-in' of techniques (David 1985, Arthur 1989) or location (Arthur 1990).

(This said, more advanced students would be well advised to read Kirman's (1997) paper as well. He notes, for example, that without replacement – in terms of the QWERTY parable, when the number of firms is finite – 'macrostructure' need not evolve, and that even with replacement, the sense in which the q_t functions tend to some q is *not* innocuous.)

Identification

As the previous section hinted, most students' exposure to the identification problem is limited to the first lectures on (linear, of course) simultaneous equation models (SEMs), a practice that, in the end, often translates into a mechanistic concern with the order condition and the exclusion of variables. Identification is broader and more subtle than this, however, as manifested, for example, in complex models of 'social interaction'. To illustrate, consider a possible discussion of the returns to education for liberal arts students, one that, for obvious reasons, will fascinate seniors and others 'on the market' for the first time. With no small pride, economics students tend to focus on choice of major, *MAJ* and *GPA* as important determinants. In fact, students will sometimes claim that *MAJ* matters for two reasons: it is proportional, more or less, to the otherwise unobservable 'commercial acumen' *ACU*, and (it is useful, at this point, to remind them that this is, or should be, a testable proposition!) students who choose economics (or statistics) are somehow more productive workers. If the direct effect of *GPA* on salaries *SAL* is 'obvious' to most students, there is a second, indirect, effect to consider – if the mean *GPA* conditional on choice of *MAJ* rises, the offers to individual students could rise, too. It follows, then, that some 'directed discussion' could produce the specification:

$$SAL = \alpha + \beta E(SAL|MAJ) + \gamma E(GPA|MAJ) + \delta GPA + \nu MAJ$$

where $ACU = \nu MAJ$. This is of course a term for term transposition of the 'school achievement' model Manski (1997) considers in recent research on the 'reflection' problem in the social sciences. As he characterizes them, b is a measure of the importance of 'endogenous' or pure 'interaction' effects, g measures the importance of 'contextual' or 'exogenous' effects, and n is a measure of the 'correlation' effect.

The problem with this otherwise plausible model, of course, is that none of these parameters is identifiable – a student's expected *SAL*, conditional on choice of *MAJ* and *GPA*, is:

$$E(SAL|MAJ,GPA) = \frac{\alpha}{1-\beta} + \frac{\gamma+\beta\nu}{1-\beta} E(GPA|MAJ) + \frac{\delta}{1-\beta}GPA + \nu MAJ$$

This tells us, more or less, that if $\beta \neq 1$, the composite parameters $\alpha / (1 - \beta)$, $(\gamma + \beta\nu) / (1-\beta)$ and ν can be identified, which in turn means that the researcher can determine whether *some* social effects are present, but not whether these are interactive or contextual and, if both are present, how much each contributes. [11]

(G)ARCH and other Nonlinear Time Series

The behavior of financial markets fascinates most students, so that data on stock market returns, in particular, provides an attractive platform for the discussion of 'structure' in economic time series. Some, perhaps most, of those enrolled in the third statistics/econometrics course, for example, have completed both the intermediate micro/macro sequence and the course in financial economics, so that the substance, if not the details, of Mandelbrot's (1963) seminal paper should be accessible to them. Students could (and perhaps should) demonstrate for themselves that the (unconditional) distribution of asset returns is 'fatter tailed' than 'normal' and, for those with the requisite preparation, consider how, if at all, the increased likelihood of 'substantial' shocks alters the basic principles of finance. The further characterization of returns as a Pareto distribution leads, for those students unfamiliar with them from the previous course(s), to an introduction to 'scaling laws' in economics.

It is also reasonable to suppose that confronted with similar data, students will, like Mandelbrot (1963), 'discover' that asset prices exhibit 'clustered volatility' – that is, periods of 'tranquility', in which small fluctuations follow small fluctuations, and periods of 'turbulence'. From here, the inference that the conditional distribution of returns *must* be heteroscedastic is almost inevitable. [12] (As Bollerslev, Engle and Nelson's (1994) comprehensive review of the literature also reminds us, the GARCH specification also captures the 'no trade period' and 'information release' effects, and the EGARCH variation can, in principle, capture the familiar 'leverage effect'.)

Since a substantial number of econometrics textbooks now include an introduction to ARCH models, the issue here is more 'motivational' than substantial. In more advanced courses, students and/or instructors could then evaluate the results of ARCH-based exercises in the context of Brock and Potter's (1993) and/or Brock and de Lima's (1996) characterizations of the literature, in which GARCH specifications fail to capture *all* the non-linear structure (and the 'residual structure' is not the consequence of a switch or switches in regime) and cannot explain *all* the 'stylized facts'.

Bootstraps and other Simulation Exercises

Brock (1999) observes that Santa Fe-inspired research often requires that researchers often 'bootstrap' hypotheses of interest onto non-linear models. There is little doubt that over the next decade or two, econometricians and their students will indeed substitute the inexpensive computational power of the 'workstation' for traditional mathematical methods more often. This trend is still not reflected in current textbooks, where serious treatments of either Monte Carlo and/or resampling methods are the exception, not the rule (Simon and Bruce 1991). This is a surprise inasmuch as the intuition and, with few exceptions, the 'mechanics' involved can be introduced to students in their *first* course, and allows some to overcome familiar obstacles.

Most statistics/econometrics students, for example, will be familiar with the multivariate linear model after several months, and will have acquired our own (excessive?) reliance on the asymptotic behavior of familiar estimators. To provide a macroeconomic example, students could discuss (say) Fair's (1999) own 'double-check' of χ^2 and F tests in his recent evaluation of NAIRU models. For purposes of simulation, he first defines a 'base model' in terms of the (initial) estimated coefficients and estimated error variance. He then 'draws' an alternative sequence of error terms, derives the associated sequence of dependent variables, and calculates the values of his test statistics for this 'pseudo-sample'. Last, on the basis of 1000 such samples, he constructs 'exact' critical values for his test statistics which, it is important for students to note, are very different (for reasons related to the presence of unit roots) from the 'traditional' values.

In conceptual terms, it is a small step from here to (for example) Monte Carlo studies of the OLS estimator for the efficient markets model $p_{t+1} = \alpha + \beta p_{t-1} + u_t$ under the null that β is 1 (Elder and Matthews 1999), or to 'bootstrap models' where the (estimated) errors are themselves resampled.

CONCLUSION

There is less here that is difficult, or much different, than first seems, but there is more, I believe, than could be covered in a two semester sequence. At the least, the 'complexification' of the statistics and econometrics curriculum presupposes a three course sequence in which the first is (as it is at Middlebury, for example) 'pattern oriented'. Even so, instructors will still be required to choose, and sometimes substitute, new/revitalized ideas and methods for old.

NOTES

*   This chapter has benifited from conversations with Brian Arthur, William Brock, David
    Colander, Duncan Foley and Carolyn Craven.
1. Durlauf and Johnsons's (1995) identification of four distinct regimes on the basis of
    'regression trees' (Brieman et al. 1984) is also innovative, and deserves some attention
    in a 'complexified curriculum'. From a broader perspective, the connections between

tests for structural breaks and tests for nonlinearities should be underscored in such courses. Quandt's (1960) extension of the usual Chow test is another obvious example. For details see Teräsvirta, Tjostheim and Granger (1994).

2. Econometricians' 'professional norms' have themselves been 'locked in' for some time. We caution students and sometimes one another (Learner 1983, Lovell 1983) not to 'datamine', but current practice reveals the distinct absence of a metanorm' (Axelrod 1986). There are exceptions, of course: some would trace the renaissance in time-series methods, for example, to the increased attention of Phillips (1986) and others to 'spurious regression' problems in macroeconometrics. There are also (Hoover 1995, for example) limited defenses of the practice. Last, for a complexified perspective on model selection itself, see Brock and Durlauf (1998).

3. The inference that the real GDP series has a 'unit root' is not a commitment, *contra* the conventional wisdom, to 'real business cycle models. I would speculate, in fact, that the 'fusion of horizons' associated with unit roots is also (more? no less?) consistant with Harrod's (1952) extension of the benchmark Keynesian model.

4. Brock (1996) also discusses Zipf's Law of Cities, which seemed to me, a Canadian, (much) more problematic than the others. On the other hand, Gabaix's (1999, p. 129) recent research provides an economic rationale for the phenomenon, which he claims 'hold [s] in virtually all countries and dates for which there are data'.

5. For more details, see Teräsvirta, Tjostheim and Granger (1994). For several meticulous case studies, see Brock, Hsieh and LeBaron (1991).

6. The intuition here is that $\hat{y}^2$, for instance, will be correlated with x_j^2 and the 'cross terms' $x_j x_k$ and if the latter should not have been omitted, its coefficent will be 'substantial when $\hat{y}$ or $\hat{u}$ is regressed on $x_1 \ldots x_k$ and $\hat{y}^2$. However 'obvious' this seems, it should be recalled that there is no specific alternative here, even if the RESET has been (re) contextualized as an LM test in the recent literature. Indeed, as this heuristic hints, the earliest versions were intended to serve as a broad omitted variables test. For more details, see Teräsvirta, Tjostheim and Granger (1994).

7. In his own brief, but useful, introduction to neural nets and other, more traditional, non-parametric methods, Kennedy (1999) refers readers to Smith (1993). For a more advanced review, see Teräsvirta, Tjostheim and Granger (1994).

8. For a review of the state of the art *circa* 1986, see Amemiya (1986).

9. Brock and Hommes' (1997) influential 'rational route to randomness' model for example, which several contributors to this volume cite, is predicated on switches between 'rational' expectations (when the benefits of computation are substantial) and 'rules of thumb'.

10. In Elder and Matthews (1999), we describe the simulation of these and other urn processes in more detail.

11. This is Manski's (1997) first proposition, more or less verbatim. For a more recent characterization of the reflection problem and its possible solution, see Brock and Durlauf (1995).

12. The 'almost' is needed here because, as Bollerslev, Engle and Nelson (1994) note, the unconditional distribution of returns' excess kurtosis is consistent with both excess kurtosis of the condition and/or random condition variance.

13. Kennedy (1998), for example, concludes that even when the use of these methods is limited to thought experiments, students master such otherwise elusive notions as the 'sampling distribution' with relative ease. Indeed, I have the sense that most Bayesians are born the moment the 'fiction of repeated samples' is understood! For some other useful classroom exercises, see Pulley and Dolbear (1984).

248   *Complexity Vision and the Teaching of Economics*

REFERENCES

Allen, B. (1982), 'Some Stochastic Processes of Interdependent Demand and Techno-
logical Diffusion of an Innovation Exhibiting Externalities Among Adopters', *International Economic Review*, **23**, 595–608.
Amemiya, T. (1986), 'Non-Linear Regression Models', in Z. Griliches and M. Intriligator
(eds), *Handbook of Econometrics*, **1**, 333–89.
Arthur, W.B. (1989), 'Competing Technologies, Increasing Returns, and Lock-in by
Small Historical Events, *Quarterly Journal of Economics*, **99**, 116–31.
Arthur, W.B. (1990), 'Industry Location Patterns and the Importance of History', *Math-
ematical Social Sciences*, **19**, 235–51. Reprinted in W.B. Arthur (1994), *Increasing
Returns and Path Dependence in the Economy*, Ann Arbor: University of Michigan
Press.
Arthur, W.B. (1994), 'Inductive Reasoning and Bounded Rationality', *American Eco-
nomic Reiew*, **84**, 406–11
Arthur, W.B. (1997), 'Asset Pricing under Endogenous Expectations in an Artificial
Stock Market', in W.B. Arthur, D. Lane and S. Durlauf (eds), *The Economy as an
Evolving Complex System II*, Reading, MA: Addison-Wesley.
Arthur, W.B., Y.M. Ermoliev and Y.M. Kaniovski (1987), 'Path-Dependent Processes
and the Emergence of Macrostructure', *European Journal of Operational Research*,
30, 294–303. Reprinted in W.B. Arthur (1994), *Increasing Returns and Path De-
pendence in the Economy*, Ann Arbor: University of Michigan Press.
Axelrod, R. (1986), 'An Evolutionary Approach to Norms', *American Political Science
Review*, **80**, 1095–111.
Baghestani, H. (1991), 'Application of the RESET test to the Original Anderson-Jordan
Equation', *Journal of Macroeconomics*, **13**, 157–69.
Bak, P. (1996), *How Nature Works: The Science of Self-Organized Criticality*, New
York: Springer-Verlag.
Bollerslev, T., R.F. Engle and D.B. Nelson (1994), 'ARCH Models', in R.F. Engle and
D.L. McFadden (eds), *Handbook of Econometrics, Volume IV*, Amsterdam: Elsevier,
pp. 2961–3040.
Bray, M.M. and N.E. Savin (1986), 'Rational Expectations Equilibria, Learning, and
Model Specification', *Econometrica*, **54**, 1129–60.
Breiman, L., J.L. Friedman, R.A. Olshen and C.J. Stone (1984), *Classification and
Regression Trees*, Belmont: Wadsworth.
Brock, W. (1996), 'Scaling Laws in Economics: A Reader's Guide', University of
Wisconsin at Madison Economics Working Paper.
Brock. W. (1999) 'Some Santa Fe Scenery' in D. Colander (ed.), *The Complexity
Vision and the Teaching of Economics*, Aldershot: Edward Elgar.
Brock, W. and S.N. Durlauf (1995), 'Discrete Choice with Social Interactions I', SSRI
Discussion Paper No. 9521.
Brock, W. and S.N. Durlauf (1999), 'A Formal Model of Theory Choice in Science',
Economic Theory.
Brock, W. and C. Hommes (1997), 'A Rational Route to Randomness', *Econometrica*,
65, 1059–95.
Brock,W., D. Hsieh and B. LeBaron (1991), *Nonlinear Dynamics, Chaos and Instab-*

ility, Cambridge: MIT Press.

Brock, W. and S. Potter (1993), 'Nonlinear Time Series and Macroeconometrics', in G.S. Maddala, C.R. Rao and H.D. Vinod (eds), *Handbook of Statistics, Volume 11*, Amsterdam: Elsevier, pp. 195–229.

Brown, R.L., J. Durbin and M.J. Evans (1975), 'Techniques for Testing the Constancy of Regression Relationships over Time', *Journal of the Royal Statistical Society B*, **37**, 149–92.

Cornwall, R.R. (1997), 'deconstructing silence: the queer political economy of the social articulation of desire', *Review of Radical Political Economics*, **29**, 1–130.

Cuthbertson, K., S.G. Hall and M.P. Taylor (1992), *Applied Econometric Techniques*, New York: Harverster Wheatsheaf.

David, P. (1985), 'Clio and the Economics of QWERTY', *American Economic Review*, **75**, 332–37.

Dufour, J.M. (1986), 'Recursive Stability Analysis: The Demand for Money During the German Hyperinflation', in D. Belsey and E. Kuh (eds), *Model Reliability*, Cambridge: MIT Press, pp.18–61.

Durlauf, S.N. and P. Johnson (1995), 'Multiple Regimes and Cross-Country Growth Behavior', *Journal of Applied Econometrics*, **10**, 364–84.

Elder, J. and P.H. Matthews (1999), 'Simulation and Time Series Methods', Middlebury College Working Paper.

Fair, R.C. (1999), 'Does the NAIRU Have the Right Dynamics?', *American Economic Review*, **89**, 58–62.

Freeman, R.B. (1976) 'A Cobweb Model of the Supply and Starting Salary of New Engineers', *Industrial and Labor Relations Review*, **29**, 236–46.

Gabaix, F. (1999), 'Zipf's Law and the Growth of Cities', *American Economic Review*, **89**, 129–32.

Geweke, J. (1985) 'Macroeconometric Modeling and the Theory of the Representative Agent', *American Economic Review*, **75**, 206–10.

Hall, R.E. (1978), 'Stochastic Implications of the Life Cycle/ Permanent Income Hypothesis', *Journal of Political Economy*, **86**.

Hamilton, J.D. (1994), *Time Series Analysis*, Princeton: Princeton University Press.

Harrod, R.F. (1952), *Economic Essays*, London: Macmillan.

Harvey, A.C. (1990), *The Econometric Analysis of Time Series*, Cambridge, MA: MIT Press.

Hommes, C. and G. Sorger (1998), 'Consistent Expectations Equilibria', *Macroeconomic Dynamics*, **2**, 287–321.

Hoover, K.D. (1995), 'In Defense of Data Mining: Some Preliminary Thoughts', in K.D. Hoover and S.M. Sheffrin (eds), *Monetarism and the Methodology of Economics*, Aldershot: Edward Elgar, pp. 242–57.

Hughes, R. (1988), *The Shock of the New*, New York: Alfred A. Knopf.

Kennedy, P. (1998), *A Guide to Econometrics*, 4th edn, Cambridge: MIT Press.

Kirman, A.P. (1997), 'The Economy as an Interactive System', in W.B. Arthur, S.N. Durlauf and D. Lane (eds), *The Economy as an Evolving Complex System II*, Redwood City: Addison-Wesley.

Klein, L. (1962), *Introduction to Econometrics*, Englewood Cliffs: Prentice Hall.

Lau, L.J. (1986), 'Functional Forms in Econometric Model Building', in Z. Griliches and M.D. Intriligator (eds), *Handbook of Econometrics*, **3**, 1515–66.

Leamer, E.E. (1983), 'Let's Take the Con out of Econometrics', *American Economic Review*, **73**, 31–43.

Levine, R. and D. Renelt (1992), 'A Sensitivity Analysis of Cross-Country Growth Regressions', *American Economic Review*, **82**, 942–63.

Li, W. (1991), 'Absence of $1/f$ Spectra in Dow Jones Daily Average', *International Journal of Bifurcation and Chaos*, **1**, 583–98.

Lovell, M.C. (1983), 'Data Mining', *Review of Economics and Statistics*, **65**, 1–12.

Lucas, R.E. (1988), 'On the Mechanics of Economic Development', *Journal of Monetary Economics*, **22**, 3–42.

Mandelbrot, B. (1963), 'The Variation of Certain Speculative Prices', *Journal of Business*, **36**, 394–419.

Mankiw, G.N. (1996), 'Discussion', *Brookings Papers on Economic Activity*, **1**, 66–70.

Mankiw, G.N., D. Romer and D.N. Weil (1992), 'A Contribution to the Empirics of Economic Growth', *Quarterly Journal of Economics*, **107**, 407–37.

Manski, C.F. (1997), 'Identification of Anonymous Endogenous Social Interactions', in W.B. Arthur, S.N. Durlauf and D. Lane (eds), *The Economy as an Evolving Complex System II*, Redwood City: Addison-Wesley.

McCloskey, D.N. (1985), 'The Loss Function Has Been Mislaid: The Rhetoric of Significance Tests', *American Economic Review*, **75**, 201–5.

North, D. (1997), 'Some Fundamental Puzzles in Economic History/Development', in W.B. Arthur, S.N. Durlauf and D. Lane (eds), *The Economy as an Evolving Complex System II*, Redwood City: Addison-Wesley.

Perron, P. (1989), 'The Great Crash, the Oil Price Shock, and the Unit Root Hypothesis', *Econometrica*, **57**, 1361–401.

Phillips, P.C.B. (1986), 'Understanding Spurious Regression in Econometrics', *Journal of Econometrics*, **33**, 311–40.

Pulley, L.B. and F.T. Dolbear (1984), 'Computer Simulation Exercises for Economics Statstics', *Journal of Economic Education*, **15**, 77–87.

Quandt, R.E. (1960), 'Tests of the Hypothesis that a Linear Regression System Obeys Two Separate Regimes', *Journal of the American Statistical Association*, **55**, 324–30.

Quandt, R.E. (1982), 'Econometric Disequilibrium Models', *Econometric Reviews*, **1**, 1–63.

Ramsey, J.B. (1969), 'Tests for Specification Errors in Classical Linear Least-Squares Regression Analysis', *Journal of the Royal Statistical Society B*, **31**, 350–71.

Romer, P. (1994), 'The Origins of Endogenous Growth', *Journal of Economic Perspectives*, **8**, 3–22.

Rosen, S. (1977), 'Human Capital: A Survey of Empirical Research', in R.G. Ehrenberg (ed.), *Research in Labor Economics*, **1**, 3–40.

Rotheli, T.F. (1998), 'Pattern Recognition and Procedurally Rational Expectations', *Journal of Economic Behavior and Organization*, **37**, 71–90.

Sala-i-Martin, X. (1997), 'I Just Ran Two Million Regressions', *American Economic Review*, **87**, 178–83.

Schroeder, M. (1991), *Fractals, Chaos and Power Laws*, New York: Freeman.

Simon, J. (1990), 'Great and Almost-Great Magnitudes in Economics', *Journal of Economic Perspectives*, **4**, 149–56.

Simon, J. and P. Bruce (1991), 'Resampling: A Tool for Everyday Statistical Work',

Chance, **4**, 22–32.

Smith, M. (1993), *Neural Networks for Statistical Modeling*, New York: Van Nostrand Reinhold.

Spitzer, J. (1982), 'A Primer on Box-Cox Estimation', *Review of Economics and Statistics*, **64**, 307–13.

Stock, J.H. (1994), 'Unit Roots, Structural Breaks and Trends', in R.F. Engle and D.L. McFadden (eds), *Handbook of Econometrics, Volume IV*, Amsterdam: Elsevier, pp. 2740–843.

Stock, J.H. and M.W. Watson (1988), 'Variable Trends in Economics', *Journal of Economic Perspectives*, **2**, 147–74.

Teräsvirta, T., D. Tjostheim and C.W.J. Granger, (1994), 'Aspects of Modeling Nonlinear Time Series', in R.F. Engle and D.L. McFadden (eds), *Handbook of Econometrics, Volume IV*, Amsterdam: Elsevier, pp. 2919–60.

Tsay, R.S. (1986) 'Nonlinearity Tests for Time Series', *Biometrika*, **73**, 461–6.

Vitaliano, D.F. (1987), 'On the Estimation of Hospital Cost Functions', *Journal of Health Economics*, **6**, 305–18.

Voss, R.V. and Clark, J. (1978), '1/*f* Noise in Music/Music from 1/*f* Noise', *Journal of the Acoustical Society of America*, **63**, 258–63.

White, H. (1984), *Asymptotic Theory for Econometricians*, New York: Academic Press.

PART FIVE

Bioeconomics, Complexity and the Teaching of Economics

16. Bioeconomics: Lessons for Business, Nations and Life

Stephen P. Magee*

The individual is foolish but the specie is wise. (Edmund Burke)

Man is an animal, technically, an alpha male primate. Man is parasitic: he practices slavery against conspecifics (other members of his specie). He is a carnivore, eating raw meat, live fish and live monkeys' brains. Man domesticates lesser animals into workers, beasts of burden and food. As man has evolved from hunters to gatherers to manufacturers, man has replaced lesser animals with robotics such as planes, trains and personal computers.

The economic center of gravity for the wealth of the Western world is in organized financial exchanges on Wall Street. There, in the most efficient market in the world, trading resembles wolverines in a feeding frenzy.

'Is man an animal?' Everything from insects to primates has strikingly human courtship behavior, territoriality and fecundity strategies; mallard ducks commit rape; chimpanzees practice war and genocide; ants have slaves; dolphins save each other and even humans from drowning; and lizards, dogs and seagulls all practice homosexuality (Wellborn 1987, p. 58). We think of modern man as different from cave men. But we are not. The change in man's genetic makeup in man's 10,000 years of recorded history is a fly speck in our six million years on earth. As we shall show, Western man's civilized appearance is a façade created by wealth. Wealth has blinded us to the reality that until recent millennia, economics was more about survival than abundance.

Man's origins are traceable to shrew-like creatures that go back 150 million years. Mammals originated with aquatic worms that go back 600 million years. Life itself descended from microorganisms that go back 3 billion years. Insects are more successful at survival than man.[1] E.O. Wilson, the founder of sociobiology, has calculated that ants have been here for a 100 million years (1975, p. 421) and that they constitute 10 percent of the weight of all living creatures.

Man's six million years on earth works out to about 300,000 generations. Our preoccupation with sex, money and time derives from our ancestors winning economic resource battles while simultaneously reproducing 300,000 times in a row without a single miss. We are survivors, but surviving is not the same as living a civilized life.

This chapter is about bioeconomics. Since this book is about complexity and the teaching of economics, let me begin by considering what bioeconomics has to do with complexity. The dynamics of chaos theory appear to be extremely fragile. Chaos theorists say that their techniques are so sensitive that they can register the effects of butterflies flapping their wings in Philadelphia on events in China. This seems implausible to the average person. However, even smaller effects are captured in the fossil records studied by paleontologists and biologists. Such butterfly effects are easily measured over periods of millions of years.

To illustrate, consider migratory birds that fly thousands of miles each way between North and South America every year. Wing length, bone densities and other body metrics are critical to survival for these birds. Consider a strong bird whose wing configuration gives it a probability of reproducing of 0.9999 compared to a 'weaker' bird with a probability of 0.9998. These two numbers appear to be trivially indistinguishable. However, the strong bird's descendants are 22,000 times more likely to survive than the weak bird's after 100,000 generations.

In short, the animal kingdom is a rich laboratory in which to learn economic lessons about complex systems. Biology teaches us that small differences in fitness have enormous effects on survival.

Bionomics changes the way we think about the economy and the way we teach economics and business. Our thinking about the economy becomes much broader, dynamic and includes wider issues. In this chapter I discuss those wider issues. We do not teach about abstract models based on some perfect conception of rationality; instead we teach about actual behavior. We teach about survival and dynamic optimization, not static optimization.

To date, bioeconomic work falls into two broad groups. The rational choice theorists look for individual maximization as a driving force. In contrast, sociobiologists look for the survival value of animal behavior and apply it to humans. Pioneering work by bioeconomists includes Alchian (1950), Becker (1976), Hirshleifer (1977, 1978), Tullock (1990a,1990b) and Ursprung (1988). Equally interesting work, but with an anthropological slant, includes Rogers (1992) and Smith (1992). Both Hirshleifer (1978) and Tullock (1990b) present important alternatives to government solutions to public good problems. Henderson (1989) and Rothschild (1992) suggest biological insights for business applications.[2] For the use of biological ideas in the development of economic theories, see Nelson and Winter (1973), Simon (1962) and my own work on endogenous policies and rent seeking in Magee, Brock and Young (1989), which took a predator-prey approach to explaining endogenous protection based on lobbying and politics.

Biology and the field of sociobiology pioneered by Trivers (1971), Wilson (1975), Dawkins (1976) and others is a fertile ground for learning both the genetic determinants of human behavior and analogies from animal social behavior for economics. The bioeconomic lessons reported in this chapter come in three areas. There are lessons for the individual, the firm and the nation.

GENETIC MEMORY AND BEHAVIOR

Gould (1983, p. 182) reports an experiment in which chicken embryos were injected with chemicals that caused the chickens to grow teeth. This excited paleontologists because birds have not had teeth like this for over 60 million years. Gould concluded that living creatures have genetic memory. Our entire genetic history going back to the beginning of time may be encoded in our DNA structure.

Genetic memory may be long-lived, but how much does it affect behavior? Brain research indicates that about half of human behavior is genetically driven and half is learned. The Minnesota study of 348 sets of twins raised separately, including 44 pairs of identical twins, found that personalities are determined as much by DNA as by society's influences. Genetics explained 40 to 60 percent of the behavior examined. About 60 percent of extroversion (versus introversion) was determined by heredity rather than culture (Wellborn 1987, p. 58).

THE NATURE OF MAN: COOPERATIVE, SELFISH, ALTRUISTIC OR SPITEFUL?

In all of nature, there are only four logically possible ways for organisms to interact with others. Behavior can be cooperative, selfish, altruistic or spiteful. My behavior is *cooperative* if I help myself and help others; it is *selfish* if I help myself but hurt others; it is *altruistic* if I hurt myself but help others; and it is *spiteful* if I hurt both myself and others.

Both altruistic and spiteful behavior are rare with animals. Most of the examples that come to mind are either reciprocal altruism (cooperation) or selfishness. Spiteful behavior is bad for the actor. For example, bee stings appear to be spiteful because they hurt the bee (who dies afterward) and the person stung. At another level, the bee's behavior is altruistic because the other bees in the colony are protected. As we shall see later, bee behavior is best explained by a selfish gene (kin selection) theory.

Selfish behavior is the dominant form of animal behavior. Almost all feeding behavior with interspecies interaction is selfish. Predators and parasites increase their welfare at the expense of prey and hosts. Within species, dominants capture food from subordinates. Cooperative behavior occurs in nature. But examples such as pilot fish with sharks and cowbirds with cows are exceptions to the rule. Altruistic behavior appears primarily between mothers and offspring.

Cooperative behavior is the civilizing differentiator between man and the animals. Cooperation is the dominant form of man's economic behavior – voluntary transactions necessarily involve mutual gain. One can think of economic relationships as horizontal, because both parties gain. Since both players gain, they are on an equal plane. Man's political relationships are selfish. One's gain in a political campaign or a lawsuit is another's loss. Politics can be thought of as vertical, because it is about rights, redistribution and power, all of which are relative. Biopolitics explores these relationships and is instructive for public choice theory. Biological relationships, especially dominance hierarchies, are insightful for vertical relationships in human society (Magee 1998).

In short, man's political behavior appears to be predatory and biologically primitive. Man's economic behavior is cooperative and a significant differentiator of man from other animals.

r VS. K STRATEGISTS

MacArthur and Wilson (1967) note that there are two basic survival strategies in nature: r strategies and K strategies. Mnemonically, r species can be thought of as roaches and K species as cows.[3] The r strategists include insects, fish and amphibians while K strategists include birds, mammals and man.

The r strategists are characterized as having opportunistic basic life strategies, short lives, many offspring, low levels of parental care for offspring, and small body sizes. K species have sedentary basic life strategies, longer lives, fewer offspring, higher parental care for offspring, and large body sizes. In general, r strategists thrive in variable environments while K strategists do better in stable environments.

Behaviorists who apply this structure to man characterize r strategists as more aggressive (for example, type A personalities), creative, accident prone, nonconformist, risk loving, irresponsible, sloppy and spendthrift. K strategists are passive, conventional, careful, conformist, risk averse, responsible, precise and frugal. The young prefer r strategies while the old prefer K. The r strategists tend to have shorter time horizons while K strategists have longer ones. See Rogers (1992) for an analysis of time preference and natural selection.

The reproduction strategies of insects is an r strategy: lay hundreds of thousands of eggs and leave the young to fend for themselves. This contrasts with the K strategy of the cow which has a nine month gestation period. There is a weak tendency for males to be r strategists and females to be K strategists. Lopreato reports that the average woman will produce only about 400 eggs in her lifetime whereas the average male can generate hundreds of millions of sperm in the course of a single day (Lopreato 1984, p. 323).

Management departments in some business schools now teach r and K approaches as business strategies. The approach employed by the r strategists is that of generalists, emphasizing adaptability; the K strategists are specialists who emphasize quality. The r strategists are more adaptive while K strategists are more inflexible. The r strategy is similar to mutation: it combines new elements and variation into behavior. The K strategy generates selective forces resisting change and mutations. Innovative r strategists populate marketing, advertising and sales departments and push creativity while conservative K strategists thrive in finance and accounting and preserve existing success by resisting change.

The r–K strategy distinction is insightful in explaining economic behavior between developing and advanced countries. Developing countries face highly variable economic and political environments. We observe that developing countries yield larger numbers of offspring per family and lower levels of parental investment; have generalists rather than specialists; have greater hierarchical (for example, political) competition; are more risk loving; have short time horizons; and employ scramble competition strategies for survival. The high variance in developing country incomes dictates the r strategy.

In r environments with low density and lower competition, less energy must be expended in protecting turf. Scramble competition describes r behavior in new product markets. In contrast, in highly competitive situations and in older product markets with excess supply, then defensive K strategies aimed at one's rivals may be necessary for survival. In business, this may explain the proliferation of antitrust complaints in commodity-type industries, which are highly competitive but overpopulated.

Higher levels of economic competition in large urban centers push individuals to specialize more, like K strategists. Country dwellers rationally opt for generalist r strategies. The basic economic strategy of r strategists is offensive while that of K strategists is defensive. Another angle is that r strategists have a comparative advantage in making money while K strategists have a comparative advantage in managing and keeping money. Newly industrializing countries which are moving up the world economic hierarchy employ r strategies while those at the top such as the United States and the Europeans adopt various exclusionary devices (for example, protectionism in the form of voluntary export restraints for older products, and so on) to fend off the entrants. The r–K dichotomy provides insight into the Olson (1982) problem: redistributive political coalitions are more prevalent in older societies with greater density and higher levels of economic competition.

DOMINANCE HIERARCHIES: THE ARCHITECTURE OF NATURE

The pyramid of nature is the ultimate dominance hierarchy: carnivores consume herbivores, herbivores consume herbs, and so on. Dominance hierarchies are almost universal.

Experiments have shown that when, say, 20 chickens are placed together for the first time, they engage in vigorous combat for about an hour until the pecking order is determined, from one to 20. Thereafter, when conflicts arise, each chicken typically defers to superior chickens. The pecking order is much more than a social process. It is a process of survival when resources decline: chicken number 20 is the first to die; number 19 the second, and so on. The strongest chicken is the last to die. The pecking order is the survival order. The dominance hierarchy is nature's great organizer.

The core concept of bioeconomics is the dominance hierarchy. It determines both political rank and the distribution of resources – food, territories and mates. There is no separation of politics and economics in the animal kingdom. They are one.There are chemical determinants of hierarchical rank. Androgen injections induce aggression in laboratory mice while testosterone injections induce the same effects in rhesus monkeys. Hens injected with testosterone can move from the bottom to the top of a hierarchy (Wittenberger 1981, pp. 144, 151).

A dominance hierarchy is biologically adaptive because it increases resources in the possession of the strongest animal, which increases its reproductive success. For laboratory mice, dominant males fathered over 90 percent of the offspring even though they were only 33 percent of all males in the experiment (Wittenberger 1981, p. 588).

Efficient hierarchies in human cultures expand the resources of the members of these groups. Seniority rules promote the values of those at the top of the hierarchy to those below. Rules enhance the fitness of the organization relative to rivals and the wealth and power of the organization increases. Hierarchical control promotes both efficient and inefficient behavior. Inefficient seniority rules prevent the elevation of successful newcomers. There is mixed evidence over whether seniority rules in the Congress are efficient or just preserve the existing hierarchical equilibrium in the face of talented newcomers to Congress. Hierarchical competition is prevalent in most bureaucracies, academic institutions and the military. For a fascinating application of hierarchies in politics, see Vehrencamp (1983).

The animal kingdom displays less of the altruism that is observed in man. Much of the third world lives in poverty. The bioeconomic prediction of steep hierarchies with scarcity describes well the unequal distributions of income in these societies. A social virtue of economic prosperity is the comfort of a flatter hierarchy and less dominance behavior.

While food and status appear to be highly correlated in the animal kingdom, these two are traded off more in human hierarchies. For example, banks reward dozens of vice presidents with titles instead of pay. A study showed that people with BAs in economics make more than MAs, and that MAs make more than PhDs. Garbage collectors make more than receptionists and other higher-status jobs. Rewards in politics are less monetary and more status. There is a long pecking order from local school board membership to the US presidency. The same is true of fame generally: academics face a direct trade-off between fame and remuneration.

What about hierarchical equilibria among species and among groups in society? In the very long term, genetic makeup must guarantee that the fastest coyote be faster than the slowest deer (otherwise the coyotes get wiped out) and the fastest deer be faster than the slowest coyote (otherwise the deer get wiped out).

This notion in predatory ecologies is also reinforced by short-run population dynamics. Coyote overconsumption of deer ultimately reduces the number of coyotes. Conversely, deer overpopulation will be offset by an expansion of coyotes. While there are cycles in the ratios of coyotes to deer in controlled environments (on islands), the equilibrium mean ratios are around one to 15.

A similar phenomenon may be at work among predatory and hierarchical groups in a society. No group can take more than some fraction of the resources of those below it, otherwise the hierarchy collapses. Magee and Kim (1997) modeled how national fitness varies with the ratios of predators to predatees. Using an intertemporal model and lawyer densities as proxies for predatory activity, they were able to solve empirically for the optimal (income-maximizing) level of predatory activity. The optimum balances the facilitative economic gains from legal activity against the predatory costs.

LEADERSHIP AND THE SELFISH GENE

Decades ago, leadership in the animal kingdom was thought to be altruistic. The example given was Arabian babblers, a territorial bird. The leaders of these birds sit in treetops and warn the flock of any impending danger. These sentinels vigorously compete for this right but the cost is that they have higher mortality rates because of greater vulnerability to predators (Wittenberger 1981).

The now discredited trait group selection theory said that altruistic signal birds might have higher mortality rates but their group would expand faster than groups without such leaders. If the group expansion offset the declining number of leaders, then the altruistic behavior would persist. However, subsequent research indicates that the altruistic leaders would be exterminated over sufficiently long periods of time. Even small increases in mortality rates of altruistic leaders would guarantee this result.

The current explanation of the altruism puzzle has been best explained by Richard Dawkins (1976, p. 97) in his book, *The Selfish Gene*. The argument is that it is the gene which is competing, not the organism. The insight is that the gene can survive if either (1) it passes itself along to the next generation through successful reproduction or (2) it passes a copy of itself along to the next generation through successful reproduction by a relative. The gene that triggers alarm calls in leader birds might have a personally higher mortality rate. But if it warns its kin, then the alarm-call gene is passed to the next generation. Specific leaders are killed off generation after generation but the gene lives on. The irony is that the selfish gene leads to altruistic behavior. This is the principle of inclusive reproductive fitness.

Return to the question of human leadership. Leadership is a public good; considerable costs are imposed by hierarchical competition on successful leaders in both democracies and despotic states. The parallel in nature is the dominant male walruses, who survive as dominant for less than a year. They are killed by younger males competing for the job. There is a parallel at the bottom of the hierarchy, as illustrated by the following story.

The sociobiologist Lopreato (1984, pp. 55–6) reports that during plagues several centuries ago in Marseilles, the citizens would choose a voluntary beggar who would be fed and housed lavishly for a year, like a surrogate leader, then carried through the streets, thrown into the sea and drowned. The parallels among walruses, sacrificed beggars and recent American presidents is striking.

The principle of inclusive reproductive fitness contains at least one metaphor for leadership. It makes little sense for leaders to climb to the top, given the high costs, for purely altruistic reasons. Leaders go to the top for thousands of reasons. The single best hypothesis, apart from testosterone, is that, like the selfish gene, leaders receive benefits. For animals, the benefit is elevated status, greater territory and more mates. The selfish gene theory of leadership states that the public receives a joint product of altruistic leadership but at a selfish gene cost. These costs are sex for the walruses, lavish meals for beggars and all of the above plus cash for political leaders.

TESTOSTERONE AND SUCCESS

One hierarchy experiment showed that when a mouse was subordinated in a social group, its body produced less testosterone (Wittenberger 1981, p. 152). This is interesting because it indicates that testosterone production is endogenous. The implication is that racism and other forms of dominance can result in the biochemical weakening of subordinates and that steeper dominance hierarchies in developing countries can have negative effects on the performance of subordinates. Dominance hierarchies are more prevalent in caged animals than for animals in the wild (Wittenberger 1981, p. 593).

It is a wonderful thought that the reverse could probably be true, that is, that superordination increases testosterone, confidence and aggression. The 20 million firms in the United States and millions of white collar and professional workers in a labor force of 130 million allows a large fraction of the work force to perceive that they are hierarchical dominants. Biochemical sources of creative energy are a potential explanation for the success of Western capitalism. If large numbers of people can feel important, then economic success is biochemically reinforced.

ECONOMIC EVIDENCE FOR AND AGAINST MAN AS AN ANIMAL

Who bears the costs of economic fluctuations in the animal kingdom? Consider the red grouse, a bird living in the central United States. There is little territorial behavior by these birds in the summer months because of an abundance of food. In the fall of each year food becomes scarce. Males establish territories and begin courting hens. However, not all cocks are successful in obtaining territories. Unsuccessful males and unmated females find themselves in undefended areas where food and covering are both in short supply. Most of these weaker birds die during the winter because of predation, inadequate cover and insufficient food. To summarize, the weakest animals live on the fringes of animal troops, with little food, unsafe territories and no mates. When food becomes scarce in the animal kingdom, those at the bottom of the pecking order die first.

How much does man differ from animals, and, in particular, the red grouse? Economists from David Hume to Amaryta Sen, a recent Nobel laureate in economics, have discussed man's care for his fellow man. The economic theory of diminishing marginal utility of income suggests that the rich in a civilized society are most able to cope with economic downturns and the poor are least able. That is, a 1,000 dollar reduction in income comes at a small cost to the rich because they already have a lot of money. A one thousand dollar reduction in the income of the poor comes at a great cost because they have so little. Economic theory predicts that the rich rather than the poor should bear more of the adjustment costs of economic downturns.

While the economic evidence is mixed, man appears to be more civilized than animals. A study by Polkovnichenko (1998) indicates that capitalists in America bear more risk than workers. His monthly data from 1965–97 indicate that real aggregate wages, real aggregate proprietary income and the S&P monthly real stock returns all increased by (in the S&P case, had returns of) 0.2 percent per month over this time period. One financial measure of risk, the standard deviation of the returns, was as follows:

real wages	0.8%
real proprietary income	1.6%
S&P 500 returns	4.2%

Using these measures, man does appear civilized relative to the animals because more economic risk is borne by the rich than by the poor.

However, within laborers and within capitalists, man is more like the animals in that the weak bear the burden of economic adjustment. Both hierarchy theory from biology and the principle of diminishing marginal productivity from economics predicts that for workers, the weakest are the last hired and the first fired. And similarly for capital, the weakest firms are the last to start up and the first to fail. The same is true for the poor: the weakest live on the fringes of the economy, with little food, no property and no mates – that is, street people. In this regard, man is an animal, like the red grouse. In an advanced society such as the United States, the high level of wealth masks our animal nature.

DOMINANCE HIERARCHIES IN BUSINESS

Dominance hierarchies, discussed above, are nature's great organizer. The same is true for business. Firms are not democratic. They are command driven, just like the old Soviet Politburo. Corporations and businesses rationally delegate control to those with the most to lose if they make poor decisions – the owners. Hierarchies in firms promote efficiency. Individuals who are loyal to the institution and promote it over their own personal interests are promoted and move up. Individuals do not move up if, in the opinion of those above them, they fail to advance the firm's interests. Hierarchies within firms are reflected both in the compensation of workers and in their job title. In general, job titles and compensation are highly correlated.

Hierarchical success in business across firms is generally measured by wealth (net worth). Witness the popular focus on the ranking of the 400 richest people in the US in Forbes magazine. Economics and biology are similar in that wealth expands in the hands of firms with successful products and efficient hierarchies, just as more fit species expand in animal populations.

A bioeconomic insight is that for both animals and humans, hierarchies become steeper (that is, substantial dominance of subordinates by superiors and/or more resources in the hands of dominants) the greater the external threat to a group. Wars, professional sports, older industries and older product markets and other highly competitive endeavors display this. The need for high conformity explains social acceptance of a steep hierarchy: nonconformists can be more quickly eliminated when authority is concentrated in a few hands. Stabilizing selection, to be discussed later, quickly eliminates poor performers. Intensely competitive industries face greater pressures from conforming selection and hence display steeper hierarchical structures within the firms in the industry. Intense competition eliminates democratically managed firms. Even minor deviations from efficiency threaten the existence of firms. Superiors fire inefficient employees and intimidate remaining employees with termination if they fail to increase their effort and behave in ways prescribed by superiors. This is a painful process but it increases firm fitness.

SPECIATION AS MARKET SPECIALIZATION

Henderson (1989) reports an experiment performed by G.F. Gauss of Moscow University in 1932. Gauss placed two difference species of protozoa in a petri dish. He discovered that if they fed on the same food source, one of the species would eventually eliminate the other. His conclusion: only one of two identical competitors will survive in the long run.

The business lesson Henderson drew from this experiment is that competitors who sell identical products (commodities) cannot coexist indefinitely. The business example of Coke and Pepsi selling an essential commodity illustrates the point. They can survive only by differentiating their products – if not in reality, then by perception through advertising. In general, the heavy advertising required for differentiation in commodity-type consumer products illustrates this principle. Apparent differentiation through advertising is important in commodities such as soft drinks, beer and banking. Both real and apparent differentiation emerges as products age and their markets become more competitive, witness automobiles, insurance and shoes.

We observe similar differentiation in the animal kingdom in the very long run. Competition for resources forces animals to specialize their foraging. Ultimately, species proliferate until every food niche is filled. The species of Australia evolved independently from those in North America. But Australia has many of the same animals. Australia has a Tasmanian wolf, a native cat, a flying phalanger (like our flying squirrel), wombats (like our ground-hogs), marsupial anteaters, marsupial moles and marsupial mice. None of these can reproduce with their North American counterparts because they are different species. But they look like the North American animals and they fill the same food niches (Baker and Allen 1982, Fig. 24.7).

In the very long run, every animal is an enemy and every animal has an enemy. Even the mighty lion, the king of beasts, has enemies. After kills, solitary lions are frequently driven from the carcass by packs of hyenas and wild dogs. Lions must hunt cooperatively to protect even their own kill. Weaker animals compensate by foraging in groups, just as individual voters enhance their political fitness by foraging as lobbies.

THE LAW OF INCREASING COMPETITION

Millions of years of natural selection lead to greater and greater competition among species for food. This is the law of increasing competition, which states simply that competition increases through time.

The previous section suggested the first major consequence of the law of increasing competition – specialization. Animals pursue increasing special-ization and narrower food sources through time to avoid competition. Mil-lions of years ago, many animals were omnivores. Omnivores are generalists that eat both plants and animals. Herbivores and carnivores are specialists in that they eat either plants or animals but not both.

Man and skunks are omnivores. But these generalists are vestigial remains of ancient animal behavior. The theory of comparative advantage of inter-national trade theory – that nations and individuals do only that which they do best – is the economic parallel. The law of increasing competition goes back billions of years to single cell organisms. The lessons of economic comparative advantage and of bioeconomic increasing competition are the same – specialize or die. The weakest industries are those without both the economic efficiency to compete and the political clout to get political pro-tection from imports. These industries die daily in the countries of the world.

This suggests a point not understood by economists. Economists judge political activity as inefficient. They fail to see political activity as competi-tion on a larger scale. The bioeconomic law of increasing competition sug-gests that competition plays on many dimensions: economic, political, social and legal. Applied to man, lobbying and political intervention are not distor-tions, just broader ways of competing. In equilibrium, we observe that indi-viduals compete on every dimension that confers an advantage. As the cliché goes, we must compete both on what we know and who we know. Those who do both are more fit. The complaint that a rival got ahead by 'playing politics' is the sour-grapes lament of a loser.

A second consequence of the law of increasing competition is that dominance hierarchies get steeper through time. The growth of inequality in the US economy in the 1980s illustrates this, even though the 1980s is a flyspeck in biological time. Lopreato notes that in both human and animal ecologies, increases in competition (population densities) lead to increased aggressive behavior, more fighting, and greater dominance conflict (Lopreato 1984, p. 61). The distribution of income in developing countries is much less egalitarian than in advanced countries, partly because of this effect. There is greater competition for survival in developing countries.

The density effect explains the Olson phenomenon of greater redistributive conflict in older nations. Older nations have greater densities than the same nation at an earlier time. We expect lobbying, tax avoidance, lawyering and other measures of redistributive behavior to increase with density.

A third consequence of the law of increasing competition is that hierarchies multiply. There are over 20 million businesses in the United States, in an economy with only 130 million adults in the entire workforce. Biologists report medium-run advantages for specialists relative to generalists, meaning they leave more descendants. The bioeconomic parallel is the principle of comparative advantage. But a cost of increased specialization is greater vulnerability to redistributive predation from other groups.

The ideas of speciation as market specialization, the filling of food niches and the law of increasing competition all illustrate the great efficiency of nature.

GENE REPRODUCTION, STABILIZING, SELECTION AND THE VALUE OF BUREAUCRACIES

Animals have bureaucracies. A surprising consideration in animal dominance relationships is the power of tradition. It has been observed that young pigs fight vigorously for teat positions on their mother during their first hour after birth. They scratch and fight and bite each other with their sharp teeth, with piglets on the three anterior teats receiving 84 percent more milk than piglets on the three posterior teats. Interestingly, once the teat order has been established, it tends to stay that way until weaning. Efforts to condition the piglets to change teat order by getting them to suckle new teats on tranquilized sows were unsuccessful (Wittenberger 1981, p. 176).

Animal bureacracies have other means of social control, including chemicals. It has been observed that workers in oriental hornet colonies are strongly attracted to the queen because they lick an alcohol extract from the queen. This pheromone is a chemical compound used by the queen to control worker behavior. If the queen is removed and they are not able to obtain this chemical, workers become disinterested in caring for broods, become increasingly combative, and neglect and may even eat the larva that they usually care for (Wittenberger 1981, p. 454).

One explanation for the long-term stability of behavior is the fidelity of DNA gene reproduction. Organisms can reproduce millions and millions of times without changes or mutations in the genes. There is adaptive value in this absence of change since an animal which has successfully mastered its environment and food niche in an ecology would be harmed by easy changes in its makeup. This absence of change is called 'stabilizing selection' and has great adaptive value.

Business and government bureaucracies have similar value. Older businesses in more mature industries have evolved successful ways of competing. Competitive pressures force successful firms to evolve through time toward lower wage employees. Firms must routinize and specialize tasks to the point where they can be performed with a minimum of training of low-wage employees. While the growth of bureaucracy and rules are chaffing to creative workers, they are necessary to perpetuate successful standardized products. Low variance is good in both nature and business.

THE NATURAL SELECTION OF NATIONS

Species which resolve conflict efficiently, either via territoriality or dominance hierarchies, have an advantage over those with neither. Wilson (1975, p. 279) indicates that straight chain hierarchies produce greater group efficiencies than more complicated ones.

There are costs and benefits of hierarchical conflict. The benefits are elimination of the unfit. The costs are the loss of life and limb by the survivors. Intra-specie conflict is one of the dimensions along which species compete. Surviving species should display efficiency of intra-specie pecking order conflict. We expect contraction of species with above and below optimal levels of hierarchical conflict. By definition, only species near some sort of optimum, given the historical environments, will be observed today.

The same is true for families, groups and nations. Political rent seeking and redistributive activities in human economics and politics are evidence of dominance hierarchies. Fighting over status in these hierarchies is a transaction cost of social and political life.

Think now of nations as different species. Competition among nations over the last several centuries has been accompanied by flatter hierarchies, less dominance behavior and greater equality within nations. For the last 500 years, nations have demonstrated the civilizing flattening of hierarchies. The first modern nation, the British empire, achieved economic success by dominating extra-territorial regions through colonialism. The evolution from selfish behavior (win–lose) to cooperative behavior (win–win) occurred around the time of industrialization. The political parallel was the decline of dominance through monarchies and the emergence of cooperation through democracy.

Democracy did not triumph just because it seemed the right thing to do. It triumphed because democratic nations were better competitors – they were more fit. Starting around the time of the French and American revolutions, the race to democratize was on. Nations which were not democratic were less fit.

For both animals and humans, hierarchy limitations on conflict appears to increase fitness. The Japanese economic miracle for part of the post-World War II period was partly driven by a limited hierarchical conflict. Their rigid social hierarchy supported group cohesion and reduced redistributive conflict. This increased Japan's national fitness, certainly relative to both competing and advanced foreign competitors.

Developing countries have more hierarchical and societal conflict than advanced countries. This contributes to lower levels of income per capita and other social indicators. Some advanced countries in Europe have become so civilized and reduced conflict so much that they fail to grow economically as rapidly as we might expect. The French rationalize their poor economic performance with friendly jabs at the United States. They say that the United States passed from being barbaric to decadent without ever passing through the civilized state.

What is the optimal level of intra-nation conflict, or what Krueger (1974) called 'rent seeking'? Magee and Kim (1997) have constructed an intertemporal model and measured conflict across 54 countries for a 25-year period. Using lawyer densities as a proxy measure for levels of conflict over property rights, they found that country economic growth rates over a 25-year period are maximized at approximately 10 lawyers for every 1,000 white collar workers. Lawyer densities below this number reflect suboptimal conflict and insufficient social turnover while those above the optimum reflect excessive conflict. Nations which are above (the United States) and below (Continental Europe) the optimum are less fit, as reflected by their lower growth rates.

POWER RULES NATURE WHILE ECONOMICS RULES MAN

While man is an animal, there are differences. One is that animals allocate economic resources by power while humans allocate more resources through cooperation. The power of cooperation is illustrated in the animal kingdom by the ants, who are similar to man in being one of the most organized and cooperative of all animals. The adaptive value of their cooperation is illustrated in Wilson's calculation reported earlier that ants constitute 10 percent of the weight of all living creatures.

Most animals are not cooperative – they dominate rather than cooperate. The same is true in poor countries – dictators dominate the populace. The results are the subsistence economies of the third world, with the populations living on the Malthusian margin of survival. With limited resources, there are steeper hierarchies and greater concentrations of resources at the top. Greater scarcity is associated with more redistributive fighting and steeper hierarchies as reflected in the higher shares of income going to the rich.

As a result, *power creates wealth* in nature and poor countries while *economics creates power* in advanced countries. In advanced countries, successful competitors amass wealth by cooperating with customers. They use their wealth to then accumulate political power. Behind successful economies are benign governments and institutions that facilitate cooperation and protect capitalism.

The same pattern has held through history: military power created economic power in ancient civilizations such as Rome while economic power creates political power today. Witness American military might.

ECONOMICS CREATES DEMOCRACY, NOT VICE VERSA

Does democracy create prosperity or vice versa? The irony is that the most powerful countries in the world have governments that give power away. By giving power back to the people, the economy thrives and creates the wealth necessary to fund military and world political power. It has not been clear historically whether democracy precedes economic success or whether economic success precedes democracy.

The dominance of economics over politics has been shown in a study by Barro (1997). He shows that a higher income per capita causes democracy and not vice versa. Thus, the causation appears to run from economics to politics. Economic success causes much more than just benign governments, it is a great civilizing force. The great art and music that we have inherited from previous centuries was funded by concentrations of wealth and the contribution of economic wealth to material civilization is obvious.The two greatest concentrations of wealth in all of history were created in ancient Rome and by the French monarchy and aristocracy of the seventeenth and eighteenth centuries. Rome's great monuments are still with us 2000 years later and the French left us the art and architecture of Paris and the great palace at Versailles.

Economic success thus appears to be a precondition for democracy. What does this predict for the political future of Russia as it emerges from the ashes of the old Soviet Union? The voluntary dissolution of the old Soviet Union was certainly an unexpected and rare event. Russia, the largest of the republics, was in economic free fall in the 1990s. A collapsing economy is not a harbinger for the emergence of democracy. If it is true that prosperity drives democracy, then Russia is ripe for a relapse into nonbenign totalitarianism. Democracy may be a political luxury good that is largely confined to prosperous nations.

AN r–K THEORY OF ECONOMIC AND POLITICAL DEVELOPMENT

Recall our earlier discussion of the r–K strategies, that is, that developing countries are r strategists because they face scarcity and highly variable economic environments while developed countries are K strategists because they face the reverse. Societies such as Japan employed r strategies to move up the world economic ladder while those in the United States and Europe adopted various exclusionary devices (for example, protectionism, and so on) to fend off the interlopers. Now that Japan is at the top, it is becoming more conservative and switching toward K strategies.

An easily verified political prediction of r–K theory is that politics will be more chaotic in developing countries. An illustration of the r strategy is Bolivia. Bolivia has had more than 190 coups in the last 160 years. Not even illiteracy precludes leadership in such a powerfully r environment. Enrique Penaranda's mother said: 'If I had known he was going to be the President of Bolivia, I would have taught him to read and write.' At the other end of the spectrum are Japan and Mexico, each of which, until recently, had a single political party in control for 50 years. It appears that these K-strategy governments conferred greater economic fitness on these countries.

An empirical implication of r–K theory is that government turnover should be higher in countries with lower levels of per capita income. This is indeed the case; government turnover is higher in countries with lower per capita incomes, even among advanced countries. This empirical relationship does not prove the r–K theory because of the small sample size, the weak relationship, the absence of controls and a plethora of other theories to explain this relationship. However, this data is not inconsistent with the theory.

An r-theory prediction of high economic variance among despotic governments and a K-theory prediction of low economic variance among democratic governments is supported anecdotally. Benevolent despots in Singapore and Hong Kong have caused their economies to outperform the democracies. In recent decades, nonbenevolent despots like Idi Amin in Uganda and

Sadaam Hussein in Iraq have done the reverse. The data show that the variance of economic growth rates is higher across despotic countries than across democratic ones.

A PUNCTUATED EQUILIBRIUM THEORY OF THE RIGIDITY OF POLITICAL INSTITUTIONS

Russia was dominated for centuries by the czars. The communist regime that followed, also totalitarian, lasted for over seven decades. The British monarchy has been around for about 1,000 years. Institutions and cultural norms in Europe, Japan and China have been intact for millennia. Nations and their bureaucracies are remarkably stable over long periods of time.

What lessons can we learn from biology on why human political and cultural institutions are so slow to change? We know that species are slow to change. Gould's (1983) story of hen's teeth, reported earlier, indicated that living creatures retain genetic memory for at least 60 million years. But institutions do not have genes, so a different explanation is required.

Our earlier discussions of the fidelity of gene reproduction, the stability of teat orders and the biology behind business bureaucracies provided insights into political rigidity. We advance another hypothesis here built on Eldredge and Gould's (1972) biological idea of 'punctuated equilibrium or phyletic gradualism' (see Gould and Eldredge 1993). Their theory suggests that a given specie does not display major change or improvement between mutations. It simply stays the same for millions of years.

Darwin himself knew that many species failed to 'improve' over long periods of time but he refused to accept this as generally true. He thought the result was an anomaly attributable to imperfections in the fossil record. Paleontologists had written relatively little about this stasis phenomenon, because, like Darwin, they thought it was counterintuitive and preferred the existing dogma of within-specie improvement. Until recently, most biologists were unaware of the widespread stasis (constancy) that exists in the fossil record.

Eldredge and Gould challenged the existing biological dogma and found that many new specie's genetics congealed rapidly after its formation and then did not change for thousands or millions of years. Technically, the theory of punctuated equilibrium is stated as the 'instantaneous origination and subsequent stability for millions of years of paleontological morphospecies'. In the theory of punctuated equilibrium there is no directional change or 'improvement' in body size, except at a point of major change, called the 'punctuated equilibrium'.

This contrasts with the theory of directional change in the right panel of

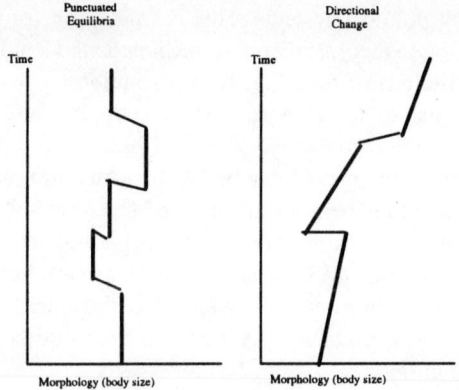

Figure 16.1 Absence of Change versus Directional Change of a Specie

Figure 16.1, in which the specie displays improvements (increases) in body size through time. Such counterexamples of the punctuated equilibrium theory are increasing brain sizes for humans and decreases in the number of toes (to a hoof) on horses, which increased their speed and foot durability. Gould (1995, p. 128) argues that these popular examples of directional change are exceptions rather than the rule.

An example supporting the theory of punctuated equilibrium is the light gray moth that existed for thousands of generations in English forests because its color blended with the light gray tree trunks. The Industrial Revolution two centuries ago brought clouds of black smoke and the trees turned black, leading to near extermination of the light gray moth within 100 years. The moth population then displayed a radical shift to black, which made them less vulnerable to birds and other predators. Recent pollution control measures have cleaned up the skies enough so that the trees are turning gray again and so the moths too are displaying a shift back to light gray. Another example of a punctuated equilibrium might be the death of the dinosaurs caused by the asteroid that smashed into the Gulf of Mexico about 60 million years ago.

The theory of punctuated equilibrium is a metaphor for political institutions. Political institutions and bureaucracies congeal rapidly after nation formation or revolutions and change only incrementally after that. Niskanen's (1976) belief was that bureaucracies have a change bias toward growth with regard to their budgets. But, he noted that while they grow, just like the economy, a bureaucracy's essential form, function and interest group basis remains unchanged.

Punctuated equilibria generate a phenomenon called 'path dependence' by economists. As in nature, institutions change incrementally until revolutions or wars shock political systems. This is frustrating for economic theorists, but it may be a fact. A lesson from punctuated equilibrium is the value of studying periods of stasis between revolutions.

An economic explanation for the stability of economic and political institutions is people's aversion to change. Thaler (1992, ch. 6) reports economic experiments in which humans display powerful status quo bias. Recall also the earlier discussion of the permanence of pigs' teat orders. The implication of all of these theories for history and politics is path dependence. Punctuated equilibria, the times of the birth and death of species, are nature's revolutions. Economic revolutions are rare events, like the emergence of a major new genus, which is a group of species. Economic revolutions are even rarer than political revolutions.

There have been three major modern economic revolutions in history: the agricultural revolution (800 BC), the industrial revolution (1700) and the current information revolution (2000). If the latter lasts several decades, its effects could override the normal Olson (1982) sclerosis which occurs in political and legal institutions.The puzzle of the 18-year mania of the American stock market (1982 to the present) might be explained by this revolution. The wealth created by this revolution may continue the economic boom for years if not decades into the twenty-first century.

MASTODONS AND THE TRAGEDY OF THE COMMONS

Man is more cooperative but also more destructive than the animals. Cro-Magnon man overkilled megafauna, driving entire herds of bison and reindeer into pit traps. One of the most inefficient animals harvests in the last Ice Age occurred where the Potomac River hits the Atlantic seaboard today (Weatherford 1985). It was a junction of north–south and east–west routes traveled by prehistoric mastodons. About 20,000 years ago, prehistoric man sat on that site and over-slaughtered migrating mastodons. There are no mastodons today. It is ironic that this inefficient slaughter of mastodons occurred near the very spot where Washington, DC, is located today. Economics conservatives point to the parellel between this and the economic inefficiency of the US government. How can we explain man's inefficient slaughter of the mastodons? The explanation for this particular example is the tragedy of the commons.

Medieval villages used to have a fenced common area in the center that contained the village's milk cows and goats. Each family had one or two cows and there were static populations and a lack of mobility across villages. All of this contributed to a strong community sense that prevented families from adding more animals to the common than their fair share.

With the Protestant revolution's emphasis on the individual, and with increased mobility in Europe, there was a decline in the power of community values. Individuals began to free ride on village interests and add more than their share of animals to the commons. More and more animals led to the overgrazing of the commons until there was insufficient grass to feed the animals. Prisoners' dilemma-style, the institution of the commons collapsed.

Hardin (1971) called this the 'tragedy of the commons'. It is a widespread phenomenon in situations in which there are free goods or underpriced resources: demand exceeds supply, so there is overutilization of the resource. It explains excessive political lobbying over the budgets of governments, government deficits (the demand exceeds the supply of free government goods), redistributive activities of all sorts, overfishing in the oceans and the overhunting of wild animals.

The solution to the commons problem which emerged in medieval times was privatization. The common was converted into private property. The land was not overgrazed when people owned it. But, the social cohesion of communities declined. The modern privatization of resources formerly owned and managed by governments reflects efficiency moves of this sort.

A COMMONS THEORY OF GOVERNMENT

Since governments allocate common goods, the tragedy of the commons provides insight into government inefficiency. Lobbies compete for government budgets, taxes, laws and regulations as if they were free. The absence of property rights means that anarchy would dominate the allocation of government goods in the absence of constitutions and institutional structure. Even so, there is still a commons problem caused by lobby competition by groups for expenditure benefits and tax reductions. The persistence of government deficits is symptomatic of the commons problem that lobbies demand more than governments can supply.

Following our notion of the nation as a specie, nations with political institutions which are more fit in dealing with this commons problem flourish relative to the rest. These nations are called 'developed economies' and they flourish relative to the rest.

MAN AS THE HIGHEST VARIANCE ANIMAL

Man's mental capability to cooperate leads to his economic superiority over the animals. The tragedy of the commons reminds us that man can also be more destructive than animals. Few mammals (hyenas, wild dogs and other group predators) are capable of organized mass destruction. Most are solitary and only individually capable of harming prey and inferior members of their own specie. It is instructive that, outside of predatory behavior, much of the pain inflicted by mammals is through dominance conflict on members of their own specie.

Do we observe commons problems in nature? One would think so because everything in nature is a commons except the territory (private property) created and defended by an individual animal or that controlled by a dominant animal in a hierarchy. But, except for group predators and some colonial animals (certain birds, penguins, walruses, and so on), an animal's ability to dominate others is limited to its own individual strength and power. Dominance hierarchies privatize what a single animal is able to appropriate.

Man's ability to destroy more than the animals comes from a combination of technology (weapons) and organization (militaries) and institutions (the state) and resources (millions of taxpayers). Man's cooperation and selfishness are both augmented relative to the animals.

In short, man has high variance. He is both the greatest creator and the greatest destroyer.

POLITICAL SELECTION: THE THEORY OF ENDOGENOUS PREDATION

The theory of endogenous predation attempts to explain how endogenous politics facilitates economic predation. Man is like the other animals in behavior toward conspecifics (members of the same specie): we are both predatory and parasitic. Individuals and groups devote resources to redistributive rent seeking so long as the expected gains exceed the costs. They invest in both production and predation until the marginal returns from each are identical. Lobbies are predatory groups. Protectionist lobbies contribute funds to a protectionist party (one which taxes imported goods) to maximize their economic gain from the political system.

When a party sponsors a special-interest policy, it gains votes using the campaign contributions from a special-interest lobby but it loses votes because voters are upset by the special-interest policy. Endogenous politics describes the process leading to the equilibrium level of the policy (for example industry protection such as a tariff against imports) which maximizes the difference to the sponsoring party between the votes gained and the votes lost. This theory of endogenous policy is a general one that explains any government policy with special interests behind it. Brock and Magee (1974, 1978, 1980), Young and Magee (1986) and Magee, Brock and Young (1989) were the first to model endogenous protection (tariffs). Their model of endogenous predation was the first model with special-interest policies formed with *all* groups behaving rationally.[4] All behavior was described by first-order conditions for all of the actors in each of the following four markets: factor markets, goods markets, lobbies and political parties. Even voters were rationally ignorant. A pyramid of nature-Stackelberg structure guaranteed game theoretic consistency, with parties at the top, lobbies next, goods and factor markets next and voters, the least informed, at the bottom of the pyramid.

The model captured the two-way causation between power and wealth: political power creates wealth and economic wealth creates political power. It is this mutual attraction between power and money that motivates predatory redistributive activity through special-interest politics.

The correct view that predatory activity is economically wasteful leads economists to a mistaken conclusion that political markets are not efficient. This view is wrong, since successful politicians, by definition, provide exactly what their constituencies want. Political markets are efficient – but they are politically efficient. Rational politicians maximize votes, not economic efficiency. We have economically inefficient policies, such as tariff protection, because they maximize the votes for the protectionist party. There is nothing that economists can do to eliminate protection because any change from the current level would generate more opposition than support.

When politicians maximize votes, they promote political efficiency. Political efficiency delivers to voters and interest groups what they want. The current debate over the quality of public education in America clarifies this point. Three-fourths of high-school graduates do not go to college and most adults cannot afford an Ivy League prep school education for their children. The wailing of the press about the sorry state of American education reflects elitist upper-class values. America's democratic system provides exactly what the majority of parents and children want: football, band and high grades. Democracy works.

There is a major difference between both economic selection and natural selection on the one hand and political selection on the other. In an animal ecology, expansion in a group of predators is self limiting because of limits on prey. The same is true for firms and industries in an economy, because of diminishing returns. At the profit-maximizing point for each firm, additions to sales will be less than additions to costs.

But, Magee, Brock and Young (1989) discovered increasing returns to political selection. That is, the more capital there is in an economy, the higher will be the rate of return to capital. The greater political power of capital through their capital lobbies results in more preferential policies for capital and greater legal protection. Magee and Magee (1994) suggest that such increasing returns to politics results in a bimodal distribution of the world's capital stocks. That is, economies bifurcate into the highly capital-abundant developed countries and the capital-scarce developing countries.

Two observations support the increasing returns to politics theory. The first is that labor-abundant countries such as India and China and the former Communist countries (all of which have low per capita capital stocks) tend to have prolabor and anticapital policies. But anti-capitalist policies lead to economic failure.

The second observation is that over half of all of the income earned in the world in the mid 1990s was earned in three countries with the most procapital policies of the twentieth century: the United States (27 percent) and two former fascist countries, Japan (17 percent) and Germany (7 percent). The striking thing about this is that both Japan and Germany are geographically smaller than the US State of Illinois. It should not be surprising that countries which protect the returns to capital will have a lot of capital. The Magee, Brock and Young model predicts and the data anecdotally supports the view that endogenous politics reinforces economic fitness. Politics causes pro-capitalist countries to get economically stronger and pro-labor countries to get weaker.

STABILIZING VS. DIRECTIONAL SELECTION AND COMMON LAW VS. CIVIL LAW COUNTRIES

There are two types of selection: directional and stabilizing. Directional selection fosters change and works best when environments are changing rapidly and species must change to survive. Stabilizing selection retards change and is the rule in stable environments. The existing traits are probably optimal in stable environments, so deviations are discouraged. The stakes are lower in economics than in biology. In biology, the less fit die; in economics they just lose their assets. Directional selection and stabilizing selection are biological bases for the r and K strategies discussed earlier.

Directional selection is the form of evolution most people recognize. It involves a mutation with superior reproductive capability. For example, mutant males among ruffs, a promiscuous European shore bird, are larger and have more exaggerated plumage. Females prefer the larger, more colorful males and this increases their ability to attract and mate with females. Directional selection changes the physical characteristics of a specie, for example, size or length or wings. The probability of mutant deviations persisting in the gene pools of many small isolated colonies is higher than that in a large population. In short, directional selection can lead to greater variety the greater the number of separate colonies.

The bioeconomic implication is that geographical separation of markets reduces the product homogenization that a competitive world market imposes. Product variety increases and economic mutations that work locally can one day spread worldwide. In this situation, the infant industry argument for protection has value, because a local industry can develop in isolation and can foster this variational effect in the long run.

Stabilizing selection is the more important form of biological selection, but less obvious because it maintains the status quo. Stabilizing selection eliminates mutants and deviants who are less successful reproducers. Through time the variability of individual members of the specie declines. Stabilizing selection is a powerful force during periods when a specie is under severe stress, such as severe weather or cataclysmic mortality, such as long bird migrations.

A study of house sparrows showed greater mortality during severe weather among birds that had either longer or shorter wings than the average. Deviations from conformity increase mortality: sparrow hawks prefer odd-colored mice because they are easier to see than normal-colored mice. Also, migratory birds whose wing lengths and bone densities deviate from the optimum are incapable of surviving the physical stress of long migrations.

Stabilizing selection is parallel to long-run economic competition. Firms or individuals that are not the most efficient are eliminated. Takeovers and bankruptcy are the vehicles by which economies perform stabilizing selection. In stable environments and older institutions, K strategists, such as journal referees, cost accountants and financial analysts rule, à la Olson (1982).

An interesting implication of stabilizing selection is the solution it provides to the economic free-rider problem. The more effective are the mechanisms of stabilizing selection, the less prevalent will be the free-rider problem. If these mechanisms break down, then other mechanisms take over, such as exclusion from the group.

How does group exclusion solve the free-rider problem? Since loners are more vulnerable to predation, the proportion of loners declines until an equilibrium is reached. There are always loners and free-riders, but their numbers are limited by predation.

Stabilization and directional selection have implications for the two major legal systems of the world: common law and civil law. Common law comes from Britain and is practiced in most former British colonies such as the United States, Australia and Canada. Common law evolves from precedent, is flexible, innovative and can change daily with new precedents. Like directional selection, it works best in variable environments, in frontier societies, such as colonies, which are just beginning their economic ascent. The common law should also facilitate more rapid economic change than the civil law. As such, we would expect the more flexible common law countries to have an advantage in the new information revolution.

Civil law is centered in Continental Europe. It grew out of ancient Roman law, as modified by the Napoleonic Code of 1805. It is statute driven, is less flexible and tradition driven. It is like stabilizing selection in preserving the status quo and the power of interest groups that influence legislation. Civil law is cumbersome to change.

The information revolution has permeated former British colony countries faster than other countries because English is the language of the internet. Protection of intellectual property is also better in these countries because of the flexibility of the common law. For both of these reasons, there is a larger number of personal computers per capita in every single former British colony (the US, Australia and Canada), and as well as in Britain itself, than in each of the other major advanced countries (Sweden, Switzerland. Holland, France, Germany, Belgium, Japan, Spain and Italy), according to the *Economist* (11 February 1995, p. 22).

BIOECONOMICS AND THE DEATH OF THE NATION STATE

Institutions of political dominance have been dying for three centuries. First monarchy, next communism and now the nation-state. The law of increasing competition and the flattening of hierarchies both predict the decline of the nation-state. While the government share of economies has risen during this century, the power of political institutions is now declining relative to business. Technology and the information revolution make the ground-based nation-state weaker and increasingly irrelevant.

What happened to American states at the end of the ninteenth century is now happening to nation-states at the end of the twentieth. In the 1890s, national corporations began to eclipse the US states. Business successfully lobbied to transfer power from state governments to the national government. The states were too small geographically to be economically efficient. The same is happening today. Business has pressured national governments into nearly 60 regional trading arrangements in this century (the European Community, NAFTA, and so on) that have reduced the power of individual nation-states over international trade. Nation-states are losing their power over business and markets (see Magee and Lee 2000).

What evidence is there of the decline of nation-states? The impeachment of President Clinton is symptomatic of this trend: the US Congress is demonstrating its frustration at its own weakened power. There were discussions in the 1990s of leadership weakness in other major countries: Germany, Japan and particularly Yeltsin in Russia. This weakness also stems from excessive intra-nation conspecific leader competition discussed earlier.

The evolution in business from corporations to virtual corporations (which coordinate product design and selling but no longer produce their own products) is being replicated by nations. Advanced democracies are being replaced with 'virtual states', whose focus has moved away from production and toward management and marketing skills. This forces the acquisition of production from overseas and switches politics from a domestic to an international focus. The optimality of producing overseas (for example in China and in labor-abundant countries) rather than at home suggests that tariffs and other forms of import protection will decline in the most efficient nations.

Rosecrance's (1996) virtual states parallel virtual corporations as innovative and efficient new political institutions. The 1996 world competitiveness rankings by the World Economic Forum ranked two of Rosecrance's new virtual states – Singapore (number 1) and Hong Kong (number 2) – as the most competitive countries in the world and more competitive than the US. The United States ranked fourth behind New Zealand. Neither Singapore nor Hong Kong are democracies; they are run by benevolent despots.

Another reason for the decline in nation-states is that countries are tied to land and land is declining in relative economic importance. Rosecrance (1996, p. 55) argues that human capital and physical capital have become the dominant forms of the world's wealth. He cites a World Bank study that 64 percent of the world's wealth consists of human capital. Less than 2 percent of American income is derived from agriculture. As a result, land wars will be a thing of the past because of the growing economic unimportance of land. Without wars, nation states are less important. The voluntary collapse of the former Soviet Union in 1990 may be a common phenomenon in the twenty-first century. Optimal country size is growing, witness the political unification of Europe, North America (NAFTA), and the pro-export focus of nearly all of the successful Asian economies in the last half century.

Do the new virtual states throw any light on whether states with benevolent despotisms will have an increasing advantage over democracies? Malevolent despots are dead or dying, witness the Soviet collapse. The downside of benevolent despotism is its violation of human rights. This plus the bioeconomic flattening of the hierarchies would give democracies the edge.

But, the spectacular success of Singapore and Hong Kong supports a benevolent despot theory. Their governments are more efficient and they mete out justice swiftly, which is increasingly rare in the world. The caning of an irresponsible American youth in Singapore was lustily cheered in America, where plagues of lawyers protect the rights of everything down to endangered pseudo scorpions. Benevolent despots are better capable of coping with competition from business, since businesses are also organized as command institutions. As business–government competition grows, governments will become more efficient. In the absence of major human rights infractions, benevolent despots will increase relative to special-interest-driven democracies. The difference between these despots and the old monarchies and communists is that benevolent despots promote efficient policies and give power back to markets. The most adaptive democracies of the twenty-first century will do the same.

CONCLUSION

Man emerged from the forest primeval six million years ago. The focus of economics over this period has evolved from survival to abundance. The theory of increasing returns to politics also suggests increasing returns to prosperity. Cooperation, altruism, democracy and civilized behavior increase with prosperity. The abolition of slavery and advance of human and women's rights all followed economic advance. Bioeconomic fitness is leading us toward an economic Garden of Eden in which the more we have, the more there will be.

NOTES

*   Copyright, 1998, Stephen P. Magee. Magee is the Bayless/Enstar Chair and Professor of Finance and Economics, Department of Finance, University of Texas, Austin, TX 78712. magee@mail.utexas.edu (512) 471-5777. The author is indebted for comments on this paper to Fran Magee and Jinkeun Yu and to participants at the Middlebury Conference on Complexity, April 5, 1998, and participants at the Conference on Dynamics in Public Choice at the Max-Planck Institute into Economic Systems, Jena, Germany, November 22, 1998. This chapter is an extension and elaboration of Magee (1984, 1993, 1998, 1999).
1.   Stephen Jay Gould according to a Kirkus Review of Dawkins' *River Out of Eden* at Amazon.com.
2.   My own work on bioeconomics develops economic metaphors from sociobiology, particularly from MacArthur and Wilson (1967), Trivers (1971), Wilson (1975), Dawkins (1976), Wittenberger (1981), Gould (1983), Vehrencamp (1983) and Lopreato (1984).
3.   The terms come from an equation describing animal populations: r is the population growth rate and K is the maximum population that the ecosystem can support.
4.   Krueger (1974) first modeled rent seeking but without endogenous policies and without endogenization of voters, parties and the resulting political process.

REFERENCES

Alchian, A.A. (1950), 'Uncertainty, Evolution and Economic Theory', *Journal of Political Economy*, **58**, 211–21.
Baker, J. and G. Allen (1982), *Study of Biology*, 4th edn, Reading, MA: Addison-

Wesley.

Barro, R.J. (1997), 'The Determinants of Democracy', Research Memo 9706, Erasmus University.

Battalio, R.C., J.H. Kagel and D.N. MacDonald (1985), 'Animals' Choices Over Uncertain Outcomes', *American Economic Review*, **75** (4), 597–613.

Becker, G.S. (1976), 'Altruism, Egoism, and Genetic Fitness: Economics and Sociobiology', *Journal of Economic Literature*, **14** (3), 817–26.

Brock, W.A. and S.P. Magee (1974), 'The Economics of Politics', A paper presented at George Stigler's Workshop on Industrial Organization, University of Chicago.

Brock, W.A. and S.P. Magee (1978), 'The Economics of Special-Interest Politics: The Case of the Tariff', *American Economic Review*, **68**, 246–50.

Brock, W.A. and S.P. Magee (1980), 'Tariff Formation in a Democracy', in J. Black and B. Hindley (eds), *Current Issues in Commercial Policy and Diplomacy*, New York: St. Martin's Press, pp.1–9.

Darwin, C. (1859), *The Origin of Species*, New York: Penguin reprint, 1979.

Dawkins, R. (1976), *The Selfish Gene*, London: Oxford University Press.

Eldredge, N. and S.J. Gould (1972), 'Punctuated Equilibrium' in T.J.M. Schopf (ed), *Models in Paleobiology*, San Francisco: Freeman Cooper, 82–115.

Gould, S.J. (1983), *Hen's Teeth and Horses Toes*. New York: W.W. Norton.

Gould, S.J, and N. Eldredge (1993), 'Punctuated Equilibrium Comes of Age', *Nature*, **336**, 223–7.

Harlow, V. (1988), *Economic Preferences and Risk Aversion*. Mimeo. Department of Finance, University of Arizona, Tucson.

Henderson, B.D. (1989), 'The Origin of Strategy', *Harvard Business Review*, **67** (6), 139–43.

Hirshleifer, J. (1977), 'Economics from a Biological Viewpoint', *Journal of Law and Economics*, **20**, 1–52.

Hirshleifer, J. (1978), 'Natural Economy versus Political Economy', *Journal of Social Biological Structures*, **1**, 319–37.

Krueger, A.O. (1974), 'The Political Economy of the Rent-Seeking Society', *American Economic Review*, **64**, 291–303.

Lopreato, J. (1984), *Human Nature and Biocultural Evolution*, Boston: Allen and Unwin.

MacArthur, R.H. and E.O. Wilson (1967), *The Theory of Island Biogeograph, Monographs in Population Biology*, No. 1, Princeton: Princeton University Press.

Magee, C.S. and S.P. Magee (1994), 'An Endogenous Political Theory of Economic Development and the Bimodal Distribution of World Capital Endowments', Working Paper, University of Texas at Austin.

Magee, S.P. (1984), *Bioeconomics: A Theory of Economic Selection*, Unpublished manuscript, 10 chapters, University of Texas at Austin.

Magee, S.P. (1993), 'Bioeconomics: The Economic Lessons of Evolutionary Biology', *Public Choice*, **77**, 117–32.

Magee, S.P. (1998), 'Biopolitics and Dynamics', Paper presented at the Workshop on Dynamics in Public Choice, Max-Planck-Institute, Jena, Germany, November 22.

Magee, S.P. (1999), 'Biobusiness', Working Paper, Dept of Finance, University of

Texas, Austin, TX, December.

Magee, S.P., W.A. Brock and L. Young, (1989), *Black Hole Tariffs and Endogenous Policy Theory: Political Economy in General Equilibrium*, New York: Cambridge University Press.

Magee, S.P. and G. Kim (1997), 'The Optimum Level of Rent Seeking in a Democracy: Theory and Evidence', Working Paper, Department of Finance, University of Texas.

Magee, S.P. and H.L. Lee (2000), 'Endogenous Tariff Creation and Tariff Diversion in a Customs Union', *European Economic Review*.

Nelson, R.R. and S.G. Winter (1973), 'Toward an Evolutionary Theory of Economic Capabilities', *American Economic Review*, **63** (2), 440–50.

Niskanen, W. (1976), 'Bureaucrats and Politicians', *Journal of Law and Economics*, **19**, 617–43.

Olson, M. (1982), *The Rise and Decline of Nations*, New Haven: Yale.

Polkovnichenko, V. (1998), 'Heterogeneity and Proprietary Income Risk: Implications for Stock Market Participation and Asset Prices', Mimeo, Department of Finance, Northwestern University, November.

Rogers, A. (1992), *Evolution of Time Preference by Natural Selection*, Mimeo, Department of Anthropology, University of Utah, Salt Lake City.

Rosecrance, R. (1996), 'The Rise of the Virtual State', *Foreign Affairs*, **75**, 45–61

Rothschild, M.L. (1992), *Bionomics: The Inevitability of Capitalism*, London: Futura Books.

Simon, H.A. (1962), 'The Architecture of Complexity', *Proceedings of the American Philosophical Society*, **106** (6), 467–82.

Smith, V.L. (1992), 'Economic Principles in the Emergence of Mankind', *Economic Inquiry*, **30**, 1–13.

Thaler, R. (1992), *The Winner's Curse*. Princeton: Princeton University Press.

Trivers, R.L. (1971), 'The Evolution of Reciprocal Altruism', *Quarterly Review of Biology*, **46**, 35–47.

Tullock, G. (1990a), 'The Economics of (very) Primitive Societies', *Journal of Social and Biological Structures*, **13** (2), 151–62.

Tullock, G. (1990b), *Hawks, Doves and Free Riders*, Discussion Paper 90–35, Department of Economics, University of Arizona, June.

Ursprung, H.W. (1988), 'Evolution and the Economic Approach to Human Behavior', *Journal of Social and Biological Structures*, **11**, 257–79.

Vehrencamp, S.L. (1983), 'A Model for the Evolution of Despotic vs. Egalitarian Societies', *Animal Behavior*, **31**, 667–82.

Weatherford, J.M. (1985), *Tribes on the Hill*, New York: Bergin and Garvey.

Wellborn, S.N. (1987), 'How Genes Shape Personality', *US News and World Report*, **102** (14), 58–62.

Wilson, E.O. (1975), *Sociobiology*, Cambridge: Harvard University Press.

Wittenberger, J.F. (1981), *Animal Social Behavior*, Boston: Duxbury Press.

Young, L. and S.P. Magee (1986), 'Endogenous Proctection, Factor Returns and Resource Allocation', *Review of Economic Studies*, **53**, 407–19.

17. Complexity, Business and Biological Metaphors

Michael Rothschild

The study of complexity can seem highly mathematical, esoteric, and irrelevant for the real world. When mathematicians do it, it can be all of those. In this chapter, however, I want to present another side of complexity, one which suggests that exactly the opposite is the case – one which suggests that the economics that follows from the complexity vision can be more relevant to business and the real world than is standard economics.

I arrived at this view early on in my studies – when I was an undergraduate student in economics. I had done well in my studies and my department chairman said to me: 'It's time to start getting those applications in to graduate school.' I looked at him rather astonished, and said, 'You don't think I'm going to graduate school, do you?' And he said, 'Well, of course – you got all As.' I replied 'I'm *interested* in economics, I can *do* it, but I don't *believe* it.' The reason why was that what I learned in my economics classes did not fit the real world economy as I knew it from my own family's small business and other jobs that I have had. There was this huge disconnect between what I saw in the pages of my economics text, and what I knew from the world around me. I was very troubled by that, as, I believe, many undergraduates are today.

I went on to business school and law school instead of graduate school in economics. Despite that choice, the questions raised by economics that fascinated me when I was an undergraduate continued to fascinate me, as did the belief that the world of business was not described by the economics presented in the standard texts. I still was puzzled by how the economy really works.

After completing law and business school, I began to work with The Consulting Group which advises large corporations on strategies. In that work I observed how they conducted business. Instead of simply maximizing profits, as my economics textbooks had suggested, businesses struggled for market share; they attempted to capture a market niche in a given market segment. This struggle reminded me of work I had done in college biology, in which organisms struggle for territory within a given habitat. So I decided that there might be some lessons from biology that I could bring into my

285

consulting practice to help business clients understand the dynamics of competition within a given market segment. I searched for writing on the topic but I found very little written.

That led me to take some time off my consulting practice and to write a book, called *Bionomics: The Economy as Ecosystem* (Rothschild 1990). In that book I raise some of the same issues as does the complexity work of Santa Fe, but I do it from a business person's perspective. From that perspective, it is useful to think of competition within a biological, rather than a mechanistic, equilibrium, a metaphor used by most texts. This is the center of what I call the bionomics metaphor and it has close substitutes to the complexity vision of the economy as an adapting, evolving system.

A central point of this chapter is to point out that businessmen's understanding of the economy reflects this evolutionary vision; their understanding does not reflect the view in most economics textbooks. In a businessman's view a product develops, mutates and competes in the manner chosen by natural selection. Thus, businessmen find the complexity vision a much easier vision to relate to than the standard textbook vision.

THE ECONOMY AS AN ECOSYSTEM

The central bionomic argument is that the economy is an ecosystem. There is no central direction to it; there is no plan; it develops, or evolves, spontaneously over time. The dynamics of that evolution are central to its operation. One difference between the economy and the ecosystem is that the economy evolves more quickly than the ecosystem, but their fundamental properties are similar.

There are a number of insights that follow from viewing the economy within the complexity vision. The first is that the evolutionary process leads to an increasing degree of complexity over time in ecosystems and in the economy. Our economy is continually changing – continually becoming more complex – and any businessperson who does not take that into account will soon no longer be a businessperson. The second is emphasized in the bionomics book; that insight is that the economy can be usefully analyzed in reference to biological or evolutionary metaphors.

Evolutionary systems can be broken out into virtual spaces, which have a variety of sublevels. In economics virtual spaces are called markets; in ecosystems virtual spaces are called habitats. Within markets are industries; within habitats are species. Within industries are firms or companies; within species are organisms. Within firms are divisions, within divisions there are teams or work groups; within organisms are cells. So the parallels are strong.

My point is that firms can be thought of as essentially multi-cellular organisms, just as individuals are essentially cooperative collaborations of zillions of cells. Many alternative organisms are possible, from a single-cell organism to huge multi-cellular organisms. The action, however, takes place at the cellular level. Within the cell are substructures called organelles; within economics, individuals play the role of an organelle in a cell.

THE OPERATION OF A CELL

To show the organelle let me trace out what happens in the life of a cell as part of the ecology, and then what happens in the life of an individual as part of the economy. The lifeblood of an organism is food – proteins, sugar and such. This food comes into an area called the lissome, which is a micro stomach of a cell. Here protein is dissolved into amino acids – pieces of proteins – going to this area called the 'endoplasmic reticulum', where they are re-assembled into a new sequence.

What determines the sequence of the re-assembly? In the nucleus, where the genes are, there's a code, and the exact sequence of that code is transported down here by molecules of RNA. Think of RNA as the chief guy who says, 'This one here, this one here, this one here, this one here.' It directs the re-assembly like beads on a string. When it is finished it goes out to this area called the Golgi apparatus which is essentially a labeling and packaging operation. After being reassembled, and labeled, the new protein goes out into the blood stream as a cell.

Sugar is dissolved into smaller pieces of sugar molecules that are then sent over to the area called the myocardia to provide energy for the process. While the proteins are being processed sugars have moved over to the myocardia area, where they are broken down and shipped as energy packets, called ETP molecules, all over the body, to keep all the other molecules going. All living cells essentially operate in this fashion.

THE OPERATION OF BUSINESS FROM A CELL PERSPECTIVE

Let us take a look at a business with the above picture in mind. I find it useful to distinguish some basic functions that exist in any economic entity, be it a team or the whole organization. Raw materials and raw information will come in on the red line. Another *special* form of information, called money, comes in on the green line. There is some kind of a receiving line where there is a disassembly process. Then there is a production operation where there is some processing or assembly. This production operation does not have to be a big factory; it could be a patent lawyer's office where documents are analyzed and packaged into something usable.

Just as in a cell, there is also the nourishment function; that is the final step in any economic process, which is taking in dollars and then disbursing them throughout the organization to keep everybody else fed and warm.

LEARNING, EVOLUTION, AND PROGRESS

Now that I have talked about some of the similarities, let me talk about an important difference, which accounts for the reason the economy evolves faster than do most biological structures. At most levels of biological structures there is no learning that goes on. The genetic code remains the same. There is slow change; at times there are genetic accidents – perhaps a cosmic ray creates a mutation – a re-sequencing of that genetic alphabet. Natural selection then chooses among the mutant and the existing organisms, and if the mutation happens to fit the environment, that organism gets to reproduce itself. But the process is very slow.

What is different about the economy is that there is conscious, endogenous learning. During this production process, while we are making that patent application, or running a ton of pig iron, or assembling a Dell microcomputer, the people who are actually involved are watching what they are doing, particularly if they have some incentives to care.

There is some learning that is going on that I call the learning loop. A worker notices: 'Gee, I can see that if I rearrange my work table so that this pile of little chips was not here, but over here, I'd be able to move a little bit faster.' Eventually some supervisor comes by and notices that the worker has rearranged his table and that he is doing better work. The change becomes policy throughout the area. Everybody now has their work area rearranged in that way. And it is written down in the policy manual that that is the way you arrange your work area. Learning is what causes firms and economies to grow, and hence learning is central to understanding how economies function. In business, this learning process is often called 'the learning curve'.

THE LEARNING CURVE[1]

Let me give a bit of history about the learning curve in business. The learning curve was first noticed by an engineer, Theodore Wright, who saw that costs consistently decreased with volume – an observation which he published in the *Journal of Aeronautical Sciences*. When he discovered it Wright already had established himself as a leading figure in American aviation. As chief engineer and general manager at Curtiss, he had designed and built a string of famous military and commercial aircraft. In early 1943, a year after Pearl Harbor, Wright was put in command of all American aircraft production. From that point forward, the '80 percent curve' became a rule of thumb throughout the aircraft industry.

By exploiting the predictive power of the learning curve to its fullest, Wright's production planners were able to accurately estimate workforce requirements for a massive buildup of aircraft manufacturing capacity. In just three years, America's factories churned out 230,000 fighters and bombers. By the spring of 1945, when production rates were at their peak, nearly 10,000 planes rolled off the line each month. The swarms of new aircraft overwhelmed enemy air defenses and were central to the Allies' victory. Without question, Wright's learning curve played a key role in bringing America's industrial potential to its full might (Yelle 1979).

After the war, the US government commissioned several studies that again validated the accuracy of the learning curve (Asher 1956, Reguero 1957, Alchian 1963). But during the 1950s and early 1960s, except for a few articles in academic journals, the learning curve was largely ignored. Since the statistical proof for organizational learning was drawn almost exclusively from aircraft production, apparently few executives in other industries believed that continuing cost reductions were possible in their own firms. Intuitively, the learning curve seemed to apply only in businesses where a high labor content and complex tasks made worker learning especially important (Andress 1964).

The learning curve languished in obscurity until 1966, when the Boston Consulting Group (BCG) – a recently formed consulting firm specializing in corporate strategic planning – conducted a study for a client in the semiconductor industry. BCG analysts found that, after adjusting for inflation, the unit costs of integrated circuits were dropping 25 percent with each doubling of experience. This cost erosion could not be attributed solely to improving labor productivity. Instead, the data revealed that *all* of the client's cost components – overheads, advertising, research, engineering, and marketing, as well as direct labor – declined with the accumulation of production experience.[2]

To distinguish this across-the-board cost erosion from the notion that learning only applied to labor, BCG rechristened the learning curve the 'experience curve'. Throughout the 1970s, as BCG grew to become one of the world's premier advisers to major corporations, the experience curve served as its creed. In confidential studies prepared for corporate clients around the globe, BCG analysts compiled historical cost data showing thousands of experience curves. Unfortunately, since a company's unit costs usually are kept secret, the great bulk of this experience curve evidence remains buried in inaccessible documents. Nevertheless, over the last two decades, dozens of studies – prepared by BCG and others – have been disclosed to the public. The data consistently show real cost declines ranging from 10 percent to 30 percent per doubling of experience (Dutton and Thomas 1984). Of course, shortages and gluts can temporarily drive costs sharply up or down, but the trends are absolutely clear. Data proving learning-curve cost declines have been published for steel, soft contact lenses, life-insurance policies, automobiles, jet-engine maintenance, bottle caps, refrigerators, gasoline refining, room air conditioners, TV picture tubes, aluminum, optical fibers, vacuum cleaners, motorcycles, steam turbine generators, ethyl alcohol, beer, facial tissues, transistors, disposable diapers, gas ranges, microprocessors, float glass, long-distance telephone calls, knit fabric, lawnmowers, air travel, crude-oil production, typesetting, oil-refinery construction, factory maintenance, and hydroelectric power.[3]

Significantly, no study has ever identified a product or service whose costs did not decline with accumulating experience (Thompson 1981). Bruce Henderson, BCG's founder and intellectual leader, wrote, 'The experience curve phenomenon is as real as gravity' (Henderson 1973, p. 4); ' [Its] effect can be observed and measured in any business, any industry, any cost element, anywhere' (Henderson 1974, p. 4).

Product or service, high- or low-tech, fast or slow growth, foreign or domestic, labor or capital intensive – learning curves are found because they reveal a fundamental property of all competitive economic organizations. Like intelligent organisms, organizations improve performance as they accumulate experience. Because they inhabit an enormous variety of economic niches, cope with a broad spectrum of technical problems, and possess varying degrees of intelligence, firms and industries exhibit a wide range of learning curve slopes. But whatever their rates of learning happen to be, the important point is that all organizations learn. In their pursuit of economic survival, organizations leave behind a data trail that reveals the evolutionary nature of technical progress (Gilder 1984, p. 158, Yelle 1979, p. 309).

During the 1970s, in presentations to top executives throughout North America, Europe, and Japan, BCG relentlessly argued that adroit use of the experience-curve effect was the key to competitive success. The curve implied that the firm with the largest share of its market would gain production experience – and reduce unit costs – faster than smaller competitors. At comparable prices, the leader's cost advantage would translate into wider profits and faster growth.[4]

BCG argued that under certain conditions, a firm could seize industry leadership with a preemptive strike against its competitors. By slashing prices below costs, winning the biggest share of industry volume and accelerating its cost erosion, a company could get permanently ahead of the pack. If its lunge for leadership was executed properly, the firm would more than recoup its up-front losses by building an unchallengeable long-term cost advantage. After 40 years of being ignored by everyone outside the aircraft industry, BCG's efforts turned the learning curve into the centerpiece of corporate strategic thinking. In all the leading business schools, lessons drawn from the learning curve effect became part of the core curriculum. To executives in search of a logically coherent framework for risky, multimillion dollar decisions, the 'first-strike' solution derived from the experience seemed to be the ultimate answer.

But by the early 1980s, several critics began arguing that grabbing market leadership did not necessarily guarantee a long-term cost advantage. They pointed out that in many industries, cost-cutting innovations spread quickly among competitors, making it impossible for an aggressive leader to hang onto its cost advantage. With managers and engineers job-hopping among competing firms and equipment makers, peddling the same state-of-the-art machinery to all firms in an industry, technology 'leaks' allowed small companies to keep pace with cost reductions achieved by the industry leader. According to BCG's critics, a preemptive strategy of slashing prices or building a new factory ahead of demand made little sense, because rapid technology diffusion meant that long-term cost savings would be too narrow to offset short-term losses.

None of BCG's critics questioned the validity of the learning curve itself. Instead, they argued that a simple extrapolation of an industry's costs cannot alone provide enough information to tell the president of Company X what to do next. By predicting cost and price trends, the learning curve furnishes decision makers with vital insights into future industry conditions, but the subtle nuances of each market niche, the relative strengths of competitors, and the potential for unpredicted technological shifts demand that a comprehensive analysis be completed before a company's strategy is plotted.

In short, the learning curve is a general observation. It cannot provide automatic, detailed prescriptions for every strategic dilemma. Consequently, after a decade in the corporate limelight, the learning curve was downgraded from 'ultimate weapon' to 'essential tool' in the arsenal of corporate planners.

The learning curve is well-known to business people, and is central to the thinking of high-tech business, because they usually only get the experience of making a couple of units and then somebody comes to them and says, 'What would be your price to me if I ordered eight million of those chips?' They have to guess where their cost is going to be by the time it gets out there, or they lose the business. If they are too low, they go broke; if they are too high, they do not get the order. What is amazing is that it is not part of the economics curriculum.

THE LEARNING CURVE AND REAL-WORLD BUSINESS

The learning curve comes into play into business in all kinds of ways that are essential to understanding what is going on in business today. For example, consider the observation I stated earlier that businesses go for market share, not for maximizing profits. Can the learning curve explain that? The answer is yes. Say you are the market share follower: you are Pepsi and here is Coke. Coke has got a lot more market share than you do which means that Coke's costs are lower. Because of the learning curve, it is very bad to be a follower. That is why well-known corporations such as General Electric sell their businesses if they are not number one or number two in its segments.

In my consulting we spend a lot of time devising strategies for firms if they are behind the learning curve. Let me consider one way used by the Japanese. They license the technology from the leader, and then leapfrog. For example, Sony licensed the transistor from Bell Labs for $24,000. And what did Bell Labs give them? A set of technical documents – coded information in my Bionomic language – and then Sony leapfrogged from that.

Perhaps because so many people are trained by economists, and perhaps because of an inherent inertia and conservatism, most organizations fail to sufficiently take into account the learning curve or to design their business to take advantage of it. One of the things my consulting firm does is to discuss how businesses can take advantage of the learning curve, by formalizing what we call the learning loop. The learning loop is important because learning takes place at an individual level. Without a learning loop there is very little dissemination of new learning across the organization. My consulting firm helps businesses structure their information systems so that they establish learning loops. Building in the learning loop helps push firms down the learning curve faster, and makes them more efficient. They are better able to slit the throat of their competitors, which of course is the name of the game in business. If you can push everybody out of your habitat, you are safe, secure, and rich.

I am currently a business consultant; I give talks about the learning curve and learning loops to business audiences all over the world. The general response is: 'Yeah, yeah, we know about learning curves – they're part of the way we think about costs, and this learning loop thing – that's pretty cool; but that's definitely what we're trying to do.' You will not get that type of response teaching businessmen from the standard economic text.

THE NEGLECT OF THE LEARNING CURVE BY THE ECONOMICS PROFESSION

Despite the studies proving its universality, the learning curve has been shunned by most academic economists. The term learning curve is not mentioned in most economic textbooks (the editor's text is an exception). It is seldom even discussed that product costs might decrease. For example, in Samuelson and Nordhaus's most recent edition, the notion that product costs might decrease is buried in an appendix to the chapter on supply and demand. Neither *learning* nor *experience* appears in the index of leading history of economic thought texts (the editor's included).[5]

This conspiracy of silence reveals far more about the sorry state of orthodox economics than it does about the learning curve. Although a smattering of learning-curve articles have appeared in economics journals, the curve has remained a fringe concept, well outside the mainstream of accepted thought. When asked about their profession's treatment of the learning curve, several respected economists, including Nobel winner Kenneth Arrow, agreed, 'It's been ignored'. No economist denies the curve's existence, and no one criticizes it. It is just that virtually no one writes or talks about it. Since economists build their careers by disputing economic concepts, the lack of discussion is almost eerie.[6] Perhaps if the learning curve lent factual support to the core concepts of Western equilibrium economics, a way would have been found to incorporate it, but it did not fit. So textbook economics simply ignored it.

Here is the problem the learning curve presents for the standard texts. There, it is presented that the supply curve depends upon marginal costs, and that the supply curve slopes upward in the relevant ranges of output. The learning curve suggests the opposite, and thus undermines the basic notion of the upward sloping supply curve. The texts solve the problem by ignoring the learning curve. Businesses cannot ignore it. When I started working in business; I could never find a president of a company who said, 'Nope, don't take any more orders. We're done; we're set. To increase production would increase our marginal costs.' If a consultant used such a model, nobody would hire him. Any consultant worth his fee recognizes that costs decrease with volume. This idea is built into basic thinking with the learning curve.

THE LEARNING CURVE AND COMPLEXITY

I am a supporter of the complexity vision because it directly relates to real-world business in a much more direct way than does the standard economic textbook. The advantage of the complexity approach to economics is that it takes the focus away from equilibrium conditions and places it back on process. And in that process, the learning curve becomes the central tool that businesses see it as. That is why Arthur's work on increasing returns has had such a positive reaction from the business community; it is the reintroduction of ideas such as the learning curve.

If there is a learning component, part of production is investment in the future and true costs differ from economists' conception of marginal costs. This explains why companies can take losses initially and still be valued very highly by the market. Those losses are simply another form of investment, which are building your market position, and can at a later date be translated into profits.

The problems has two levels – one, the learning-curve component, and the other, simply a conception of marginal cost – that marginal costs are much more complicated, and change much quicker than do the marginal costs of textbooks.

If adding complexity to economics can add this simple insight it will have made a large contribution to students' understanding of the economy.

NOTES

1. This section is based on Chapter 16 of my book, *Bionomics*.
2. Conley (1970, p. 8), Henderson (1973, p. 1), 'The cost characteristics of experience curves can be observed in all elements of cost whether labor costs, advertising costs, overhead costs, marketing costs, development costs, or manufacturing costs. It seems to be immaterial whether the value added is labor or capital intensive' (Henderson 1980, p. 2). Wright reported the same finding in his 1936 article (p. 125). He found that as labor costs fell on an 80 percent curve, the costs of raw materials and 'purchased' materials were on 95 percent and 88 percent curves, respectively. In effect, the term *experience curve* was a marketing gambit by BCG to attribute recency to the old but obscure discovery of the 'learning curve'.
3. Learning curves have been published for steel, soft contact lenses, life insurance policies, automobiles, bottle caps, gas ranges, refrigerators, gasoline refining, room air conditioners, TV picture tubes, aluminum, optical fibers, vacuum cleaners, motorcycles, steam turbine generators, ethyl alcohol, beer, facial tissues, transistors, microprocessors, float glass, long-distance telephone calls, knit fabric, lawnmowers, air travel, crude-oil production, typesetting, oil-refinery construction, factory maintenance, and hydroelectric power.
4. The author was a consultant with the Boston Consulting Group from 1977 to 1980.
5. 'Judging from current textbooks and casual observation, the 'learning' phenomenon receives almost no mention in the standard treatments of production costs in economics or industrial engineering courses' (Preston and Keachie 1964, p. 105).
6. But see Kenneth Arrow. 'The role of experience in increasing productivity has not gone unobserved, though the relation has yet to be absorbed into the main corpus of economic theory' (1962, p. 156). See also Hirsch (1956), Preston and Keachie (1964), Ghemawat and Spence (1985), Ross (1986, pp. 337–53), Spence (1981),

Barloff (1966), Fudenberg and Tirole (1983). Regarding the relationship between the learning curve and conventional economic theory, the following comments are drawn from telephone interviews with three Stanford University faculty members: Kenneth Arrow (May 3, 1989): 'It's kind of ignored.' Nathan Rosenberg (January 16, 1989): 'There is a huge literature on the learning curve, but it is very formalistic and it is within a static framework. Most of the literature is from the mid-1960s to the mid-1970s. It is no longer at the forefront of economic thinking.' Marvin Lieberman (April 25, 1989): 'The learning curve is outside the mainstream. You can't derive it from a theoretical model. It's not a theory, and it's the theories that get published. It's a topic at the fringe. The learning curve is not explainable within the normal confines of economics, so it's ignored.' But see Ross (1984).

REFERENCES

Arrow, K.J. (1962), 'The Economic Implications of Learning by Doing', *Review of Economic Studies*, **29** (3), June, 155–73.

Alchian, A. (1963), 'Reliability of Progress Curves in Airframe Production', *Econometrica*, **31** (4), October, 679–93.

Andress, F.J. (1964), 'The Learning Curve as a Production Curve', *Harvard Business Review*, January–February.

Asher, H. (1956), 'Cost-Quantity Relationships in the Airframe Industry', Santa Monica, CA: RAND Corporation, July, Report 291.

Barloff, N. (1966), 'The Learning Curve – Some Controversial Issues', *Journal of Industrial Economics*, **14** (3), 275–82.

Conley, P. (1970), *Experience Curves as a Planning Tool: A Special Commentary*, Boston: Boston Consulting Group.

Dutton, J.M. and A. Thomas (1984), 'Treating Progress Functions as a Managerial Opportunity', *Academy of Management Review*, p. 238.

Fudenberg, D. and J. Tirole (1983) 'Learning-by-Doing and Market Performance', *Bell Journal of Economics*, **14** (2), Autumn, 522–30.

Ghemawat, P. and A.M. Spence (1985), 'Learning Curve Spillovers and Market Performance', *Quarterly Journal of Economics*, **100** (5), Supplement, 839–52.

Gilder, G. (1984), *The Spirit of Enterprise*, New York: Simon & Schuster.

Henderson, B.D. (1973), *The Experience Curve Reviewed II: History*, Boston: Boston Consulting Group.

Henderson, B.D. (1974), *The Experience Curve Reviewed III: Why Does It Work?*, Boston: Boston Consulting Group.

Henderson, B.D. (1980), *The Experience Curve Revisited*, Boston: Boston Consulting Group.

Hirsch, W.Z. (1956), 'Firm Progress Ratios', *Econometrica*, **24** (2), 136–43.

Preston, L.E. and E.C. Keachie (1964), 'Cost Functions and Progress Functions: An Integration', *American Economic Review*, **54** (2), 100–7.

Reguero, M.A. (1957), 'An Economic Study of the Military Airframe Industry', Wright-Patterson Air Force Base, OH: Department of the Air Force.

Ross, D.R. (1984), 'Policy Implications of the Learning Curve', Chicago: Northwestern University, PhD dissertation. University Microfilms #8411184.

Ross, D.R. (1986), 'Learning to Dominate', *Journal of Industrial Economics*, **34** (4),

337–53.

Rothschild, M. (1990), *Bionomics: Economy as Ecosystem*, New York: Henry Holt.

Spence, A.M. (1981), 'The Learning Curve and Competition', *Bell Journal of Economics*, **12** (1), Spring, 49–70.

Thompson, D.N. (1981), 'The Experience Curve Effect on Costs and Prices: Implications for Public Policy', in F.E. Balderston, J.M. Carman and F.M. Micosia (eds), *Regulation of Marketing and the Public Interest*, New York: Pergamon Press, p. 62.

Wright, T.P. (1936), 'Factors Affecting the Cost of Airplanes', *Journal of the Aeronautical Sciences*, February, 122–8.

Yelle, L.E. (1979), 'The Learning Curve: Historical Review and Comprehensive Survey', *Decision Sciences*, April, 302–28.

Index

abduction, and
  complexification 232
  decisions 128, 198
abstract models, vs. actual behavior 256
accelerator 181, 182, 183
activism, increasing returns and 83
  laissez faire 82–5
  lock-in 83
  path dependency 83
advanced economies
  bioeconomics 269
  r-K strategies 259–60
African economies 201–2
aggregate demand, the nonfinancial side 197
aggregate outcome, modeling of 191
animal kingdom, as laboratory to learn economics 256
anthropological economists 164
anti-trust law, Austrian view 106–7
anti-trust laws 86, 89
Apple, and Microsoft 110
Aquinas, T. (St.) 153
ARCH models
  bootstrap tests 42–4
  financial markets 245
Aristotle 153, 160
Arrow, K.
  complexity research 4
  learning curve 293
Arrow–Debreu model 75, 82
Arthur, B.
  complexity research 4–5
  complexity view summarized 5–8
  teaching economics 9
'artificial life', approach to economic analysis 74–5
  approach to problems 216
  computer simulations 164
artificial stock market 242
Asian economies 201–2
association, meaning 53–62

types of 58–61
Austrian economics 137–45
  the Big Player 107, 114–15
  complexity viewpoint 77–8
  'ignorance argument' 83
  laissez faire 97
  naive view 97–9
  pro-market policy 97–115
autocatalytic sets 74
automatic stabilizers 184
Auyung, S. 2
average, vs. marginal 154–9

Bach, J.S., music and complexity study 236
Bak, P., self-organization 83
Baumol, W.J., and innovation 89–90
Bayes factor 87
BDS statistic 232, 236–7
Bertalanffy, L., complexity theory 139
Big Players, defined 107, 114, 115
  impossibility of modeling them 114–15
bioeconomic fitness, the future 282
bioeconomics 260–76
biological selection, as slow process 288
Böhm-Bawerk, E. 139
bootstrap-based specification testing 88
bootstrapping
  Santa Fe research 245–6
  statistics 43–6
Boston Consulting Group and learning curve 289–91
Bourbakism 191
Box-Cox test, 239, 240
Britain and bioeconomics 272
Brock, W.
  economic policy 10
  teaching economics 8
Brussels School approach 73
Buchanan, J., and the emergence of order 102

297

298   *Complexity Vision and the Teaching of Economics*

168, 232
North, D. 78, 79, 81
Nurkse, R. 201–2

Okun's Law 191, 196–7, 234
Olson phenomenon 267
Orcutt, G. 78

Paradox of Saving 179
Pareto optimality 78, 79
Pareto–Levy distributions, 32, 235
Pareto's Law 236
path dependence 22
    as familiar concept, 177–8
    punctuated equilibrium 272–4
    as standard economics 178
path dependency 78
    activism 83
    the multiplier model 135
    QWERTY 85
pattern completers 54–6
pattern development theory 75
patterns
    of beliefs 58
    in complexity 19
    detection of 39–41
    econometrics, hunt for in 234–8
    econometric literature 233
    emergence in the economy 25–6, 29
    financial markets 41–3, 168
    micro vs. macro 34
    positive feedback 21–3
    Santa Fe approach 31–3, 46–7
    scaling laws 29–30
    search for in complex curriculum 233–5
pedagogy
    development economics 206
    introduction of complexity 185–6
    mathematical economics 209–13
    its subsidiary pleasures 185–6
Peirce, C. 128
Pepsi and learning curve 292
Petty, W. (Sir) 190
Phelps, E. 80
Phillips curve 46, 191, 196, 234
Planck, M. 51, 147
policy
    Austrian view 105
    Austrian view of socialism 99–101

complexity 113, 184
policy analysis
    constantly changing data 91
    self-organizing patterns 91–2
    social capital 90
political activity and efficiency 266–7, 268–9
political behavior and bioeconomics 258
political institutions and punctuated equilibrium 272–4
political unification and optimal country size 281
politics and economics 270–2
Polya Processes 88, 143
    urn process 243
positive feedback, econometrics of 232, 233
    fundamental principles 180–5
    stabilizing policy 185
Prasch, R., and teaching specific courses 12–13
price
    fixed 144
    'just' 149–54
    'right' 75–8
    Walrasian clearing 160
prisoner's dilemma 157, 220
    bioeconomics 275
privatization 275
pro-market policy and Austrians 97–115
problem solution
    stochastic dynamic programming 51–2
    strategies 51
problem-solving and complex strategies 20–1
production possibility curve
    Santa Fe approach 132
prosperity and democracy 270–1
Pryor, F., and comparison of analytical methods 9
public choice model 82
    biopolitics 258
public good problems and bioeconomics 256, 262
punctuated equilibrium 272–4
Putnam, R.D. 78, 81
    social capital 90, 91

Quantity Theory of Money 190, 191
Quesnay, P. 190